PATTON Uncovered

By B. E. Boland

Melody Publishing Co.
Voorhees, NJ

Patton Uncovered. **Copyright © 2002 by Barbara E. Boland.**
Library of Congress Control Number: 2002105924

FIRST EDITION

Library of Congress Cataloging in Publication Data

Boland, B. E.
    Patton Uncovered/B. E. Boland
ISBN 0-9720470-0-X
    1. Patton, George S. (George Smith), 1885 – 1945 2. Military
        History – WWII. 3. Generals – United States – Biography.

Dedicated to my parents

PATTON'S FAVORITE PSALM

Psalm 63

1 O God, thou art my God; early will I seek thee: my soul thirsteth for thee, my flesh longeth for thee in a dry and thirsty land, where no water is;

2 To see thy power and thy glory, so as I have seen thee in the sanctuary.

3 Because thy loving kindness is better than life, my lips shall praise thee.

4 Thus will I bless thee while I live: I will lift up my hands in thy name.

5 My soul shall be satisfied as with marrow and fatness; and my mouth shall praise thee with joyful lips:

6 When I remember thee upon my bed and meditate on thee in the night watches.

7 Because thou hast been my help, therefore in the shadow of thy wings will I rejoice.

8 My soul followeth hard after thee: thy right hand upholdeth me.

9 But those that seek my soul, to destroy it, shall go into the lower parts of the earth.

10 They shall fall by the sword: they shall be a portion for foxes.

11 But the king shall rejoice in God; every one that sweareth by him shall glory: but the mouth of them that speak lies shall be stopped.

TABLE OF CONTENTS

MAPS

Chapter One

CONQUEROR

Stalemate had befallen the armies in Normandy. For a month the allies had clung desperately to the shore, barely even daring to hope that they might ever leave Normandy's isolated cliffs and advance into the farmland beyond. They had all heard about the beauty of French farm villages, but all they knew was the cold rain, the English channel behind them, and the wind that whistled through the enemy pillboxes and whipped across the rugged cliffs.

And then, suddenly, an army broke free of the German coastal defenses and raced across France, sweeping all opposition before them. Like a fiery bolt of lightning it blazed in one direction, then another, so quickly that observers could scarcely believe it. This army, "the liberators" and "saviors" as the grateful French called them, in one incredible stroke had broken the stalemate of months and captured the important French ports of St. Brieuc, Quimper, Morlaix, and Nantes.

The Germans reeled at their defeats and pondered what incredible force the Americans had just released upon them. For from all reports the Third Army was an army like any other, only greener. It had known only three weeks of combat and yet in seven days had stolen 10,000 square miles from the "victorious Reich." "Who was in command of Third Army?" the Germans wondered. For whoever he was, he had just made the fastest advance in history with a green army!

The commander of the Third Army, General George S. Patton, Jr., looked every inch a conqueror. He was tall, 6 foot 2, and sixty years old – old for an American general. His whole life had been spent preparing for this moment. His whole career had been devoted to war. Leading a victorious army in battle had been his one ambition.

Yet a few months ago his career had been hanging in the balance. Eisenhower was pondering the value of this, the commander that had just broken the stalemate on the beaches and advanced faster than the German blitzkrieg.

To his commanders, Patton was always a liability. He was too honest and too talkative. What was worse, he was extremely successful. They needed him militarily. But politically he was their worst nightmare. One never knew when he might tell people what was actually happening at Eisenhower's headquarters.

Always completely honest, Patton was nevertheless not naive. He was surrounded by evil, corrupt and dishonest men, and he was not oblivious. A keen observer of human nature, Patton recorded all of his thoughts in his diary. It remains the only thoroughly honest, unabridged and pure source to emerge from WWII. It is true that it shows us only Patton's perception of the war; but this is his wholly honest opinion, not a manufactured after-war coverup.

A major factor in all of Patton's life was duty. While to most military men this means duty to officers and to authority, Patton took this one step further and often spoke of his duty to the American people. They had a right to know what was going on in Europe, he would often say. Eisenhower's staff had reason to fear what he knew, and what he was clearly unafraid to say.

Patton was destined to lead the Third Army in some of the most spectacular victories of military history. This army would trap eleven German divisions at Falaise, save the Allies from disaster during the Battle of the Bulge and rescue the stranded Americans in Bastogne, surround and cut off ten complete German divisions in the Hunsruck Mountains, cross the Rhine with a mere 28 casualties, uncover the barbarity of the Nazis by liberating the first concentration camp, and discover the German gold reserve. This unheard of and inexperienced army, by virtue of its unmatched commander, would liberate France, Belgium, Luxembourg, Germany, Bavaria, Austria and Czechoslavakia.

No other commander, before or since, can match Patton's record. In spite of this, Patton was still denied supplies and forced to beg for permission to advance through undefended enemy territory. Because of his honor and despite his incredible military performance, Patton would be removed, demoted, disgraced and relieved.

But all this was to come. Right now Patton was at the height of his glory. He was the idol of his men, the liberator of France, and the commander of the dreaded Third Army. The German army was retreating before him, wondering which way he would release this catapult of his own creation. Never before had war moved faster. Patton had reason to be proud.

This was August 1944, and Patton's second great victory. His first had been a year earlier, as commander of the Seventh Army in what looked like a doubtful situation in Sicily. We will now go back to that time, when a victory like the one Patton had just achieved in France seemed worse than impossible.

Chapter Two

THE PLAN

The plans for the invasion of Sicily were being drawn up. This would be the first large amphibious operation the Allies would be trying, and so naturally the plan for Sicily presented many problems. Sicily's terrain did not lend itself to invasion; there were few beaches and many rugged mountain cliffs. It quickly became clear to the planners that Sicily's two major ports would have to be taken first in order to supply the troops.

The first port, Syracuse, had proven itself the key to many earlier battles. Alcibiades had said, during the Peloponnesian war in 415 B.C., "If Syracuse falls, all Sicily falls also, and Italy immediately afterwards." The same idea was in the mind of the Allied planners. The second port, Palermo, had a long waterfront and an excellent harbor. Palermo was lightly defended so the planners were quite pleased with their choices. The seasoned and battle-hardened British Eighth Army would take Syracuse in the east, and the novice American Seventh Army would capture Palermo. With the two most accessible ports taken, the armies would then head to the better defended Messina and cut off the German armies in Sicily.

This was the plan that everyone had agreed on when Patton left Tunisia to take charge of the planners. His assignment was to refine the plan's tactical details. But before Patton even got a chance to work on the plan it was scrapped.

The Eighth Army, Montgomery's army, had just emerged triumphant, not only in battle, but also in all the newspaper headlines. Montgomery was called the "Victor of El Alamein" and this battle was hailed as the "first major British victory." The fact that other armies, both American and British, had contributed to that victory was largely ignored, and the British Eighth Army received all the credit. Montgomery was resting on his laurels when he discovered that the plan for Sicily would give Palermo, the seat of the ancient Sicilian kings, to the American Seventh Army.

Montgomery quickly flew to Algiers for a conference with Eisenhower and Alexander. He had never seen the plan in detail so his criticisms were limited to generalities like, "Possibly some sort of compromise will be necessary in order to get ourselves out of the mess we are now in" and "The preparation for the operation must be gripped firmly, and be handled in a sensible way." As Alexander, the British Commander of the Allied forces, listened, he knew immediately the exact nature of Montgomery's "objections" to the Sicily plan.

While Montgomery was away trying to discredit a plan he had never seen, his offensive in Tunisia had ground to a halt from which it was never renewed. Montgomery was not disturbed, however. He had won the battle at headquarters.

At Cairo, for the first time, Monty was shown the plan for which he had so many pre-conceived reservations. General Gairdner, the British General who had designed the plan, was dismayed at Montgomery's superficial comments and ludicrous objections. The invasion of Sicily was less than 81 days away, and Gairdner had been working on "Husky Eight"[1] for months.

Clearly Montgomery would not be able to persuade the Allied High Command to withdraw the current Sicilian invasion plan, "Husky Eight," unless he had another substitute plan. While his Tunisian offensive had bogged down, Monty had been working on a new plan, which he now began campaigning vigorously for.

In Montgomery's plan, according to Alexander, "the more spectacular assignment of taking Syracuse, Augusta and possibly Messina was to be assigned to General Montgomery's Eighth Army."

---

[1] The codename for the Sicily Invasion plan devised by General Gairdner.

This plan fixed all the strategical "errors" of "Husky Eight" by placing the Americans in a defensive position at the horrible beachhead at Gela. At this beach, it would be impossible for the Americans to ever advance, while the British Eighth Army went on to capture everything of value on the island.

Later Monty would claim that from the moment he saw "Husky Eight," "I had my own ideas about the American landings, but did not think the moment was yet opportune to put them forward." Montgomery had a way of dealing behind the scenes and undermining the authority and credibility of commanders and operations. Few knew what his exact methods were, but all were sure of his underhanded conceit, and that he had chosen "Husky Eight" as his target.

While Montgomery was to lead the British Eighth Army in the coming invasion, a virtually unknown commander, Patton, would lead the American Seventh Army. Patton had made a favorable impression on the British, especially Alexander, who liked his daring operations and inspiring leadership. He had already observed Patton's remarkable effect on the morale and deportment of the Americans in North Africa, which had changed overnight from slovenly and disobedient to polished and efficient.

On the personal level, Patton and Alexander had become close friends. Patton was one of the very few educated and well-read Americans. Most of the American generals claimed to be poor boys who had been given a second chance in the military, and none seemed to have learned or read anything since West Point. But Patton was different. He had an almost aristocratic background combined with an amazingly sharp intellect. For him the army was more than the calling he had chosen; it was the profession he had been called for; he had not entered it for monetary reasons like his fellow generals. He was a real warrior who read, studied, lived and breathed war, yet also a student of history who possessed an almost uncanny perception into human nature. He seemed to understand about Europe, and what made it different from America, rather than simply assuming that all peoples were the same. For all these reasons, Patton became the favorite American general among the British.

But Alexander had uncovered another facet of Patton's personality, one rare on the British side, and almost nonexistent in the American high command. Patton was a deeply religious, highly moral man. Early on Patton's honesty, justice, sense of duty, personal bravery and unimpeachable honor had manifested themselves. Though the two had only known each other for a few months, they had covered topics Patton couldn't even speak about with Americans. In fact, Patton noted in his diary that Alexander "is a good soldier and much more talkative than he's supposed to be." The rumors of Eisenhower's illicit liaison with Kay Summersby, his driver, had undoubtedly been the subject of their conversation when Patton told Alexander how wrong and unwise it was for a soldier of high standing to have any intimate association with women during wartime. Patton went to church every Sunday, read the Bible and believed that it was God, and God alone, who could bestow victory. He believed that God was watching everything that happened, and that when he died he would be personally accountable for all of his actions. This was what made him so scrupulously honest and honorable, and it was also what caused his downfall.

Patton, for his part, admired Alexander. Most of their military ideas were in accordance, and Patton was duly impressed when he learned that Alexander had fought for ten full years – four years in World War I, 2 years in Russia fighting the Reds, one year on the Northwest frontier of India, and three years in World War II. Soldiers spend most of their careers in preparation for fighting. The years they actually do fight are considerably fewer.

The sudden rash of "objections" to "Husky Eight" caused Alexander to summon a high-level meeting on the subject at St. Georges in Algiers. This was not what Montgomery wanted; it was not in line with his shadowy way of ruining operations. Now he would have to attend and present his tactical objections.

Patton arrived at the meeting on time, only to find that Montgomery, the reason for the meeting, was having one of his famous "coincidental" influenza attacks and couldn't make it. As was his condescending habit, he would send his Chief of Staff to "explain everything." This was always a headache because de Guingand was not authorized to make any agreements and could not always be relied on to be expressing the wishes of his boss. This time, however, de Guingand's plane couldn't land, so another of Montgomery's generals, Sir Oliver Leese, would come instead.

Leese was held up by fog, and in desperation Alexander postponed the meeting until the next day. Patton had just witnessed the inside workings of the British command system, and Montgomery's avoidance of it.

Chapter Three

THE SEVENTH ARMY MAY ONLY DEFEND

The next day, April 29th, the meeting started as planned. Gathered in the room were the leaders of the British Navy, Army and Air Force. Only Patton and Nevins, a member of Eisenhower's staff, were American. This seemed fitting to the British, who hoped to squelch Montgomery's new plan before it reached fruition.[1]

As senior in command, General Alexander began the meeting. The purpose of the meeting, he announced, was to consider the changes in the Sicily invasion plan proposed by Montgomery. The assembly already knew why they had been called, and furthermore were annoyed by Montgomery's conspicuous absence.
"We've already agreed to the plans," grumbled British Chief Admiral Cunningham. "Isn't it too late to change?"
"We will hear what the Eighth Army wants," replied Alexander.

Leese, standing in for Montgomery, rose and read to the generals a paper detailing Montgomery's objections. Monty objected to having his

---

[1] The names and ranks of those who attended are: Admiral Sir Andrew Cunningham of the Royal Navy, his chief of staff, Commodore Royer M. Dick, Vice Admiral Sir Bertram Ramsey of the Royal Navy, Air Chief Marshal Sir Arthur Tedder of the RAF, Air Vice Marshal Coningham of the RAF and Eisenhower's air chief, Air Vice Marshal Horace Wigglesworth of the RAF, Major General Frederick Browning, Ike's airborne adviser, General Gairdner, the general in charge of the planning of "Husky Eight," and his deputy, Brigadier Arthur A. Richardson, and of course Alexander, Leese, Nevins and Patton.

army split and wanted to attack as a united Army in the vicinity of Syracuse, he announced. The Germans will move four divisions from Italy to Sicily, predicted Montgomery, and those divisions will undoubtedly reinforce the airports at Licata. If that happened, and Monty was sure it would, Patton's Seventh Army would be stranded in the west without supplies. Leese corroborated Montgomery's statement by saying that his XXX Corps of two divisions was far too weak to attack near Licata and capture the needed airports.

Monty's new plan which Leese eagerly read to the dismayed generals placed Patton's Seventh Army in a totally useless defensive position on Eighth Army's flank. Besides removing anything of value from the Americans' path, the plan also cut the Seventh Army off from naval and air support making it a defenseless target as well as a useless appendage of Eighth Army. When Leese was finished reading the new plan, the British began to vigorously oppose leaving Patton without proper naval and air support.

Patton, of course, was also more than a little concerned about this. But what was more worrying was how Montgomery had forsaken common sense strategy and was selfishly trying to stuff the Seventh Army into a virtually undefendable corner of the island while his Eighth Army went on to capture the famous cities of Palermo and Messina.

Clearly Montgomery was just trying to make the Sicily invasion "a sure thing attack for the Eighth Army and its 'ever victorious General,' and to heck with the rest of the war," Patton wrote in his diary. The British already knew how arrogant and selfish Montgomery was, so those in the room were not surprised like Patton, but annoyed.

Tedder, the British Air Chief Marshal, said, "Really, gentlemen, I don't want to be difficult, but I am profoundly moved. Without the capture of the airports near Licata, the operation is impossible."
"From a naval point of view," Cunningham chimed in, "the massing of so many ships in the Siracusa area is to invite disaster, and besides, the chief merit of amphibious attack is to do so on a broad front and disperse enemy effort. I am definitely opposed to the plan."
Alexander replied, "But if from our viewpoint, that is, the army, it is necessary, we must do it."
"We are all in it," Tedder objected, "it is not an army show, but three arms are in it. Besides, we can't support Patton unless we get these airfields."

14

Patton, silent until now, spoke up. "I would like to stress that point because I am sure that without the airfields, while I may get ashore, I won't live long."

Cunningham now suggested that perhaps Leese could capture the needed airfields if he were given an extra division. Leese's answer was hasty and see-through, "Montgomery would never consent to splitting his Army."
"My force is split by more than four miles," Patton whispered to Tedder.
"Say it out loud," Tedder said, and Patton did.
"That the man on the ground must decide," Alexander replied, remaining infuriatingly official.
"In view of General Alexander's remark, I withdraw mine," Patton said, "But I feel sure if I refused to attack because my force was split, I would be relieved."
"I am sure of it in your case, and there would be a file of aspirants to take your place," Leese said. It was a strange remark and Patton couldn't tell if he was trying to be insulting or not.

As if hearkening back to a few years before when the Americans hadn't been in the war, Alexander said, "I think we should send a wire to the Prime Minister."
"Why not ask Eisenhower?" Cunningham said, "After all, he is Commander-in-Chief." Ironically, while Churchill would have disciplined Montgomery's extraordinary selfishness, Eisenhower was "allied" and would allow Monty to destroy the plan's strategic value.

The British argued among each other for almost three hours. Most of them were fed up with Montgomery's small-minded and very selfish attitude. Before he had used his wiles to destroy fellow British army commanders, but now he was trying to ruin the whole American contribution in the coming operation. Patton recalled that the arguing was "quite hot" and eventually no conclusion was reached. How could one be, when Montgomery hadn't attended? Alexander suggested that they go "visit Montgomery and argue with him."
Cunningham said, "I shan't go. I also have things to do."
Then someone suggested that Conyngham go. Tedder said, "Fine, it will be good for Monty to hear his master's voice."

"About then, the telephone rang and Alexander apparently got some bad news, for he and Conyngham left at once and the meeting ended in an impasse, all due, in my opinion, to lack of force on the part of Alexander, who cut a sorry figure at all times. He is a fence walker. After the meeting broke up, I asked Cunningham if I had been too frank. He said, "Not at all. You were the only one that said anything and, in spite of your tactful retraction, what you said had a profound effect." *Patton's diary*

Tedder overheard Patton's question to Cunningham and came over to them. After saying he was for Patton, he took them to lunch. After lunch they were talking and Tedder made an interesting revelation. "It is bad form for officers to criticize each other, so I shall. The other day Alex, who is very selfish, said of General Anderson, 'As a soldier, he is a good plain military cook.' The remark applies absolutely – to Montgomery. He is a little fellow of average ability who has such a build-up that he thinks of himself as Napoleon – he is not."

"I believe this meeting is of momentous import and may result in a complete change in the high command. I am sure that such a change must eventually take place." *Patton's Diary*

That evening, as was his custom, Patton wrote to his wife,

"Alex presided and Sir Andrew [Cunningham] protested, and dear old Monty was sick[1] so Sir O. Leese pinched in for him. Tedder and Conyngham were also there. In fact, I was the only foreigner, it was quite an internecine war, and all I had to do was listen and make three well chosen remarks. Strange to say I was on the side of Tedder and Andrew… It ended in a stalemate. It was one heck of a performance. War by committee. If old Monty won't give in, I don't know what will happen. I should not be too surprised at a change in the top."

Patton was used to the American military tradition, where a higher rank gives a command and those below him obey. The British, on the other hand, could choose to disregard a command from those above if they deemed it unadvisable or foolish. For this reason, before plans were enacted they needed to be agreed upon by everyone and arguing was

---

[1] Obviously the British had alerted Patton to the strange nature of Montgomery's timely "sicknesses."

endemic. Patton was quite surprised, for Americans could debate with the commander, but once the commander issued an order, it had to be obeyed.

There had been a change in the American system of commanding, however. Raising so many objections and threatening a plan which would be executed in only a few weeks would have been intolerable in an American. But the American high command didn't even seem fazed by Monty's irascibility. In fact, they had scheduled a meeting in Algiers for May 3rd where his objections would be heard and addressed.

Bedell Smith had called Patton to inform him of the new meeting, and Patton wrote in his diary that,

> "There are probably going to be some big changes in the Husky plan, and that Montgomery will be there to present his ideas, and that he thinks that... I should have a chance to be heard. In view of the last meeting, I fancy that Monty will insist on his plan, which means that the airfields at Gela will not be taken. This situation can be solved either by our taking them or else by delaying our landings until the British eventually take them, or by raising an ad hoc plan. I intend to do a heck of a lot of listening, but will not sacrifice American lives to save my job. I will get there as early as possible and see Cunningham and Tedder."

Unfortunately for Patton, his plane was caught in a storm on the way to Algiers. By the time he finally arrived, the fate of the Sicilian operation had already been decided. "I am sorry I am late for the meeting, but I did the best I could," Patton told Eisenhower.
"Oh, that's all right," Ike replied, "I knew you would do what you were ordered without question and told them so. We had better get hold of Alex and Hewitt and show you the new setup."

Hughes, Alexander and Bedell Smith ushered Patton to the map where the destruction of "Husky Eight" and the impending doom of the new plan was clear. Seventh Army, Patton's army, would be given the impossible beachhead at Gela from where it would be close to impossible to supply, just as Montgomery had wanted.

"Monty, so far as I can gather, simply refused to play ball, so Alex yielded in spite of the fact that the supply people say that the plan Monty wants is logistically impossible." *Patton's diary*

Some apologists, to make up for his stunningly poor performance in strategy, have called Montgomery a "master of logistics." I am sure the logisticians would disagree.

The new plan, which had been agreed upon in Patton's absence, had been designed and dreamt up by Montgomery. It had the British capturing eastern Sicily,[1] while the Americans were supposed to take the southern. Montgomery would land at Syracuse and Augusta, while Patton would come ashore at the tiny villages of Scoglitti and Gela. These two ports weren't large enough to supply the Americans, so they were expected to move on and capture the airfields with two divisions,[2] then take the small port of Licata. Perhaps, with all these things taken, it would be possible to supply the Seventh Army, but only in a defensive position. Montgomery had reserved the easiest landing beaches and the quickest route to the biggest cities for his "victorious Eighth Army."

Montgomery's plan had made any hope of a Seventh Army advance impossible. Patton's objectives, the little port villages, were so tiny that even several of them couldn't adequately supply him. Besides that, so many tiny Sicilian villages were embarrassingly small objectives for a whole American army. It seemed that the British were intent on maintaining the attitude they had assumed in N. Africa: namely that the Americans couldn't capture difficult military objectives.

If this was what they were implying, Patton meant to show them. According to the plan he was only allotted the miniscule objectives of Scoglitti and Gela. He was then to sit and watch Montgomery take Messina and Palermo, the famous Sicilian cities. This may have been the plan, but the plan hadn't reckoned on Patton.

It was at this time, when it seemed as if Montgomery had succeeded in dooming the Seventh Army to a defensive role, that the British brigadier Cecil Stanway Sugden, a planner for Eisenhower, said,

---

[1] See map of Sicily
[2] Incidentally what Leese had said was impossible.

18

"I say, you don't need to worry, old chap. With the dispositions as they are, old Patton will soon have poor Monty bloody well surrounded!"
Another British planner remarked, "That Patton bloke is sure cooking with gas – on all burners!"

Even the British were rooting for Patton. And who wouldn't? With the stakes piled so highly against him, only Patton could possibly manage to turn the tables so effectively!

Chapter Four

ASHORE!

At the meeting Patton had attended on April 29th, Leese had stated unequivocally that he could not take the air bases at Gela. Now, with a wave of the hand, Montgomery had ordered Patton to do it. Either Leese was lying, and could easily have taken the airfields; or they were admitting that Patton was quite an amazing general.

Even though Patton had arrived at the May 3rd meeting late, there were still details in the plan that had to be negotiated. Patton had been handed a mission, impossible from strategical and logistical aspects; yet he had every intention of pulling it off. He informed them that he was going to land four divisions and two parachute regiments and take Licata straight off. Because his objectives were inadequately small, though, he would need the British to supply him through Siracusa. The British quickly agreed.

> "They promise easily, but even so it means we have to supply more than two divisions over the beaches, without ports, indefinitely; yet the Navy says that after September 1st, beach supply is impossible. Well, we will do it anyway." ***Patton's diary***

Patton had no other choice; the plan had been accepted by the American and British commanders that mattered. The Sicily plan was bad from so many aspects that it is a credit to the soldiers who fought there that it succeeded.

Unable to change what had already been agreed on, but still worried about supplies, Patton suggested a signed agreement. This would enforce what decisions had been reached at the conference and have the "binding effect of a treaty." Bedell Smith quickly backed Patton up on this. Smith told Patton afterwards that Lord Gort had warned him that "In dealing with [Monty] one must remember that he is not quite a gentleman."

> "Spent the night with Ike. Kay[1] came to supper. Ike and I talked till 0120. He is beginning to see the light but is too full of himself. I was quite frank with him about the British and he took it." *Patton's Diary*

Montgomery's incredible power and the way his superiors feared him troubled Patton, who asked Bedell Smith about it.

> "Bedell Smith says that the reason everyone yields to Monty is because Monty is the national hero and writes direct to the Prime Minister; and that if Ike crossed him, Ike might get canned. Also that Monty is senior in service to Alexander,[2] and taught Alex at the staff college,[3] and that Alex is afraid of him." *Patton's Diary*

As time passed, Patton would see the peculiar back-handed dealing that was customary of Montgomery, and would soon learn how easily Monty could curtail the operations of those he hated. Yet Patton, being a different type of man, would never fear Montgomery.

The men who had formulated the original plan for Sicily, members of Alexander's staff, were very angry that their plan had been rejected. They gave Patton a paper full of objections to the new plan, some of which were, in his opinion, sound.

Nevins, Hewitt, Muller, and Patton went to see the British General Gairdner. Gairdner had worked on "Husky Eight" for months only to watch it be destroyed in a matter of weeks.
Patton said to Gairdner, "We are on the same side and I want your help in putting up our side when Monty's chief of staff comes up. Specifically, I want all the paratroops and a definite written promise of

---

[1] Eisenhower's WAC and girlfriend.
[2] This was incorrect.
[3] This was correct.

supplies, via Siracusa, to make up the service for what we can't get in [over the beaches]; also, I want a definite boundary between Eighth Army and Western Task Force."

Gairdner was sympathetic and said he would help. Someone has suggested that only two paratroop battalions are necessary, he added.

"While I have the highest respect for the valor of the U.S. troops," Patton replied tongue-in-cheek, "I do not feel that they are so superior to the British that a third as many paratroopers and infantry can succeed in an attack which the XXX Corps[1] considered impossible."

"They saw the point," remarked Patton in his diary.

Contrary to popular belief, Patton did not know Eisenhower well. The two were never friends, although they had known each other briefly in the past. Too much was different between the two men for them to have ever been close; and gradually their attitudes, about both war and peace, would take sharply different paths. Patton would come to condemn Ike as a weak and traitorous politician, while Eisenhower would adopt a condescending and haughty attitude when speaking or writing about "Georgie."

The pattern of the war had already established itself. Montgomery had destroyed a plan due to envy and jealousy and Eisenhower was too weak to stop him. Eisenhower, Patton decided, had been placed in charge because he didn't have the guts to contradict the British.[2] The British could do as they liked and Eisenhower "says, 'Yes, sir.'"

Another more disturbing problem was that Eisenhower had never fought, in *any* war. He had simply begun a meteoric rise in rank starting in 1942, which averaged to be a new rank every *6 months*. Because he had never had any actual experience, he relied too heavily on the advice of others. He could not judge the merit of their advice because he was not a student of war, like Patton.

The contempt of the true soldier and student of war for the arm-chair general is immeasurable. On April 23rd, Patton wrote to his wife,

---

[1] Leese's XXX Corps was British.

[2] In reality, as Patton would learn, Eisenhower was given command because he would not contradict the politicians in Washington. Ike was chosen deliberately because of his weakness; the fact that he would be weak when dealing with the British did not seem to worry Washington.

"People who have not seen death should not make war, especially when they are too proud to learn... Either D[1] is nuts or else he is under wraps. I can't make it out. He is suffering like hell and can't look at you. 'Uneasy lies the head etc...' "

Patton wrote on May 7th,

"Monty is a forceful, selfish man, but still a man. I think he is far better than Alexander and that he will do just what he pleases, as Alex is afraid of him. Montgomery is a very forceful man."

Patton's remark on Montgomery was perceptive. He respected the fact that Montgomery *fought* for his side of the argument;[2] Patton was becoming increasingly disgusted with Eisenhower's weakness.

Since Eisenhower was supposed to be American, Patton had thought that he would stand up for American participation in the coming operation. But Ike hadn't. He had withdrawn behind a complex network of "cooperation" and "allies" which made Patton's patriotic soul sick. "I fear Eisenhower has sold his soul to the devil on 'Cooperation,' which I think means we are pulling the chestnuts for our noble allies," he wrote in his diary, "It is clear that I too must 'cooperate' or get out."

"Went to see Ike in the morning and found him much elated over his 'great victory.' I had bet him that we would not be in Tunis and Bizerte till after June 8th, and a second bet that we would not tie in on May 8th. I lost both with great pleasure, so got a new 50 franc bill and presented it to him on a tray with a red rose and the remark 'Hail Caesar.' He walked the floor for some time, orating, and then asked me to mention how hard he had worked – what great risks he had taken – and how well he had handled the British, in my next letter to General Marshall. I wrote a letter which largely overstated his merits, but I felt that I owe him a lot and

---

[1] D stands for Dwight, Eisenhower's first name. Eventually Patton would use the pseudonym "Divine Destiny" (a play on Ike's initials) when writing to his wife so as to avoid censorship.
[2] Even if unfairly!

24

must stay in with him. I lied in a good cause. As a matter of fact, I know of no one except myself who could do any better than Ike, and God knows I don't want his job." *Patton's diary*

Clearly nothing in Tunisia had escaped Patton's observant eye. There were many generals there, all out for themselves; and then there was Eisenhower, the epitome of a weak leader. Further in his diary entry Patton wrote, "[Ike] needs a few loyal and unselfish men around him, even if he is too weak a character to be worthy of us. But if I do my duty, I will be paid in the end."

Patton visited Alexander's planning headquarters and found panic raging uncontrolled due to weak leadership. Patton admitted in his diary that the upcoming Sicily operation was impossible and he, too, was scared, "I have to exude confidence I don't feel every minute."

"Monty is all set to make Americans defend his left flank and to do it by [having the Americans] landing at the most difficult beaches. From a logistical aspect [the operation] is impossible, both the landing and the supply, but I feel that by God's help, and only by His help, we will do it."

Because of his faith in God, and his abhorrence of disorder, Patton was able to avoid the panic of Alexander's HQ. Even though he prayed for success, Patton was ultimately a realist, and he wrote that, "If the Germans succeed in getting two divisions in place, I think that the operation is impossible. But the President and the Prime Minister will insist on it anyhow. Well, one cannot live forever. I got two extra [divisions] out of the British."

Meanwhile the press had already built a reputation for Patton based on his performance in N. Africa. They called Patton "Blood and Guts," a nickname which Patton hated. The nickname implied that he didn't care for his men and required them to expend themselves more than other commanders, which was the very opposite of the truth. He felt that "Brains and Guts" would have been a better nickname. They were the two qualities necessary for victory. After all, every side had blood.

Along with the nickname was the very incorrect assertion that Patton was a martinet, a commander who demanded useless "parade-ground" discipline. The newspapers claimed all these things and more, and as time went on their attacks against Patton would become more and more ferocious.

To a friend Patton wrote,

> "This 'Blood and Guts' stuff is quite distasteful to me. I am a very severe disciplinarian, because I know, as you as an old soldier know, that without discipline it is impossible to win battles, and that without discipline to send men into battle is to commit murder. This war makes higher demands on courage and discipline than any war of which I have known. But when you see men who have demonstrated discipline and courage, killed and wounded, it naturally raises a lump in your throat and sometimes produces a tear in your eye."

The incorrect idea of Patton which the newspapers had broadcasted had prompted a preacher to write to Patton.

> "He hoped I thought about Jesus and reminded me that I would die and go to Hell if I did not. I wrote him that I was amazed at his temerity in writing me such a letter when I was a far better Christian than he was."

Oddly enough, of all the great commanders that have led in battle, few have had the great faith in God that Patton had. He believed that it was God which made an army victorious, and for that reason he prayed and read the Bible every night. Before the Gafsa attack in N. Africa, Patton had made his now famous announcement, "Gentlemen, tomorrow we attack. If we are not victorious, let no man come back alive." He then retired to pray.

Bradley, who had been present, remarked later in his book that he found this one of Patton's contradictions. "For while he was profane, he was also reverent. And while he strutted imperiously as a commander, he knelt humbly before his God." In fact it is no contradiction at all. Patton was a man who knew his place and his worth. While never doubting his own capabilities, he also never underestimated God's hand in the world.

As a commander Patton always had to present to his men, including his staff and Bradley, a picture of confidence, which he admitted often in his diary he did not feel. He did this because he knew that his men would never be victorious if their leader had doubts. On the one hand Patton always seemed supremely confident, so confident that some people mistook his confidence for arrogance. But on the other hand we have Patton's diary, full of doubts and reservations, providing living proof that Patton was not foolishly over-confident; he was simply inspiring his men with confidence.

Patton was increasingly disgruntled with Eisenhower's "leadership." He wrote in a letter, "AFHQ is really a British headquarters with a neuter general, if he is not pro-British. Some day some one at home will stumble on what is going on." He was to continue on a similar theme twelve days later on May 22nd in his diary,

> "Under the present arrangement for Husky, we have a pro-British straw man at the top [Ike], a British chief admiral and senior vice admiral, Cunningham and Ramsey. This makes our Admiral Hewitt third. Tedder controls air with Spaatz, a straw man under him… Conyngham commands the tactical air force and close support air force by another British vice air marshal. Our close air support is commanded by a Colonel. Browning is an airborne advisor [to Eisenhower] and trying to get command of the paratroops. Alexander commands all the ground troops. His chief of staff is British, but we have a Director of Operations in Brigadier General Nevins and a Deputy Chief of Staff in Major General Huebner, which may help. General Montgomery, a full general, commands [Eighth Army]. I command – a poor last. I cannot see how people at home don't see it. The U.S. is getting gypped. All Seventh Army supplies come either over beaches or else through Siracusa, a British port, and I am told to arrange with Monty as to amounts [that I will get]. Only an act of God or an accident can give us a run for our money. On a study of form, especially in the higher command, we are licked. Churchill runs this war and at the moment he is not interested in Husky. The thing I must do is to retain my SELF-CONFIDENCE. I have greater ability than these other people and it comes from, for lack of a better word,

what we must call greatness of soul based on a belief –
an unshakable belief – in my destiny. The U.S. must win
– not as an ally, but as a conqueror. If I can find my
duty, I can do it. I must. This is one of my bad days."

It is clear what Patton is expressing here – profound patriotism,
coupled with shocked disbelief at how naive his country could be. "The
U.S. must win – not as an ally, but as a conqueror." Eisenhower, it was
clear, was intent on being only an "ally." Well, if Eisenhower couldn't
show the British how Americans fought, then Patton certainly would.
Not only would the enemy be surprised, but so would the "ally."

On June 1st Eisenhower called up to tell Patton that,
"My American Boss will visit you in the morning ..."
To which Patton replied, "When did Mamie arrive?"[1]

Recounting the incident in his diary Patton added,

"Man cannot serve two masters. 'My American Boss.' "

Patton found the title both amusing and disturbing. Eisenhower
was calling Marshall, "My American Boss." Who was his British boss?

On June 22nd Alexander said that it was foolish to consider the
British and Americans as one people, "as we are foreigners to each
other." That Alexander dared express this wildly politically-incorrect
theory shows partly why Patton liked him so much. For after Alexander
had said this, Patton jumped right in, agreeing wholeheartedly and saying
that,

"It was so, and the sooner everyone recognized it the
better. I told him that my boisterous method of command
would not work with the British no matter how
successful with Americans, while his cold method would
never work with Americans. He agreed."

In Patton's letters to his wife, Patton referred to Eisenhower in
code. Eisenhower's initials, Dwight David, were changed to "Divine
Destiny," or sometimes just D. Eisenhower was certainly Patton's
"Divine Destiny." The British were sometimes called "the cousins."

---

[1] Mamie, Eisenhower's wife.

Patton wrote to his wife on June 26th, "Poor D is having a hard time with politics." Two days later, Patton reported to Eisenhower. Eisenhower was "full of praise for the 3rd Division" but never mentioned the fact that Patton had made it what it was. "I fear I was untactful," Patton wrote.

Poor Patton! He longed to hear the praise he so richly deserved, but Eisenhower consistently refrained from doing so. In fact, after the capture of Messina, Patton would receive compliments from Alexander, Churchill, and Roosevelt, but Ike remained silent. We will never know the reason for sure, but Patton attributed this lack of gratitude to Eisenhower's new "allied" attitude, and praise for his American partner did not fit into this mode.

On July 3rd, Patton went to say goodbye to "General Ike." Eisenhower started out by giving Patton a long lecture on the bad discipline of the 1st Division. "I told him he was mistaken and that, anyhow, no one whips a dog just before putting him in a fight." Then Eisenhower started talking about criticism of the Air Corps…

> "I told him that, due to his efforts, we were apparently
> going to get air support. This was a fib, as I was the one
> who attacked them and made them come across. At no
> time did Ike wish us luck and say he was back of us –
> fool. After others… left, I told him that I was very
> appreciative of being selected [for Husky]. He said,
> 'You are a great leader but a poor planner.'"

This comment of Eisenhower's was mystifying, for, as Patton replied, "except for Torch, which I had planned and which was a high success, I had never been given a chance to plan." Was Eisenhower deliberately being rude to Patton? Many books have told of their alleged friendship, but nothing among their papers really substantiates this. Later on in the war, Patton and Eisenhower would become quite determined enemies, mostly because of this strange attitude of Eisenhower's.

Eisenhower then said that if,

> "… Husky turned into a slugging match, he might recall
> me to get ready for the next operation and let Bradley
> finish Husky. I protested that I would like to finish one

29

show. I can't make out whether he thinks Bradley is a better dose fighter than I am or whether he wants to keep in with General Marshall, who likes Bradley. I know that Bradley is completely loyal to me. Ike has never asked me to a meal since I have been here, one week. However, it turns out I would not change places with anyone I know. I am leading 90,000 men in a desperate attack and eventually it [my Army] will be over 250,000 [men]. If I win, I can't be stopped! If I lose, I shall be dead."

This attitude of Patton's, "If I lose, I shall be dead," has been called theatrical. In fact the attitude was completely realistic. He was going to fight with his men; if they died, he would be at their head. For this reason Patton loved the desperate attack, and always won. He was as unafraid of dying as he was of losing.

The invasion of Sicily began on July 10th. Patton was duly excited and had "the usual shortness of breath before a polo game." A strong wind was blowing over Sicily and most of the airborne troops were unable to find their objectives: a bridge near Syracuse in the British sector and an important crossroads in the American sector. Instead the airborne troops proceeded to cut telephone wires and ambush small groups of enemy soldiers. At 2:45 more than seven Allied divisions landed along 100 miles of Sicilian shore.

Montgomery's Eighth Army landed in the sheltered Gulf of Noto and got ashore quickly. Leese's XXX Corps turned west to link up with Patton's Seventh Army, while Dempsey's XIII Corps prepared for what they thought would be a quick capture of Syracuse, Augusta and Catania. Meanwhile Patton's Seventh Army was running into all of the predicted problems, along with incredible gale-high winds. Middleton's 45th Division went ashore at the fishing village of Scoglitti and Allen's 1st Division landed at the minor port of Gela. Truscott's 3rd Division invaded near the port of Licata. This first part of the invasion, the landing, was successful and relatively easy. Lucas and Keyes, Patton's generals, had both been at the beaches personally directing their units.

The Germans and Italians quickly surmised that they could not counter all of the Allied landings. Guzzoni ordered the Germans near the east to defend Syracuse while an Italian and German division prepared to launch a counterattack against American-controlled Gela.

The Seventh Army had achieved all of its objectives. Licata, Gela and Scoglitti had been captured. Meanwhile the British troops had become bogged down along a hastily erected defensive line before Syracuse. On July 11th the Germans and Italians launched their attack against Gela, in their most coordinated effort to force the Americans out of Sicily.

Patton was in Gela while the battle raged for the city. Watching from the top story of a tall building, Patton could see the enemy moving across the field, "perhaps 800 yards away." American infantry, paratroops, rangers, engineers, tankers and artillerymen were all involved in the fighting. The ships supported the American troops well, although soon the fighting was so internecine that they could not fire without endangering Americans. Patton's group was cut off from the 1st Division during the fighting. Both sides were firing at point blank range. At length, however, the Axis was unable to cross the coastal road, and with sixteen of their tanks burning on the battlefield, they were forced to withdraw. As they retreated, the Navy opened fire again.

Patton's building was hit twice, but no one was hurt. Patton then sent word to his general, Gaffey, to close the gap between the 1st Division and the town and to send tanks to reinforce Colonel Darby, the commander of the Rangers who were defending Gela. Darby used these tanks to counterattack and took 500 prisoners, thereby defeating the Axis attempt to recapture Gela. Patton's personal presence at Gela during the height of the attack, and his well-timed orders, saved Gela.

Patton toured the battlefields, inspecting his generals' commands, and sometimes even giving personal instructions to soldiers. He laid mortars, inspected the front, advised his generals, and then drove back to Gela. On the beach at Gela he saw "the most stupid thing I have ever seen soldiers doing." There were three 500 pound bombs and seven tons of high explosive shells piled on the sand, and,

> "These soldiers dug themselves foxholes in between the
> bombs and boxes of ammunition. I told them that if they
> wanted to save the Graves Registration burials, that was
> a fine thing to do, but otherwise, they better dig a
> foxhole somewhere else. About the time we got through
> explaining this to them, two bombers came over and
> strafed the beach, and all the soldiers jumped right back

into the same holes they had dug. I continued to walk up and down and soon shamed them into getting up."
Patton's Diary

Thus victory the first day was secured. Even on this first day Patton was out with the men, facing the same dangers, taking the same risks: seeing for himself the enemy counterattack and taking the necessary measures to prevent it. Part of the reason no other commander has been as successful as Patton is because so few have dared to be with their men in the line of fire, personally commanding.

Chapter Five

PALERMO

Early in the morning on July 11th, Patton noticed that the Axis seemed to be trying a serious attempt at dislodging his beachheads. He ordered a regiment of airborne troops to be flown from Africa and dropped inside his front. This was the quickest and easiest way to reinforce the beachhead. Patton called a meeting aboard the Monrovia to discuss his plan. Ridgway and Lucas attended the conference.

Even though Patton had planned for weeks to have the 82nd Airborne reinforce his beachhead, he had been unable to secure from them the exact route that the paratroopers would be taking. This was a fatal mistake on the part of the air corps, for such information was vital to the anti-aircraft gunners on the ground. Patton had a message sent to all of his major subordinate commanders – Bradley, Middleton, Allen, Galley, and Truscott warning them to "expect flights of friendly troops" on any of the first six nights of the invasion.

The Axis air forces had launched almost 500 missions against the Seventh Army. The anti-aircraft gunners had been firing all day long at the enemy planes overhead. On July 11th at dawn, a heavy German air attack was launched against the beaches. Another at 6:35 compelled the ships to weigh anchor and take evasive action. Four planes strafed the Gela beaches at two in the afternoon. Half an hour later, four bombers appeared over Scoglitti. Two hours later thirty German Junkers 88s began flying over Gela and strafing the area. Then at 9:50 p.m. so many German planes flew over Gela that the American ships were forced to disperse. Needless to say after so many attacks the anti-aircraft gunners were jumpy. Patton wanted to stop the airdrops but found that he could not get radio contact and was "terribly worried."

Meanwhile at the beaches the noise of the last raid had scarcely died down when the Allied transports carrying the 2000 paratroopers crossed the coastline near Sampieri. The first group jumped and landed fine. The second flight was just across the shoreline when a single machine gun on the ground opened fire on the formation. Within minutes a chain reaction occurred and it seemed that every Allied antiaircraft gun below was hysterically spitting bullets at the troop transport planes. Squadrons broke apart and scattered. Six planes took direct hits as the parachutists were trying to get out of the door to jump. Altogether, of the 144 planes that had departed Tunisia, 23 never returned. Among the paratroopers, there were 82 dead, 135 wounded, and 16 missing.

The paratroopers did not know the current countersigns and paroles, thus making the other Americans on the ground even more suspicious and likely to fire on them. Patton quickly sent an order down the chain of command that "extreme caution must be used to identify before firing on personnel."

The next day, July 13th, Patton received a "wire from Ike, cussing me out" because of the unfortunate incident during the night of the 11th. "He demanded an investigation and statement of punishments for those guilty of firing on them." It was tragic that Americans had fired on Americans. But Patton could see no way that the accident could have been avoided. The gunners had been bombed and shelled all day; their mistake, however regrettable, was also understandable.

> "It is my opinion that every possible precaution was taken by this headquarters to obviate firing on our own airborne troops and that the failure to do so was an unavoidable incident of combat. As far as I can see, if anyone is blameable, it must be myself, but personally, I feel immune to censure. Perhaps Ike is looking for an excuse to relieve me. I am having a full report made but will not try anyone [by court martial]. If they want a goat, I am it. Fortunately, Lucas, Wedemeyer, and Swing are here and know the facts... Men who have been bombed all day get itchy fingers. Eisenhower has never been subjected to air attack or any other form of combat.

However, he is such a straw man that his future is secure. The British will never let him go." *Patton's diary*

"Eisenhower has never been subjected to air attack or any other form of combat." How was it that he would come to lead millions of men in an environment he had never been in?

In World War Two, the U.S. decided that old generals should not retain command. People believed that the disasters of WWI were due to tired, old men leading. In WWII, it was decided, younger generals would command. At fifty five, Patton was the oldest American general. When America entered the war, he was sure that the "old general" fate would befall him and he would be disqualified from an active combat position. But Patton's brilliant performance in the war games saved his career from the fate his age would have otherwise doomed it to.

But now Patton was surrounded by his juniors. Whereas Patton had fought in the Mexican American War, WWI, and WWII, Eisenhower had neither fought nor commanded in any war. Most of the generals Patton was speaking to had only a textbook knowledge of war, and those with experience could claim only to have served a few months in WWI. No wonder they were intimidated by the British generals![1]

It is no accident that it was Patton who showed the British that the Americans were not amateurs playing at war. Only Patton had the experience necessary, and only Patton had updated his knowledge between wars, learning from the masters of war. It is really not surprising that the British didn't respect Eisenhower; after all, he had never fought at all!

On July 12th, General Ike came in a light cruiser.

"When I took him to my room to show him the situation [on the map], he was not much interested but began to compare the sparsity of my reports with the almost hourly news bulletins of the Eighth Army. I have intercepts of many of them, and they are both non-essential and imaginary in the majority of cases. Furthermore, they are not fighting, as we are. I directed

---

[1] Part of the reason the Americans were being treated as amateurs by the British was due to their obvious lack of experience as well as knowledge.

Gay to send in three reports in addition to the regular 16:00 situation reports. Ike also told me that I am too prompt in my replies and should hesitate more, as he does, before replying. I think he means well, but it is most upsetting to get only piddling criticism when one knows one has done a good job. Ike is now wearing suede shoes a la British ...."

On July 12th, in the Eighth Army area, Dempsey's XIII Corps was able to move into Augusta because the Germans had withdrawn to better defensive positions. The Germans had decided to set up a defensive line south of Catania which was effectively blocking all of Montgomery's attempts to breach it.

After a bit of thought, Montgomery decided to start a secondary thrust with Leese's XXX Corps on the left taking an interior road reserved to the Americans, going around the western slopes of Mt. Etna, and then attacking behind the enemy troops blocking Catania. For this left-hand thrust, Montgomery needed the Vizzini-Enna road which Alexander had placed in the American zone. Without consulting Alexander, he took it, and then demanded that the army boundaries be altered to confirm the accomplished fact.

Alexander caved in, infuriating the Americans. The Vizzini-Enna road was crucial to their advance. Montgomery had foreseen this and had sent a message to Alexander suggesting that the Americans be shifted westward to Gela[1] so that he could use their interior road. Monty recommended that the Seventh U.S. Army face westward and "take defensive positions." There would be nothing for the Americans to defend at Gela; Monty simply wanted the American army to stand still while he used its road to advance and take Messina.

Montgomery needed to have the American road, because the Germans had created an effective defense in front of him, and he felt that the grass was greener on Patton's side. Montgomery liked to act as if the Americans did not exist, and as much as he could he ignored them. Up until this point all his plans had the British taking the important objectives and the Americans "covering." Even in December of 1944 in Operation Market Garden, he had the British taking the largest bridges.

---

[1] Practically hemming the Americans in and making it impossible for them to advance.

Patton recorded the day in his diary.

"Bradley wanted to get Lt. Col. Darby to command the 80th Regimental Combat Team of the 45th Division with the rank of colonel. Darby preferred to stay with the Rangers. This is the first time I ever saw a man turn down a promotion. Darby is really a great soldier. I gave him the D.S.C. [for his action at Gela]. General Wedemeyer asked to be reduced to a Colonel so he could get the 8th. I sent him up to command it as a Brigadier General. I have no real authority to do this, but like to help a fighting man. Went to lunch at 12:50. General Alexander... and members of his staff arrived at 13:10, so I had to quit eating and see them. They gave us the future plan of operations, which cuts us off from any possibility of taking Messina. It is noteworthy that Alexander, the Allied commander of a British and American Army, had no Americans with him. What fools we are." *Patton's Diary*

At this meeting Patton could easily have lost his temper and stated how ridiculous denying him roads and forcing him to wait was. But he wisely restrained himself. Arguing with Montgomery would be futile. Montgomery had "proven" himself at El Alamein, and so far the Americans really did seem to be amateurs compared to their British counterparts. Patton was determined to change that; but for the moment, he would be quiet and wait. When the moment was ripe, he would seize the chance for victory.

Patton knew that after several days had gone by, Alexander would be annoyed with Montgomery's non-existent progress. Then Patton could ask Alexander for permission to "help."

"I asked General Alexander permission to advance and take Agrigento, which is beyond the line specified for the front of the Seventh Army. He stated that if this could be done through the use of limited forces, in the nature of a reconnaissance in force, he had no abjection. It is very essential to capture this port as, by so doing, we can obviate the necessity of using Siracusa as a base, thus saving a turn around of 140 miles [by trucks] over

bad roads, and also obviating the necessity of using a
port in conjunction with the Eighth Army which could
use all the supplies coming through Syracuse. If we take
Agrigento, we can supply all the Seventh Army forces
through ports. This will permit abandonment of
[unloading at] the beaches which are difficult and
distant." *Patton's Diary*

At this juncture it is worth pointing out that Montgomery had
designed the plan for Sicily. In his original plan, he had said that he
would take Messina by way of a coastal road. But now, in the middle of
the operation, he had decided he also needed Patton's inland road. This
clearly shows what a poor planner he was. Patton was now pushed into
the corner (literally) and forced to wait while Montgomery crawled.

"Seventh Army was forced to take their front to pieces
and re-shape it further west. Their distress could have
been mitigated by allowing them to fight for more
elbowroom against the Germans in the west, having
been deprived of it by Montgomery in the east, but
Patton was still held in check. Alexander permitted him
to reconnoitre in the direction of Agrigento, but told him
that he must not become involved in heavy fighting.
Palermo was still forbidden territory. It was now that the
flaw in Montgomery's plan became apparent. Only three
good roads led northwards from the beaches, and
Montgomery had taken two of them. Seventh Army was
cramped for space, their strength only half used, and
humiliated by this overt demonstration that they were
not to be trusted with a major role. During the next few
days the relative missions of the two armies did not
change. Eighth Army pushed up the two main routes in
an attempt to encircle Etna as Alexander had planned,
and Seventh Army conformed by occupying the centre
of the island in the Enna-Caltanissetta triangle. They
were still forbidden to strike for Palermo, although by
this time there was not even the excuse that Eighth Army
required them as a flank-guard, for all German
formations had moved eastwards. When Alexander told
him that he must wait until Eighth Army had secured
their base (presumably Catania), Patton drew himself up

and replied, 'Yes, General.'" *"Alex, the life of the Field Marshal Earl Alexander of Tunis," by Nigel Nicolson.*

Bradley remembered that they were "within easy artillery range of the Vizzini-Caltagirone road that would open a path to Enna" when he was called to Seventh Army HQ at Gela. He says he "found Patton wreathed in cigar smoke, scanning a map with his G3."
"We've received a directive from Army Group, Brad. Monty's to get the Vizzini-Caltagirone in his drive to flank Catania and Mt. Etna by going up through Enna. This means you'll have to sideslip west with your 45th Division."
Bradley whistled. "This will be horrible for us. I had counted heavily on that road. Now if we've got to shift over, it'll slow up our entire advance. May we at least use the road to shift Middleton over left of Terry Allen? It'll be easier to move around to the left of the 1st rather than shift both divisions over. In that way we can probably keep Terry going and maintain the momentum of our attack. I don't want the enemy to get set anywhere."
"Sorry, Brad," Patton answered, "but the change-over takes place immediately. Monty wants the road right away."
"But that leaves you in a pretty tough spot. Middleton is now within 1000 yards of that road. If I can't use it to move him over to the other side of Allen, I'll have to pull the 45th all the way back to the beaches and pass it around Terry's rear."

At this point Patton handed Bradley Alexander's directive. "The enemy was falling back in disorganization, I didn't want him to regain his balance," Bradley recalled. But the directive was clear enough. Montgomery was to advance toward Messina on two diverging paths; one up the rim of the island on the east coast road, across the marshes, through Catania, and beyond along the narrow shelf between Mt. Etna and the sea, and the other to the west, north of Mt. Etna toward Messina. But because of this change, Bradley now had to shift the 45th Division by trucking it back to the beaches and placing it into position on the left of Allen's 1st Division. This would be a long and difficult maneuver, during which the enemy would have a change to reorganize and reconnoiter.

Weeks after the Sicilian campaign had ended, Patton visited Monty at the latter's CP. During their conversation, Patton complained of the injustice of Alexander's Army Group directive on the Vizzini-Caltagirone road. Monty looked at him with amusement. "George," he said, "let me give you some advice. If you get an order from Army Group that you don't like, why just ignore it. That's what I do."

> "Montgomery, of course, had oversimplified his explanation. He was first a good, if sometimes perverse soldier. He didn't ignore his orders,[1] though sometimes he tried to skirt them, while being careful to avoid a showdown. Basically, Montgomery's comment to Patton reflected a common attitude in the British command, a view sometimes difficult for an American soldier to understand. Unlike the U.S. Army, where an order calls for instant compliance, the British viewed an order as a basis for discussion between commanders. If a difference of opinion developed, it would be ironed out, and the order might be amended. In contrast, we in the American army sought to work out our differences before issuing an order. Once an order was issued, it could not be changed except by the issuing authority. Had I known of this British characteristic I most certainly would have appealed to Patton to protest the Army Group decision on the road." *"A Soldier's Story," by Omar N. Bradley.*

It was the 14th of July, and it looked as if Messina was going to be taken by the British. But there was still Palermo, a large city on the western end of the island. If Patton could take Palermo very quickly, his army would be in a great position for capturing Messina – provided that Montgomery had still not taken it. And that was Patton's secret dream.

For this purpose, Patton assembled a provisional corps consisting of the 3rd Division, the 82nd Airborne Division, and a regiment of the 8th Division "which is due to arrive tomorrow." He gave command of the corps to Keyes, whom he authorized to go all the way. Even though he was squeezed into the narrow southern section of Sicily, Patton would now have two corps operating on two routes, just like Montgomery in the west. Bradley was moving toward the northern core of Sicily while Keyes was moving toward Palermo.

In his diary, Patton said,

---

[1] It is customary of Bradley not to be forthright, as he is clearly doing here. There are many times when Montgomery ignored his orders, but as he explains this is not as big an offense as it seemed anyway.

"It is my opinion that when the present line of the combined armies is secured, which will probably be around the 19th, it will be feasible to advance rapidly with the 3rd Division and 2nd Armored Division and take Palermo. I will bring this question up to General Alexander when the time is ripe."

Patton had bet the British Vice Air Marshal Wigglesworth a bottle of whiskey against a bottle of gin that the Americans would take Palermo by midnight of the 23rd.

"He was very skeptical, but I believe without logical reason, that we can do so because I am sure that the enemy, German or Italian, cannot resist *our* continuous attacks. One Italian prisoner, an officer, is alleged to have said in a captured letter that the Americans were strange people; they attacked all day, marched all night, and fired all the time." *Patton's Diary*

To date the Seventh Army had captured 14,000 men. "Monty is trying to steal the show and with the assistance of Divine Destiny[1] may do so," he told her, "but to date we have captured three times as many men as our cousins."[2] Patton is blaming Eisenhower, not Alexander, because he felt that it was Eisenhower's duty to stand up for American participation in the operation.[3]

On the 17th, Patton wrote in his diary,

"General Alexander... directs that the Seventh Army protect the rear of the Eighth Army, thus putting the Americans in a secondary role, which is a continuation of such roles for the whole campaign and may find the war ending with us being overlooked, I am flying to Tunis to see General Alexander. I am sure that neither he

---

[1] Patton's codename for Eisenhower.
[2] His codename for the British.
[3] Eisenhower did not have much of a role in the Sicilian operation, although it is his fault that the Navy was under-deployed and the Germans were allowed to escape from the island. This basic flaw in Montgomery's original plan was apparently not noticed, and since Eisenhower approved this plan, he bears responsibility.

nor any of his British staff has any conception of the power or mobility of the Seventh Army, nor are they aware of the political implications latent in such a course of action." *Patton's diary*

Patton realized that the British simply didn't know what he was capable of. He could turn the Seventh Army into an incredible thrusting device and drive the Germans from the island – but not without Alexander's permission.

"I shall explain the situation to General Alexander on the basis that it would be inexpedient politically for the Seventh Army not to have equal glory in the final stage of the campaign. Arranged a map showing our proposed operation and attached a copy of the order we believe should be written. General Wedemeyer and I left... at 12:10, arrived at Tunis at 13:09, and saw General Alexander. He explained that he had planned to do just what I asked but that his chief of staff had failed to tell me when issuing the order.[1] He gave me permission to carry out my plan if I would assure him that the road net near Caltanissetta would be held... If I do what I am going to do, there is no need of holding anything, but 'it's a mean man who won't promise' so I did."

At last Alexander had given Patton permission to advance. Nigel Nicolson points out that Patton's later career "has made it difficult to associate him with reticence," but there was a crucial difference between Patton in Sicily and Patton in France. Patton was willing to wait in Sicily because he was dealing with the British and he was asking them to accept a gamble and let his untried army free. But later in France he would be dealing with the American high command, who already knew his value and what he was capable of. After the British saw how quickly Patton could advance they were in awe; as General Lemnitzer said, "whatever friction there may have been in the early stages of Husky, all was forgotten... as Alexander realized for the first time what a thruster he had under his command."[2]

---

[1] Patton found this a "pretty weak" excuse.

[2] Think of what could have taken place had Eisenhower been in command now, instead of Alexander. Similar situations occurred many times in France, but Eisenhower always held Patton back when Montgomery wanted him to. It is to

In his diary, Patton compared the differences between the Americans and the British.

> "I think that the British have the bear by the tail in Messina and we may have to go and help. Had they let us... take Caltagirone and Enna ourselves, instead of waiting for them, we would have saved two days and been on the north coast now. Alex has no idea of either the power or speed of American armies. We can go twice as fast as the British and hit harder, but to save British prestige, the XXX Corps had to make the envelopment, and now I think they are stuck. They attacked Catania with a whole division yesterday and only made 400 yards... Our method of attacking all the time is better than the British method of stop, build up, and start, but we must judge by the enemy reaction. I can do it here. Alex can't in Tunis." *Patton's Diary*

The attacking method that Patton is calling "American" is really his own, and it was not characteristic of American attacks before or since. *Patton* was certainly better than the British, but whether or not the Americans were is open to conjecture. Their later massive casualties at Normandy, Hurtgen and the Ardennes compare favorably to Montgomery's Arnhem and Caen.

On July 20th, the Seventh took Enna at 9:43 in the morning. The Canadians came eight minutes later.

> "I sent a dispatch to General Alexander saying that we arrived at the same time. I will bet they claim to have got there first."

Patton sensed that the British "have a pretty bloody nose south of Catania." They had asked for the 78th Division to come to Sicily from North Africa, "which last week they had said they did not need."

Alexander's credit that after Montgomery failed to advance he let Patton take the prize – Messina.

On the 22nd, Patton's tanks rolled into Palermo, capturing what was to be their first in a series of many headlines. He wrote jubilantly to his wife:

> "By the time even the censor sees this [letter] the name of the town will be in all the papers so he can fill it in here _____. We have out blitzed the Bosch[1]... It is really a great show. I am flying to the front after lunch to see the kill. I feel that future students of the Command and General Staff School will study the campaign of Palermo as a classic example of the use of tanks. I held them back far enough so that the enemy could not tell where they were to be used; then when the infantry had found the hole, the tanks went through in large numbers and fast. Such methods assure victory and reduce losses, but it takes fine leadership to insure the execution. General Keyes provided perfect leadership and great drive. The praise should be his. After dusk we got to the command post of the 2nd Armored Division and Colonel Perry, chief of staff, told me he thought Palermo had fallen and that Generals Keyes and Gaffey had entered it. He volunteered to guide me in, so we started. It is a great thrill to be driving into a captured city in the dark. We got to the Headquarters at the Royal Palace at 10 p.m. and found Keyes and Gaffey had gone to bed, and Combat Command A and elements of the 3rd Division had the town under control. I saw Keyes and Gaffey and congratulated them. We had a small flask and each took a drink."

The victory was sweetened by a message radioed from Alexander. It read: "This is a great triumph. Well done. Heartiest congratulations to you and all your splendid soldiers." Patton wrote next to the message in his diary, "I told him once that Americans needed praise and here it is." The Americans had proven themselves and won, from the British at least, the praise they deserved.

---

[1] Germans

Chapter Six

VICTORY

The American blitz across Sicily and victory at Palermo was splashed across all the headlines. Patton's victory was incredible in its speed, and he was called a "brilliant and mobile" general. The papers didn't know why Montgomery had halted to the east in Sicily, although they were careful to say that he was up against the "brunt of the resistance." Soon they would be writing that the areas Patton took had not really been defended, something that annoyed Patton, but spurred him on.

Patton's "Account of the Capture of Palermo" makes for interesting reading.

Account of Capture of Palermo, July 23, 1943
We went through an almost continuous village. The street was full of people shouting, "Down with Mussolini" and "Long Live America." When we got into the town the same thing went on. Those who arrived before dark... had flowers thrown on the road in front of them, and lemons and watermelons given them in such profusion that they almost became lethal weapons.... The bag of prisoners for the day must have been close to 10,000. On the morning of the 23rd, when I was inspecting the harbor, I passed a group of prisoners, all of whom stood up, saluted, and then cheered. The harbor is not too badly damaged; but the destruction around the lip is really appalling. We took over the so-called Royal

Palace for a headquarters and had it cleaned by prisoners for the first time since the Greek Occupation.[1] We are also having the prisoners remove the rubbish from the streets and plug the holes in the dock. The Cardinal's Vicar came to call on me and I assured him that I was amazed at the stupidity and gallantry of the Italian army: stupid because they were fighting for a lost cause, and gallant because they were Italians. I asked him to tell them that and to spread the rumor. I further said that we had demonstrated our ability to destroy them; and if they failed to take the hint and surrender, we would certainly do so. As a matter of fact, I called off the air bombardment and naval bombardment which we had arranged, because I felt enough people had been killed, and felt that with the drive of the 3rd Armored Division we could take the place without inflicting unproductive losses on the enemy. I believe... that historical research will reveal that General Keyes' Corps moved faster against heavier resistance and over worse roads than did the Germans during their famous blitz. We did not waste any time, however, and started this morning capturing the north road and also moving artillery to support the final effort[2] of the II Corps which will begin in a few days.

Patton also wrote in his diary,

"The British have given me [Routes] 113 and 120 [leading to the east, toward Messina] and are damned glad we are there... The Seventh Army has taken most of the island."

Patton wrote to his wife the next day, again commenting on the reticence of Eisenhower.

"So many big shots have told me how great I am that I am in danger of believing and that might cramp my style. Of course under the circumstances there is danger in too much success, but I can't help it if the cherries fall

---

[1] The ancient Greeks
[2] The final effort was to be an American drive along the northern shore toward Messina!

46

in my mouth. So far I have heard nothing [of praise] from D, but suppose that in time it will come? Tomorrow I go to see Alex and Monty. I hope it comes out all right. I always feel like a little lamb on such occasions but so far I have gotten by. Some day I hope I can fight a nice war alone but fear that it is too much to hope for. Anyhow, I love wars and am having a fine time."

Heubner had been relieved as Alexander's deputy chief of staff, "largely, I know, because he stood up for American interests." Patton was worried that the same fate might befall him. I need "to report at Siracusa Airport tomorrow at 11:00 to see Alex and Monty. I fear the worst, but so far have held my own with them."

At the meeting the next day,

"Monty was there with several staff officers. I made the error of hurrying to meet him. He hurried a little too, but I started it. He then asked me to look at a map on the hood of his car. On this he had drawn a boundary. He agreed so readily that I felt something was wrong, but have not found it yet. When this much had been arranged, Montgomery did not see why we did not take all of route 117. As it is useless to both of us, he did not have any objection to our taking it." *Patton's Diary*

Patton needed the coastal roads, Highway 113 and 120 to take Messina, which was about 20 miles inland.

"After all this had been settled, Alex came. He looked a little mad, and, for him, was quite brusque. He told Monty to explain his plan. Monty said he and I had already decided what we were going to do, so Alex got madder and told Monty to show him the plan. He did and then Alex asked for mine and agreed, but said there were supply difficulties which General Miller [G-4, AFHQ] would explain. All Miller wanted to do was to cut my LSTs to 35. I held out for 45, to which Miller reluctantly agreed, but said it was up to Admiral Cunningham. On this, Bedell Smith broke in and told Miller that AFHQ would make the division [of LSTs between the Armies] and that he, Miller, was too prone to forget the existence of AFHQ. (So is everyone else, as it never asserts itself.) I then said I wanted LST's for at least a reinforced battalion for small amphibious operations [along the north shore]. Alex did not think much of this but agreed to try. I also said I needed cruisers, and Richardson said he would see that we got them. I doubt if he does. He also asked me if I knew Huebner had been relieved, and I said I did. He said, 'I want to assure you that [Alexander's] 15th Army Group is completely Allied in mind and favors neither Army.' I know this was a lie, but said I felt that he was right – God pardon me. The meeting then broke up. No one was offered any lunch and I thought that Monty was ill bred both to Alexander and me. Monty gave me a 5 cent [cigarette] lighter. Some one must have sent him a box of them."

The tone of this passage is sarcastic, and Patton seems more and more frustrated with the British.

"We flew back to Palermo in just one hour, arriving at 2:30 p.m., at the same moment that the rest of the staff came in by motor. Keyes met me with a Guard of Honor from the 3rd Division and a band. We occupied the Royal Palace. I am in the King's Room and there are, by count, seven ante-rooms between my room and the State dining room. My bed has three mattresses on it, but it is uncomfortable, and there is a bathroom with warm water and electric lights. Many fine oil paintings on the walls and much golf furniture, mirrors, etc.... There is also a grand staircase – very dirty. All sorts of retainers live in holes about the place and give the Facist [sic] salute. Stiller has no flair for history and said he was sure he could find me a nicer place in some good boarding home. I prefer the historical lift of sleeping in a royal bed and cleaning my teeth in a mirror etched with the Arms of Savoy." *Patton's Diary*

Patton called on the Cardinal. He was living in a convent because his palace was bombed.

48

"He is very small and quite intelligent. They took a lot of pictures of us in the bosom of the church. I offered to kiss his ring, but Keyes says no, only the faithful do that – he did it. We went into a chapel and prayed. The Mother Superior is a French woman and we talked a little... I feel that he [the Cardinal] is on our side and this fact will have a good effect on the inhabitants."

Patton felt that part of his duty as a general was to visit the wounded soldiers at the hospitals. Patton did not enjoy the visits because there were always some gruesomely mangled soldiers which made him upset. It seems amazing that someone who is often viewed as a tough, rough man would cry, but Patton felt he had responsibility for each and every man under his command. The sight of men who had valorously shed their blood for their country moved him to tears. Unfortunately Patton's hospital visits have become associated only with the slapping incidents. In reality, Patton visited the hospitals long before those incidents, and would continue to throughout his career.

"The other day... I apparently performed a miracle. I was at the hospital seeing the men... I presented a lot of Purple Hearts. Finally I came to a man with an oxygen mask on, which is the last stage, so I took off my helmet, kneeled down, and pinned the Purple Heart on his pajamas – he got well."

Palermo's capture had not gone unnoticed. Roosevelt had sent Patton a signed picture, Churchill had sent Congratulations, and so had General Alexander. Eisenhower, however, seemed determined to remain silent. In a letter to his wife on July 27th, Patton wrote,

"The war is far from over but we are going to win it in a big way. At the moment we are having a hard race with our cousins. I think we have an edge on them. I am quite curious to see what comes out at home. BBC just barely admits that we exist. I have not the least notion what will happen next time [after Sicily] but I don't care where, when, or who I fight so long as I keep fighting. It is the greatest of all games. FDR sent me a signed picture of he and I, and the PM has wired congrats, but Divine Destiny [Eisenhower] is still mute."

On the 27th of July Patton inspected the Coast Artillery Corps Anti-aircraft. The colonel who was in command there did not know where his firing batteries were. Patton insisted that he visit all of them at once. When Patton arrived a few days later, the colonel was able to guide him personally over the grounds.

Montgomery visited Patton and told him that *if* the Americans got to Taormina first, they were to turn south. Always before Monty had insisted that the Americans were not to go as far as the east coast. But now Monty was admitting that the Americans might get to Taormina or even beyond. This was a sign that Montgomery realized what trouble his front would soon be in; his troops had only crawled since Patton had left the beaches. Patton, for his part, refused to let the pressure off his men; they had done well, but they were to continue conquering – quickly. "I spurred both Bradley and Middleton a little today. I felt they were getting sticky, but probably I am wrong."

On July 28th, 1943, Patton sent an often misunderstood message to his general, Middleton. The message read, "This is a horse race, in which the prestige of the U.S. Army is at stake. We must take Messina before the British. Please use your best efforts to facilitate the success of our race." Here, say many biographers, Patton is clearly showing his petty-jealousy and rivalry with the British. In reality, Patton's meaning is clear, for he states his motives, "The prestige of the U.S. Army is at stake."

This was literally true. Unless the Americans proved themselves in a glorious and spectacular victory, the British would always treat them like amateurs. Patton had waited quietly for a week while Montgomery was halted by the thick German resistance that he had allowed to build up in front of him. Then, to get around that resistance, Montgomery took the American road without either permission or consideration... you get the picture. If Patton didn't do something incredibly quickly, the Americans would be treated forever like a very sorry appendage of the British army. As Nigel Nicolson, an Englishman, said, "It is to Patton's credit that he wished not merely to capture 'real estate in the empty west,' but share in the real fighting for Messina; not to just look good on maps, but to excel." Yet, amazingly, some of Patton's biographers would make this a crime.

Patton felt that Middleton's attacks were not audacious enough. He thought that Middleton looked tired and his attacks lacked drive. Patton said to him, "I think I will give the 45th a rest and use the 3rd." Middleton said, "I would never ask for a rest."
Patton replied, "It is my duty to see that the best interests of the United States are served, so I shall give you a rest."
Middleton answered, "I think that is what you should do."

> "I thought this was an excellent example of willingness to play ball and unwillingness to ask for help. I wired Truscott to come up and talk over with Middleton the question of [division] relief. Bradley called up and I told him... I was going to relieve the 45th as I had talked about with him yesterday. Drove to the command post of the leading battalion... just west of S. Stefano. They were attacking. I talked to the men and said, 'I hope you know how good you are, for everyone else does. You are magnificent.' I also told the engineers what fine work they have done. They have, but love to be told."

Eisenhower arrived to inspect the Seventh Army on July 31st. Patton had a scout car escort and a Guard of Honor from the 15th Infantry. This was Eisenhower's old battalion, "the only unit he ever commanded," Patton commented dryly in his diary. The guard of honor "was the thought of General Gay, and Ike was quite pleased with the compliment." Patton noted that Eisenhower was "quite relaxed but did not compliment us." Eisenhower told them that after Sicily the Eighth Army would cross at Messina and the Fifth U.S. Army land at Naples with an American corps and the X British Corps. "If things get serious, the Seventh Army will land later near Florence, otherwise we will go to the UK for the big push."[1]

On August first, Patton wrote a message for his troops and ordered it read to them. Patton was always concerned with the well-being of his men, and this message was to be morale-lifting: a kind of "eve of victory" announcement.

> "Soldiers of the Seventh Army and XII Air Support Command: Landed and supported by the navy and air force, you have, during 21 days of ceaseless battle and

---

[1] the Normandy invasion.

unremitting toil, killed and captured more than 87,000 enemy soldiers, you have captured or destroyed 871 cannon, 172 tanks, 928 trucks, and 190 airplanes – you are magnificent soldiers! General Eisenhower... and General Alexander... have both expressed pride and satisfaction in your efforts. Now in conjunction with the British Eighth Army you are closing in for the kill. Your relentless offensive will continue to be irresistible. The end is certain and is very near. Messina is our next stop!"

Patton was very happy with the progress his army was making.

"We have started to move and move and move... The mountains are the worst I have ever seen. It is a miracle that our men get through them but we must keep up our steady pressure. The enemy simply can't stand it. Besides, we must beat the Eighth Army to Messina."

Alexander came the next day, and Patton was "very much amused with his statement that he was delighted with our ability to carry out his plans for the early capture of Palermo." Patton felt that Alexander had done "everything to prevent not only its early capture but its capture at all." Patton would soon get used to senior commanders taking credit for his victories.

Patton wrote to his wife,

"We have had all the hot shots to visit us, first Monty, then D, and today Alex. The first is much less condescending then he was – he ought to be, as a study of the map will show. D was very nice and while not complimentary failed to criticize – first time. Alex is always good company and much interested in ruins.[1] I showed him my palace... there is a parliament room 140 feet long by 60 feet broad, with all the labors of Hercules on the walls at one end and on the cealing [sic].

On August 3rd Patton once again visited an evacuation hospital. He,

---

[1] Some people say Patton hated the British?!

"...talked to 350 newly wounded. One poor fellow who had lost his right arm cried; another had lost a leg. All were brave and cheerful. A first sergeant... was in for his second wound. He laughed and said that after he got his third he was going to ask to go home. I had told General Marshall several months ago that an enlisted man hit three times should be sent home..."

In a letter to his brother-in-law, written on August 6th, Patton said,

"We have taken a town that we have been attacking for three days, so I feel pretty good, especially as Bernard [Montgomery] had wired that he was coming to my assistance. Now he doesn't need to. We are having a horse race to see who will get to the last big town first – it will be a close match, but I hope to beat him and so make a clean sweep."

In an interesting diary entry, Patton wrote that,

"I stopped to inspect a field hospital... and saw two men completely out from shell shock. One kept going through the motions of crawling. The doctor told me they were going to give them an injection to put them to sleep and they would probably wake up alright. One man had the top of his head blown off and they were just waiting for him to die. He was a horrid bloody mess and was not good to look at, or I might develop personal feelings about sending men to battle. That would be fatal for a General."

This entry is of special interest because it proves that Patton *did* believe in shell-shock. He knew and understood it, but knowing what it was, he also knew what it was not.

On a completely different note, Patton said,

"The Germans are firing at the command post regularly with a long range gun ... I was a little worried for a few seconds, and I felt ashamed of myself but I got over it. I have trained myself so that usually I can keep right on talking when an explosion occurs quite close. I take a sly pleasure in seeing others bat their eyes or look around."

The number of entries in Patton's diary about hospital visits are amazing, especially when one considers that other commanders did not take the trouble to visit this part of their command. And all of these examples are of Patton visiting the hospital, *before the slapping incidents.*

"At another evacuation hospital... one boy with a shattered leg said, 'Are you General Patton? I have read all about you." All seemed glad to see me... Most of them are in good shape, and I saw only two who the medical people said were going to die."

In a daring operation called an "end-run," Patton planned to load his men onto ships and land in front of the opposition holding up the 3rd Division. An operation of this sort was both daring and risky, but it was typical of Patton. These were the sort of operations that separated Patton from the mediocre generals. He was not afraid that the landing army might be cut off and annihilated. His generals told him it was risky, but what was war, if not risky? He deemed another risk far more dangerous: the one caused by waiting while the German opposition slowly ate away at their troops. Patton's generals, however, didn't agree. Bradley and Truscott wanted to call off the end-run because they said that the 3rd Division had not moved fast enough to support it.

On the British side of Sicily, Churchill had sent a telegram to Montgomery. He wanted him to advance using what he called "cat's claw," or what the Americans called an end-run. Montgomery, after experimenting, cancelled both landings. He thought they were too risky.

On the American side, Patton was trying to convince his generals that end-runs were not risky, if they were followed by a quick advance. He told Keyes that the landings had to go on. Maybe the Americans had heard that Montgomery had cancelled his, who knows. If they thought their boss would do so too, they completely misjudged Patton.

Another of Patton's generals, Truscott, requested to speak to him. Truscott strongly protested continuing the landings. Patton told him they would go on. Truscott replied, "Alright, if you order it."

Patton answered, "I do."

Patton surmised that his generals were altogether too nervous, so he decided to go up and see General Truscott at his Command Post with General Gay. There they would "see that the boats got off," as Patton put it.

The first person Patton met outside Truscott's C.P. was Captain Davis, the U.S. Navy chief of staff to Admiral Davidson. He said the landing should be called off as it had started an hour late and could not land before 4 am. "I told him that if it did not land until 6 a.m., it still had to go on." This was a crucial moment; the anxiety that occurs before a daring operation can turn into pandemonium if the commander does not demonstrate confidence in his army's abilities.

Inside the Command Post, Truscott was pacing up and down, "holding a map and looking futile."

Patton confronted him. "General Truscott, if your conscience will not let you conduct this operation, I will relieve you and put someone in command who will."

"General, it is your privilege to reduce me whenever you want to," Truscott answered.

"I don't want to. I got you the DSM and recommended you for major general, but your own ability really gained both honors. You are too old an athlete to believe it is possible to postpone a match."

"You are an old enough athlete to know that sometimes they are postponed."

"This one won't be," Patton replied. "The ships have already started."

Truscott replied, "This is a war of defile, and there is a bottleneck delaying me in getting my guns up to support the infantry. The infantry will be too far west to help the landing."

Patton looked at him. "Remember what Frederick the Great said?"

"What's that, General?"

"L'audace, toujours l'audace."[1] Patton paused. What had happened to Truscott? He couldn't be afraid?

It was at moments like this that Patton demonstrated why he was able to command the best from his men. Truscott was an old friend, and he was urging Patton to forsake the landing. But Patton knew that the landing was necessary and not as risky as Truscott seemed to believe. He needed to bolster the confidence of his general, and to do so, he said, "I

---

[1] Audacity, always audacity.

know you will win and if there is a bottleneck, you should be there and not here."

Patton always believed that the commander should be at the sight of the action, personally directing and ordering from a position where he could best see what was happening.

Just then Bradley called to ask whether or not the landings were on. At this moment Patton must have wondered what manner of fear had overtaken his generals; his best men, the men he had so much confidence in, were weak with fright. Patton immediately and unhesitatingly told Bradley that they were certainly going to attack. If the landings failed, he insisted, "I will take full responsibility." And if things went well, Patton added, Bradley could have the credit along with Truscott. This technique was Patton's last line of defense in overcoming his generals' fears. He would insist that he had total confidence in the success of an operation, and to prove it he would sacrifice his career if it failed.

Bradley would always resent Patton's insistence on these end-runs in Sicily, even though they turned out to be incredibly successful. The fear that Bradley felt during these operations, and his anger that Patton insisted on the end-runs and was right, permeates his record of this time. Bradley was to write, quite unjustly, that,

> "The techniques of command vary, of course, with the personality of the commander. While some men prefer to lead by suggestion and example and other methods, Patton chose to drive his subordinates by bombast and by threats. Those mannerisms achieved spectacular results. But they were not calculated to win affection among his officers or his men." *"A Soldier's Story," by General Omar N. Bradley*

This statement could not be farther from the truth. As has already been shown, Patton would drive to the scene of action and personally assist his men in assuring victory. Whether by pointing out to a colonel that he should know where his men were located, or by calling in additional troops at the crucial point in a desperate battle, Patton *always* led by example. In fact he is the only commander who dared go the front and risk himself along the lines. He said that he could not have ordered his men to do anything he would not do himself. As for "affection" from "his officers or his men," Patton's men were so loyal and devoted that the books they have written have been condemned by modern biographers as being too "biased." There is not a single example that can be given of Patton driving "his subordinates by bombast and by threats." This must be Bradley's own opinion, often disguised as someone else's. In France, where Bradley was in command of Patton, instead of the other way around, "Instead of replying huffily as he might have a year before, George merely crinkled his eyes and chuckled, 'You're right, Brad, actually, you're always right.'" Bradley then concludes that this was *new* behavior on Patton's part. It was not. The difference between Sicily and France is that in Sicily, Patton commanded Bradley, whereas in France, Patton was Bradley's subordinate. In other words, in Sicily Patton could force Bradley to undertake a daring and successful operation, whereas in France Bradley could forbid such a one to Patton.

Bradley wrote another strange statement concerning Patton, probably incited by Patton having to force him to carry out the end-run operation. "At times I felt that Patton, however successful he was as a corps commander, had not yet learned to command himself," Bradley wrote. This statement is ridiculous. *Eisenhower* could clearly not control himself, yet there is no word of criticism for him anywhere in Bradley's book; in fact he is often weakly defended. Patton's command of himself was exemplary. He was afraid of neither fire nor bullets. There are many witnesses who have said that airplanes would be dropping bombs all around, but Patton would not even flinch, even as higher ranks ran for cover. He often stood bravely up against Eisenhower when a lesser man would have backed down. In France Patton and Bradley would get along relatively well together. But in Sicily Bradley did not agree with Patton's daring tactics or his stand on Montgomery. In fact Bradley did not become convinced of Montgomery's terribly WWI-like tactics until after Normandy. And Bradley did not properly appreciate Patton until Patton rescued him in the Ardennes operation. Bradley was, to put it mildly, a typical West Point graduate, slow, cautious, and convinced that Clausewitz tactics would undoubtedly triumph. This, no matter how many times audacity had proven otherwise.

Patton's generals were still nervous about the end-runs, so Patton told Truscott that he had complete confidence in him, and, to show it, he would leave him in command and go home to bed.

"On the way back alone I worried a little, but feel I was right. I thought of Grant and Nelson and felt O.K. That is the value of history. I woke General House up to be sure we would have air cover for the Navy in the morning, as we may need their support [for the landing]. I also told him to put all his air cover in front of the 3rd Division. I may have been bull-headed, but I truly feel that I did my exact and full duty and under rather heavy pressure demonstrated that I am a great leader." *Patton's Diary*

Patton did not know that Montgomery had just cancelled his own similar end-run landings. Patton certainly did show his ability as a leader, in a "competition" with Montgomery that neither was aware of.

Churchill knew that he had recommended end-runs to Monty, but that Monty had cancelled them after deciding they were "too risky." Because of this, and because Patton had shown with dazzling clarity the effectiveness of end-runs, Churchill would always regard Patton as the general who had been willing to take risks in Sicily – and succeed.

British vehicles were very poor, and the Americans could move much more rapidly. Their poor equipment was just another factor that was slowing the British down. It is not, however, as important a determinant in the campaign as Montgomery's poor planning and worse leadership.

Montgomery, however, was happy to blame the inferior equipment for his lack of progress; equipment was the one area that he admitted the Americans were superior in. General Gay's aide, Murnane, remembered this amusing tale,

> "You'll remember that during the North African campaign, Monty, almost like a senior prefect in school, used to call in various commanders, including some of ours and deliver lectures. He used to call this a 'military critique.' This one was even more high, mighty and objectionable than usual. In it, he said that whereas American equipment was magnificent, our troops were inadequately trained and rather poorly led. He made the modest proposal, therefore, that these troops should be taken out of Africa for more training, and that our equipment be turned over to him, so that he could get on with the war. I leave you to imagine the steam that was coming out of Patton's ears. He managed to obtain a sort of half-baked apology; but it was far from satisfactory, and he did not forgive. When we hit Sicily the plan was

for Patton to move up the center a certain distance and then hold, while Monty drove for the south all the way to the north coast at Messina. That was the plan, but [Patton] had another; he told us we were going to reach Messina before Monty, if it killed him and all of us.[1] It didn't and we did. In fact, Monty had hardly moved at all. Of course, he was facing mostly Germans, and we had fought mostly Italians, but victory was no less sweet. We were in some olive grove, or other, hoping it would be nice camouflage against bombers. Your uncle and 'Hap' Gay were off to one side.

Suddenly, Patton yelled, 'Hey, Murnane.'

I hurried over. He pointed at a five-gallon jerry can.

'You see that can, Murnane?'

'Yes, sir, of course.'

'Well, I want you to take it to Monty, down at Taormina and give him a message from me. Now listen.'

'Yes, sir.'

'The message is as follows: 'Although sadly short of gasoline myself, I know of your admiration for our equipment and can spare you this five gallons. It will be more than enough to take you as far as you will probably advance in the next two days.''

'But, my goodness, General, I can't do that.'

'Yes you can, because that's an order. You hear?'

'Yes, sir.'

Well there I was, a first lieutenant, ordered on an errand to insult a Field Marshal, but I took off by jeep anyway. I managed to reach 'Pete' de Guingand, Monty's Chief of Staff, who, thank heavens, had a sense of humor, and explained the thing to him. He told me that insofar as my boss was concerned, the can and message had been delivered." *"Before the Colors Fade," by Fred Ayer.*

The next morning Patton did not go to the front, although he was worried. He felt going to the front would be showing lack of confidence in Truscott, "and it is necessary to maintain the self-respect of generals in order to get the most out of them." Unbeknownst to Patton, the

---

[1] Does it make sense now why Patton wanted to take Messina? If the Americans hadn't, it is certain that Montgomery would have continued his condescending treatment of the Americans. The British may have even occupied center-stage the rest of the European war. We owe Patton more than we like to think.

infantrymen had made it ashore at 2:30 in the morning. They were behind the German front, and advanced quickly into the hills, undetected. The Germans realized too late that the Americans were behind as well as in front of them. The Germans attacked, but lost. The next day, the 15th, Patton planned a third amphibious operation, at night. Montgomery, recovering his nerve, had also decided to launch an amphibious operation, and early on August 16th, British Commandos came ashore and sped toward Messina. On the same day,

> "Truscott and Bradley again tried to call off the landing operation due to the fact that elements of the 3rd Division had passed Falcone.[1] I insisted that the landings go on because the plans had been made and also so we would get an extra regiment to the front without effort."

Middleton's 45th Division landed at Bivio Salica. Truscott's 3rd Division had already taken Bivio Salica and was pushing toward Messina. The race was on!

> "We received a message from Truscott at about midnight that leading elements of the 3rd Division entered Messina at 11 p.m. ...I immediately sent a message in clear [uncoded] to General Alexander and one to General Eisenhower. Phoned Bradley at 3 a.m. on the 17th that we would enter Messina in the morning at 10 p.m. I also phoned Truscott to make the necessary arrangements."

Victory on the heels of speed had been achieved at last. At 7 a.m. on August 17th, on the hill just west of Messina, Truscott received the municipal dignitaries. He sent his assistant division commander, William Eagle, into the town to organize the troops and, as Eagle later said, to see that the British did not capture the city from the Americans. The British did not arrive until 10 a.m. on August 17th. At daybreak they were still two miles from Messina, halted by a demolished bridge. The bridge went over a deep ravine, and they just managed to get a jeep across the gap. When they arrived they were to find that Messina was already in American hands.

To Patton's dismay, Bradley did not have the pleasure of entering the town in the victory procession. Patton telephoned him, but

---

[1] The landing site.

Bradley must not have gotten the message.[1] Patton described the victory procession thus:

> "On the way, the enemy shelled the road from the Italian side [of the straits]. One of these shells hit the second car behind me, wounding all the occupants, including the G-2 of the 3rd Division. The next car behind that, in which Truscott's aide was riding, had all four tires blown off without injuring the car or anyone in it. In the town of Messina we met three British tanks and a few men who had arrived at 10:00 o'clock under the command of a general. It is very evident that Montgomery sent these men for the purpose of stealing the show. They landed from one LCT about 15 miles south and had come directly up the road. I think the general was quite sore that we had got there first, but since we had been in for 18 hours when he arrived, the race was clearly to us."
> We then went to the town hall and saw the Mayor, the Chief of Police, etc. I told Truscott to do the honors as he had captured Messina. The town is horribly destroyed – the worst I have seen. In one tunnel there were said to have been 5,000 civilians hiding for over a week. I do not believe that indiscriminate bombing of towns is worth the ammunition, and it is unnecessarily cruel to civilians." *Patton's Diary*

The Americans had been there for 18 hours! This simple fact is so often overlooked by British and even American authors. "The British arrived minutes after the Americans," is a fallacy that has been repeated many times in several books. Eighteen hours could hardly be termed "minutes," but many authors prefer to overlook that.

An armored column of Montgomery's repaired the bridge and entered the town. The senior officer walked over to Patton, shook his hand, and said, "It was a jolly good race. I congratulate you."

This gesture proves that Patton was not being petty or jealous, and that it was a race enjoyed by both sides.

---

[1] This would become a particularly bitter part of Bradley's gripe against Patton. Bradley would always maintain that he had not been invited to the victory celebration.

"On the way back we met General Bedell Smith and General Lemnitzer. Smith had stopped back of the crest, just why I do not know, although it would be reasonable to suppose because the road beyond the crest was under fire.

Patton would not know the reason until almost a year later, on May 22nd, 1944. After Keyes, Gay, and Patton left to enter the town, Smith and Lemnitzer arrived and decided to follow him "if it was quite safe." Murnane, Gay's aide, took them.

"When they got to the top of the pass, Smith asked if we were under fire and was told it could happen. Just then one of our batteries of 155 [mm.] guns let go, firing [across the strait of Messina] into Italy. Smith thought it was enemy shells arriving and jumped from the car into the ditch in one leap, and refused to leave it, even when Lemnitzer and Murnane told him it was quite safe. When I got back he was still pale, gray, and shaky." *Patton's Diary*

Of course, the most disturbing part of this incident is that Bedell Smith was a general on Eisenhower's staff. How terrible for battle-hardened men to know that the generals who decided their fates could not even stand shells!

According to Ladislas Farago, Patton's remarkable six day occupation of Sicily was a "disintegration of Alexander's strategic plan.... His job was so clearly to remain firm in the face of his two prima-donnas. He let the campaign continue haphazardly without a firm and purposeful design."

This was really not true. The plan for Sicily, Montgomery's plan which Eisenhower adopted, was fatally flawed. It allowed the Germans to escape into Italy with most of their men and materiel. Alexander simply adjusted the plan to fit the circumstances, and the commanders he was leading.[1] For as Nigel Nicolson wrote,

"It is true that twice Alexander had allowed Montgomery to have his way (in the change in the overall Husky plan, and in the switch of the inter-army

---

[1] Something Eisenhower notoriously failed to do in the coming campaigns.

boundary) and twice Patton (in releasing his army
westwards, and allowing him to double back towards
Messina), but in each case he was responding to
circumstances, and the most that could be charged
against him is that those circumstances might have been
foreseen. What was his alternative: To dismiss the victor
of Alamein, the hero of El Guettar? Far from
relinquishing a purposeful strategy, the strategy only
began to make sense when the two prima-donnas were
ranged side by side on the approaches to Messina.
Montgomery's summing-up of the campaign is also less
than just: 'There was no master plan... The army
commanders developed their own ideas of how to
proceed, and then 'informed' higher authority. The
Seventh US Army, once on shore, was allowed to wheel
west towards Palermo. It thereby missed the opportunity
to direct its main thrust-line northwards in order to cut
the island in two.' It is this sort of mangling of history
which makes one suspect Montgomery's loyalty to his
chief. In Alexander's original orders, Eighth Army, not
Seventh, was to cut the island in two, but it was the
Seventh who did so. Patton was not allowed to wheel
west 'once on shore'; for a whole week he was kept on a
tight leash. The only army commander who acted first
and told Alexander afterwards was Montgomery
himself." *"Alex, the life of the Field Marshal Earl Alexander of
Tunis," by Nigel Nicolson.*

Here it is, the real truth. Montgomery often covered up his own
tracks, either by denying his own role, or saying, in effect, "everybody's
doing it." I believe that Alexander's *original mistake* was letting
Montgomery proceed with his flawed plan for Sicily. The Seventh Army
being held back was part of that plan, and Montgomery was angry and
jealous that the Seventh was released – and took the feather from his cap,
Messina. Alexander had realized that Montgomery was getting nowhere,
and after a week he let Patton go. We should give Alexander credit for
this. In France there would be many occasions where Montgomery had
promised Eisenhower much and delivered little, while in the south Patton
would be straining at the leash. The difference between Eisenhower and
Alexander, though, is that when Montgomery didn't carry through,
Alexander released Patton. Nationalities seem to make no difference
here. One would have expected the American Eisenhower to let the

American Patton go in these instances, but Eisenhower never did. On the other hand, one would expect the British Alexander to restrain Patton while waiting for the British Montgomery to get a move on. In reality, though, it was each leader's own personality and charisma that determined how they dealt with unfulfilled promises – in short, how they dealt with Montgomery.

> "The overrunning of the west was a necessary part of the campaign, to provide Patton with a port instead of the open beaches to which Montgomery's plan had restricted him. It was an independent operation which had no effect upon the cutting of the island in two. Patton and Montgomery were each determined to be the first into Messina, and Alexander, with an amusement that can be presumed, saw no reason to dampen their rivalry for such a prize." *"Alex, the life of the Field Marshal Earl Alexander of Tunis," by Nigel Nicolson.*

This is another interesting point. Consider this scenario: Montgomery and Patton, racing to take Europe, seeing who would get to Berlin first. Unrestrained, unhampered, unhindered, free to go where they pleased, take what they pleased and go as fast as they pleased. Although in the majority of the cases Patton would probably have won, it is interesting to note that in "the race to Messina" Montgomery was only *18 hours* behind Patton. Compare this with *one whole month* behind Patton in France! A good commander-in-chief would have noticed this trait and exploited it.

On August 17th, Patton drove to the 8th Division where he had lunch with Bedell Smith. They had a discussion about promotions. Smith told Patton that the Seventh Army staff had not qualified. Patton replied that he knew that, "But now that we have demonstrated our ability, we demanded recognition, not as a favor but as a right." Patton felt sure Smith would do his best to prevent it, "but I will get them anyhow. Smith is a typical s.o.b."

> "Well, I feel let down. The reaction from intense mental and physical activity to a status of inertia is very difficult... I feel that the Lord has been most generous. If I had to fight the campaign over, I would make no change in anything I did. Few generals in history have ever been able to say as much. So far in this war I have

been a chip floating on the river of destiny. I think I had best keep on floating. I will surely be used some more, though at the worst, things look gloomy. For the moment the future of the Seventh Army does not look bright but I trust that the same fortune which has helped me before will continue to assist me. I have been very lucky."
Patton's Diary

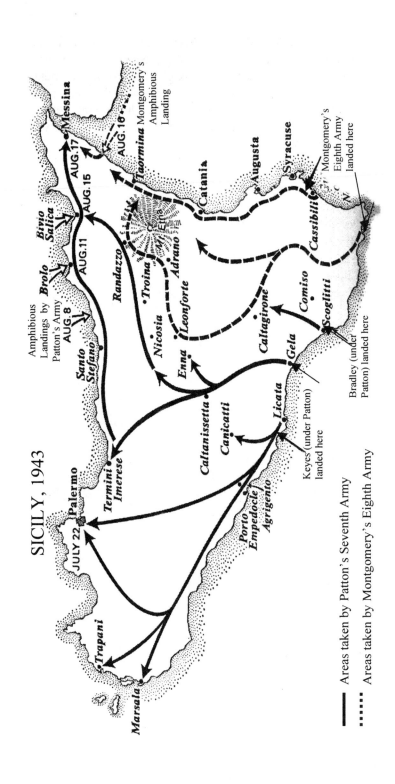

SICILY, 1943

Amplibious Landings by Patton's Army
AUG. 8

Amphibious
Landings

Montgomery's
Amphibious
Landing

Montgomery's
Eighth Army
landed here

Bradley (under
Patton) landed here

Keyes (under Patton)
landed here

Messina
Bivio
Salica
Brolo
Santo
Stefano
Randazzo
Termini
Imerese
Palermo
JULY 22
Trapani
Marsala
Porto
Empedocle
Agrigento
Licata
Canicatti
Caltanissetta
Enna
Nicosia
Troina
Leonforte
Adrano
Mt. Etna
Catania
Augusta
Syracuse
Cassibili
Comiso
Scoglitti
Gela
Caltagirone

AUG.17
AUG.15
AUG.11
AUG.18

Taormina

_____ Areas taken by Patton's Seventh Army

········ Areas taken by Montgomery's Eighth Army

Chapter Seven

LUCK AND FATE

Patton's incredible victories in Sicily left the world holding its breath, while Patton wondered where he would fight next – in mainland Italy or Normandy. Fate, however, had other things in store for him. That August Patton would descend from the height of fame to the depths of misery and the brink of relief.

It all started on August 3rd when Patton drove to a hospital, something that no other combat commander did. It was Patton's custom to cheer up the sick and wounded men that he found there. It was also very typical of Patton's style as a leader that he would go among the men and find out for himself what was actually happening. On this day he discovered to his chagrin that a malingerer was wasting time at the hospital.

> "In the hospital I met the only arrant coward I have ever seen in this Army. This man was sitting, trying to look as if he had been wounded. I asked him what was the matter, and he said he just couldn't take it. I gave him the devil, slapped his face with my gloves, and kicked him out of the hospital. Companies should deal with such men, and if they shirk their duty, they should be tried for cowardice and shot. I will issue an order on this subject tomorrow." ***Patton's Diary***

The man he slapped that day at the hospital, Kuhl, would cause Patton to almost lose his command and just barely survive the attacks upon his name and character to fight another day. Kuhl, by his own admission, was afraid. Calling him a coward, a malingerer or just a "sick patient" makes no difference, when it is clear by Kuhl's own admission the nature of his "sickness."

The order that Patton had issued reads as follows,

"SEVENTH ARMY MEMO TO CORPS, DIVISION, AND SEPARATE UNIT COMMANDERS, AUGUST 5, 1943

It has come to my attention that a very small number of soldiers are going to the hospital on the pretext that they are nervously incapable of combat. Such men are cowards and bring discredit on the army and disgrace to their comrades, whom they heartlessly leave to endure the dangers of battle while they, themselves, use the hospital as a means of escape. You will take measures to see that such cases are not sent to the hospital but are dealt with in their units. Those who are not willing to fight will be tried by Court-Martial for cowardice in the face of the enemy."

On August 10th, Patton went to another evacuation hospital and,

"saw another alleged nervous patient – really a coward. I told the doctor to return him to his company and he began to cry so I cursed him well and he shut up. I may have saved his soul if he had one."

Patton next heard about what he considered to be his fully justified actions on August 17th, when he received a letter from Eisenhower.

Before I quote the letter, which I am going to do in full, I would like to point out a few details, which would make this ordinarily depressing letter terrible.

> The letter is from Eisenhower. Eisenhower had *still* not complimented Patton, even though Patton had taken two thirds of Sicily, and international leaders had recognized his accomplishment.[1]

> Patton made it a point to visit hospitals every day, something that few, if any, commanders bothered to do.

> Eisenhower did not visit hospitals, nor did anyone on his staff.

The letter went as follows:

"I am attaching a report which is shocking in its allegations against your personal conduct. I hope you can assure me that none of them is true; but the detailed circumstances communicated to me led to the belief that some ground for the charges must exist. I am well aware of the necessity for hardness and toughness on the battlefield. I clearly understand that firm and drastic measures are at times necessary in order to secure the desired objectives. But this does not excuse brutality, abuse of the sick, nor exhibition of uncontrollable temper in front of subordinates.

In the two cases cited in the attached report, it is *not* my present intention to institute any formal investigation. Moreover, it is acutely distressing to me to have such charges as these made against you at the very moment when an American Army under your leadership has attained a success of which I am extremely proud. I feel that the personal services you have rendered the United States and the Allied cause during the past weeks are of incalculable value; but nevertheless, if there is a very considerable element of truth in the allegations accompanying this letter, I must so seriously question your good judgment and your self discipline as to raise serious doubts in my mind as to your future usefulness. I am assuming, for the moment, that the facts in the case are far less serious than appears in this report, and that whatever truth is contained in these allegations reports an act of yours when under the stress and strain of winning a victory, you were thoughtless rather than harsh. Your leadership of the past few weeks has, in my

---

[1] Including personal letters of congratulations from both Roosevelt and Churchill.

opinion, fully vindicated to the War Department and to all your associates in arms my own persistence in upholding your pre-eminent qualifications for the difficult task to which you were assigned.[1] Nevertheless, you must give to this matter of personal deportment your instant and serious consideration to the end that no incident of this character can be reported to me in the future, and I may continue to count upon your assistance in military tasks.

In Allied Headquarters there is no record of my letter to you, except in my own secret files. I will expect your answer to be sent to me personally and secretly. Moreover, I advise that, provided there is any semblance of truth in the allegations in the accompanying report, you make in the form of apology or other such personal amends to the individuals concerned as may be within your power, and that you do this before submitting your letter to me.

No letter that I have been called upon to write in my military career has caused me the mental anguish of this one, not only because of my long and deep personal friendship for you but because of my admiration for your military qualities, but I assure you that conduct such as described in the accompanying report will *not* be tolerated in this theater no matter who the offender may be."

Patton's reaction to the letter was predictably unhappy that he had upset Eisenhower.

"General Blesse... brought me a very nasty letter from Ike with reference to the two soldiers I cussed out for what I considered cowardice. Evidently I acted precipitately and on insufficient knowledge. My motive was correct because one cannot permit skulking to exist. It is just like any communicable disease. I admit freely that my method was wrong but I shall make what

---

[1] "Your leadership of the past few weeks has, in my opinion, fully vindicated to the War Department and to all your associates in arms my own persistence in upholding your pre-eminent qualifications for the difficult task to which you were assigned." Ok, sure. Take credit for someone else's achievement, and then act like you said so all along.

amends I can. I regret the incident as I hate to make Ike mad when it is my earnest study to please him."

One of the men Patton had slapped, Private Charles Kuhl, was first admitted on August 2nd. He was diagnosed with "Exhaustion." He had already been admitted three times for exhaustion in the Sicily Campaign. A note from the E.M.T about him says, "Psycho-neurosis anxiety state – moderate severe (soldier has been twice before in hospital within ten days. He can't take it at the front, evidently. He is repeatedly returned.)" According to Kuhl himself, then, *He couldn't take it at the front.* The debate here must then be: is "not taking it at the front" considered being a coward? And if so, was Patton right to slap him? According to the dictionary, a coward is a person who lacks courage in facing pain. War is evidently full of pain, and going to the hospital so as to avoid it is lacking courage. Someone who can't take it at the front is necessarily placing an additional risk on his fellow soldiers who have to make up for his "anxiety." Every soldier has anxiety, but he has to brave it. Imagine if everyone thought he could go to the hospital because he was nervous!

After Patton slapped Kuhl, the doctors found Kuhl had a temperature of 102.2 degrees and had a history of chronic diarrhea for about a month. He was found to have malarial parasites. For this reason, many authors say that Patton had slapped a "sick" man. But when Patton came to Pvt. Kuhl, according to the official report, Patton asked him what was the matter, and Kuhl replied, "I guess I can't take it." So Kuhl, on his own admission, was there because he was afraid – a coward's plea.

Should Patton have slapped him on the face with his gloves? One author points out that this was the usual procedure, but it was administered by one of the hospital staff. Many agree that Kuhl was a coward, and that slapping was not so terrible, but that for Patton to do so was below the role of a general. It seems that Patton himself took this stand as well. For he says, "My motive was correct, for one cannot permit skulking to exist… I admit freely that my method was wrong."

The other man that Patton slapped was Private Paul G. Bennett. He had served for four years in the Field Artillery. Bennett never had any problems until August 6th, when his buddy was wounded. According to the report,

"He could not sleep that night and felt nervous. The shells going over him bothered him. The next day he was worried about his buddy and became more nervous. He was sent down to the rear echelon by a battery aid man and there the medical officer gave him some medicine which made him sleep, but still he was nervous and disturbed. On the next day the medical officer ordered him to be evacuated, although the boy begged not to be evacuated because he did not want to leave his unit."[1]

According to Dr. Donald E. Currier, Bennett had wanted to return to his unit although he "had a temperature and he was sick." This statement, however, is in direct contradiction to that of General John A. Crane, to whose brigade he belonged. Crane stated, *"That the man was absent without leave and had gone to the rear by falsely representing his condition to the battery surgeon."* Bennett's record also stated that he was "Absent Without Leave." The medical report sent to Eisenhower also says that, "Showing symptoms of dehydration, he was fatigued, confused, weak, and listless." But if this was the case, why did he reply to Patton's question of what was wrong with him, "I guess it's my nerves." Why did he, like Kuhl, believe he was scared when the doctors were saying he was sick? They had gone to the doctor in the first place because they were afraid. (Or *nervous.*) One of the doctors who wrote the report of the Bennett case seemed to have written a much more fantasy-like style, for, unlike Kuhl's report, Bennett's is full of descriptive conversations and explicit adjectives. It was not written in the matter-of-fact style that Kuhl's report was, but in a manner like that of a novel. Kuhl's report says that Patton called him "all types of a coward," but Bennett's is written much more graphically.

"Lt. General George S. Patton, Jr., entered the receiving tent and spoke to all the injured men. The next patient was sitting huddled up and shivering. When asked what his trouble was, the man replied, 'It's my nerves,' and began to sob. The General then screamed at him, 'What did you say?' The man replied, 'It's my nerves, I can't stand the shelling any more.' He was still sobbing."

---

[1] I don't understand why they call him a boy when he was twenty one.

Before we go any further with the account, are we supposed to have pity on him? Why do they inform us that "he was still sobbing?" Some man.

> "The General then yelled at him, 'Your nerves, blank; you are just a blank coward, you yellow blank.' He then slapped the man and said, 'Shut up that blank crying. I won't have these brave men here who have been shot at seeing a yellow blank sitting here crying.' He then struck the man again, knocking his helmet liner off and into the next tent. He then turned to the admitting officer and yelled, 'Don't admit this yellow blank; there's nothing the matter with him. I don't have the hospitals cluttered up with these blanks who haven't got the guts to fight.'"

The author is being a trifle dishonest here by saying that Patton then "struck the man again." In fact, he only slapped him with his gloves, and Bennett was unhurt. The next sentence seems, once again, designed to make us feel sympathy for Bennett.

> "He then turned to the man again, who was managing to sit at attention though shaking all over and said, "You're going back to the front lines and you may get shot and killed, but you're going to fight. If you don't, I'll stand you up against a wall and have a firing squad kill you on purpose. In fact," he said, reaching for his pistol, 'I ought to shoot you myself, you blank whimpering coward.' As he left the tent, the General was still yelling back to the receiving officer to send that yellow blank back to the front line. Nurses and patients attracted by the shouting and cursing came from adjoining tents and witnessed this disturbance. The deleterious effects of such incidents upon the wellbeing of patients, upon the professional morale of hospital staffs, and upon the relationship of patient to physician are incalculable. It is imperative that immediate steps be taken to prevent a recurrence of such incidents."[1]

---

[1] Bennett's report was peppered with curses which I edited. I have a hard time believing that Patton used twenty curses in two seconds. For the full account see the "Patton Papers" edited by Martin Blumenson.

The usual procedure for these nervous (or scared) men, was to give them drugs and send them back. I would like to stress that a slap on the face with leather gloves could not hurt two grown men at all. And, the psychological damage would have been "Oh, boy, I'd better not go back to the hospital." *Big* deal.

Was Patton right to slap them? Patton believed that he was wrong; because it wasn't the appropriate action of a general. Ordinarily, the men would have been treated and sent back to the front. Some books on Patton have concluded that men like Bennett and Kuhl should have stayed at the hospital undisturbed; it is difficult to tell whether Eisenhower disagreed with this concept or not – only one shirker was executed for cowardice under Eisenhower, even though there were hundreds of notorious cowards under his command.

There is another medical witness of the slapping incident who is almost never quoted. After talking with another medical officer present at one of the incidents, General Wallace said that, "As for the so-called 'slapping incidents,' General Patton made frequent visits to the hospitals to see that the wounded were being properly cared for. One day he visited a large hospital in Sicily when he commanded the Seventh Army. As he came to the last ward, having been much distressed by the sights he had seen of the severely wounded and how bravely they were bearing up, he saw suddenly a young soldier sitting on the edge of his cot, apparently crying. Patton went over and said, 'What's wrong, soldier, are you hurt?' Without rising, but burying his face in his hands, the soldier whimpered, 'Oh, no, I'm not hurt, but, oh, it's terrible - terrible - boo-hoo-hoo." With that the general, disturbed after seeing all the badly wounded and mutilated soldiers, commanded, 'Stand up.' The soldier got to his feet and the general slapped him across the neck with his gloves and said, 'Why don't you act like a man instead of a sniveling baby? Look at these severely wounded soldiers, not complaining a bit and as cheerful as can be, and here you are, a crybaby.' I was told by the medical officer that it was the best thing that could have happened to the boy and that he was discharged from the hospital in less than a week, perfectly normal and well."[1]

This conception of Patton, and the man he slapped, while closest to the truth, remains the most untold. Incidentally, this version was *not* sent to Eisenhower.

---

[1] For more see "The Unknown Patton," by Charles M. Province.

When the press heard about the slapping incidents, they first went to Eisenhower. With typical press behavior, they felt that Patton should be court-martialed. Eisenhower told the press officials that he would punish Patton, but they should keep it out of the papers so that Patton's terrific leadership would be insured for the rest of the war. Eisenhower told them that if they published the story, he might have to relieve Patton.[1] The men promised to not publish it.

Meanwhile, Patton's press image was already none too good. The press had heard that when Patton was training his men in America, he had said that to win wars you needed blood and guts. Immediately, across the headlines were the words, "Old Blood and Guts," even though Patton hated the nickname and no one ever called him it. The press had liked Patton's flamboyant manner, but they soon amended their opinion and considered Patton to be "undemocratic." They portrayed him as "swaggering", "pistol-packing," and a martinet. Although Patton was immensely popular with his men, the newspapermen felt that Patton was an autocrat. However, even with the newspapers' black picture of Patton, American opinion did not change. Family and friends of soldiers in Patton's army were staunchly loyal, and this attitude was contagious. When the slapping incidents leaked out, however, the press felt that it was in line with their idea of Patton. Wasn't this the Patton who had fined "innocent" soldiers for not wearing their helmets and shot a poor Sicilian farmer's donkey?

Patton was not happy. Being out of the newspapers would help, of course, but Ike's opinion was first and most importantly where his job rested. General Lucas had told him of Ike's attitude, and Patton "felt very low." How many generals in history, he no doubt wondered, on the pinnacle of their triumph, were outcast from the final battle? What crime would deserve this punishment? What country would inflict such a penalty on their hero, their victor, and their conqueror? The Byzantines had, but everyone knows they suffered the consequences. The Romans, who had honored and revered their champions, had lived to see many such victories.

Had the fate of the slapping incidents been up to Bradley, no one would ever have known. Bradley received a report of the incident but decided not to bypass the chain of command by sending it to

---

[1] Stand up for Patton? Sorry, not an option.

Eisenhower. Bradley simply buried the report in his safe. The hospital, however, had no such qualms. When they saw that Bradley did nothing, they then bypassed the chain of command and went through medical channels directly to Eisenhower.

On August 21st, Patton voluntarily submitted to the humiliation of shaking hands with Private Paul G. Bennett. In his diary he wrote,

"I had Pvt. Paul G. Bennett... in and explained to him that I had cussed him out in the hope of restoring his manhood, that I was sorry, and that if he cared, I would like to shake hands with him. We shook. General John A. Crane, to whose brigade he belongs, stated to me afterwards that the man was absent without leave and had gone to the rear by falsely representing his condition to the battery surgeon. It is rather a commentary on justice when an Army commander has to soft-soap a skulker to placate the timidity of those above. Bob Hope and his troupe called on me at the office later and we had them to dinner and they sang and carried on until after midnight. I put myself out to be amusing and human as I think it may help, particularly if this business about the shirkers comes up."

According to Patton's aide, however, Patton amused and outperformed Bob Hope. Mr. Block, Hope's writer, was especially fascinated. After hearing one of Patton's "sallies" he said, "But, General, that's *beautiful* – Bob! Did you hear that reading? And what *timing* – General can we use that one in next Thursday's show?" He exclaimed a little later, "You might as well bow out, Bob – he's topped your every line so far." Hope thoroughly agreed with his writer's assessment of Patton. Patton began speaking again; eloquent, then sentimental, he brought them to the verge of tears. When Hope saw this he remedied the situation quickly with, "Not the old blood and guts *I've* heard about!"

Patton told them about his campaigns, and according to Codman was "very modest" saying that "he just prays he's done his job as well as he could."
Hope lent over conspiratorially. "Look, General, if you should ever be out of a job, I believe – I believe I could get you a solid week at Loew's State." As the troupe was leaving, Patton told them that entertaining the

troops was a fine thing. "You can see how they enjoy *anything* in the way of entertainment."

"How do y'mean, *anything?!?*" Hope rejoined.

Patton thought for a moment and then said, "Well, let's say *everything*."

Mr. Block, the writer, chimed in, "It's beautiful – see what I mean, Bob? Beautiful. Now he's *double* topping you."

The next morning Patton gave his most famous orders to the Seventh Army.

> "Soldiers of the Seventh Army: Born at sea, baptized in blood, and crowned in victory, in the course of 38 days of incessant battle and unceasing labor, you have added a glorious chapter to the history of war. Pitted against the best the Germans and Italians could offer, you have been unfailingly successful. The rapidity of your dash, which culminated in the capture of Palermo, was equalled by the dogged tenacity with which you stormed Troina and captured Messina. Every man in the Army deserves equal credit. The enduring valor of the Infantry, and the impetuous ferocity of the tanks were matched by the tireless clamor of the destroying guns. The engineers... Maintenance and Supply... Signal Corps... Medical Department... The Navy... our Air. As a result of this combined effort, you have killed or captured 113,350 enemy troops. You have destroyed 265 of his tanks, 2,324 vehicles, and 1,162 large guns, and in addition, have collected a mass of military booty running into hundreds of tons. But your victory has a significance above and beyond its physical aspect – you have destroyed the prestige of the enemy. Your fame shall never die."

Patton's reaction to the mental and physical exhilaration and its sudden ending can only be imagined. He was also worried about Eisenhower's reaction to the slapping incidents, though he thought that volunteering to apologize ought to make him more lenient. That day he wrote to Beatrice, "As usual I seem to have made Divine Destiny[1] a little mad but that will pass, I suppose. It [Eisenhower] has a lot of worries

---

[1] "Divine Destiny" was Patton's code name for Eisenhower that would escape the censors.

which it has to pass on…" He again commented on Eisenhower's silence in regard to his stunning victory, although he seemed to have resigned himself. "I have had telegrams from George [Marshall] and Harry [Stimson] and a host of others, all but from D[1] who is, I suppose, too international." Patton could see clearly Eisenhower's progression from soldier to politician. He could see even clearer how Eisenhower was not a "simple soldier," or, if he was, he certainly was not "simply a soldier." Patton could see even before Berlin or France that Eisenhower had quickly made the leap from "Supreme Allied Commander" to "Inter-Allied Mediator." Seeing a man who had never fought rise to command millions of men was probably similar to the Germans astonishment that Hitler, a corporal, would command their armies. But then, at least Hitler had some battle experience!

Patton wrote to his wife on the 22nd that, "At the moment things are pretty quiet as the natural reaction which invariably follows active operations has set in." He also told her that he had not "the least idea of what is to happen next. In fact I think that what we do is so contingent on political reactions that any thing can happen."

Meanwhile, he was busy trying to find out what the battle experiences of the rank and file had been so as to "get the real dope from people who actually did the close in fighting. If I succeed, it will be the first time in history where the ideas of the little fellow will have a chance to be articulated." Here is where Patton showed his true prowess, and his true calling as a democracy's war leader.

He also understood the faults of generals, how many stressed loyalty from the bottom up, but that loyalty from the top down was much more valuable and even rarer. He knew that generals could be timid. It was important, he said, that they should not consult their fears. Of all traits, Patton valued daring and audacity most. Patton always knew the terrain where his men would fight, and made his plans to fit the area, not the other way around. He said that many generals would make a plan and just use it on any terrain, rather than making a plan with the terrain in mind.

Patton also felt that in generals, "I find moral courage is the most valuable and most usually absent characteristic. Much of our trouble is directly attributable to 'The fear of they.'" Audacity, daring

---

[1] D, Dwight, and Divine Destiny all mean Eisenhower.

and boldness were the trademarks of Patton's plans, and it was these three characteristics which made him so successful.

Also on August 22nd, Patton spoke to the doctors and nurses and enlisted men who had been onlookers during the slapping incidents.

> "I told them about my friend in the last war who shirked, was let get by with it, and eventually killed himself. I told them that I had taken the action I had to correct such a future tragedy."

He also expressed his regret for "my impulsive actions." To Dr. Currier, who was summoned to Palermo, and along with other medical personnel escorted into Patton's office, the general sat behind "an impressive desk," and Patton's remarks sounded like "no apology at all," but rather "an attempt to justify what he had done." It seems that Dr. Currier did not like Patton. I do not understand the significance of Patton sitting behind "an impressive desk." I rather suppose that Eisenhower's was probably even bigger and more impressive. And as for his remark that Patton had made "no apology at all," anything and everything Patton said to them was voluntary.[1] The slappings had clearly been misjudged but as for Patton's "attempt to justify it," that was merely his way of showing that he had not acted without thinking. How many people would have done what Patton did to prevent an ugly process they recognized from occurring again? It is interesting to note Dr. Currier's unending sympathy for Bennett.

The next day, the 23rd, Patton apologized to Kuhl. He wrote in his diary,

> "I have acquired lots of fame and also sustained a great deal of mental anguish, which was, in the light of subsequent events, quite unnecessary. However, with a few brief lapses I have retained my self-confidence. I have always done my duty and have trusted to my destiny. At 10:00, Private Charles H. Kuhl ... came in. He was one of the two men I cussed out for skulking. I told him why I did it, namely, that I tried to make him mad with me so he would regain his manhood. I then asked him to shake hands, which he did."

---

[1] Eisenhower had merely *suggested* it.

Kuhl later admitted that Patton had apologized, saying that "he didn't know that I was as sick as I was." And, if Kuhl's opinion matters more than the thousands of other privates who served under Patton, he thought that Patton was "a great general," but also "a glory hunter. I think at the time it happened, he was pretty well worn out... I think he was suffering a little battle fatigue himself."[1]

Patton wrote to his wife with a dose of self-praise. He undoubtedly was writing to her things that he would have told no one else.

> "I have been a passanger [sic] floating on the river of destiny. At the moment I can't see around the next bend, but I guess it will be all right. Once in a while my exuberant personality gets me in a little lame with Divine Destiny [Patton's nickname for Eisenhower], which seems to have the trait... of believing the worst of every one on insufficient evidence."

Lucas sent a letter to Patton that same day stating that,

> "Everything is OK. The people who were making the fuss have been told to stop yelling and have agreed to do so. Ike just read me a report to General Marshall on the campaign in which he recited your achievements in glowing terms. The situation is in hand."

These glowing terms were, "First, Patton. He has conducted a campaign where the brilliant successes scored must be attributed directly to his energy, determination, and unflagging aggressiveness." He told Marshall that the campaign demonstrated "swift conquest" for future students at the Army War College. "The prodigious marches, the incessant attacks, the refusal to be halted by appalling difficulties" were "something to enthuse about." And this came "mainly from Patton," who refused to "seize on an excuse for resting or refitting," or recuperating to bring up more strength. When an order from Alexander appeared to keep him "rather quiescent... he immediately jumped into a plane, went to Alexander, got the matter cleared up, and kept on driving."

---

[1] Um ... please. Does Kuhl understand the meaning of battle fatigue? He thought he had it. And for that matter, I guess he thinks everyone has it.

Of course, how could Eisenhower keep on praising Patton? Almost immediately he wrote that Patton continued "to exhibit some of those unfortunate personal traits of which you and I have always known." This is amazing. Patton had never slapped any other enlisted man nor did he later. These "personal traits," whatever they may have been, should have had no effect on Patton's promotions or anything else. Wartime cannot afford the sacrificing of heroic individuals because of *personal* traits. Think about it. They're personal.

Eisenhower continued his derailing account, "His habit of impulsive bawling out of subordinates, extending even to personal abuse of individuals" occurred twice, and Eisenhower had to take "the most drastic steps." If he is "not cured now, there is no hope for him. Personally, I believe that he is cured – not only because of his great personal loyalty to you and to me but because fundamentally he is so avid for recognition as a great military commander that he will ruthlessly suppress any habit of his own that will tend to jeopardize it." Here it was again. The image of Patton as the glory-hunter. But in this statement Eisenhower is revealing himself. It was Eisenhower who would suppress any personal habits so as to be promoted or to become famous.[1] Not Patton, though his alleged love of glory is oft-repeated. Patton was, at heart, literally and truly a soldier. Oh yes, he might suppress his "bad" habits, but it was so that he might lead men in battle! Patton really loved war, and he also loved his country. He felt that America needed him now more than ever and that to take American pay for all the peace years and then to quit when he was most needed would be worse than dishonorable. Patton not only wasn't "avid for recognition as a great military commander," he didn't need it. He already was a great military commander.

Eisenhower continues his lecture, and one is forced to wonder where the "glowing account" that Lucas was talking about is. The first paragraph was just, in light of the rest of the letter, a grudging recognition of the first great American victory in WWII. Ike continues in the strain that Patton had qualities that they could not "afford to lose unless he ruins himself." Patton, he said, could be classed as an Army commander whose troops would "not be stopped by ordinary obstacles."

---

[1] Or later so as to become President.

Patton visited all his division commanders between August 24th and 30th in order to address all the officers and men. The first division he addressed, the 2nd Armored Division, was Patton's old division. Patton noted in his diary that he "gave a talk on how good they were." One unmentioned purpose was a sort of incomplete apology, "for any occasions when I may have harshly criticized individuals," although he undoubtedly thought hard before he delivered it. He made no mention of the "slapping incidents," which would have been unnecessary since everyone had already heard about them. He praised the Seventh Army's courage at length, and then the apology,

> "In my dealings with you I have been guilty on too many occasions, perhaps, of criticizing and of loud talking. I am sorry for this and wish to assure you that when I criticize and censure I am wholly impersonal... for every man I have criticized in this Army, I have probably stopped, talked to, and complimented a thousand, but people are more prone to remember ill usage than to recall compliments; therefore, I want you officers and men who are here to explain to the other soldiers, who think perhaps that I am too hard, my motives and to express to them my sincere regret..."

Some authors criticize Patton for making what they call a "round-about" apology, but the apology was voluntary. They say the troops could not have cared less what he told them, and also that they didn't like his "half baked apologies." However the reaction of the 3rd Division a few days later stands in stark contrast to their opinions.

Patton continued speaking,

> "In the Sicilian campaign we lost some 1,500 of our comrades, killed in action. I do not grieve for their death because I thank God that such men have lived, but I do say to you all that it is our sacred duty to see that each of our dead comrades is escorted through the Pearly Gates by a large, a very large number of enemy dead. It is up to us now and hereafter to produce these escorts for our heroic slain. You know that I have never asked one of you to go where I feared to tread. I have been criticized for this, but there are many General Pattons and there is

only one Seventh Army. I can be expended but the Seventh must and will be victorious."

Middleton discussed with Patton Clark's role in Salerno, where the Americans would be covering (again!) for the X British Corps. "I am quite sure from my experience that the British should always do the covering and the Americans the attacking, but others do not agree with me." Patton said that Alexander "came to see what he could steal" for the invasion of the Italian mainland. Forlornly, he wrote that "If I suggest to Ike that this is the case, he will tell me I don't see the 'big picture.' I wish to God he was an American."

A day or so later, Patton spoke "to all 1st Division" and remarked upon their improved discipline since Huebner took over. Huebner, however, later recalled Patton's visit,

> "I assembled 18,000 men, and Patton made a speech, a very good speech, in which he explained that he was sorry. But when he was finished, not one man clapped or said anything. There was no applause. They knew Patton was wrong, but they also knew it was something to get over with and forget as soon as possible."

On August 28th, Patton talked to "selected officers of all grades on their battle experience. I have done this with every division and hope to get a good cross section of how wars are fought..." Patton was also worried about replacements, which so far had been few and far-between.

Patton wrote to Eisenhower the same day,

> "I want to commence by thanking you for this additional illustration of your fairness and generous consideration in making your communication personal [rather than official]. I am at a loss to find words with which to express my chagrin and grief at having given you, a man to whom I owe everything and for whom I would gladly lay down my life, cause for displeasure with me. I assure you that I had no intention of being either harsh or cruel in my treatment of the two soldiers in question. My sole purpose was to try and restore in them a just appreciation of their obligation as men and soldiers. In World War I, I had a dear friend and former schoolmate who lost his

nerve in an exactly analogous manner, and who, after years of mental anguish, committed suicide. Both my friend and the medical men with whom I discussed his case assured me that had he been roundly checked at the time of his first misbehavior, he would have been restored to a normal state. Naturally, this memory actuated me when I inaptly tried to apply the remedies suggested. After each incident I stated to officers with me that I felt I had probably saved an immortal soul."

On the 29th, Patton went to Catania to meet Eisenhower, Montgomery, Bradley and Truscott. To his relief, Eisenhower put the letter in his pocket and did not read it in front of Montgomery. As he wrote in his diary,

"Ike had just landed and was most effusive. We had lunch with Monty, who was, I think, trying to make up for not feeding me last time. Ike decorated him with the big cross of the Legion of Merit. Then I handed Ike my letter about the incidents of the two soldiers. He just put it in his pocket. Well, that was a near thing, but I feel much better." *Patton's Diary*

On August 30th, Patton visited the 3rd Division, the one he had chosen to be the last to hear his apology. This was a special division, for it had captured Agrigento, Palermo and Messina. Patton especially loved them, and they loved Patton even more than any other division. Patton intended to give them the same speech he had given all the divisions. But as he began, they sensed that he was going to give them his apology and began to chant, "No, General, no, no; no, General, no, no," with increasing insistence, "no, General, no, no." They would not listen, nor would they let him go on. His speech was drowned by their chanting, and tears came to his eyes. The roar swelled in volume. "No, General, no, no." Choked with emotion, Patton left the speaker's stand abruptly and drove away.

This incident, more than any other, shows the intense love that the men had for Patton. And because of this, many biographers have claimed that it was stage-managed, that Truscott arranged for his men to cheer Patton. I find this assumption frankly absurd. Just as the slapping incidents weren't arranged to discredit Patton, neither was this spontaneous cheering arranged. Martin Blumenson is ridiculous enough to assert that if it wasn't stage-managed then it was completely made up and never occurred. He does not seem to understand the loyalty that troops have for their commander, especially troops that are constantly "spoiled" with victory. I once saw a book on Patton that had been marked by an engineer who had been with the Seventh Army in Sicily. The engineer had underlined all of the complimentary sentences about Patton, but whenever the author said anything derogatory, the engineer had crossed it out with a pencil and had written comments to the effect of "What does he know?" on the margin. This type of loyalty has been demonstrated in many ways similar to this – and this is only the loyalty that Patton's men carried home with them long after Patton's own death. Imagine their reaction at a scene of such intense emotion from Patton! Could men so loyal not react as they did? They loved Patton. There is nothing more to it. Whatever you may argue that Patton did nothing for his men to deserve such undying devotion,[1] Patton's soldiers still loved him immeasurably and would do anything for him.

On September 2nd Eisenhower sent for Patton. Maybe he had read Patton's letter, but in any case, Patton flew to Algiers. Patton says that Eisenhower "Lectured me" but "I realize that I acted precipitately[2] and accepted his remarks in the spirit intended. I feel that he likes me. Of course he should." The slapping incident had occurred a month ago, and things looked like they had settled down. Eisenhower told Patton that the Seventh Army would be dispersed and that "Brad was to go to England to form a new Army and plan. I told him I was a pretty good planner, but he said I did not like to do it – in that, it seems I am like him, or so he said (compliment?)." It would have been better of Eisenhower to have told Patton now that Bradley had been promoted and he effectively demoted in the coming operation, but Eisenhower chose to wait.

Why had Eisenhower chosen to make Bradley an Army Group Commander and not Patton? And why Bradley, one of Patton's generals, over Truscott, Lucas, and Wedemeyer, his other generals? Bradley had not captured any important city. The only convincing explanation is that Bradley's personality was suited best to the role he was to be given. He would not argue no matter how stupid the plan he was forced to use was, nor would he complain if he and his men were treated unjustly. Bradley only stiffened in France after continued attacks from Montgomery and

---

[1] And the newspapers of the time argued it bitterly.

[2] In the slapping incident.

Patton's constant backing. But even then he was weak, and a meeting with Eisenhower was all it would take to put him back on track.

Right now, however, Patton could not have known that the remainder of his career would be under Bradley, four years his junior, Patton's own general in Sicily. Patton probably expected that he also would command an Army group. It is still a mystery why Eisenhower did not give him one, Patton being *the* most qualified American barring not even Eisenhower. The Germans were waiting, and based on Patton's performance in Sicily, they had decided that Patton would certainly command an army group on the continent.

Patton hated the feeling he had in Algiers: the feeling of weak leadership and the casual air the generals there took about the war. Of course, there usually was that laid-back attitude in a command post far from the action: a laissez faire demeanor because they knew there were other generals doing the real work. The political nature of Eisenhower's headquarters was upsetting. Eisenhower never had any backbone, Patton thought, and so he takes orders from Monty and anyone else who cares to give them.

> "Flew back to Palermo... A day or two in Algiers almost kills me. No one there seems to be interested in the war, and one cannot escape the feeling that the so-called Allied Headquarters is a British headquarters commanded by an American... Only Hughes, Lucas, and [T. J.] Davis made any complimentary remarks concerning the activities of the Seventh Army in Sicily. It was so apparent that it is probably intentional, the most charitable assumption being that since the Seventh Army made the Eighth Army look like thirty cents, it is felt inadvisable, from an inter-Allied standpoint, to give any credit to the Seventh Army. In the clippings from the U.S. ...the fall of Messina received scant notice."

In the newspapers there already was an attempt to rewrite what was going on. Newspapers of the time have several large columns devoted to the meager Russian gains, whereas there is only a side note on the Americans, even on days when they won great victories. In one instance, the Germans actually gave bigger headlines to Patton's victory (their defeat) than we did.

For the next two days, the only entries in Patton's diary are that he "recovered from Algiers" and "recovered some more." Montgomery's 8th Army was the first to land on the European continent, as it landed in Italy on September 3rd with minimal opposition.[1] Patton must have been very disappointed not to have been there. Patton wrote to his wife, still "recovering" from Algiers, and the tone of the letter is anxious as well as humorous.

"This is the first battle since I left home that I have had to listen to on the radio, and it is quite trying. Of course Monty has a habit – a good one – of never letting out any news till it is big news. So thus far we only know that the landing was O.K. Some of our guns... supported it. It always takes me about three days to get over a trip to Algeria. One should wear chain mail to avoid the knife thrusts. It would be amusing if it were not serious. Of course, one can never tell, for strange things happen, but I rather believe I will be out of circulation along with the ever victorious Seventh for a while. Omar is going to see Jake[2] and John Lucas gets his outfit. I was told that I was too impetuous to do what Omar has to do. Apparently I am a man of deeds not words. Except when I talk too much. Well, luck and fate have been with me thus far, so I don't worry. I wish I could be less criptic [sic], but if I ever return, I will keep you awake a lot talking over my experiences. Don't worry. I love you."

Patton next received a cable that must have crushed him. It read simply: "Seventh Army will not continue as an Army."

---

[1] So far, all operations had been in Sicily, or N. Africa.
[2] Jake Devers in London, who commanded ETOUSA.

Chapter Eight

THE NEW ARMY GROUP COMMANDER

Patton had been relieved. He wrote in his diary that night that the last telegram from Marshall announcing the end of his command of Seventh Army had ruined him. "It is very heartbreaking. The only time I have felt worse was the night of December 9th, 1942, when Clark got the Fifth Army. I feel like death but will survive I always have." Patton called in his chiefs of staff and had the telegram from Marshall read to them. He told them, "Gentlemen, what you have heard is secret and will not be discussed nor mentioned to your assistants. I believe in destiny and that nothing can destroy the future of the Seventh Army. However, some of you may not believe in destiny, so if you can find a better job, get it and I will help you all I can. You may be backing the wrong horse or hitched your wagon to the wrong stars. In any event, we must go right on like we knew nothing, so that the enemy will fear the potential threat of the Seventh Army." Patton was giving his staff leave to go, even though he believed that none of his staff would leave him. He was right, none of them did.

Eisenhower sent two inspectors over to question soldiers about Patton's alleged brutality to them. "He said he did it in my behalf, to counteract untrue stories. I think this may be true but fear that it is to protect" him.

In reference to this inspection Patton wrote to his wife on September 7th that,

"Your saying that I learned how to make our men fight is amusing as now it is held against me, that I made the Seventh Army too bloody minded – you can't please every one... I know why we were soft pedaled [in the press]. It was in consonance with the oriental custom of face saving and possibly necessary. I hear that in London we stole the show."

Eisenhower wrote a letter to Marshall with the promotions he felt should be made. Martin Blumenson apparently felt that Eisenhower was doing Patton a favor by mentioning his name, I however can not understand how he could make a list without Patton's name at the top.

"With respect to Patton, I do not see how you could possibly submit a list, on combat performance to date and omit his name. His job of rehabilitating the II Corps in Tunisia was quickly and magnificently done. Beyond this, his leadership of the Seventh Army was close to the best of our classic examples. It is possible that in the future some ill-advised action of his might cause you to regret his promotion. You know his weaknesses as well as his strength, but I am confident that I have eliminated some of the former. His intense loyalty to you and to me makes it possible for me to treat him much more roughly than I could any other senior commander... In the last campaign he, under stress it is true, indulged his temper in certain instances toward individual subordinates who, in General Patton's opinion of the moment, were guilty of malingering. I took immediate and drastic measures, and I am quite certain this sort of thing will never happen again. You have in him a truly aggressive commander and, moreover, one with sufficient brains to do his work in splendid fashion... Incidentally, I think he will show up even better in an exclusively American theater than in an allied one."

Although it was "nice" of Eisenhower to mention Patton, it wasn't smart that he was taking credit for the impossible, namely, shutting Patton up. When Patton had something to say, he said it, because he was not a politician. He mentioned Bradley after Patton as "In my opinion, the best rounded combat leader I have yet met in our service. While he possibly lacks some of the extraordinary and ruthless

90

driving power that Patton can exert at critical moments ... he is among our best." Bradley was a dependable number two, you could rely on him to be quiet and "do what he was told."

Bradley would travel to the United States before going to England, and on September 8th, he came to tell Patton goodbye. It was not exactly a meeting of teacher and student, it was more like the meeting of a former superior with a former junior, neither of which could understand the turn around in fortune. "We had quite a long talk and I told him a lot of my best ideas to tell General Marshall. I suppose I should have kept them to gain reputation by springing them myself, but I am not built that way. The sooner they are put into effect, the better for our army," Patton wrote. One of these ideas was very similar but even more audacious than the Cobra plan, which was put into effect later in Normandy. Bradley always said that he had created the idea himself, but the nucleus was planted in him now. When Patton showed Bradley his own bold version in England, Bradley rejected it as too daring, but some of the key parts he saved for his pet plan, Cobra. "Bradley has a chance to help or hurt me with General Marshall. I hope he chooses the former course, but I did not ask him to."

Patton was still depressed. He did not yet know if they would even use him at all, and Ike purposely withheld that information from him. It was to be his punishment. The agony of not knowing his future proved to be excruciating, for he knew that is was not beyond them to just leave him to rot in Sicily. "My resilient nature worked all right and today I am almost back to normal. But I have to keep working on my belief in destiny, and poor old destiny may have to put in some extra time to get me out of my present slump."

The Italian armistice had just been declared, and Patton noted that "I fear that as a soldier I have too little faith in political war. Suppose the Italians can't or don't capitulate? It's a great mistake to inform the troops, as has been done, of the signing of an armistice. Should they get resistance instead of friendship [during the amphibious landings at Salerno], it would have a very bad effect."

Once again Patton "prophesied" correctly. Although the soldiers were warned that Germans on the mainland would oppose them, they let down their guard and suffered many casualties. While Clark's Fifth Army landed ashore, Patton worked all day on his report of operations in Sicily.

Patton had been left out of all future invasions, left to ponder his fate in the ancient palace where he had landed. Eisenhower and Stimson said there "was important military reasons" for Patton's detainment, but to Patton they seemed vague. Because allied intelligence showed German fear and respect towards Patton, Eisenhower said that Patton was detained in Sicily to "mislead" the Germans.

"I almost believe that there is a deliberate campaign to hurt me; certainly it is hard to be victimized for winning a campaign. Gay[1] thinks the cousins[2] are back of it because I made a fool of Monty," wrote Patton. How could he know that it was the Communists? He was still waiting. Waiting one almost senses, until the slapping incidents exploded into the headlines.

Patton was still performing the duties of an officer of rank, although he had no army. He went with Alexander to see the surrendered Italian battle fleet sail by on their way to Malta. There were many jokes "among the British officers to the effect that the ships passing us were ghost ships, since the Royal Air Force and the Royal Navy had definitely sunk them all on various occasions."

Many of Patton's diary entries at this time are depressing accounts to the effect that "I am waiting to see what fate will bring me." The most intuitive one he wrote on November 17th, "I have seldom passed a more miserable day. I have absolutely nothing to do and hours of time to do it. From commanding 240,000 men, I now have less than 5,000... well, pretty soon I will hit bottom and then bounce."

---

[1] Patton's general
[2] Patton's code name for the British

Chapter Nine

A DISCREDITED JOURNALIST

Meanwhile, at home in America, something extremely far removed from Patton was happening, something that would connect to him amazingly – because it was connected to Drew Pearson, the man who was to "reveal" to the Americans what had occurred in Sicily.

"According to reports of Drew Pearson's personality, even by his friends, he was at best, a 'bastard'. He was similar to a copperhead snake. It made no difference 'who' he bit as long as he bit 'someone.' It was his nature. Pearson would attack friend or foe alike. Pearson's only requirement was that it would benefit Pearson." *"The Unknown Patton," by Charles M. Province.*

It was Province who first discovered the real reason why Pearson chose to discredit Patton, a man he didn't know at all.

It would be nice to think, as so many authors do, that Pearson revealed the story out of concern for the welfare of the American soldiers, but the facts reveal that he did it instead to save his own reputation by smearing another man's.

First of all, the journalist Pearson was extremely pro-Communist. He was constantly advocating a second front in France (what Stalin wanted.) He demanded that we assist our Russian "friends" immediately, and he became angry when his demands were not addressed.

Pearson was a friend of Sumner Welles, then Undersecretary of State. There was intense rivalry between Hull, secretary of state, and Welles, the undersecretary, over foreign policy, and in particular, how to deal with the Russians. Rumors were circulating around Washington that Welles was bisexual. Hull saw an opportunity for ridding himself of his opponent. In those days homosexuality and bisexuality were extremely hated and if it was proven that Welles was indeed bisexual, Welles would be forced to resign. Hull discovered that Roosevelt had had an investigation done and he asked Hoover to see it. Hoover informed him that the FBI report was in the hands of McIntyre, an aide of Roosevelt's.

Hull did not want any embarrassing publicity in case the rumors proved true, so he did not act right away. Meanwhile the FBI report had been given to the Attorney General, Biddle, who was unsure how to handle it. One of Roosevelt's former aides, Rowe, suggested that he take it to the President, but the Attorney General was reluctant. Finally Biddle mustered the courage to take it to FDR. When Biddle returned he was shaken. He told Rowe that the President had "frosted" him and ordered him to "leave it alone." Roosevelt did not want the truth known about Welles because the election was coming up. FDR had always known that Welles was bisexual; moreover, he did not care. What he truly feared was what the voters would think if Welles was discovered.

Welles' other rival, Bullitt, had heard of the FBI report and was urging Hull to action. Hull was being excluded from talks being held with Welles, Hopkins, Wallace, and Roosevelt. This enflamed Hull's jealousy, and he was more open to Bullitt's advice. Bullitt told him that if he threatened to resign, Roosevelt would be forced to deal with him rather than Welles. Welles would probably have to resign in disgrace.

The rivalry between Hull and Welles had now reached a stand-off. One or the other would have to go, as they could not work together. A Republican, Brewster, had by now heard of the FBI file, and he asked Hoover to see it. Hoover refused. Brewster then threatened to have the Senate investigating committee headed by Truman open an investigation. Brewster then asked Hull the question many had been secretly wondering. Why hadn't he gone with the report to FDR? Hull told him that he had but Roosevelt refused to act.

A month later Hull informed Roosevelt that "everyone knew" that Welles was being blackmailed. Welles soon fell ill and while he was gone Bullitt confronted FDR with the charges against Welles. A violent altercation took place. Roosevelt roared that Bullitt was being "un-Christian" and he was afraid that he had already leaked it to the newspapers. Roosevelt then argued that he needed Welles, he was the "only man in the State Department who really knew what was going on" and that he could not trust "that old fool Hull." "It is my duty, as friend and supporter, to point out that Welles can be blackmailed," Bullitt retorted. FDR then had himself wheeled out of the room. Bullitt then dictated a memorandum about his second "furious row" with Roosevelt. Roosevelt later told a friend about the meeting, "I told him I was going to play St. Peter. Two men stood before him at the Pearly Gates. Welles confessed and was admitted. Bullitt also confessed but FDR told him: 'Bill, you've tried to destroy a fellow being.' With a gesture of his thumb he added: 'Get out of here and don't come back.' I don't suppose he'll ever forgive me," FDR concluded, laughing.

Roosevelt may have thought he had gotten the better of Bullitt, but he was wrong. The *New York Times* printed a front page story on the scandal on August 4th. Hull saw his chance and he told Roosevelt that either Welles or he would have to go. Welles angrily met with Hull for the last time before Welles' own resignation. Roosevelt had told Welles that it was Hull who wanted him to resign. "Why didn't you tell me yourself?" Hull asked him. "Stop right there!" Hull cried. "I didn't speak to you because you're an intimate friend of the President, much closer to him than I. I based my request on your personal habits. For more than two years, I concealed it from my wife. It was brought to her attention by wives of prominent members of Congress. You knew it was known to them, to the Soviet government, the Free French, the British and South American countries. You should have come to me. Your continuation in office would be, for the President and the State Department, the greatest national scandal since the existence of the United States." It was the last time Welles and Hull would ever speak to each other.[1]

Welles met with Drew Pearson to ask him for advice. Pearson's brother, a radio journalist, reported Welles' resignation and immediately the left-wing press made Welles the hero. "The only friend of Russia, the sole bulwark against a Fascist State Department," the radios trumpeted. Drew Pearson himself stated that Hull was politically maneuvering so as not to have a second front and that Hull secretly wished to see "Russia

---

[1] For more detail, read "Sumner Welles: FDR's Global Strategist" by Benjamin Welles.

bled white" by the Germans; note the reference to *white* Russia. Hull retorted that, "Pearson's allegations are pure falsehood; monstrous and diabolical lies." Although in private Roosevelt had been for Welles, he now publicly denounced Welles' most vocal supporter, Pearson, by branding him a "chronic liar." Roosevelt then said that the Russians would be offended by Pearson's untrue remarks about Hull.

Pearson, being so outwardly pro-Communist, was worried about the President's remarks on his credibility. So Pearson consulted his lawyer, Earnest Cuneo. Cuneo thought that Pearson should create a "distraction" so as to take the public's attention away from Roosevelt's insult and Welles' immorality. Pearson decided to create a sensation, an uproar that might do even more than just restore his credibility – might it also not put the best Allied general (known to be anti-Communist) out of work? Cuneo suggested to Pearson that he use the "slapping incidents" which Pearson had heard third hand.

And so something as unrelated to the combat in Europe as the resignation of the bisexual undersecretary of State was to be connected, amazingly, to Patton's career reaching the brink of an early close. Thousands of other correspondents knew about the incidents but had obeyed Eisenhower and left the story unpublished. As Province says, "Pearson had no scruples about any story at any time. Pearson was one of the masters of 'yellow journalism.'" And he was certainly using this knowledge to his own disgusting advantage now. Though the story was known by other newspapermen for three months, Pearson broke the story as a "scoop" on November 21. Pearson predicted in his broadcast that "Patton would never again hold a responsible war assignment." Pearson certainly hoped that this would be the case, but he was wrong. He usually was.

Once the story was out, the American[1] newspapermen wrote columns calling for Patton's relief. Walter Winchell said that one of Patton's men would murder him. Another incorrect prediction.

"It is difficult to believe that a muckraker like Drew Pearson and the firing of a homosexual[2] government employee could almost cause the destruction of the

---

[1] To be distinguished from the newspapermen who were in Europe and who were thus much better acquainted with the facts.

[2] According to his son, Benjamin Welles in "Sumner Welles: FDR's Global Strategist," Welles was actually bisexual.

career of one of the greatest military figures in the history of the United States, but it is true." *Charles M. Province*

As Patton said, "If the fate of the only successful general in this war depends on the statement of a discredited writer like Drew Pearson, we are in a bad fix. Of course I am worried, but I am quite confident that the Lord will see me through... I am perfectly certain that this is not the end of me." Patton, as usual, was right.

Chapter Ten

INDIGNATION AT HOME

Patton never knew about Pearson's ulterior motives or what had caused the eruption at home, but he wrote in his diary that:

> "Apparently Drew Pearson has made certain allegations against me in Washington. I had been expecting something like this to happen for some time because I am sure that it would have been much better to have admitted the whole thing to start with, particularly in view of the fact that I was right."

Patton did not think that the slapping of two cowards was wrong. Eisenhower did; which was why he did not want the incidents exposed.

The correspondents in Washington were demanding Patton's relief without even investigating the facts. In Washington, Patton had been nominated to the permanent rank of major general. Though Patton was made a temporary lieutenant general in Algiers, his permanent promotion should have been made long ago. He was still only a permanent Colonel of Cavalry! But now that the slapping incidents had come to light, his pending promotion caused an uproar among the press and in the government.

The representatives demanded that Eisenhower give them an explanation. They wanted to know if Patton had been punished and how. Eisenhower was not there, so, in his absence, Bedell Smith (an enemy of Patton's) said that Eisenhower had administered a reprimand, but that it had been personal, not official. This smelled to the journalists of a cover-up, and they wrote it up as such. Important documents were not released until years after the war, when Eisenhower's letter to Patton, the medical corps' letter to Eisenhower, and other important documents were released. Before that, it was conjecture and Patton's diary.

At the request of Congressman Andrews of Indiana, Secretary of War Stimson asked Eisenhower for a report on the incidents. Eisenhower replied on November 24th, giving the account he had received of what had happened. The mainspring of the sustained Seventh Army drive from Gela to Messina, he said, was Patton. Patton's "absolute refusal to accept any excuses for delay or procrastination" was a large factor in the early collapse of the Axis resistance in Sicily. He drove himself as hard as everyone in his Army and became "almost ruthless in his demands upon individual men." Eisenhower told them that "twice, while visiting the wounded in the hospitals, Patton encountered patients suffering from nerve difficulty or what is commonly known as 'battle anxiety." Both times he "momentarily lost his temper and upbraided the individuals in an unseemly and indefensible manner." Eisenhower then wrote that after "learning of these indiscretions from a medical report, which was followed by a report from "three reputable newspapermen"[1] he immediately asked Patton about the allegations, expressed "extreme displeasure," and informed him that any repetition would result in his "instant relief." He ordered Patton to make "proper amends" to the individuals involved and to his whole Army, meanwhile reserving for himself the decision on whether to relieve Patton until he could determine the effectiveness of Patton's "corrective action."

Eisenhower justified this decision in his report by saying that he did not want to relieve Patton if he didn't have to "thus losing to the United Nations his unquestioned value as a commander of an assault force." He pointed out that Patton had apologized to the individuals concerned. Eisenhower said that he had discussed the matter with the three newspapermen who had reported the incident, and they were convinced that "the measures taken were adequate in the circumstances." Since the men who had been sent to find out about any resentment on the part of Patton's men had found that Patton had done "a splendid over all job and no great harm had been done," Eisenhower said that he felt justified with the punishment he had administered for Patton's "indefensible" conduct. "I took those steps that seemed to me applicable

---

[1] What value their opinion would be, I have no idea.

in the circumstances, because I believe that General Patton has a great usefulness in any assault where gallantry, drive, and loyalty on the part of the Army commander will be essential."

Representative Jed Johnson of Oklahoma wrote to Marshall about "the despicable incident" and said he was "amazed and cha-grinned" that Patton still commanded the Seventh Army. Patton's "unprovoked attack" should have brought about an immediate relief.

Representative Charles B. Hoeven, Republican of Iowa, said in the House of Representatives that, "If our boys are to be mistreated, let's import Hitler and do it right." This was an amazingly callous statement, both in regard to Hitler's horrendous crimes and the remarkably small "crime" of Patton. Other legislators chimed in, some quoting the Bible, one demanding that Patton be removed from command of the Seventh Army to command of the Japanese Evacuation Centers on the West Coast. He could apparently think of no lower assignment for the disgraced general, and did care how Patton would slap the faces of "those Japs." This was another astonishingly prejudiced statement that shows the amazing cruelty of the legislator. These were the men who were pretending to have apathy for two crybabies in Sicily; men who were willing to send a man they thought acted like "Hitler" to torture "Japs."

Some of the politicians were trying to treat Patton like one of themselves. Patton was a soldier. He wasn't supposed to worry about what he said, or how his actions would look when exaggerated by the press. Besides, America needed Patton whether they liked to admit it or not. The Secretary of War continually pointed out that America needed battle-tested men.[1] Stimson told them that only the Germans would be happy about Patton's relief. But the politicians were adamant, and continued to rail Patton from their respective posts.

There were congressmen who thought that they, not the Germans, would be happy about Patton's relief. However, by December, the President, Secretary of War, and others in the executive branch of the government had received around 1,500 letters relating to Patton. The majority of them were decidedly in favor of the general, and many also called for his promotion.

---

[1] One might also point out that they are not expendable.

Too many biographers say that, "Americans were outraged when they learned of the slapping incidents." Some people in America may have been outraged, but according to Patton's aide, Codman, the letters that they received, discounting Patton's friends and family, were: letters of protest, 11%; letters in support, 89%. Codman found this amazing in light of the fact that Patton was grotesquely misrepresented in the United States.

In spite of this, you will find a considerable number of authors who say, "Many Americans wrote to their Senators and Congressmen and called for Patton's dismissal. For example, one said that Patton made his blood boil. A superior officer striking American boys

> 'proves he is as low and has the same heart in him as Adolph Hitler, only difference he is afraid to go quite as far as Hitler. His great progress (as I understand from men over there) is made at the cost of his men, beating, storming, and driving them as a bunch of slaves into things that will put his name in the headlines. For all, it seems too that a man that has no more heart or self control than he, is not capable of being over our boys.'"

No matter what authors say, a Gallup poll conducted a short while later showed that 77% of Americans liked Patton, 19% did not, and 4% were uncertain.

Eisenhower sent Patton a cable informing him to make no statements to the press, and that he was handling the situation.

The next day, Thanksgiving, Patton wrote, "Thanksgiving Day. I had nothing to be thankful for so I did not give thanks."

General Lucas wrote to Patton that,

> "I am told that you have been subjected to a scurrilous attack in the United States by some SOBs who would rather vent their personal spite against a famous soldier than help the war effort by keeping their mouths shut... If this is true, I know it has hurt you very much and has therefore hurt me too. I cannot believe that any harm can be done you, as your reputation is too assured for that."

General Summerall (an old friend of Patton's) was also "indignant at the publicity given to a trifling incident. Whatever you did, I am sure it was justified by the provocation." He knew what it was to see troops disintegrate when men drifted to the rear and were "coddled in hospitals. Such cowards used to be shot, but now they are encouraged. Only those who carry the responsibility of winning battles know the difficulty of making men fight and so far, you have excelled all others in this accomplishment... The country would suffer a calamity in not having your continued leadership... Your place is already made in history." But it might also end now, observed Patton wryly.

Patton had been Pershing's aide in WWI. Pershing was Patton's idol, the antithesis of Eisenhower, the man whom Patton told his wife would know how to handle the British where Eisenhower had miserably failed. But now came a crushing blow. Pershing, who was going senile, had openly denounced Patton's behavior in the slapping incidents. When Patton heard, he stopped writing to him. "How I dislike Drew P[earson]," Patton mourned to his wife. Beatrice, for her part, wrote at the time to a friend, "I wonder that Pearson does not die of his own poison. The only excuse, and it is not an excuse, that I can see for his existence, is that the world is made up of forces of good and forces of evil, and that without the latter there would be no struggle, and people might get soft. I cannot explain him any other way. I have followed his predictions now for some time, and am convinced that he is a traitor to America." She was right.

Amusingly, Patton wrote a letter to Bedell Smith, a man whom he had always disliked, and who was to become anathema in his eyes in a very few months, that, "Although, as you know, I have not personally known you so many years, yet I have heard so much of you from General Marshall that I feel far better acquainted than the length of time would indicate... I have always felt in complete accord with you since our first meeting." Not strictly true, but Patton needed to enlist his support. Patton also wrote to Stimson,[1] "This letter is not intended as an excuse for obvious mistakes or as a plea for sympathy... I have, to the best of my ability, undergone all the risks of my troops. I love and admire good soldiers and brave men. I hate and despise slackers and cowards. I am quite tender-hearted and emotional in my dealings with wounded men. Like all commanders I am constantly faced with the problem of malingering. If it is not checked, it spreads like a prairie fire."

---

[1] Secretary for War

He continued and said that he had,

"inspected some 300 freshly wounded men who had gallantly and unflinchingly done their duty, and who, in spite of their wounds, were cheerful and uncomplaining. The last man I came to was a forlorn individual sitting on a box, apparently waiting to have a wound dressed. I asked him where he had been hit. He replied that he had not been hit but that he 'just could not take it,' and had come to the hospital to avoid combat. The contrast between this cur, who was not only skulking by himself but was by his cowardice forcing other loyal and brave men to do his duty, and the heroes I had just been talking to, so moved me that I hit him across the face with the gloves I was carrying in my hand, shook him, and called him a coward, and told him to get back to his outfit and try to be a man. When I left, I told the officer who was with me that I hoped I had made a man of that thing, and that if so, I had saved an immortal soul. The other practically identical incident... I had just talked to over a hundred wounded, the last of whom had lost his right arm and was joking about it when I came on a second of these human jackals, who also told me 'He could not take it.' I simply shook him, cussed him out, and told the hospital to return him to his outfit. There is no doubt that my method was too forthright. They will not be repeated. General Eisenhower wrote me a forceful personal letter very rightly calling my attention to the bad effects my action had on public opinion and directing me to make certain amends."

This is Patton's record of the incident. It deserves to be heard. He wrote each incident in his diary at the time, but this record is more detailed because it was written after the press explosion. It explains his motive, which he thought at the time was obvious.

"I apologized to the two men. I called in the medical personnel who witnessed the incidents, explained to them the reasons for my action, and my regret for the same. I made a speech to each of the divisions telling the men what great soldiers they were, explaining to them what they were fighting for, and emphasizing how proud

I was of them. I ended by saying that if any of them felt I had been too severe, I apologized, but for every man I had corrected for his own good, I had complimented a thousand. Any other prejudicial statements concerning me as an officer or soldier are not true."

Patton wrote that, "Ike and Beedle are not at all interested in me but simply in saving their own faces. I might act the same if the case were reversed, but I doubt it... Naturally I am worried but I am really more angry than uneasy. My side is not being shown and my friends must be having a hell of a time. So far as I can see, there is nothing for me to do except read the Bible and trust to destiny. I certainly do not intend to read any of the dirt published in the papers or broadcast over the radio. There is no use in giving myself indigestion for nothing."

Chapter Eleven

"HE MADE YOU, IKE"

No combat troops would stay under Patton. They were all removed either to the United Kingdom, or to Italy under General Clark's command. One can only imagine how Patton felt. We must remember that this is the way that America was rewarding her hero; her victor, the captor of Messina and conqueror of Palermo, was being rewarded by losing his army and remaining out of combat for close to a year.

Did Eisenhower think that he was punishing Patton for his conduct concerning the two soldiers he slapped? Even if he did, the harm caused to America by Patton's skill not being utilized for eleven months far exceeds any punishment that could have been administered to him.

There are those who say that Eisenhower was very gracious in not relieving Patton on the spot after the incidents. They portray this as an example of the gallant and chivalrous Eisenhower defending his friend against the onslaught of the press. The movie "Patton" expresses a similar outlook, and there are hundreds of books that say the same. They overlook, however, that Eisenhower was planning on becoming president, even at this early date. Every move he made in Europe was carefully done so as to be politically correct. A Gallup poll that was conducted at the time said 77% of Americans liked Patton, 19% did not, and 4% were uncertain. So even though what had happened was grossly misportrayed in the newspapers at home, 77% of Americans still liked Patton, and for Eisenhower to have opposed the wishes of that mass of voters would have been unthinkable. The books that state Eisenhower stood up for Patton against the press and also against the outraged

American people are not accurately portraying events. The only outraged people were certain senators and the press corps.

It should also be noted that when Eisenhower first heard about the slapping incidents, he told the press to not publish it because he would lose a valuable commander. He had no intention whatsoever of standing up for Patton. Politicians never stake their reputation on that of another's, especially one as unreliable as Patton's. That is, until a poll is conducted.

Even if Eisenhower had decided to save Patton before the poll was conducted, it was hardly a courageous deed. Patton was Eisenhower's best general; Patton was much more experienced and better able than Eisenhower. Patton had fought against Pancho Villa, he had fought in WWI as Pershing's aide; where the fighting was, Patton had always been. Patton was also, according to the Germans, the Americans most modern general, a man who applied the tactics of mobile warfare even better than the Germans themselves. No matter what may be said for Eisenhower or Bradley, they were hopelessly tied to the idea of a "broad front;" they had never ventured beyond traditional West Point caution; the idea of a swift advance or unguarded flanks frightened them.

Patton was also the oldest American general; he had the most experience and he should have had Eisenhower's position. The only convincing argument I have heard as to why he did not have it is that the Supreme Allied Commander needed to be tactful and make decisions with important political consequences. Basically, they wanted (and got) a politician. The fact that a politician would make tactical and strategic decisions would have struck us as absurd, so they found a man who was a graduate of West Point.[1] They could tell people that he was a "simple soldier" and, incidentally, they always did so when he made terrible political decisions.[2] But the millions of men who lost their lives due to poor military[3] management have Eisenhower to thank. He didn't even listen to sound military advice from Patton. And if one of his generals

---

[1] Eisenhower had trained tankers in the US during WWI while Patton was in France fighting with those tankers. At the start of WWII he was a mere Lieutenant Colonel. After 1942, however, he had risen (on average) a rank every 6 months!

[2] Like not taking Berlin.

[3] Let's not even get into political decisions.

said something politically incorrect – why, look at Patton! He relieved the general who had saved him.

Patton was *the* general when a situation arose that was desperate. Although Eisenhower was constantly taking armies from Patton and ignoring his advice, when the Battle of the Bulge became serious, Eisenhower's first reaction was, "Get Patton and give him as many armies as you can."[1] If Eisenhower had relieved Patton after the slapping incidents, the war would certainly have been many years longer.[2] Eisenhower himself would have been relieved (because of the Battle of the Bulge) and there would have been many similar costly battles like the Bulge.[3] Eisenhower didn't "rescue" Patton from the attacks of the Press, saving him from destruction for some gracious reason: the reason was that *Eisenhower* needed Patton more than Patton ever needed Eisenhower. In fact, this was duly recorded by someone in London. He was walking along the corridor at Eisenhower's headquarters and he overheard a heated discussion between General Wedemeyer and General Eisenhower about Patton. Eisenhower was telling the story, oft-repeated by historians, of his having saved Patton, when General Wedemeyer burst out, "Heck, get on to yourself, Ike; you didn't make him, he made you."

The British influence on Patton's retainment is larger than supposed. The fiasco at Anzio proved that not all American generals knew the technique of a swift advance. When Churchill said he had wanted a lion, but had been given a whale floundering on the beach, he meant that what he had needed was a Patton. And even though the British generals could not replicate Patton's daring themselves, they admired those tactics, like they admired Rommel. The Royal Air Force and Navy men especially liked him. Had Patton been relieved, the only one who would have been happy would have been Montgomery.

The statement that Patton was a better general is proven by the fact that in France, when Patton was merely an army commander, his name was mentioned in headlines along with those of Montgomery and

---

[1] As soon as things started going well, he went back to his old self and gave half of Bradley's army to Montgomery.
[2] If on the other hand, Patton had been in Supreme Command, the war would have been at least a year shorter.
[3] 80,000 Americans died. Patton predicted to Bradley an attack in the exact sector where it occurred but was ignored. More on this later.

Bradley who were Army group commanders.[1] None of Patton's equal ranks excelled in the way he did, their names didn't even appear in the headlines. This proves that Patton was put in a position far below his true worth.

Patton received a telegram from Marshall stating that "The prestige of Seventh Army would prove to great advantage in that follow up" of the Normandy invasion. This did not make Patton any happier, that along with the news that Bradley was to be the American Army Group commander. Not that Patton was jealous, his later amicable role as Bradley's general proves that he was not, it was just that he was senior to Bradley, had been in command of Bradley in Sicily, was more qualified and had proven his excellence where Bradley had not.

We owe much to Patton that he didn't quit at this stage in the game. If he had, who knows what may have happened to the future of the European campaign? He remained only to save American lives in the coming campaign.

---

[1] They had several army commanders under them.

Chapter Twelve

RELIEVED

"I guess I am the only one who sees glory in war ..."

Patton's command since the start of the war had captured, wounded, or killed 177,000 Germans, Italians and French. The Seventh Army's average losses had been one American for 13 1/2 of the enemy. "It would be a national calamity to lose an Army commander with such a record," Patton observed sadly in his diary.

Eisenhower wrote to Patton and told him that he thought the noise at home was dying down. General Joyce told Patton that he should tell the newspapers the exact truth about the slappings, "George, tell them the exact truth in these words, 'I had been dealing with heroes. I saw two men whom I thought were cowards. Naturally I was not too gentle with them.'" Though perfectly true, Patton felt there was no use repeating it. He would leave the talking to Eisenhower and his staff.

General Joyce told Beatrice, Patton's wife, that "Wars were won by leaders who were "hard men." The "niceties" of life had to be left to "the softer times of peace." Why were the newspapers and the high command surprised at Patton's behavior? He was, after all, a fighting man. He was a tough commander who demanded toughness on the part of his men. A coward could only.be tolerated under the command of a cowardly man. Patton's toughness and discipline had been touted by the newspapers, even exaggerated; and then they were surprised that he did what a tough, disciplined commander does: discipline.

Patton's side of what had happened was never heard. The newspapers only listened to the Pearson version. There were even cartoons showing Patton as Adolf Hitler, something that must have made Patton sick. He wrote to his wife, "The thing that hurts me is that as far as I can see, my side of the case has never been heard. It is like taxation without representation... However, I am sure that my move is to make no move." "On occasion it is best to do nothing, and however repellent that is to my nature, I am doing exactly that," he wrote to Keyes.

> "I am now not so sure that my luck has held in view of all the bunk that seems to have appeared in the papers about me. Also if the war ends now, I hate to be out of the last act. Of course we still have Japan and that should be a nice fight..."

Patton had nothing to do, and he spent most of his time worrying over what Congress would do with him – and how well Eisenhower would defend him.

Many decisions that would have impact on Patton's career were taking place now in Teheran. The "Big Three," Churchill, Stalin and Roosevelt met on the 28th of November, 1943 in Teheran. It would be Roosevelt and Stalin's first meeting. Churchill had no illusions about Stalin's intentions, but Roosevelt believed that he could "control" Stalin. Ever since WWI, Churchill had campaigned for armies to invade the Soviet Union. At a time when many people were awed by what they thought were its achievements, Churchill openly denounced them. The only deal he ever made with Stalin was that each would not make a separate peace. In the speech he made explaining why he did it, Churchill said that he still had not changed any of his opinions on Stalin, and that he felt Hitler and Stalin were equally evil, but that the most aggressive evil had to be dealt with first. Churchill was, quite frankly, extremely desperate, for they were in the dark days of the battle of Britain. Now, however, with the Americans on their side, they could not fail, and Hitler knew it.

In Roosevelt's declining years, when sickness was devouring his fragile body, many close advisors of his were Communists. He might not have been aware of their danger, or perhaps he did not know that his wit was dimming. In any event, Roosevelt was determined to negotiate with Stalin. The opening remarks at the conference show the weight that each man placed on what he was doing. Roosevelt began lightly, welcoming Churchill and Stalin. Churchill, showing the gravity with which he held the meeting, said, "In our hands we have the future of mankind." Stalin said, almost ironically, "Now let us get down to business." Though Roosevelt was at ease, Churchill was very ill throughout the conference as well as nervous. Stalin had wanted to meet Roosevelt on his own, and Churchill was obviously afraid of the consequences that this could have. Stalin had told Roosevelt that he and Churchill "got into each other's hair."

> "Only Roosevelt, who had long hoped to meet Stalin face to face, travelled to Teheran with the expectation of smoothing the rough edges of collaboration. For all the President's notorious charm, the first contacts were awkward. He wrote to his wife of the atmosphere of 'great distrust' emanating from Stalin when they first met. Arnold, Roosevelt's air force Chief-of-Staff, was struck by Stalin's patronising treatment of the British, 'half-humorous, half-scathing.' Roosevelt decided to side with Stalin in these exchanges in order to break the ice. At the plenary meeting on the second day of the conference the President began by ignoring Churchill and chatting to the Soviet delegates; he began to poke fun at the British, and the more Churchill scowled the more Stalin smiled. When Stalin finally burst out laughing at Churchill's discomfiture, the tension between the two leaders was broken." *"Why the Allies Won," by Richard Overy.*

Stalin wanted the allies to invade France, and invade it now. He said it would take the pressure off the Soviets. So would invading the Mediterranean, pointed out Churchill. But Stalin was adamant. The reason, when one looks at the map, is clear. With an invasion in France, Russia could take huge tracts of Eastern Europe. If the allies landed in Turkey or Italy[1] the Americans and British could split their forces in two, one going for Eastern Europe, the other for Western Europe. This would take away the Russians' dream of encompassing other countries and leave them with the dismal task of conquering no other country besides their own. Their lust for Eastern Europe made them vigorously oppose any Mediterranean landings that might eclipse their dreams of empire.

Teheran was the scene of one of the most dramatic incidents in the war. At dinner on the second day, things seemed to be going better. However, Stalin "could not leave Churchill alone" and kept saying that

---

[1] Mass landings, not diversions

Churchill was unable to appreciate the Red Army, and did not want to establish a second front. According to Churchill, "Stalin indulged in a great deal of "teasing" of me, which I did not at all resent until the Marshal entered in a genial manner upon a serious and even deadly aspect of punishment to be inflicted upon the Germans. The German General Staff, he said, must be liquidated. The whole force of Hitler's mighty armies depended upon about fifty thousand officers and technicians. If these were rounded up and shot at the end of the war, German military strength would be extirpated." Churchill colored and denounced his host in a torrent that concluded, "The British Parliament and public will never tolerate mass executions. Even if in war passion they allowed it to begin, they would turn violently against those responsible after the first butchery had taken place. The Soviets must be under no delusion on this point." Stalin pursued the point. "Fifty thousand," he said, "must be shot." Churchill was, in his own words, deeply angered. "I would rather be taken out into the garden here and now and be shot myself than sully my own and my country's honor by such infamy." Roosevelt, perhaps in jest,[1] said, "How about a compromise? Not 50,000 should be shot, but 49,000." Many in the room were motioning to Churchill that it was all a joke, but then Roosevelt's son, Elliot, rose. He made a speech saying how he agreed with Stalin's plan and how he was sure the United States Army would support it. At this, Churchill got up and left the room. Stalin persuaded Churchill to come back, "Although I was not then, and am not now, fully convinced that all was chaff and there was no serious intent lurking behind."

This ominous incident tells us a lot about what the allies already knew of the maniacal obsession the Russians possessed, and their vindictive nature against the Germans. The entire American staff of the War Department were against attacking the Mediterranean. They said it would result in another Gallipoli.[2] Their narrow-minded strategic policy was in line with the theories of Claueswitz and Napoleon. They overlooked the attacking nature of campaigns and could see only in terms of a "broad front." The staff had approved the N. African campaign only as a sideshow while the army got ready to attack. They had wanted as early as 1942 to attack Normandy (potentially disastrous) and were angered that Roosevelt's "politics" had got them stuck in Italy. Too narrow-minded to see the potential of an aggressive attack in Italy and Sicily or in the Baltic region, American strategists, both political and

---

[1] Perhaps not, based on his son's reaction.

[2] Overlooking that none of the area was defended, and that in this war the Turks were sympathetic to the allies.

military, had decided the main effort would be put into France and any other excursions would simply be sideshows. They deemed the N. African and Italian campaigns as British ploys designed to annex countries and extend the "Empire."

To an extent, Patton agreed with his peers. He mentions in his diary about the political and British nature of the Sicilian campaign. But, unlike his peers, he could see that when one had the advantage, one should take it, and take it fully. In 1943, Patton was not in a high enough position to see that taking France would help the Communists, but taking Italy would harm them. From his vantage point, it *did* look like a British ploy. However, during the German occupation in 1945, the reader gets the sense that Patton had begun to perceive what had happened, and his constant disgust with Eisenhower reflects this. "I have seen the untoward of things," he wrote.

Chapter Thirteen

OUSTED

On December 7th Patton heard that Eisenhower was going to the United Kingdom. Contrary to the opinion of the time, Marshall was not going to command the Normandy invasion. He had decided some time ago that Eisenhower would lead the invasion. Marshall was remaining in Washington as Army Chief of Staff. Sir Henry Maitland Wilson, commander of the British Middle East Command, would succeed Eisenhower in Algiers. Patton asked the Assistant Secretary of War Mc Cloy what would become of him. Mc Cloy skirted the question. Patton knew that Eisenhower was commanding the invasion as Supreme Allied Commander, and that Bradley and Montgomery would have Army Groups. What would he have?

Mc Cloy told Patton that he "had in his makeup certain chemicals no other General had; that he was a great fighter and an inspiring leader, though probably not a Moltke, and that he must be used... He was not to worry about what was said about him as that would hurt his efficiency."

> "He also said that I look and act like a general and that no one else we have does... 'You have color, personality, and size. Men like to follow a man they can respect.'"

Then Mc Cloy broke the news. Patton would have an army. "I should have a group of armies," Patton wrote, "but that will come. I think that my luck is in again." Harry Hopkins took Patton aside and said to him, "Don't let anything that s.o.b. Pearson said bother you."

Patton wrote to his sister that he didn't want her or anyone else making excuses for him. "If I cannot stand on my record, very few people can." He said that, "The thing for all of us to do is to do nothing and say nothing." He also warned his wife not to defend him. It was very cold in Sicily, "and as we have no fires and no heat, the only thing one can do is to shivver... [sic] Send me some more pink medecin. [sic] This worry and inactivity has raised heck with my insides."

"Everyone and his brother" was visiting Sicily, and Patton was giving them tours of where the Carthaginians beat the Romans. After tiring of that, Patton decided to see the Holy Land, and so took a "flight into Egypt." General Wilson, who they stayed with, was British and "I liked him – he is more impressive than either Alex or Monty. There is a very definite effort on the part of all the staff except General Wilson, to run Monty down and to try to get me to agree with them, but needless to say, I did not commit myself. Apparently the Regular officers of the British Army do not like Montgomery at all." This was news to Patton. Throughout the war, Monty's officers hated him. He would relieve anyone who dared to question his orders. Often he would relieve them without reason. When he took over the Eighth Army, before getting to know the old staff, he fired them and replaced them with his own "yes men."

Patton also learned something of the Russians now. He became friendly with General Anders, commander of the Polish II Corps. Anders told Patton jokingly that if his corps was caught between a German and a Russian Army, they would have difficulty figuring which one they wanted to fight the most. Behind the joke, though, was a sinister reality. The actuality of the threat of the Communists was already beginning to dawn on Patton.

Patton visited Egypt which he said was the filthiest city he had seen yet. The pyramids were not as impressive as the ones in Mexico. He said however, that there was a Roman forum ruin nearby which was dwarfed by the impressiveness of the Egyptian ruin.

When Patton returned he wrote about the slapping incidents' long term effects to his wife. "The incident will still further frighten weak commanders and will cramp my style for a while with new troops, but I have the gift of leadership and will get them back as I always do. As you say, Destiny [Ike] has never backed me up and never will, but I manage some how... When my turn comes, as it surely will, I have no debts to pay. When the new set up come out [Overlord] you will be surprised how well our relatives [the British] have done. It is realy fantastic. How long, Oh! Lord, how long?"

Patton wasn't too happy on Christmas. He had just learned that, even though given the option, none of his staff had left. "My men are crazy about me, and that's what makes me so angry with Drew Pearson ... my destiny is sure and I am a fool and a coward ever to have doubted it. I don't any more. Some people are needed to do things, and they have to be tempered by adversity as well as thrilled by success. I have had both. Now for some success." And though Patton had recently said he was getting to like Smith better, he wrote that, "I wish to God Ike would leave and take Smith with him. They cramp my style." Seemingly in a depressed mood, he wrote on December 29th to his wife that "I guess I am the only one who sees glory in war .... Over 80% of the letters I have received are for me. Only one letter by a person of education is hostile. The rest are cranks and unsigned mostly." The night before New Year's Eve he wrote, in a type of allegorical remark, "Destiny will keep on floating me down the stream of fate."

Eisenhower rated Patton 5th out of 24 lieutenant generals. This was close to an insult. Who had taken Messina? Palermo? Or did he so quickly forget upon whom his career had rested? Eisenhower wrote that Patton "Should always serve under a strong but understanding commander."

For Patton, New Year's was hardly happy. Clark, an old enemy of Patton's and friend of Eisenhower's, who incidentally had never had any combat service before WWII, was going to command Seventh Army when he "thinks he should quit Italy." It was insult added to injury.

> "I feel very badly for myself but particularly for the staff and headquarters soldiers who have stood by me all the time... I suppose that I am going to England to command another Army, but if I am sent there to simply train troops which I am not to command [in battle] I shall resign... I cannot conceive of anything more stupid than to change staffs on a General, nor can I conceive of anything more inconsiderate than not to notify him

where he is going. It is just one more thing to remember when the time comes to pay my debts. A Hell of a Happy New Year.'"

Patton would always remember what Eisenhower had done on that New Year, not to him, but to his staff. To give those constant and loyal men to Clark, the failure, was the unkindest cut of all. The change of staffs was "unfair and insulting to me, but is heartbreaking for the staff of Seventh Army who have been utterly loyal, and now find that their efforts get them nowhere. It is damnable. I have contemplated asking to be relieved but will stick with it at least for the present..." Happily, Patton would get most of his staff back in France by special request. "Wellington had many adversities. His staff also changed several times. Fate."

Lord Gort asked Patton to come to Malta and see the Crusader castles, and so on January 4th Patton accepted the invitation and flew over his old battlefields in Tunisia, and "hundreds of memories surged up and all were of success." No trace of the old battle could be found in the desert. There was no trace of the desperate actions, nor the courage with which they had been fought. There were no remains from the fuel dumps at Tebessa, the tanks, the guns, the tents, the command posts; the historic battles and their trappings, like the men that had fought in them, were gone forever. The way that the Americans had treated Patton was similar to this scene of the unending desert: harsh and forgetful.

On his vacation he observed the various battlegrounds where in medieval times the knights had fought the Saracens. He returned on January 6th, in time to hear Gay read the order that relieved him. He gave his staff a short speech. They should be as loyal to Clark in Italy as they had been to him here in Sicily, he said. Patton's staff begged him to get them back when and if he was given another campaign, and two men began to cry. Patton thanked them for their loyalty, but then he "choked up and quit." The worst part of it all was that the man who would be taking Patton's army, Clark, had like Eisenhower, no battlefield experience. Patton was worried that Clark wouldn't promote or decorate the officers from Seventh Army who would be going with Clark to Italy, so he tried to treat Clark nicely even though he was "most condescending and treated me like an undertaker treats the family of the deceased. It was rather hard to take, especially as I am certain that they pulled the wires which got me removed from Anvil..."

Now that we can look ahead, we can see what a mistake it was to give Patton's army to Clark. Anzio is the disaster that proves why constantly underestimating and underrating Patton would finally come back to haunt the commanders that did so.

Patton's shrewd discernment of General Lucas' nature deserves mention only to show that Patton was not only good at predicting the enemy's moves, but also his own country's. "I hope he is successful... but I am not sure that he has sufficient drive." Lucas would command the Anzio assault, in which the opportunity to advance through undefended Italy was lost. The landing at Anzio thoroughly stunned the Germans, but Lucas failed to exploit the surprise he had gained and the Germans soon reinforced the beachhead, turning Anzio into one of the most famous fiascoes of WWII. All this was due to what Patton had originally noted: Lucas' lack of "sufficient drive." Eisenhower was not blessed with this kind of foresight. Had he been, we might have not suffered as many disasters, fiascoes, and needless waste of life as we did.

A shell landed only nine inches from Patton's toe, but it just spun around on the ground. As all these close calls with eternity did, Patton felt reassured in his destiny that was yet to be fulfilled. "Mathematically I should be dead as none of the four craters was more than 30 feet from me," wrote Patton, "but I am not dead or even hurt. It gave me great self-confidence. The Lord had a perfect cut for me and pulled his punch." The near miss greatly bolstered Patton's spirits about his new position under Bradley as well. As he wrote to his wife, "Well I have been under worse people and I will surely win. You have no idea how much that near miss cheered me up."

Patton was also thinking about people. What would their reaction be at the end of the war? Would they react as they had at the end of WWI? Already they seemed to be heading in that direction. "I have already met several quite intelligent men who say 'Now we will have no more wars.'... The avowed purpose of the treaty of Vienna in 1814 was to see that that was the last war. Around 1700 BC, the Hittites, Cretans, and Egyptians had a tri-party treaty to avert wars, and we lerned [sic] about it in 1914. Some explorers discovered the Hittite capital and in the library discovered the bricks with the treaty on them – yet before the mud had dried, the Egyptians and Cretans had ganged up and destroyed the Hitites [sic]. If we again think that wars are over, we will surely have another one and damned quick. Man is WAR' and we had better remember that."

121

It was now a certainty. Patton had heard on January 18th that Bradley would be commander of all the American ground troops landing in England. Patton correctly surmised that Bradley would be American group commander. He was disappointed, but he had long suspected that he would not be given any posts. It gave him time to reflect on Bradley, whom he termed, "a man of great mediocrity."

"At Benning in command he failed to get discipline. At Gafsa, when it looked as though Germans might turn our right flank he suggested that we draw corps headquarters to Feriana. I refused to move. In Sicily, when the 45th Division approached Cefalu, he halted them for fear of a possible German landing east of Termini. I had to order him to move and told him that I would be responsible for his rear, and that his timidity had lost us one day. He tried to stop the landing operation #2 east of Cap d'Orlando because he thought it was dangerous. I told him I would take the blame if it failed and that he could have the credit if it was a success. Finally, on the night of August 16-17, he asked me to call off the landing east of Milazzo for fear our troops might shoot at each other. He also failed to get word to all units of the II Corps on the second paratroop landing.

On the other hand Bradley has many of the attributes which are considered desirable in a general. He wears glasses, has a strong jaw, talks profoundly and says little, and is a shooting companion of the Chief of Staff [Marshall]. Also a loyal man. I consider him among our better generals."

It seems that the last paragraph might be sarcasm, although the last two sentences seem to be Patton's estimation of him. Bradley was a quiet man who kept his opinions to himself and thus gained favor. But Bradley was not as smart as Patton (Bradley completely misunderstood the Russians) nor as brilliant (Bradley's tactics were mediocre at best.) Bradley was not a good judge of men (he thought Patton and Hodges were equal in ability), but he was dependable, and he was just the man Eisenhower could rely on to obey his orders without question.

In the morning on January 26th, Patton arrived in England.

Chapter Fourteen

27th START FROM ZERO

On January 26th Patton was given command of the Third Army. He was destined to take this army to extraordinary heights. At this time, though, the members of Third Army were, in Patton's words, "novices." They had not yet had any combat experience in WWII. Patton could not foresee the Third Army's eventual fame. In the coming operation, they were slated merely to support Bradley's First Army. Had its commander been less dynamic, the Third would merely have wiped up behind the unspectacular tail of Bradley's First Army.

That night Eisenhower asked Patton to dinner. Ike took along Kay Summersby. She was his driver, before the war she had been a model. Kay was in her twenties and engaged, but in love with Eisenhower, whose much older wife was in America. Of course the rumors about the two were rampant. When asked if Eisenhower was really committing adultery, an officer remarked that he thought it unusual for a general to kiss his driver. Patton said in his diary that Eisenhower was very nasty and "show-offish – he always is when Kay is present." Eisenhower criticized Lee (A general on Ike's staff) for his flamboyance, "which he would give a million to possess." In the newspapers Kay was often beside Ike or in the not too distant background. Eisenhower's wife Mamie wrote to her husband asking about Kay. Eisenhower told her that, "You must realize that in such a confused life as we lead here all sorts of stories, gossip, lies etc. can get started without the slightest foundation in fact." That was a lie which became obvious when he visited her in Washington. Eisenhower began calling her Kay by mistake. They argued and Ike told her he couldn't wait to get back to "my theater where I can do what I want." Mamie was upset and angered. She was not the only one who, by the war's end, would feel betrayed by Eisenhower.

Kay's presence made Patton nervous, and she wrote later that he was the only really manly general she had seen. He was also the only one who treated her well because she was a woman. She noted the special effort he made not to curse in her presence.

Around his own headquarters Patton had one firm rule. He would not have any female, no matter what age, nearby. He had told his nephew, Fred, that the people who didn't like him at home would try in some way to destroy him.

> "He felt that it was quite possible for someone to use a woman and a slanted press release to blacken his reputation. Obviously, he was unpopular in some quarters and did have a constant and often expressed feeling that someone or some group of persons was 'out to get him.'" *"Before the Colors Fade," by Frederick Ayer.*

He followed this rule strictly throughout the rest of his life. Patton's unusual foresight was proven correct. Thirty six years later, in "War Between the Generals," David Irving[1] would accuse Patton of having an affair with *his niece*, Jean Gordon. But even with her Patton had observed his strict rule, making these unfounded statements ridiculous.

Authors have been trying to justify Eisenhower's affair with Kay for a long time. One of their attempts has been to implicate Patton. One can see the desperate lengths to which they would go in this, their feeble attempt at accusing Patton of an affair with *his relative*. Whereas men close to Eisenhower believed that he was fooling around, men near Patton are vehement. According to Charles Codman, Patton's aide, "Any serious interest on the General's part in any women other than the members of his own family would be news to me." It would be difficult, if not impossible, to hide something from an aide. Patton's record, unlike Eisenhower's, is clear.

---

[1] David Irving's works on Hitler have recently been discredited; he was convicted by a British court of trying to falsify the historical record and denying that the Holocaust took place.

"Well, I have an Army and it is up to me," Patton wrote. "'God show the right.' As far as I can remember this is my twenty-seventh start from zero since entering the U.S. Army. Each time I have made a success of it, and this one must be the biggest" success.

On February 3rd Patton was given quarters at Grosvenor Square. According to Codman's description, the entrance to their new quarters was "unobtrusive, the vestibule small and dark."
"Since they mean to keep me under wraps, this should do fine," Patton commented. But their new quarters would be somewhat different from what the outside portended. A corporal saluted, and swung open the door on what would be the salon. Wooden panelling covered the hallway, exotic prints plastered the walls. There was a thick carpet and "soft, indirect lighting." Codman said it was more "period sitting room than salon."
"Who the heck picked this place?" the General said.
"General Lee himself, I believe, sir," the corporal answered.
"I might have known," the General muttered to himself. Then he straightened. "Where's my room?" he asked crisply.
They followed the corporal to another closed door which the corporal threw open. "Your room, sir," he said, stepping aside and to attention.

> "Rooted to the threshold, the General surveyed the white bear rug, the walls and curtains of pink brocade, the triptych-mirrored dressing table, and beyond through an open door the glint of nickel fixtures and two-tone seafoam tile. Then, as his eye caught the reflection in the mirror on the ceiling of the enormous bed lying low and lascivious under its embroidered silk coverlet, the silence was broken by a single highly charged exclamation." *"Drive," by Colonel Charles R. Codman, page 137.*

They eased back along the corridor and inspected the floor above.

> "Three more master bedrooms. Two baths. Servants quarters. By the time I got down again, General Patch had arrived. Over a couple of Scotches he and the Old Man were deep in Generals' talk."

"This morning at SHAEF," Codman overheard General Patch saying, "Beetle [Bedell Smith] claimed that particular matter was high-level stuff. He said I would get instructions in due course."

"That whole headquarters is so darned high level you have to carry an oxygen tank to live up there." General Patton's voice rose. "To hell with Beetle, see Ike himself. Though by now, they've probably got him completely isolated."

"I'll keep that in mind, George."

"Look, Sandy," he said, "I'd rather be shot than spend the evening sitting around this Anglican bordello." They decided to see a play.

At the theater Patton was given a standing ovation. Half the people stared at him, he noted, "it is quite pleasant to be famous." Patton paid a visit to Major Liecester-Warren, whose son-in-law was General Sir Oliver Leese. Leese was serving in Italy with Montgomery's Eighth Army. Patton reported that "they are very nice people." Patton is frequently accused of being an Anglophobe, but that is far from the truth. He despised Montgomery, but not Montgomery's nationality. British military tactics were slow and cautious, and the best Britons detested their own tactics.

The man who came up with blitzkrieg, Liddell Hart, was British, but his countrymen for the most part detested the strategy and ignored him throughout the 1920's. The Germans read his books and realized the sense in his strategy. Instead of fixed or "set piece" battle plans, Liddell Hart realized that the next war would be a fluid one, with the lines in constant motion. He pioneered the fast tank advance and quick, pincer drives where the enemy *was not*. In comparison with WWI, this was revolutionary. But military colleges like West Point and Sandhurst laughed at his theories. Some bright military minds, however, were reading his books. Rommel was one, Patton another. Patton read every book by Liddell Hart between wars, and developed his own attacking method from it.

But for the most part, men like Napoleon and Clausewitz were the anointed "geniuses" that the officers followed. It was their strategy to attack the enemy head-on, it was Liddell Hart's strategy to take his land and cut him off. Napoleon had revolutionized war, and since his time, war has been associated with mass murder. His strategy made it so. Patton's strategy, by contrast, had relatively few casualties with huge dividends in land and munitions. Where Napoleon would say defeat the enemy by killing his men, Patton defeated the enemy by capturing his land and armories, and forcing him to surrender.

Is it surprising that Eisenhower, Bradley and Montgomery were "disciples of Clausewitz?" Bradley (and Eisenhower eventually) accepted but did not apply the new theories of "lightning war." Montgomery, however, was a hard-liner. Eisenhower never used the tactics, but Montgomery vetoed use of them by his subordinates. Bradley adopted a few, but for the most part, he did only what he was taught at West Point.

On February 12th, Patton went to see Eisenhower. Ike said to Patton that Devers was ".22 caliber," but Patton commented in his diary that "some others are not over .32 caliber." Eisenhower told Patton that "You are fundamentally honest on the larger issues[1] but are too fanatical in your friendships." Eisenhower was displeased because Patton was rewarding the loyalty of his Seventh Army staff by getting them assigned to the Third Army.

---

[1] Patton wrote dryly in his diary, "It's a good thing someone is."

Chapter Fifteen

BRITISH PRAISE

A few days later Patton's career was almost incredibly altered. At 1:30 in the morning, he received a telegram from Eisenhower. They left immediately and were in London by 10:45.

Patton walked into Eisenhower's office.
"I am afraid you will have to eat crow again for a little while," Ike said.
Patton, alarmed, asked, "What have I done now?"
Ike, laughing a little, said he'd done nothing wrong, but "You might have to take command of the beachhead in Italy and straighten things out."
"That's not eating crow. That's a great compliment! You know I'd command anything from a platoon up in order to fight!"

Eisenhower then handed Patton a radiogram from General Alexander. Alexander was still fighting in Italy. Alexander had always wanted Patton for the Anzio operation, but General Clark[1] hated Patton.

After Lucas' miserable failure at Anzio, Alexander said to Clark, "You know, the position is serious. We may be pushed back into the sea. That would be very bad for both of us – and you would certainly be relieved of your command." After this "gentle injunction" (Alexander's words), Clark permitted Alexander to ask for a new commander of Lucas' VI Corps.

---

[1] An American

This message went to Brooke, Chief of the Imperial General Staff.[1] Brooke showed the message to Churchill, who said, "Why not send Alexander to command the troops at the bridgehead?"

Brooke lost his temper and cried, "Can't you trust your commanders to organize the command for themselves without interfering and upsetting the chain and sequence of command?"

Churchill apparently accepted Brooke's advice. He had read Alexander's radiogram. "How about sending General Patton?" he asked.

Brooke agreed. Churchill convinced Brooke that Patton would remedy virtually overnight the situation at Anzio-Nettuno. Churchill always remembered that Patton had successfully pulled off the end-run he had advised Montgomery to do. They then sent the radiogram for approval to Eisenhower.

The radiogram said that at Anzio the men were "negative and lacked the necessary drive and enthusiasm to get things done. They appear to have become depressed by events. What we need is a thruster like George Patton." As a coups fourre, he added that "If you cannot send me a thruster like George Patton, I recommend putting a British officer in command. I have already sent a British major general to the headquarters… to spur them on a little." Eisenhower reacted predictably. He didn't want a British officer in command, so Eisenhower said he would "loan" Patton to them for a month.

It is the only time where someone requested, specifically, for Patton. Patton's talents were finally being acknowledged "as the only fighting general in the army," and by an Englishman! "I had the best compliment I ever had today," he wrote his wife.

The next day, an aide phoned and told Patton that he could return to Knutsford.

> "Nothing more. He did not even think it worthwhile to tell me what had happened. We are all very sorry that the show has been called off – it would have been risky, but much honor could have been gained. No man can live forever."

Patton would not know until the spring of 1945 that Clark had cancelled his trip. When Clark had seen Eisenhower's telegram, he had

---

[1] Brooke's American counterpart would be Marshall, U.S. Army Chief of Staff.

exclaimed, "This won't do! I don't want Patton in my theater." He arranged for Truscott to be sent instead of Patton. His mutual animosity would not allow for Patton's genius, even when it was needed. And this was an American.

Chapter Sixteen

FUROR AWAKES!

Patton found that Eisenhower overrated all British, and any Americans who were not under his command. "I wish to God he was more of a soldier and less of a politician." It was February 18th, 1944.

He was disillusioned with Eisenhower. "We suffer very much from lack of command. No one is running the show... Ike has no conception of physical command, as he has never exercised it."

Hughes has been considered by many as Patton's friend, but in Patton's diary, Patton wrote that Hughes had come to London to be Eisenhower's representative, "in other words, his [private] eye."

On March 1st Eisenhower told Patton that while he would not order him, he definitely wanted him to replace Gay with a different chief of staff. He told Patton that he didn't believe Gay had the presence of mind to take over if Patton should be killed. Patton now had a terrible dilemma. Keyes, his other faithful general from Sicily, had always felt the same way about Gay. "I am very reluctant to supersede Gay, but it looks to me and to Hughes, and others with whom I have talked, that if I don't, I will be superseded myself, so I will have to make the change."

That night Eisenhower and Patton dined alone. Eisenhower was drinking too much, Patton observed, but was terribly lonely. "I really feel sorry for him – I think that in his heart he knows he is not really commanding anything."

Patton felt very bad about having to relieve Gay. "I fear that Hap will have to give place to some one with more 'IT' and play deputy. I hate to do it but forces like Destiny seem bent on bringing it about and one is a fool to fly in the face of providence, or destiny, or whatever you call the thing that shapes our ends."

On March 6th, he went to the London pound and chose a bull terrier pup. Its first owner, an RAF officer, had crashed in Europe. The puppy was 15 months old, and Patton called it "William the Conqueror." It was white "except for a little lemin [sic] on his tail which to a cursary [sic] glance would seem to indicate that he had not used toilet paper." The dog, Patton would soon discover, was hardly a fighter so he changed his name to "Willie."

That same day, Patton told Gay the truth – that he had not wanted to relieve him, but Ike had ordered him to. Gay took it well, but Patton felt disgraced. He thought he should have resigned – but I doubt Gay would have let him. Lee told Patton that he had phoned Beedle Smith, recommending General Middleton for his chief of staff.

> "The alleged grounds [were] that since General Marshall had great confidence in Middleton, it would strengthen my position. I told Lee I was quite able to take care of myself and that for the future he would not meddle. He is either a conscientious doer of good deeds or has some ulterior motive. I am rather inclined to the latter belief."
> **Patton's Diary**

Bradley and Patton then went to see Ike. Patton never called Eisenhower "Ike" in person, although everyone else did. It was always "General Eisenhower." In the privacy of his diary, though, he often wrote "Ike," or his code-name for Eisenhower, "Divine Destiny." They walked in on a heated telephone conversation.

Eisenhower was furious. He yelled into the receiver, "Now, listen, Arthur [Tedder], I am tired of dealing with a lot of prima donnas. By gosh, you tell that bunch that if they can't get together and stop quarreling like children, I will tell the Prime Minister to get someone else to run this darned war. I'll quit."

> "He talked for some time longer and repeated that he would 'ask to be relieved and sent home' unless Tedder

could get the British and American Air and the two Navies to agree. I was quite impressed as he showed more assurance than I have ever seen him display. But he should have had the warring factions in and jumped them himself, and not left it to his Deputy, Tedder... It is always depressing to me to see how completely Ike is under the influence of the British. He even prefers steel to rubber tracks on tanks because Monty does." *Patton's Diary*

In the Wehrmacht High Command's "Kriegstagebuch" (War Diary), Patton was the first general (other than Eisenhower) to be specifically mentioned so early on. It stated on March 20th that "General Patton, who was formerly employed in North Africa and is highly regarded for his proficiency, is now in England." Highly regarded by the Germans, certainly. Throughout the war Patton – a lieutenant general – would be mentioned in German memorandums expressing more fear about the location of his army than the armies of Group Commanders.

On April 7th, Patton went to a briefing on the invasion. Montgomery spoke for two hours. Patton noticed that he was the only army commander Monty mentioned by name. Montgomery mentioned the others by the number of the army they commanded. Then came Air Marshal Sir Leigh-Mallory, Admiral Sir Ramsey and then they ate lunch. After that Bradley, Gerow, and Collins gave their presentations. Dempsey and his corps followed, "as usual they were much more prolix than we are."

"The Prime Minister made the last talk and the best. He said, 'Remember that this is an invasion, not a creation of a fortified beachhead.'"

That was what they had made at Anzio, a "fortified beachhead." Both Churchill and Patton knew that only by swift advance would they retain what they had stormed. And both had a lot of worries about the Normandy invasion.

All the British were convinced that had Patton been given Clark's role in Italy all would have been well. Eisenhower told Patton he wasn't yet sure who would be Army Group Commander. But he was. And Patton knew that. It would be Bradley.

A ladies' club in Knutsford had asked Patton to speak. Patton declined, because as he said, he was "a ghost." Patton had orders to remain in the background because the Germans wanted to know where he was. (In the event, the Germans already knew he was in England.) But since the ladies entertained American troops and were starting a club for this purpose he said he would attend the meeting. He arrived 15 minutes late hoping it would be over – but they had waited for him. He was handed a schedule which said:

1) Introduction
2) An explanation of the purpose of the club
3) General – opens the club
4) God Save the King

Miss Jeffery turned to Patton and asked him "to say a few words." Mrs. Smith then rose and said that he was speaking in a "purely friendly way and that his presence is not to be disclosed. I now have the pleasure of introducing someone who really is not supposed to be here, and I feel that if he will give this club his blessing, the club will be a success. I have the pleasure of introducing General Patton."

Patton rose and began speaking. "Until today, my only experience has been to welcome Germans and Italians to the infernal regions. In this I have been quite successful. I feel that such clubs as this have a very real value, because I believe with Mr. George Bernard Shaw, who said that the British and Americansare two people separated by a common language, and since it is the evident destiny of the British and Americans[1] to rule the world, the better we know each other, the better the job we will do." His remarks continued a little while longer on the benefits of the club.

The next day, the 26th of April, Patton was sitting down to lunch when the phone rang. It was Ike's public relations staff and they asked Patton what he had said in his talk the day before. Patton was confused and not sure what they meant. Then Gay got on the line and got to the

---

[1] Patton said the next day that he had said "the British and Americans, and of course, the Russians." The chair people at the meeting corroborated his evidence. It's difficult to tell whether or not he really did add "the Russians," because he later said that "anyway, anyone who wants the Russians to run the world is a damned fool."

point, asking Patton what he had said about the British and Americans ruling the world.

> "I told him that I said, 'Since it was the evident destiny of the British and Americans, and of course the Russians, to rule the world, the better we knew each other, the better it would be.' Gay told me that some papers said I mentioned the Russians and some did not."

Patton learned that newspapers had exploded over his remarks. "Leaving out the Russians" was akin to a crime and newspapers and congressmen were once again calling for his neck. Patton had no idea that they were going to quote what he said. Not mentioning the Russians at a British and American social club hardly seems a matter to relieve a general (or anyone) over.

At 10:30 the next day Bedell Smith called and gave Patton a verbal order from Ike that he was never to talk in public without first submitting what he was saying to him and Ike for censorship, "thereby displaying great confidence in an Army commander – if I have not been relieved."

Bedell Smith continued his telephone conversation with Patton.

> "Beedle also said that due to my 'unfortunate remarks,' the permanent promotion of himself and me might never come off. How sad. In consonance with this order, I am unable to talk with either the 79th, 80th, 83rd, or 7th Armored Divisions, a restriction that will surely cost lives. Yet if I break it, I will get relieved, and that would mean defeat and a still larger loss. 'God show the right,' and damn all reporters and gutless men."

There follows in Patton's diary a complaint about the British, but a few days later Churchill would stand up for Patton to Eisenhower. Maybe Patton thought that the English were behind the attacks but in 1945 he would learn that it was the pro-Communist American press.

> "So far as I am concerned, every effort is made to show lack of confidence in my judgment and at   the   same time, in every case of stress, great confidence in my fighting. None of those at Ike's headquarters ever go to

137

bat for juniors, and in any argument between the British and the Americans, invariably favor the British. Benedict Arnold is a piker compared to them, and that includes Lee as well as Ike and Beedle."

It was today that Patton sent Ruth Ellen[1] his "most pitiful" letter. After reading it, she said she thought "that it is just awful. Gosh, I wish they would invade before something worse happens to him."

"Apparently I am again an incident due to a three minute talk I made at a gathering of some 50 people at which, by the way, the chairman (she was a woman) said I was unofficial. I really feel pretty bad today as anything may happen, but at least I still have the When and If.[2] I may be using it soon. It is a horrid thought that one may be deprived of doing the only job one is good at due to the exercise of free speech, but that thought is always with me – it is a wonderful morale builder!?!?!

I guess my trouble is that I can never realize that anyone should be interested in what I say.

I have caught nothing but hell for nearly a year now. All I want to do is win the war and everyone seems to think that all I want is notoriety which I despise.

When one knows one is good, it is not necessary to have people say so. I know I am. I have never asked a favor or shunned a detail or spared my neck, the soldiers think I am wonderful, but the Press??? Bah! Jesus only suffered one night but I have had months and months of it, and the cross is not yet in sight, though probably around the corner.

Of course, if and I say IF I get into this next show, all will be well as long as there is fighting to do. I will have to take bigger chances than usual but either you do get it or you don't, so what the heck. A nice clean grave would be better than surviving another victory, so far as I'm concerned, but frankly I don't think I will be killed. I have a job to do and I am going to do it. I still believe in fate if not in destiny [Eisenhower?]."

---

[1] His daughter

[2] The "When and If" was a boat he had acquired between wars. He said "*When* I fight in the next war, *and If* I survive I will sail it around the world."

Eisenhower was cabling Marshall. He told Marshall that he was upset that "Patton had broken out again." He is "unable to use reasonably good sense in all those matters where senior commanders must appreciate the effect of their actions upon public opinion." He had doubts about "the wisdom of retaining him in high command despite his demonstrated capacity in battle leadership." Was a battle commander's position to be determined by public relations? We enter a new age in war history.

Eisenhower admitted to Marshall that Patton's remarks had been misinterpreted, but "I have grown so weary of the trouble he constantly causes you and the War Department, to say nothing of myself, that I am seriously contemplating the most drastic action." How typical. Even now, Eisenhower had too little backbone to enumerate what the "most drastic action" would be in case it differed from Marshall's opinion. Then he posed the question the answer to which he so desperately needed. "Do you consider that his retention in high command will tend to destroy or diminish public and governmental confidence in the War Department?" Ambiguity returns: "If so, stern disciplinary action must be taken."

Eisenhower was so worried that he sent another telegram without waiting for an answer. "The fact remains that he [Patton] simply does not keep his mouth shut." Is a soldier a mannequin, that he may never express his opinion but only do what he was built for? Eisenhower may have preferred it this way since he was a terrible speaker but there are people among us who would like to use the right that has been guaranteed to us – namely, freedom of speech.

Marshall's answer was that he had been considering the issues but Patton was Eisenhower's. Marshall preferred not to wreck his reputation on a defeat caused by Patton's skills not being employed – but he also did not want another Patton outburst blamed on him. Patton was Eisenhower's problem child, best to leave it that way.

Eisenhower next wrote to Patton. He told him that he deplored his "habit of dramatizing yourself" and "committing indiscretions for no other purpose that of calling attention to yourself." *"All I want to do is win the war and everyone seems to think that all I want is notoriety which I despise."* So Patton had written to his daughter.

April 30th dawned with nothing new in sight. Bedell Smith told Patton to report to General Eisenhower at 11:00 the next morning. "It can be anything from a reprimand to a reduction [in grade], or a new plan of campaign. These constant pickings are a little hard on the nerves, but great training. I feel that if I get reduced and sent home, it might be quite important, as I w[ill] get into politics as an honest and straight spoken man and would either be a great success or a dismal failure." Incredible! It was the first time in his life that Patton was considering politics, and the main reason was because he knew Eisenhower was going to run after the war, and he wanted to inform the public. In 1945 there is evidence that Patton may not have given up the idea of running. Certainly, he was still planning on going home, retiring, and "telling the truth" about Eisenhower – if he lived.

To Marshall, Eisenhower wrote saying that he would have a meeting with Patton. He would probably relieve him and had every faith that Hodges would run Third Army and do a "fine job." Eisenhower asked whether he should reduce Patton to colonel or keep him at his temporary rating of lieutenant general.

140

Chapter Seventeen

SIMPLY TELLING THE TRUTH

"My final thought on the matter is that I am destined to achieve some great thing – what, I don't know, but this last incident was so trivial in its nature, but so terrible in its effect, that it is not the result of an accident but the work of God. His will be done."

All was dismal in England. The powers that be were reviewing what deserted outpost to send Patton to. Marshall replied to Eisenhower's telegram that if Patton was retained at his rank of lieutenant general, he would have the problem of finding a place for him. It was conceivable that a situation might develop during the invasion "where this admittedly unbalanced but nevertheless aggressive fighting man should be rushed into the breach."

Was Patton's moment of glory over already? Would the conqueror be sent home disgraced? A better question might be why Patton, our best general, always had to review his career in the service while men like Bradley, Eisenhower and Montgomery – mediocre men at best – were secure in their seats?

Eisenhower had qualms about dismissing Patton reduced rank or no. What if something happened at Normandy? If Normandy failed people would never forgive him. And they would remember the man whose career he had made a failure – a man who so far was the best proven American general. Had Patton's offence, a public relations faux pas concerning the Russians, merited his dismissal? What would the American people think? The Russians were not popular at home, and Patton was. Eisenhower was not a man of decision and he undoubtedly vacillated between the two choices. He asked Churchill what he thought about the furor that Patton's statements had caused. Churchill told Eisenhower that he could not understand it, since "Patton had simply told the truth." This was absolutely true. Today we know that anyone who wanted the Russians to rule the world was very, very wrong. But in 1944, Churchill and Patton were lone voices against the evil power of Communism.

When Churchill and Stalin made a declaration stating that they would not make a separate peace with Hitler, Churchill made a speech stating that he considered Stalin and Hitler's evils the same, but that *at the moment* Britain would support anyone who fought Hitler. Yet immediately newspapers would not allow anyone to publish articles critical of Stalin. They said that they were merely supporting their government's declarations. As soon as America entered the war newspapers spoke of the "Big Three Alliance." There was no alliance and there never was. Newspapers said they had to preserve "allied unity." Allies? Where?

When Patton left out the Russians – accident or no – he was stirring up a hornets nest which had been seething for a decade. Communists wanted Russia to look amiable and they wanted no voice in opposition. Patton annoyed them. Here was a soldier who couldn't shut his mouth, they said. Yes, he couldn't keep his mouth shut, especially when he had something to say.

Patton headed off to Eisenhower's office on May 1st. "In spite of my possible execution this morning, I slept well and trust my destiny. God has never let me, or the country, down yet." Patton arrived on time, and walked into Eisenhower's office. Ike was cordial, and asked Patton to sit down. Patton relaxed a little.
Eisenhower looked up at him. "George, you have gotten yourself into a very serious fix."
"Before you go any farther, I want to say that your job is more important than mine, so if in trying to save me you are hurting yourself, throw me out."
"I have now got all that the army can give me," Ike said, "It is not a question of hurting me but of hurting you and depriving me of a fighting Army commander."[1]
Eisenhower continued speaking, informing Patton that General Marshall had told him in a telegram that his repeated mistakes had shaken the

---

[1] Was this what Eisenhower had planned on saying?

confidence of the country.[1] Marshall had even gone back to the Kent Lambert incident [several years before]... certainly a forgiving s. o. b."

Eisenhower also told Patton that he had decided that if he relieved Patton he would not reduce him to colonel. He felt the relief would be sufficient punishment. Situations might even arise, he hinted, where it would be necessary to put him in command of an army.

Patton then said, "I am perfectly willing to fall out on a permanent promotion so as not to hold the others back."

"General Marshall has told me that you've destroyed all your chances of getting a permanent promotion. Even if you were the best tactician and strategist in the army, your lack of judgment makes you unfit to command."

> "He [Eisenhower] said that he had wired General Marshall on Sunday washing his hands of me. (He did not use those words exactly, but that is what he meant.)
> *Patton's Diary*

"If you reduce me to colonel, I demand the right to command one of the assault regiments [in Normandy]. It is not a favor, but a *right*," Patton said.

"But surely we need you to command an army," Eisenhower said.

"I am not threatening, but I want to tell you that this attack is badly planned and on too narrow a front. It may easily result in another Anzio, especially if I'm not there."

Eisenhower replied, "Don't I know, but what can I do?"

> "That is a heck of a remark for a supreme commander. The fact is that the plan which he has approved was drawn by a group of British in 1943.[2] Monty changed it only by getting 5 instead of 3 divisions into the assault, but the front is too short. There should be three separate attacks on at least a 90 mile front. I have said this for nearly a year."

The Normandy invasion was, in fact, a very haphazard plan. The idea of taking barren cliffs in the north of France had been considered

---

[1] A gross exaggeration. It had only shaken the confidence of the politicians, and General Marshall held a political post. (U.S. Army Chief of Staff)

[2] In 1943 the British did not want to launch the assault at all and were campaigning vigorously for an assault from the Balkans and Southern France. The Americans had chosen the location – Normandy – at an earlier date.

ridiculous. It was. That we managed to pull it off is a miracle and we partly have Hitler to thank. When the Allies stormed ashore, Hitler would not release ready and waiting panzer divisions. The Normandy invasion's foolhardiness is not in the scope of this book. Patton had nothing to do with its location and its design, and he had very little to do with its execution. For more on the Normandy invasion – who originated it, designed it, approved it, and fought it – read Cornelius Ryan's book, "The Longest Day."

Returning to Eisenhower and Patton, Ike then told him that he had written a "savage" letter,

> "... but wanted me to know that his hand was being forced in the United Sates. He had talked to the Prime Minister about me, and Churchill told him that he could see nothing to it, that 'Patton had simply told the truth.' Ike then went on to excuse General Marshall on the grounds that it was an election year, etc. It is sad and shocking to think that victory and the lives of thousands of men are pawns to the "fear of They," and [to] the writings of a group of unprincipled reporters and weak-kneed congressmen, but so it is.
>
> When I came out, I don't think anyone could tell that I had just been killed. I have lots of competitions in the sporting way, but I never did better [in dissembling his apparent loss of the Third Army.] I feel like death, but I am not out yet. If they will let me fight, I will; but if not, I will resign so as to be able to talk, and then I will tell the truth and possibly do my country more good.
>
> All the way home, 5 hours, I recited poetry to myself...
>
> My final thought on the matter is that I am destined to achieve some great thing – what, I don't know, but this last incident was so trivial in its nature, but so terrible in its effect, that it is not the result of an accident but the work of God. His will be done."

The next day, Patton wrote that he "felt very much like a Thanksgiving turkey waiting for the axe to fall, but no news." He didn't want to work, and "luckily" had little to do. He wrote a letter to his wife, "This last incident was 'most unkindest cut of all.' What I said was at a private party and I had been assured that no reporters were there, but it may be the end. At least as others see it. For me it is only a new beginning. I have been so upset that my digestion went, but is coming back. Even I can be pushed just so far... If I survive the next couple of days, it will be O. K. and things look brighter. But still I get in a cold sweat when the phone rings... Well we ain't dead yet. I love you and need you."

On May 3rd, the next day, Patton was out getting his teeth cleaned. When he returned, he found a telegram from Eisenhower. It said, "Since the War Department has placed the decision of relieving you on me, I have decided to keep you. Go ahead and train your army."

The telegram also said that he had reached his decision "solely because of my faith in you as a battle leader and from no other motives." Eisenhower's later claim that it was from a sense of friendship is demonstrably untrue. Eisenhower had saved Patton so as to save himself from a disaster that might occur in Normandy. The decision paid off a hundred fold. Patton lead the breakout in Normandy, he took Paris, Bavaria and Czechoslovakia, staved off disaster during the Battle of the Bulge and could have easily taken Berlin or Prague.

Patton went out to celebrate with his staff. Eisenhower met him in person and "was very nice. Sometimes I am very fond of him, and this is one of the times." He wrote exuberantly to his wife that,

> "Everything is O.K. because Divine Destiny came through in a big way. I am sorry that in some of my recent letters I sounded whiney. I don't often indulge. I guess my trouble is that I don't realize that I am always news, but you can bet I know it now. The whole thing was so silly and started in a perfectly harmless informal talk to a group of local ladies who thought I had said such a nice thing, from their purely local point of view of course, that they quoted me. Well the Lord came through again but I was realy [sic] badly frightened as you could gather from my letter... I actually had a nut in my pocket [for good luck.] I have youthed thirty years since my last letter."

"I certainly will not say another word," Patton vowed. "What a stink over nothing. Poor Harry [Stimson, Secretary of State] had a time about me. I hate to bother him so, but God knows I was inoscent [sic] that time. We all feel the overrriding influence of politics even here. It is rather amusing to note how many people are interested in it even more than war. I wish we could have a moratorium on it, but I suppose that is impossible." He also gave up his ideas of running for office immediately and telling people what was going on. But he was still planning, after the war, on telling the Americans what Eisenhower was really up to.

Patton could now concentrate on training his troops. He went to a rehearsal and was dismayed at their performance. The infantry were hanging behind, and their occupation was poor. The placement of their anti-tank guns was "awful." He showed them their mistakes, and the paper he was writing on armored divisions. He asked for comments but got none – the officers had never been in battle. Patton was in charge of a green army now but he was determined to train them well.

He attended a demonstration the next day and they performed much better. He was worried that if he was not with them, they would not know what to do: "it is a very sad commentary on our system" of training men for battle.

Chapter Eighteen

POOR STRATEGY

*"Sometimes I think that I will go mad waiting
and I know I could do a better job."*

May 15th was the day when all senior commanders and their chiefs of staff assembled for the briefing of the attack on Normandy. The King, Prime Minister and Field Marshal Smuts of South Africa attended as well. Eisenhower started with a "short talk" emphasizing the fact that any disagreements between the army, air and navy would have to be smoothed out today. Admiral Ramsey then said how difficult it was going to be to get the troops ashore. Then Air Marshal Leigh-Mallory made a speech explaining the efforts of the Air Force in the coming operation. Bradley and Spaatz "made short and good speeches." The 0King also said a few words, "but it was rather painful to watch the efforts he made not to stammer."

"At lunch I sat opposite Mr. Churchill who asked me whether I remembered him, and when I said I did, he immediately ordered me a glass of whiskey. After lunch there were more talks. Admiral Kirk [Senior American naval commander] made a weak, stilted one, and the British opposite number made a fine fighting talk. Smuts talked a lot, but repeated himself and was not impressive. Finally the Prime Minister made a really great fighting speech, worth all that preceded it. He took a crack at overstressing Civil Government, and said that his views would hurt the feelings of his dear friend, General De Gaulle. Also that we were worrying too much about governing France before capturing it. It was a very fine fighting speech, and I intend to write him a letter about it." *Patton's Diary*

Patton made no comment on Montgomery's presentation, but it's quite clear he thought Churchill gave the best speech.

Patton wrote the next day that he made a talk to the troops, "as in all my talks, I stressed fighting and killing." There have been versions of very profane speeches allegedly made by Patton circulating for some time. However Patton never actually wrote his speeches down so the copies in existence were reconstructed from different sources. Often writers would interview a Third Army man, then write what they *thought* a Patton speech would have sounded like. Since they know Patton cursed, it seems they figured they would freely pepper the speech with curses and then – voila, it was a Patton speech. I don't believe their speeches at all.

An author well-acquainted with Patton's works would easily be able to fake a speech. I found a stunning example in one of these alleged speeches[1] where Patton says, "A man must be alert all the time if he expects to stay alive. If not, some German son-of-a-bitch will sneak up behind him with a sock full of shit!"

That excerpt is incredibly similar to a story which Patton's aide Codman told, where Patton came up to a soldier on the beach in N. Africa. This soldier was lying on the beach resting. Patton told him that,

> "The next beach you land on will be defended by Germans. I don't want one of them coming up behind you and hitting you over the head with a sock full of silt. Only that was not quite that word he used." *"Drive," by Colonel Charles M. Codman.*

The author of the speech took liberties with Codman's story and peppered it with curses to make it sound more "Pattonesque." While the first account seems stretched, the second rings true.

Here's what one of Patton's soldiers said of the speech Patton gave his company in 1942,

---

[1] This one is told by Martin Blumenson.

"Suddenly he appeared out of nowhere, polished boots, pistol and all, and marched like a one-man parade up to the stand, then trotted up its steps. Before any protocol could be observed, Patton bellowed into the microphone, 'Is there any man here among you who's afraid to die?'

Believe me, there were plenty of us, and the following silence grew more silent still: then he launched into one of those speeches of his. He talked about the enemy and how we must hate him; he told us never to forget that our job was to kill and to keep on killing. Then he changed pitch and soared up into his firm belief in the God of battles and to his certainty that the only sure best heaven was for the soldier fallen in action. When he finished every man present was on his feet (or standing on a bench) cheering his head off. They were ready to invade Hell, then. I, personally, had never been so moved in my life." *"Before the Colors Fade," by Fred Ayer, page 149*

This, indeed, would have been a stirring speech. It is a shame that we can only imagine what one may have sounded like. Still, with a vivid recollection like the one above, we have something to go on.

Patton had told his Public Relations officer that he "did not want publicity except from the Germans and he was to see that I did not get it. If I hit the Huns as hard as I hope to, they will tell the world." And so it would happen.

Back in America, the Senate tabled Patton's promotion. The newspaper furor had worked. Patton was only a Lieutenant General and would not be called to any of the important meetings on the coming invasion. Isn't it amazing that newspapers (and politicians) can have more say in what happens to a general than the army?

Montgomery invited the four army commanders to spend June 1st and 2nd with him. Montgomery was especially interested in Patton's operations, "and it was very fortunate that two nights ago I had rehearsed the whole thing for Simpson, so I was very fluent." Montgomery said twice to Bradley, "Patton should take over for the Brittany and possibly for the Rennes operation." This would come to pass, no thanks to Montgomery.

Patton noted that the men around Montgomery were timid "yes men." De Guingand, his chief of staff, was "very clever" but also very nervous. The truth was that Montgomery relieved any man who even slightly disagreed with them. This created huge resentment on the part of competent British officers. Montgomery replaced them with weak, timid men who wouldn't question his orders. These men, however, were second-rate and handicapped by their own inability to say no.

At dinner Montgomery brought out a betting book and asked Patton whether or not he thought England would be at war again in ten years after the end of WWII. Montgomery bet that England would not be, so Patton "to be a sport, I had to bet she would. Also his Quartermaster offered to bet me $40 that an American horse would not win the next Grand National. In order to stick up for my country, I had to risk the $40."

General Montgomery then toasted the four Army commanders. Everyone was silent. Then Patton rose and said, "As the oldest Army commander present, I would like to propose a toast to the health of General Montgomery and express our satisfaction in serving under him."

"The lighting did not strike me [for lying]. I have a better impression of General Montgomery than I had. At breakfast I told Monty good bye. He said, 'I had a good time and now we understand each other.'" *Patton's Diary*

On June 5th Patton sent congratulations to Alexander, Keyes and Clark in Italy. They had captured Rome.

D Day was an incredibly disappointing day for Patton. The soldiers were landing in Normandy and he wasn't fighting. He wasn't even planning. He was merely waiting, waiting, waiting as always. For a high-strung soldier like Patton waiting was close to impossible. "It is terrible to be on the side lines and see all the glory eluding me, but I guess there will be enough for all. I guess I will read the bible."

It was at this time, while Patton sat anxiously on the sidelines, that Summerall defended Patton. He wrote that Patton was,

"...a general in the hearts of his soldiers and will be the leading figure in history by virtue of his own superiority.

I would have wished for him an independent command in the south of France, but he will dominate wherever he is. The men will resent the treatment he has received and will fight for him all the harder. He stands alone in all the world in knowledge, ability, and leadership." *"Patton Papers," edited by Martin Blumenson.*

On the 12th of June the Germans mistakenly announced that Patton was in command of 59 divisions in France. "It was a distinct shock to me."

A few days later Patton went to the theater with Lady Leese. The leading man, Leslie Henson came on stage after the show and said that he had played in Africa before the Eighth Army and that the wife of its general, Leese, was in the audience. Everyone clapped. Then he said that with her was "the most famous American general, a man noted for his blood and I will not say guts in front of the ladies." Throughout the theater people cheered and yelled for a long time. When they tried to leave there was a huge crowd around the car and "we had quite an ovation."

Eisenhower came to inspect Patton's men on the 26th of June.

"Ike made an inspection by walking through the ranks and talking briefly to numerous men. He tries to find points of common interest with them and is clever at it. Then he gets the loud speaker and tells the soldiers to gather around. He talks very familiarly to them, but uses 'I' 'mine' and 'me' too much, usually exhorting them to fight well, 'So that we can end this war and I can go home and go fishing.' The men seem to like it and usually clap and cheer a little. It is the style of an office seeker rather than that of a soldier. Two movie and two still photographers accompany him and take shots of his conversation and get the names of the men he is talking to. I presume these are later sent to the home town of the person, which, I think, has a very good effect. His theory is that by this method one gets on a level with the men. A commander cannot command and be on the same level. At least that is my opinion, I try to arouse fighting emotion – he tries [for] votes – for what?" **Patton's Diary**

It has been recorded that Eisenhower would go among the troops and say, "What were you before the war, son?"

The answer was invariably, "A farmer."

"What do you grow?"

"Corn (or whatever)," the soldier would reply.

"How many bushels to an acre?" Ike would ask.

"Umpteen bushels."

Eisenhower would look amazed. "Really? After the war I'll be coming to you for a job!" Then he would say, "Now listen. I want you to finish off this war – and *quick* – so I can go fishing."[1]

Witnesses have recorded that he used the same procedure over and over again – no matter how many bushels the man said he would always look surprised. What an actor.

It was the second of July and Patton was still not fighting. He wrote a paper on the striking similarity of the allied position with the Schlieffen Plan in WWI. "All we have to do is change the pivot from Alsace to Caen, and you have it." This idea would be later credited to Montgomery, who would spend months "pivoting on Caen." Patton wanted them to turn east and strike at Germany but for some peculiar reason Montgomery wanted to pivot west. Patton realized the harm of a too slow advance, "we will die of old age before we finish." He had a plan that would stave off such a disaster.

Patton suggested that a provisional corps consisting of two infantry divisions and an armored division be landed at Moralix 100 miles west of the Cherbourg peninsula. The corps would attack the Germans in front of First Army, then race to Alencon and Argentan. Then, "depending on the circumstances" they would go to Evraux and Chartres in "a great coup."

Such a brilliantly daring move would take the Germans totally by surprise. It would make travail through the difficult bocage[2] area unnecessary. Patton had been to France many times and knew that the bocage was very hard for tanks to maneuver through.

---

[1] From "Drive" by Colonel Charles R. Codman

[2] The *bocage* were the grapevine hedgerows planted in Normandy for wine. Tanks could not pass over the hedgerows without a lot of difficult maneuvering. The Germans would place men with machine guns on the other side of the row. They could then easily attack the delicate underbelly of the tank with no risk to themselves.

Patton worried that such an amphibious landing would be disregarded right away – so he came up with another plan. This one called for an offensive going exactly south to Avranches with two armored divisions. Patton chose Avranches as the objective of all his plans because it had many roads going through it and this would make it difficult to defend.[1]

Were Patton's plans used? Of course not. They were too daring, too audacious and too practical. Bradley would spend months in the bocage, then spring a plan remarkably similar to Patton's but with infantry divisions going in a horizontal direction. He would call "his" plan, "Cobra."

> "Following the possible course of [Patton's] plan, and comparing it with what was actually planned and done [by Bradley], one senses the difference between a work of art and a mere piece of craftsmanship. But Patton's design was not sheer fantasy and artistry. It also had solid realistic craftsmanship. I have no doubt that had it been adopted and carried out, the course of the war in Normandy and Brittany would have been changed and accelerated, and history's course would have been altered." *"Patton: Ordeal and Triumph," by Ladislas Farago.*

By July 5th, more than a month since D Day, the advance had slowed to a halt and was looking more and more like stalemate. Patton was trying to persuade Eisenhower to take personal charge. "He cannot bring himself to take the plunge," Patton wrote. Eisenhower was fed up with Monty's lack of drive, or so Patton wrote.

> "His current plan is [eventually] for four American armies, with one small American Army for Montgomery, as the British have reached their limit of 14 divisions; Bradley's to have three large American Armies with me on the southern flank. Why an American Army has to go with Montgomery, I do not

---

[1] When Patton went through the hedgerows, he had an armorer weld razor-sharp steel rails in a V and attached these rails to the outside of the tanks. They worked like a plow and allowed the tank to go through the hedgerows like "a bullet through cheese." No one else had thought of this. This was *another* reason for Patton's rapid torrent advance through the hedgerow region.

see, except to save the face of the little monkey." *Patton's Diary*

The next day, Patton flew to France. He could barely see through the fog in the plane, but he made out Cherbourg. He landed at an airstrip near Omaha Beach. He would not be fighting but he was happy to be in a combat area again – he could hear the shells going off from his CP.

Patton visited the site of one of the two prefabricated harbors. They had been towed across the Channel – a very time consuming and laborious process. A bad storm had destroyed one of the harbors along with all the ships and cargo. Patton wrote that there was "a tremendous pile of shipping, the terrible site of hundreds of wrecked ships." It would "certainly have shocked all honest and God-fearing taxpayers in America or England."

At around this time, Eisenhower and Bradley were showing Churchill the new M1 rifles. Churchill suggested a shooting match, at which he would shoot from 25 yards, Bradley from 50 and Eisenhower from 75 yards. They agreed to the conditions and proceeded with the match. All of Churchill's bullets hit the bulls-eye, and Bradley did only slightly worse. Eisenhower, the Supreme Commander of the Allied Forces, completely missed the target. Those who were watching hurried them away from the area without announcing the winner.

Patton was immensely impressed by the empty German pillboxes. It proved, he said, "that good American troops can capture anything and that no beach can be defended if seriously attacked." Everything had been against the Americans – even the defensive nature of the Norman cliffs. Probably nothing so naturally formidable had been stormed in history.

Bradley and Patton spoke together. Collins, one of Bradley's generals, was telling divisions where to put their battalions. Patton told Collins that that was going too far, but Collins disagreed. Bradley then informed Patton that he had to tell Montgomery the location of each battalion every day. Both Patton and Bradley agreed that this was stupid – and they were only beginning to feel Montgomery's iron rule.

That night Patton had a hard time sleeping. He could hear the artillery batteries going off near his tent. Several times that night, he and his dog Willie went outside to look around. While they were sleeping (or trying to) Third Army HQ was being moved across the channel.

Chapter Nineteen

MONTGOMERY'S DISASTER

Montgomery had boasted that he would take Caen on D Day. It was now over a month later, and Monty was trying to explain away why Caen was still untaken. Montgomery was the overall ground commander in Europe and Bradley's group of armies was still under him. Montgomery decided on a new operation to take Caen, which he called "Goodwood."[1] It was to be a heavy bombardment, which, like all Montgomery's plans, would use the thoroughly WWI idea of blasting, bombing and basically pushing through by brute force alone. Montgomery had all that America and the British Empire had to offer behind him, and he struck with 1,500 tanks and 250,000 men against the German defenses he had allowed to harden at Caen. American, British and Canadian bombers dropped 45,000 shells on the 2nd SS Panzer Corps alone. Over 800 fighter bomber missions flew to support the army while 1,800 RAF and RCAF squadrons flew against German tanks and artillery emplacements. "My whole Eastern flank will burst into flames," he told Eisenhower. Montgomery coordinated this attack with Bradley's Cobra.

A day after Goodwood had commenced, Montgomery announced to the press that he had broken out. But by the 20th of July he had been stopped dead. The Germans had not been idle during Montgomery's month of inaction. They had built pillboxes, sewn the area with landmines and had bordered the front with 88s. The British infantry were among the best in the world and they fought hard. But it is very difficult to penetrate heavy fortifications and Montgomery always

---

[1] Operation Goodwood was launched on July 1st.

had hopelessly bad strategies. Goodwood was a failure which Montgomery called off after a week of intense fighting. Caen, the largest harbor in northern Europe, was still untaken and desperately needed for Bradley's ever extending lines. Eisenhower was furious. "With 7000 tons of bombs dropped in the most elaborate bombing of enemy front-line positions ever accomplished only seven miles were gained – can we afford a thousand tons of bombs per mile?" Eisenhower's fury was "blue as indigo" according to Butcher, or "red as a hot coal" as Bradley put it. He was mad at Monty for now – but he had still not learned his lesson and would fall for Montgomery's expensive, over elaborate, cautious plans again and again and again.

Montgomery had totally failed in his original objective; yet he would later claim that operation Goodwood was a success. How? Since he timed it with Bradley's Operation Cobra he claimed that the purpose of Goodwood had been to draw German fire off of Bradley's sector onto his own. He claimed Caen was never the objective of Goodwood. Had this been true Eisenhower would never have approved Goodwood. Eisenhower had approved this expensive operation only because Montgomery had given him the impression that he was going to take Caen and finally end the stalemate in his sector. If Montgomery had been trying to draw the German divisions away from Bradley he would not have intended nor wanted to break out. Yet why did Montgomery tell the press that he had broken out a day after the operation began – unless it was what he intended to do? Had he truly meant to draw German fire he would not have doused the Germans with those millions of expensive bombs on *his* sector. They would have been dropped on *Bradley's*. In fact Montgomery was not even effective at holding the Germans in front of his lines, and two divisions wandered from his front to Bradley's.

Montgomery was to say that Goodwood had been successful. According to Montgomery all his operations were successful even when they completely failed to take the objective and cost thousands of lives. Montgomery later wrote that,

> "Many people thought that when Operation Goodwood was staged, it was the beginning of the plan to break out from the eastern flank towards Paris, and that, *because* I did not do so, the battle had been a failure. But let me make the point again at the risk of being wearisome. There was never *at any time* any intention of making the breakout from the bridgehead on the eastern flank.

Misunderstandings about this simple and basic conception were responsible for much trouble between British and American personalities." *"Memoirs," by Sir Bernard L. Montgomery*

Certainly. If you tell generals you are going to use difficult-to-maneuver, expensive equipment and then you fail to capture anything with it, you can expect to be in "much trouble."

By any standard, Eisenhower should have dismissed Montgomery. Goodwood was truly a grand-scale disaster. There were better British commanders, even British attack-oriented generals like Wavell. Eisenhower had merely to lift his finger and the British would have removed Montgomery. Eisenhower *chose* not to.

It should be pointed out that in spite of Patton's stunning successes no one ever thought of sharing such massive materiel with him – though he would have ensured instant success. Montgomery would repeat similar disasters throughout the rest of the war and Allied headquarters would continue giving him the most and the finest that they had to offer.

The Russians must have shared Patton's doubts about Montgomery's capabilities. Their troops were reported to have put up a roadsign near Minsk saying "1,294 Kilometers to Caen."

Bradley was secretly hoping that if Cobra succeeded he would be removed from under Montgomery.

> "Neither Ike [n]or Brad has the stuff. Ike is bound hand and foot by the British and does not know it. Poor fool. We actually have no Supreme Commander – no one who can take hold of a situation and say that this shall be done and that shall not be done. It is a very unfortunate situation to which I see no solution." *Patton's Diary*

Bradley told Patton that he would allow Patton's army to fight as soon as he could. "He could do it now with much benefit to himself, if he had any backbone. Of course, Monty does not want me as he fears I will steal the show, which I will." As a matter of fact, Bradley didn't want Patton either. When Eisenhower told Bradley that he would have Patton as one of his army commanders, Bradley was filled with secret misgivings.

> "Had Eisenhower asked for my opinion, I would have counseled against the selection. For not only did I question George's conduct in the Sicilian campaign,[1] but I seriously doubted the wisdom of his forcing Patton to stomach this reversal in roles of command. In Sicily George had commanded my corps from Seventh Army. Now the tables were to be turned and I was to command his Third Army as part of the new army group. Ike assured me that George would submit without rancor. 'All he wants is a chance to get back into the war. For a time he thought he was through.' *A Soldier's Story," by General Omar N. Bradley*

Eisenhower was unfairly using Patton's willingness to fight against him. He knew that Patton would not resign because the urge to fight was too strong. Ike knew that Patton would submit to this and many other humiliations so as to fight for his country.

> "Like Eisenhower I did not dispute George's brilliant dexterity in gaining ground – and there was much of it to be gained between the Channel and Berlin. But even this striking talent of Patton's could not offset the misgivings I felt in having him in my command. However, I did not speak to Eisenhower of these reservations. If Eisenhower wanted Patton, certainly I would not stand in his way. To this day I am chagrined to recall how hesitatingly I first responded to Patton's assignment. For when George joined my command in August 1944, he came eagerly and as a friend without pique, rancor, or grievance. My year's association with him in Europe remains one of the brightest remembrances of my military career." *"A Soldier's Story," by General Omar N. Bradley*

Patton felt disheartened with the whole system of command.

> "Sometimes I get desperate over the future. Bradley and Hodges [Bradley's other army commander] are such

---

[1] Bradley questioned Patton's conduct – not in the slapping incident – but in the campaign. Patton's daring was too nerve-wracking for him.

nothings. Their one virtue is that they get along by doing nothing. I could break through in three days if I commanded. They try to push all along the front and have no power anywhere. All that is necessary now is to take chances by leading with armored divisions and covering their advance with air bursts. Such an attack would have to be made on a narrow sector, whereas at present we are trying to attack all along the line." *Patton's Diary*

No, Bradley and Hodges were *not* audacious enough nor had they read the new doctrines of warfare. An examination of the German front at this time shows that a narrow, directed attack would indeed have broken through – but would Bradley and Hodges listen? No – "pushing all along the line" was all they knew how to do – and all they would do. Patton wrote sadly in his diary, "Sometimes I think that I will go mad waiting and I know I could do a better job."

There was still no progress by mid-July. When would they let Patton loose? He worried that the war might be over without him – but not the way they were progressing. "Half of July and no progress, but only casualties. The British are doing nothing in a big way, not even holding the German divisions in front of them, as two have left their front and come to ours."

On the 23rd of July Patton visited Bradley, Stimpson and Hodges about Cobra. Cobra "is really a very timid operation by Bradley and Hodges consider themselves regular devils for having thought of it. At least it is the best operation which has been planned so far, and I hope it works." The best operation planned with exception to his own, of course. Patton doesn't even mention that in his diary. He merely writes,

> "I am sometimes appalled at the destiny of human beings. I am also nauseated by the fact that Hodges and Bradley state that all human virtue depends on knowing infantry tactics. I know that no general officer and practically no colonel needs to know any tactics. The tactics belong to battalion commanders. If generals knew less tactics, they would interfere less."

On July 24th 1943, Patton had started along the north coast of Messina. It was a year later. "My long period of inactivity has been a terrible waste of brains." But he knew that that would be over soon. Cobra would be launched the next day.

Bradley had advance bombing to precede Operation Cobra but they were so disorganized that American bombs killed 111 Americans and wounded 490. The infantrymen had great difficulty maneuvering and the Germans held out. The next day Collins[1] gambled by sending his *mobile divisions* forward. They discovered a gap in the German divisions caused by the bombing the day before. Through it poured three American divisions. Patton flew over the battlefield the next day and was surprised at the mildness of the craters. They were "not anywhere as great" as in 1918.

On the 27th Bradley issued new orders. Cobra had come off so well that he decided to let the mobile forces *go to Coutances and down through the Contentin to Avranches!*[2] Since the Germans had been caught so unexpectedly all of France was open. Bradley also decided that even though Third Army would not become operational until August 1st, Patton could unofficially command the VIII Corps. Patton wrote that he "felt much happier over the war."

Patton decided to have Wood and Grow move the 4th and 6th Armored Divisions[3] to the front. The two divisions drove together side by side and captured Coutances in a day! Middleton had been striving to take that city for over a month.

Now Patton sent his armored divisions after Avranches. He went to see what was happening to Grow, whose advance had slowed down.

> "He was sitting on the side of the road and General Taylor, his assistant, had a large group of officers studying a map. I asked Grow what he was doing, and he said that Taylor was in charge of the advance guard and that he, personally, was doing nothing. I asked him whether he had been down to look at the river, and he said, 'No.' So I told him that unless he did do something, he would be out of a job. I then went down and looked at the river and was not fired at, although you could see a few Germans on the hill. So I directed the division to

---

[1] Lt. General Collins commanded the VII Corps under Bradley.

[2] Just as Patton's original plan had called for.

[3] He was finally getting a chance to prove the worth of *armored divisions!*

advance and cross the river. The fact that the bridge was
out didn't matter as the river was not a foot deep."
Patton's Diary

What Patton had told Grow he would tell many commanders
throughout the war – namely, go look and see. Don't study maps and
waste time vacillating. Patton would always check up on his units and
thus always knew what problems there were and how to fix them. He
advised his officers to do the same.

ADVANCES MADE BY THE ALLIED ARMIES THE WEEK OF AUGUST 1st, 1944

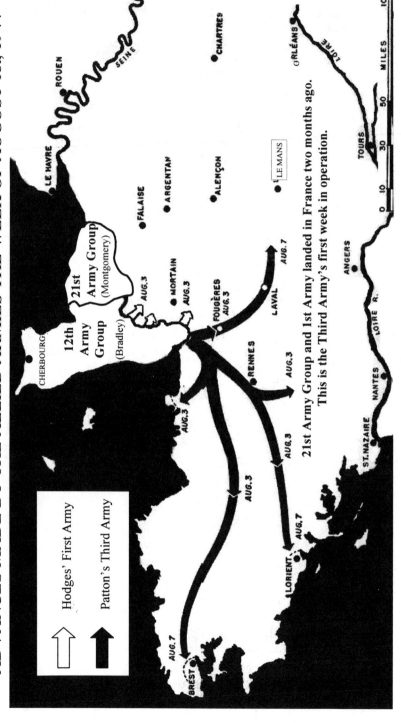

21st Army Group and 1st Army landed in France two months ago. This is the Third Army's first week in operation.

Chapter Twenty

PATTON'S TRAP

Eisenhower was angry with Montgomery. On the 27th of July he had met with Churchill and others to discuss Monty's disturbing lack of progress. Eisenhower told them that Montgomery was sitting still and on the defensive with mounting casualties. He disliked Monty's basic strategy: fight on the left so as to draw the Germans there and then push out with the right. The British told Eisenhower that he had approved the strategy, but if he now disapproved of it he should tell Montgomery himself.

Eisenhower did not want to tell Montgomery as he thought it would hurt him[1] but Montgomery already knew of the meeting and all that was said. It infuriated him that Eisenhower criticized his strategy behind his back and then supported it in front of him.

Since Eisenhower would not tell Montgomery, Monty continued "drawing" the German divisions away from Bradley's front. This alleged drawing was merely a cover-up to explain why he had not moved since D Day. He writes with pride that "the bulk of the German armour had been kept at the British front." What was the purpose of war? To keep the enemy in front of you? When you break out you will need three times the amount he has! Going around the enemy makes a lot more sense. But then, when you've been sitting in the same place for three months that might be impossible to do.

---

[1] Eisenhower's incredible capacity for leadership has always amazed me.

The British were decrying Montgomery as well. Tedder and Coningham, men who had never liked Montgomery, knew that now was a good time to remove him. Certainly the Allies would have suffered far less casualties had they done so.

Montgomery wanted to claim a share in the victory of Cobra. He said that the British had helped by keeping the Germans where they were. It was help they couldn't have withdrawn had they wanted to. In fact, the British were not keeping the Germans where they were. It was the *Germans who were keeping the British!* Montgomery angrily decried the American press who he says portrayed Cobra as a strictly American victory. If Montgomery wanted press he should have tried an advance, an attack, and this time – a victory.

At the daily briefing of the Staff that morning, Patton rose to give a speech which typifies his philosophy of war.

"We become operational officially tomorrow and doubtless from time to time there will be some complaints that we are pushing people too hard. I don't care at all about such complaints. I believe in the old and sound rule that an ounce of sweat is worth a gallon of blood. The harder we push, the more Germans we'll kill, and the more Germans we kill, the fewer of our men will be killed. Pushing means fewer casualties. I want you to remember that.

There's another thing I want you to remember. Forget this business of worrying about flanks. We must guard our flanks, but not to the extent that we don't do anything else. Some fool once said that flanks must be secured, and since then idiots all over the world have been going crazy guarding their flanks. We don't want any of that ridiculousness in this Army. Flanks are something for the enemy to worry about. Not us.

Also, I don't want to get any messages saying, 'I am holding my position.' We're not holding anything. Let the Hun do that. We are advancing constantly and are not interested in holding anything, except onto the enemy. We're going to hold onto him and kick the hell out of him all the time.

Our basic plan of operation is to advance and to keep on advancing regardless of whether we have to go

166

over, under, or through the enemy. We have one motto, 'Audacious, audacious, always audacious.' Remember that. From here on out, until we win or die in the attempt, we will always be audacious."

Patton paused, surveying the silent Staff before him. Then he smiled,

"You've done some outstanding work, gentlemen, and I want to thank you for it. I am very proud of you. But, after all, what you really have done has been to perform very well doing nothing. From now on, I want you to perform equally well doing something."

That evening, Patton's tanks rolled into Avranches. Patton told Middleton to head for Brest and Rennes. "Bradley simply wants a bridgehead over the Selune river. What I want and intend to get is Brest and Angers."

After capture, the German Major General Richard Schimpf of the 3rd Paratroop Division would say of Patton, "We can always rely on Allied hesitancy to exploit successes to give us the time to withdraw and regroup in order to slow up the next thrust. But with your General Patton it was different. He was very aggressive in exploiting penetration. His breakthrough at Avranches was an example of this. So was his phenomenal campaign in the Palatinate."[1]

On August 1st Third Army became operational under the codename "Lucky" and immediately blazed in two directions. He wanted to celebrate with a drink, but "the only thing we could find was a bottle of alleged brandy... we tried to drink this, but gagged."

Eisenhower had given Bradley the option to move from under Montgomery's temporary command whenever he chose to. Bradley would then be in charge of the American Army Group and Montgomery the British one. Bradley became his own Army group commander the day Patton got the Third Army, August 1st. But then SHAEF decided that Montgomery would still have Bradley, the Army Group Commander, underneath him temporarily.

---

[1] Patton's Palatinate campaign was yet to come – it would take place in February 1945.

Bradley was still worried about a counter-attack from the west of Mortain. He told Patton he knew that he would concur.

> "I said that I would concur, but that I did not agree with him and feared that he was getting the British complex of over-caution. It is noteworthy that just about a year ago to the day I had to force him to attack in Sicily."

South of Caen, the wall of heavy German Artillery mowed the British infantry down among tremendous casualties in men and tanks. After all of June and July in an all-out effort Caen was taken. But in the process all of the British Armour divisions had been annihilated.

Two prongs of Third Army burst out of the gap between the hills and the sea at Avranches.[1]

> "One of the oldest cities in Normandy, Avranches sits on a hill dominated by an ancient castle. The gap is at the mouth of a narrow coastal corridor extending south from Coutances and compartmented by three small but deep streams, the Seine, See, and Selune, the last south of Avranches. South of the Selune is a great plain that leads west into Brittany, south to the Loire, and east to Paris."
> *"Lucky Forward," by Colonel Robert S. Allen*

That night, the very first night of Third Army's operation, 4th Armored was within range of Rennes and 6th Armored was halfway to St. Malo.

Bradley visited Patton's HQ and allowed him to commit the XV Corps. Patton sent it eastward toward the Mayenne-Laval line. He knew that the next day he would be ordered towards the Seine. Powerful German reserves were in the Mortain area, 20 miles due east of Avranches. This area had only one good road – and all of Third Army's supplies had to pass over it. This made it extremely vulnerable. The hundreds of units that were rushing forward to exploit the breakthrough and all of their supplies relied on this road. XV Corps was given the mission of securing the German held area that the road passed through.

---

[1] The story of the Avranches Gap includes many unfamiliar French city names and also a lot of corps movement. You may wish to look at the map.

Patton attempted a dangerous maneuver by sending the XV Corps to capture the line St. Hilaire du Harcouêt-Fougères-Rennes.

> "St. Hilaire is eight miles southwest of Mortain; Fougères halfway between St. Hilaire and Rennes. Moving the Corps through the overloaded corridor was a perilous task, particularly as it required passing 5th Armored through 90th, already partially through the gap. But it was accomplished without mishap and the divisions reached their concentration areas on schedule. A big chunk of luck accompanied Lucky on this hazardous feat. Fifteen rocket-equipped enemy planes suddenly swooped down on the bridge at Avranches and a dam at near-by Ducey. The destruction of either would have raised havoc, but thanks to effective AA[1] fire the hit-and-run raid was abortive. The dam was not struck and the slight damage to the bridge was quickly repaired. But it was a hair-raising few minutes." *"Lucky Forward,"* **by Colonel Robert S. Allen**

Patton decided to reinforce the already effective AA defenses with extra automatic weapons and 90mm gun battalions which had to be borrowed from First Army.

Patton's intuition was amazing. It was his intuition even more than his daring that made him such a successful commander. In the next two days, 291 German planes attacked this area! Thanks to his foresight, the area held and the anti-aircraft knocked down 33 German planes.

The Germans continued attacking this area well into August. They realized correctly that their best strategy would be to cut off the American supply lines, especially Third Army's. They poured most of their best equipment into this area, including SS Panzer divisions. They used radio controlled glider bombs to capture one of the bridges across the Selune. It was the first time they were used against a land target. The raids, though unsuccessful, were causing a lot of casualties. It was now that Patton had the idea of rushing southward, east, and then north in a huge bag that would connect in the north with Montgomery's troops at Falaise. When he closed the bag almost the entire German army would be inside it, cut off from Germany. Patton would not need the XV Corps, the XII or the XX for wiping up in Brittany. His idea was to sweep

---

[1] Anti Aircraft

eastward and upwards encircling all of the German armies that had hardened around Montgomery. Patton ordered the commander of the XV Corps, General Haislip, to bypass all resistance. There was none. XV Corps continued surging forward.

To execute this plan, however, he needed to capture the major airfields and supply centers in the Orléans-Chartres region.

"In an effort to stem this ominous penetration, the enemy hurriedly reinforced west of the Sarthe. The 5th U.S. and 2nd French Armored Divisions hit this strong resistance and a slugging tank battle ensued. The two divisions lost 39 tanks. But the enemy was driven across the river with heavy casualties in dead and POW. With XV Corps on the Sarthe, the first link of the giant Argentan-Falaise encirclement was forged. Patton lost no time in getting the second under way." *"Lucky Forward," by Colonel Robert S. Allen*

XV Corps was now ordered to take Carrouges, 50 miles north of Le Mans and 25 miles south of Argentan. This line was the southern pincer of the fatal trap.

In Brittany Patton's VIII Corps was clearing up all opposition. They swiftly captured the important ports of St. Brieuc, Quimper, Morlaix, and Nantes. The bigger ports of St. Malo, Brest, Lourient, and St. Nazaire were still resisting. They were cut off from any additional supplies but they were big cities and well fortified. With direct radio exhortations from Hitler, these ports continued to resist.

But by August 10,[th] St. Malo, the second largest port in this area, was cleared. Ten tons of German medical stores were captured there. Lorient and St. Nazaire would continue under siege until the end of the war.

There is an important debate over the ports. Should the allies have continued besieging the ports, tying up vital men and equipment? This is basically a question of strategy. According to the Clausewitz theory, all resistance should be crushed, especially when the enemy would lie behind the rear of the attacking army. Eisenhower and Bradley insisted on taking these ports, not only because they believed in Clausewitz, but also because they wanted to use the ports for transfer of supplies. Because of the sit-down fighting right after Normandy, the Germans had had a chance to heavily fortify these ports. In order to take these cities, the Allies would need a heavy air bombardment which would render the ports useless.

Patton felt that taking those particular ports was unnecessary. The main thing was to cripple the Germans so that they would give up. This could only be done by taking Germany, not French ports. The ports were necessary only for supply purposes. However, other ports, such as Dieppe and Antwerp were not fortified.[1] In a lightning advance they could be taken before the enemy had a chance to demolish the port facilities. Patton also felt that if the Germans tied up forces trying to defend a completely surrounded city, well and good. While the Germans were defending a French port, he would take Berlin.

There is a fallacious claim made by later historians that the Allies' inability[2] to take these ports caused the supply "crisis" of September. We will get into the supposed "crisis" later but it should be known that no matter how many armies were used to take St. Nazaire, Lorient, and St. Malo, these were wasted because the ports were completely useless for supply purposes when they were taken – not because of insufficient men attacking them, but due to the lack of advance in June.

Patton was alone in his belief about the ports, but he was justified by history and vindicated by events. It is interesting to read Montgomery's book on warfare because it demonstrates very clearly that he missed this point in historical examples; thus showing that understanding what *has* happened is the best way of understanding of what *will* happen.

Hitler finally released the forces from the Pas-de-Calais area, where he had been convinced for so long the main offensive would begin. The Germans quickly reinforced the area near Montgomery and the American supply line. Eleven divisions, most of which were infantry, began pouring into this area.

After only a few days of fighting, German radios were resounding with two words. "Third Army." They didn't know who was

---

[1] At this time
[2] For they did not take Patton's advice

leading it or where it would head next, but they knew that it was overrunning Brittany. In seven days it had taken 10,000 square miles from the "victorious Reich," a faster advance than any in history. The Third's stunning advance was far faster than the German blitzkrieg.

Montgomery's troops in the north were now halfway toward Falaise. First Army was regrouping. XV Corps' northward thrust at the battered enemy's rear forced the enemy to reinforce strongly the Carrouges-Sées area. They needed to keep their escape route open. If XV Corps closed it, Patton's bag would be closed and the Germans cut off in his trap. The German resistance was desperate – they must not be cut off.

A traveler along the highway that leads to Alencon would have seen destroyed American tanks, burning Panzers and abandoned artillery. Alencon was important because it was a road and rail center twenty miles south from Sees. It was captured on August 11th. Two days later the 2nd French and 5th U.S. Armored, followed closely by infantry divisions, seized Carrouges and Sees after heavy fighting. German resistance after the fall of Alencon was non-existent. Argentan was twenty miles north.

Bomber pilots now reported a massive withdrawal from the Argentan-Falaise Gap. One squadron reported around 1,000 motor vehicles west of Argentan. Swooping down with their bombs and guns, the squadron of P47s scored their biggest kills of the month. The routed Germans were helpless against the bombers. They were desperate in Patton's trap and heading for the trap's opening to the one place they would be welcomed – Germany. All that remained was to spring the trap.

Chapter Twenty One

LYING FOR DEFENSE

The closing of the trap would lead to the downfall of all German resistance on the Eastern front. Eleven German divisions were completely surrounded by the bulk of the Allied armies.

The trap would be closed in a matter of hours. Scouts had it that XV Corps had reached Falaise. A solid armored barrier could travel the 18 short miles between Falaise and Argentan in a matter of hours.

One of the most idiotic orders of the war would be issued on that day. What the German soldiers could not do, the American High Command did. Eisenhower stopped Patton in his tracks.

Think of all the people that could have been saved had the Falaise-Argentan gap been closed. Not just the hundreds of thousands of American and British soldiers that would continue fighting for several more months in bitter battles. What of the Jews in the concentration camps? The closing of this gap would have lead to *the complete downfall* of the Third Reich. There is absolutely no doubt. The cream of the German army was inside the trap. The fruit was ripe. Patton merely had to stretch his hand and the entire German army on the Eastern front would have fallen into it. Those responsible for the failure to close it have blood on their hands.

Why was such a foolish order given? Who bears responsibility?

Patton was helpless as the Germans fled through the gap. On August 12th he repeatedly telephoned Bradley's headquarters. He reached Allen who relayed Bradley's message to halt on the line which had been assigned between the armies and consolidate his forces.

> "I believe that the order... emanated from the 21st Army Group and was either due to jealousy of the Americans or to utter ignorance of the situation or to a combination of the two. It is very regrettable that XV Corps was ordered to halt, because it could have gone to Falaise and made contact with the Canadians north of that point and definitely and positively closed the escape gap." *Patton's Diary*

Richard Rohmer, author of "Patton's Gap" notes that there is a crucial factual discrepancy between Eisenhower's "recollections" when he wrote "Crusade in Europe" and a memorandum he wrote at the time. Eisenhower says in "Crusade in Europe" that he was with Bradley when he telephoned Montgomery, but in his diary he says he found that Bradley had already acted on the idea of turning north and *had already secured Montgomery's agreement.*

Rohmer also points out that Bradley's memory is clearly faulty on certain events which he wrote seven years later in "A Soldier's Story." Therefore Rohmer doubts Bradley's memory of verbatim telephone conversations which are told in "A Soldier's Story." It is also worthwhile pointing out that in 1951, the year the book was written, Montgomery was still alive.

> "Meanwhile Monty labored on the north with slackening success. After five days of attack he had pushed his Canadian pincer only half the way to Falaise. Thus when Haislip [commander of XV Corps] reached Argentan on the evening of August 12, he found Monty stalled on the north with an 18-mile gap separating the British and American forces. Patton telephoned me that evening from LUCKY FORWARD [his HQ] near Laval.
> 'We've got elements in Argentan,' he reported. 'Let me go on to Falaise and we'll drive the British back into the sea for another Dunkirk.'
> 'Nothing doing,' I told him, for I was fearful of colliding with Montgomery's forces. 'You are not to go beyond

Argentan. Just stop where you are and build up on that shoulder.'" *"A Soldier's Story," by Omar N. Bradley.*

Bradley justified his decision to hold Patton at Argentan with, "I was reluctant to chance a head-on meeting between two converging Armies as we might have done had Patton continued on to Falaise. For any head-on juncture becomes a dangerous and uncontrollable maneuver unless each of the advancing forces is halted by a pre-arranged plan on a terrain objective."

Certainly Bradley knew that the Canadians and Poles were checked from advancing by Panzers and German infantry. These divisions had been there for months. It didn't make sense for the British to go up against the same, hardened resistance when Patton's lane was completely open. The boundary line, the alleged reason why Patton couldn't advance, was not Bradley's responsibility to move. It was Montgomery's.

Yet, as Rohmer points out, Montgomery had granted Patton permission to go 12 miles north of this boundary to Argentan. The line which was created between the armies was so that bombers would know, for sure, where the armies were. Bradley could not authorize Patton to pass this line without first receiving permission from Montgomery. Montgomery was the *only* one who could allow an army to pass this boundary. Montgomery's forces were 18 miles to the north. He knew as of August 10th that his forces would be unable to move south from Falaise. It was only Patton who could move, and it was only Montgomery who could give him that order.

Bradley makes an odd statement however. He says that, "In halting Patton at Argentan... I did not consult with Montgomery. The decision to stop Patton was mine alone. It never went beyond my CP." But Bradley couldn't make a decision like this – even if he had wanted to. Bradley also says that he was dismayed that Montgomery didn't close the gap (he shouldn't have been surprised) and that "Monty had never prohibited and I had never proposed that U.S. forces close the gap from Argentan to Falaise. I was quite content with our original objective and reluctant to take on another."

Bradley's "memory," only seven years later, is very wrong. By refusing to move the bombline between the armies, Montgomery prohibited Patton from closing the gap. It was a rigid line that could *only* be moved by Montgomery. It was Montgomery's responsibility to move it. Had he done so, the bulk of the German army would not have escaped through the Falaise Gap.

If Eisenhower moved the bombline, he would be taking command of the ground forces and then Montgomery would only have been in charge of the 21st Army Group. Eisenhower was never ready to do this. He writes that,

> "I was in Bradley's headquarters when messages began to arrive from the commanders of the advancing American columns, complaining that the limits placed upon them by their orders were allowing the Germans to escape. I completely supported Bradley in his decision that it was necessary to obey the orders, prescribing the boundary between the army groups, exactly as written; otherwise a calamitous battle between friends could have resulted." *"Crusade in Europe," by Dwight D. Eisenhower*

Why does Bradley claim that he didn't discuss the bombline with Montgomery? Bradley later said that he doubted that Patton could have held the gap. But the simple fact was that the Germans were routed and in a panic. They were simply not capable of organizing a worthy attack anywhere.

Patton actually had reconnaissance parties near Falaise when he was ordered to withdraw. On August 16th Montgomery telephoned Bradley and ordered him to go towards Trun and Chambois. But Montgomery still did not move the boundary northwards past Argentan. This northeast thrust which Monty ordered would be a "trespass" of that boundary. This proved that Montgomery certainly knew the Americans wouldn't collide with his sluggish troops.

On August 16th Montgomery allowed Patton to drive east to Dreux. Bradley claims not to have asked Montgomery to move the bombline. But certainly Montgomery could have asked Patton to drive north. He did not. The gap was not closed until August 19th.

There was one force that Montgomery could not keep from Falaise. Fighters and bombers swooped down over and over the gap hitting the helpless target that the Germans were. They had to squeeze through the narrow bottleneck between Falaise and Argentan to escape and it was here that the air scored again and again. However there were so many targets that the airplanes hardly knew where to attack next. Eight Thunderbolts spotted a large Panzer column and they raced for the juicy target. But suddenly out of nowhere nine Typhoons swooped down. The Thunderbolts assisted them in liquidating the Panzers.

Later ground was broken when some P-51s began chasing a long column of marching Germans. The airplanes then chased the survivors so persistently that they began waving their coats and handkerchiefs to surrender. The fighters then rounded them together and radioed some near-by tanks to collect them. It was the first known time that ground units had surrendered to airplanes.

The remnants of eighteen German divisions were trapped in the Falaise Gap. Nine were Panzer, eight Infantry, and one Paratrooper. They fought fiercely to escape. Most of the Germans were deployed against Patton's divisions who were at such close range that they could fire over open sights.

The Germans needed to salvage the Panzers and Paratroops and so they sacrificed their lesser units. Even with all the vacillating in the American and British High Command, 135,000 Germans were killed and wounded. Over 10,000 guns, tanks, and vehicles were destroyed or captured.

Montgomery actually chose not to close the gap. Although he knew his forces were pinned down, he didn't want the Americans to close it for him. He had already been criticized for Goodwood and his host of other failures. He had been leaving the fighting to the Americans, the press had said. Now he chose not to allow the Americans to fight. Montgomery's extreme pride and jealousy made him allow the Germans to escape.

Montgomery hoped against hope that his forces would close the gap before the Germans escaped. But he was willing to allow the Germans to escape rather than suffer the humiliation of moving the bombline and allowing the Americans to close the gap.

But Montgomery did more than simply *not move* the bombline. Pogue, an American military historian, interviewed Brigadier E. T. Williams, a member of Montgomery's staff renowned for his clear memory, just three years after the event. Williams recalls that Leclerc[1] had advanced toward Falaise from Argentan on August 12th. These are the notes from the interview.

> "Falaise Gap – Remembers was in Freddie's[2] truck near Bayeux when 2nd French Armored made its swing up and crossed the road towards Falaise. Monty said tell Bradley they ought to get back. Bradley was indignant. We were indignant also on Bradley's behalf. De Guingand said, 'Monty is too tidy.'[3] Monty missed closing the sack. Freddie thought Bradley should have been allowed to join the Poles at Trun. Bradley couldn't understand. Thought we were missing our opportunities over inter/army rights. However, it should be pointed out that Monty regarded Bradley as under his command; therefore his decision was not made on the basis of inter/army considerations. Master of tidiness. He was fundamentally more interested in full envelopment than this inner envelopment. We fell between two stools. He missed the chance of closing at the Seine by doing the envelopment at Falaise."

This shows two things. First: that Montgomery gave the order not to advance and Bradley was forced to comply. Second: that Bradley *did* protest the decision. It is clear who failed to move the boundary line *and* gave an *order* – ordering Bradley and Patton not to advance. The blame for the Falaise Gap, the hundreds of thousands of Germans who escaped and the hundreds of thousands of deaths that were their consequences belongs to Montgomery.

One certainly is left to wonder why Bradley in "A Soldier's Story" and Eisenhower in "Crusade in Europe" lied about this. Bradley knew that he had protested the decision and Montgomery had remained firm. Why not let the blame fall where it was deserved?

---

[1] 2nd French Armored, under Patton

[2] de Guingand, Monty's chief of Staff

[3] Montgomery always said he was "tidying up" his forces. He would always be regrouping and reassigning the areas different divisions could and could not go to so he'd know where they were. This was what slowed him down so incredibly.

Why, indeed, except for the fact that Eisenhower had already told that lie. "Crusade in Europe" was published in 1948, three years before Bradley's book. Eisenhower says that he was *there* when Bradley made the decision to not close the gap. Bradley's very nature proves that he would not contest this in his book. Although Bradley's book shows the war more or less from Bradley's perspective, there is nothing in his book that disagrees with Eisenhower's telling. In 1958, when Montgomery published his memoirs, he says that, "Patton's remarks from time to time did not help [in American-British amity]. *When stopped by Bradley at Argentan* he said, 'Let me go on to Falaise and we'll drive the British into the sea for another Dunkirk.'" We know now that this is a lie; for Montgomery did not merely neglect to move the bombline, but he also actually *ordered* Patton to halt.

THE FALAISE GAP

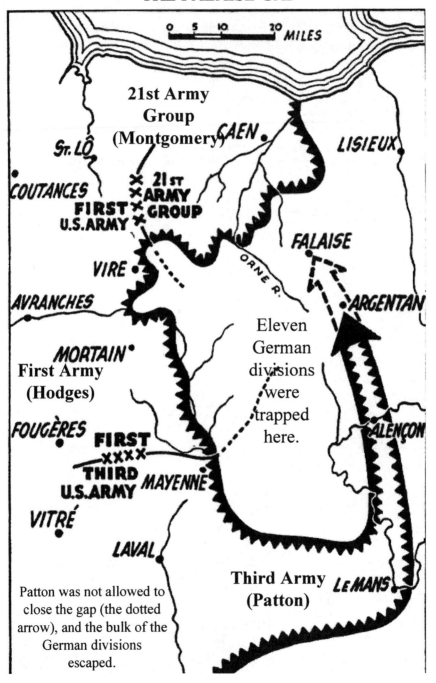

0 5 10   20 MILES

21st Army Group (Montgomery)

St. LÔ

COUTANCES

× 21ST
× ARMY
FIRST × GROUP
U.S.ARMY ×

CAEN

LISIEUX

VIRE

ORNE R.

FALAISE

AVRANCHES

MORTAIN

First Army (Hodges)

FOUGÈRES

FIRST
××××
THIRD
U.S.ARMY MAYENNE

Eleven German divisions were trapped here.

ARGENTAN

ALENÇON

VITRÉ

LAVAL

Third Army (Patton) LE MANS

Patton was not allowed to close the gap (the dotted arrow), and the bulk of the German divisions escaped.

Chapter Twenty Two

ONWARD

Patton watched in dismay as the Germans escaped through the Falaise gap. He was not one to wait when there was nothing to do, however. Patton was on the move again. If he was denied the chance to crush the German army, then he would liberate France from Germany.

Bradley allowed Patton to send the XV Corps to take Dreux, XII Corps towards Orleans and the XX Corps on Chartres. "It is really a great plan, wholly my own, and I made Bradley think he thought of it. 'Oh, what a tangled web we weave, when first we practice to deceive.' I am very happy and elated. I got all the corps moving by 10:30 so that if Monty tries to be careful, it will be too late." It was a practice Patton would repeat throughout the rest of the war. He would do anything to have Bradley approve his plans, even if Bradley got the credit. On the other hand, he would go through great lengths, including not reporting his position and "not receiving" messages, so as to carry out his plans. Montgomery was very bitter after the war when he learned what Patton had done. But Patton's actions were done in a good cause. Montgomery had proven his total and utter inability and Eisenhower's Headquarters had shown that they would look blindly on as Monty stumbled from blunder to blunder. Patton simply used the old maxim, "What he doesn't know can't hurt him." If Patton didn't report the locations of his corps, then Montgomery wouldn't be able to stop them.

Patton was constantly directing the front. Patton's wars were corps wars. He would send a corps in one direction, the rest in another. He was always aware of what was happening; if a commander slowed down or ran into resistance he would be there personally directing. Patton's rapid advances necessitated a fluid front. His army was in perpetual motion, fighting now, advancing now. This type of war suited Patton best for he could keep up with the constant motion.

There is a big difference between Montgomery's leadership and Patton's. Montgomery directed *everything*; he'd tell corps commanders how they must attack, when to hold, and when to withdraw. Patton, on the other hand, practiced the American dictum of telling commanders *what* to do, not *how*, "You will be surprised at their ingenuity." In the event that a commander was too slow in acting out his orders, Patton would visit the front and see what was delaying him. In this manner valuable time would not be wasted and the commander would not lose confidence. Montgomery rarely visited the front but relied on Intelligence reports.[1] The commanders under him did not use their creative ability because he would not let them, and often the more skilled commanders were relieved after trying something on their own. Even if these commanders accomplished a successful feat, Montgomery could not stand anyone else planning besides him. Therefore the skill of his commanders mattered little since they were being used in as robots.

Bradley visited Patton at his headquarters. Patton's record of the visit is mixed with humor and sarcasm.

> "Bradley came down to see me, suffering from nerves. There is a rumor, which I doubt, that there are five panzer divisions at Argentan, so Bradley wants me to halt my move to the east on the line of Chartres, Dreux and Chateaudun. His motto seems to be, 'In case of doubt, halt.'[2] I am complying with the order, and by tomorrow I can probably persuade him to let me advance. I wish I were Supreme Commander." *Patton's Diary*

On the next day, August 16th, Patton had reason to celebrate. Chateaudun, Dreux, Chartres, and Orleans were captured by Third Army. That day also ended Third Army (and Patton's) anonymity. Eisenhower officially announced that it was the Third under Patton that had taken Brittany, Nantes, Angers, Le Mans, Alencon, Argentan, Brest, St. Malo, and many other famous French cities. Patton's loyal general from Sicily,

---

[1] That had a history of being faulty

[2] To be contrasted with Patton's motto, "In case of doubt, attack."

Keyes, had long suspected as much. He sent Patton a telegram with the simple, "Hooray, hooray, hooray!" Americans now knew to whom they owed so much.

It was also on that day that Patton's promotion to Major General was announced. Perhaps they felt they had to announce what Patton had done in the last few months so that people would understand his promotion.

The local parson at Knutsford, the town Patton had stayed at when he was in England, wrote to him and said that he had "changed the whole face of the war." Not only that. Patton had changed the course of history by changing the fortunes of the army of the Third Reich.

Patton went that day to see the newly captured city of Chartres, then to visit Haislip, commander of the XV Corps which was near Mantes. When he returned to his headquarters at night, Bradley called up and directed that Patton use the 2nd French, 90th and 80th American divisions to capture "a town called Trun about halfway up in the gap." He would meet the Canadians there and thereby seal the almost empty gap. "I delivered this order. Life is rather dull."

Leclerc, the General of the Free French 2nd Armored had been pestering Patton about driving on towards Paris. Patton told him that he would not accept complaints from his commanders about where to attack.

Patton wrote on August 18th to his wife, Beatrice, that,

> "The family got Falaise... I could have had it a week ago but modesty via destiny made me stop... This Army covers so much ground that I have to fly in cubs most places. I don't like it. I feel like a clay pigeon... I have no apetite [sic]. I never do when I am fighting. Courtney[1] is realy [sic] a moron. Omar is O.K. but not dashing. All that I have to do [I do] over protest. I just pushed on a lot and will be warned of over extension when the phone works. Luckily it is out for the time. Omar was picked for his present job long before the slap."

---

[1] Courtney Hodges, Bradley's other army commander, was in charge of First Army.

Bradley and Eisenhower alike would worry that Patton was "over extending" his lines and it is true that Third Army was the hardest army to keep supplied. Its supply lines would cover hundreds of miles and it is a tribute to the ability of his staff[1] that he was always well supplied.[2] SHAEF[3] would worry about Patton exposing his flanks to the enemy and overextending his lines. For this reason, Patton would rarely report his location (except when ordered). To avoid being asked he would disappear to the front.

Cook, the commander of the XII Corps, was in the hospital because of his bad arteries. His circulation was so bad that he had lost all feeling in his hands and legs and his toes were turning black. It was impossible for him to walk 100 yards. Patton had a long conversation with him in which he explained that it was impossible to keep him in command "in justice to you and your men." It must have been very hard for Patton to dismiss a victorious commander, and he in fact says that, "It was a great blow to us both."

Bradley had gone to visit Montgomery and Eisenhower. He now thought that there were Germans east of Argentan. Bradley asked Patton to move the 5th Armored Division north to the west bank of the Seine near Louviers. The XIX Corps of First Army would come up on the left. "The British were asked to do this," Patton commented, "but said they could not move fast enough." It was belated frankness.

Patton realized that if he took Melun-Fontainebleau and Sens, any land on the other side of the Seine River would be useless to the Germans. Even though Patton explained this, Bradley still felt that taking these cities was too risky. However, Patton was able to talk Bradley into a compromise. If he didn't receive a "stop order" by midnight of the 20th, he would attack the next day. Patton had obtained what he wanted – Bradley's reluctant permission for the Third Army to capture a bridge at Mantes.

Bradley also gave Patton the latest news – that Eisenhower was "to placate Montgomery" by giving him the Ninth Army.

---

[1] Which Bradley labeled "mediocre."

[2] Until SHAEF cut off his supplies.

[3] Supreme Headquarters of the Allied Expeditionary Force, Eisenhower's Headquarters.

Patton's 79th Division was the first over the Seine River. Patton told his corps that a codename, "proset," would be used "in case Bradley loses his nerve at the last moment." Patton himself was nervous; it is always risky sending divisions across a river. He wrote that, "I always have funny reactions before a show like this. I think of the plan and am all for it, and then just as I give the order, I get nervous and must say to myself, 'Do not take counsel of your fears,' and then go ahead." This is well contrasted with Montgomery's remark: "I am not a bit anxious about my battles. If I am anxious I don't fight them. I wait until I am ready."

Two hours before midnight of the large river-crossing operation, Patton was writing a letter to his wife. "On paper it looks very risky but I don't think it is."
Eddy had taken over XII Corps from Cook. He asked Patton, "How much shall I have to worry about my flanks?"
"It depends how nervous you are," was his answer. "If I had worried about flanks, we'd all still be sitting in the hedgerows in Normandy. You have an open flank, but it's nothing to worry about. First of all, the enemy is on the run. Second, he has nothing south of you mobile enough to make an attack in strength before our planes will spot it and knock it out. The thing for you to do is to advance in depth, one division echeloned behind the other. That will give you striking power and at the same time cover your flank." Patton wrote in his diary that, "He has been thinking that a mile a day was good going. I told him to go fifty and he turned pale."

Meanwhile, Patton was getting a hero's welcome. As he drove through the French towns the crowds would cheer, throwing flowers and offering all sorts of presents. "I used to wave back but now I just smile and incline my head – very royal."

Patton was heading for Paris in one of his most brilliant operations yet. Hitler was screaming at his commanders to hold Paris and the Seine. The Germans were fighting fiercely, but could not withstand Patton's withering advance. Patton's plan depended on the XII and XX Corps – and at the critical moment some of Patton's divisions were borrowed by Bradley's armies – stripping the XII and XX Corps down to only two divisions each. The fierce fighting came to an end on August 21st when the 4th Armored punctured through the German lines, dooming Paris.

The annals of war record no greater achievements than those that Third Army had already won by fire and sword. The Third's incredible feats in Brittany remained unmatched – until Patton's genius and the Third Army's sinew combined to encircle Paris in a grip of steel.

Over 350 miles long and 120 miles wide, Third Army straddled France while she waged war in four directions – at once attacking everywhere. In the north in Brittany, the Third Army was attacking Brest and several other fortress cities. Along the Loire, from Nantes to Orleans, it was holding 200 miles of open flank for all the northern Allied Armies. And on its 120-mile Seine front, "Lucky"[1] was enveloping Paris, holding a bridgehead and interdicting the river north of the capital, conducting an aggressive war of movement and carving out bridgeheads south of the city.

Yet all these audacious, spectacular, and unmatched achievements were accomplished by an army only three weeks in action and with only 12 divisions, four armored and eight infantry. This bold, intrepid army would, under a less dynamic commander, have been considered "green;" because three weeks is very little experience for combat soldiers. Yet these three weeks had witnessed the liberation of almost all of France, the crippling and demoralization of the entire German army, and the Allied armies placed in a great position for conquering Germany. Where in the history of war has so great an achievement been achieved by men so inexperienced?

But what of the experienced armies? The armies who were considered so good that they were entered into the fighting before the Third? First Army and the 21st Army Group were still "mopping up" the Falaise area and had just started inching towards the Seine.

Once again glory would be stolen unjustly from the Third Army. Had they not fought brilliantly for Paris? Were not the casualties expended for it on Third Army's roster? In London in the days before D Day, SHAEF had originally planned for First Army to take Paris on or around September 6th and that a British corps would be "loaned" in order to participate in the triumphal parade. But Third Army had upset this politically correct theory by enveloping Paris without either First Army or the 21st Army Group anywhere nearby. So SHAEF made a quick adjustment. They snatched the XV Corps from Patton and transferred it

---

[1] Lucky was the code-name for Third Army.

to Bradley's First Army so that it could "liberate" Paris along with a British division on August 25th.

Early on August 23rd an announcement was made on the BBC. It said that Patton's Third Army had liberated Paris. "Poetic justice," Patton commented, "It will be refuted, but no one will pay any attention."

Patton was planning for the next campaign. He was sure that the best place to surge through the Siegfried line would be at the Nancy Gap, which had plenty of good roads going through it. An area which is accessible is always far easier to take. The Nancy Gap opened into central Germany: where the industry was. Patton was not worried about the Siegfried line "because I believe that American troops can break any line." Patton always moved so swiftly that by the time he arrived at a spot the enemy had not even had time to regroup, let alone fortify. "... I have always gotten to the place he expected me to come about three days before he got there." Thus by outrunning the enemy he did not have to worry about outmaneuvering him.

Montgomery had another plan. He was busy selling it to Eisenhower. Monty's part of the Siegfried line was well fortified thanks to his hopeless lack of initiative. Montgomery wanted to go through Belgium and Holland so as to bypass the stronghold. The flaw in this plan was that Belgium and Holland were full of canals which would make tanks useless. This may have not occurred to Montgomery, an infantryman, but Patton recognized this flaw right away. Had Montgomery looked into the history of unsuccessful attacks on Holland, he would have known that the German's great panzer forces were crippled by an inadequate Dutch army only a few years before in that exact area. However, if Metz, the fortress city that historically held the Nancy Gap, fell, all of fertile, flat, industrial Germany would be open.

Eisenhower, weak as always, was intimidated by Montgomery's dictatorial manner. Without any combat experience he needed to rely on the advice of his commanders almost entirely. Along with their advice he had his West Point infantryman's book learning. They advised a frontal assault along all fronts "pushing" the enemy back. With Patton declaring heart and soul for a quick advance into the heart of Germany "we could be there in ten days" and Montgomery vigorously demanding that he do the thrusting, Eisenhower had only cloudy visions of strategy.

ADVANCES MADE FROM AUGUST 14 to AUGUST 25

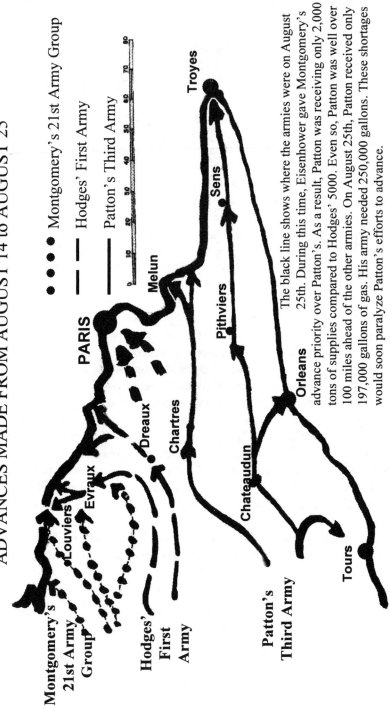

●●●● Montgomery's 21st Army Group

— — — Hodges' First Army

——— Patton's Third Army

The black line shows where the armies were on August 25th. During this time, Eisenhower gave Montgomery's advance priority over Patton's. As a result, Patton was receiving only 2,000 tons of supplies compared to Hodges' 5000. Even so, Patton was well over 100 miles ahead of the other armies. On August 25th, Patton received only 197,000 gallons of gas. His army needed 250,000 gallons. These shortages would soon paralyze Patton's efforts to advance.

Chapter Twenty Three

THE BROAD-FRONT POLICY

Now came a fierce struggle between the Americans and Eisenhower. Montgomery had originally planned the Normandy invasion. In the plan, the allies would be at the outskirts of Paris at D+90.[1] It was now D+93 and Patton had already taken Paris and was across the Seine. Montgomery had not planned for so swift an advance, nor had he planned past the D+90 date. Eisenhower was now supposed to take over operational command – start really commanding in the field rather than being advised at a desk. Eisenhower never did actually *command*. He was incredibly intimidated by Montgomery, even though Churchill had told him he could pick which British commander would be in charge. Montgomery *did* command, even bully, and by now he had discovered that Eisenhower was a push-over.

It was primarily a question of strategy – how should they take Germany? There was no determined resistance[2] anywhere; it now remained to decide where the main attack should come from. Patton believed in a well-directed, lightning advance in the south of France via Troyes to the Saar into the fertile, flat, industrial center of Germany. This seemed to him the most feasible since the Third Army was 100 miles ahead of the other armies. Bradley wanted Patton to direct this advance,

---

[1] Ninety days after D Day.

[2] "There was no determined resistance anywhere" is a commonly used expression. It should not be taken to mean that the Germans would not put up a fight, nor that some areas weren't better defended than others. What it means is that the Germans were badly organized and were in the process of retreating on all the fronts, some places more than others.

and First Army to assist. Under Bradley's plan Montgomery would secure the vital port of Antwerp – which was *still* uncaptured.

Montgomery had other ideas. Why should the single thrust be in Patton's sector? *He* wanted to execute the main thrust. What did it matter that their *was* resistance in front of his army, that his part of the Seigfried line was well-manned, and that after crossing they would run into a network of rivers before being able to strike at the German capital? Surely British prestige was worth more than practical strategy? At this time Churchill wanted Montgomery to take Antwerp, as well as other vital ports, because it was essential that the Russians be denied access to the English Channel.

Montgomery was also demanding that Bradley's nine divisions back up his advance.[1] He also demanded that three of Bradley's American corps be transferred to his command. Not only that, but Montgomery wanted Patton's Third Army to merely hold what it had taken. This seemed like adequate revenge for Patton's recent stealing of the spotlight. For under his plan, while 21st Army Group gloriously captured famous city after city and First Army assisted, Third Army would have to hold its position, forcing it to remain out of the headlines. Montgomery didn't need all of the supplies and armies he was asking for, but he knew that if he had them there was no way Patton could advance.

Cornelius Ryan, author of "A Bridge Too Far,"[2] realized the ludicrousness of the situation facing Eisenhower.

> "In his zeal, Montgomery had narrowed his rivalry down to Patton alone: a British field marshal in charge of an entire army group was trying to out race an American lieutenant general in charge of a single army." *"A Bridge Too Far," by Cornelius Ryan.*

Both men seemed to have enjoyed the competition, even though the distribution of armies was hardly equal. Eisenhower would have been wise to allow them to race each other to Berlin, thereby giving both an incentive to move as fast as possible; this was what Alexander had done after the two uneventful weeks in Sicily, with admirable results.

---

[1] Similar to his plan in Sicily
[2] An excellent book on Montgomery's worst disaster, Operation Market Garden. The movie "A Bridge Too Far" was based on this book.

But supply priority would have to go to Bradley's Army Group or Montgomery's, and thus Eisenhower would have to decide on one of their strategies. But decisions always came hard on Eisenhower. He was receiving a lot of criticism in the American press for not being firmer on the British. Eisenhower couldn't directly say no to Monty, for then it would look as if he was favoring the Americans. On the other hand, how could he possibly support the ridiculous idea of breaking through the Germans in the Seigfried line and then swimming into Berlin? The idea of risking a single thrust didn't seem advisable either, resistance or no. He much preferred the doctrines of West and proposed that all the armies push along all the fronts. This outraged all of the generals, Americans included, for this would waste all of their efforts and give the Germans time to offer organized resistance.

Montgomery saw that he would need to enlist more support for his strategy. So he resorted to Brooke and Churchill. He told them of Eisenhower's stupidity, but then told them that this was the "American strategy" and of course his plan looked good beside it. He told them that he was the only one who wanted a single thrust. He told them that the issue was having a single thrust or not, rather than where that single thrust would come from. This was a lie of course, for Bradley and Patton obviously wanted a single lightning thrust *in the south*. Now, however, Montgomery had Churchill arguing to Eisenhower that they should obviously have a single thrust into Germany and *also* that obviously that would have to be the northern thrust led by the 21st Army Group.

In British books to this day authors say that Montgomery wanted a "single thrust into Germany." They add that this bit of strategic genius was Montgomery's and that he was vindicated. They heavily criticize (as would anyone) Eisenhower's "broad-front" policy, failing to realize that Patton hated it as much, or more, than Montgomery. Bradley, in his book, never criticizes Eisenhower, and therefore never criticizes the "broad-front" policy, even going so far as to say that he supported it.

According to General Westphal, then the Chief of Staff of *OB West*, the German army was now in complete, terror-stricken panic. "It appeared hopeless to expect that the flood could be stemmed *even at the Rhine crossings...* The much vaunted and so-called West Wall thus possessed merely symbolic value. It offered not even the slightest obstacle, yet evidently impelled the Allies nevertheless to approach it with a carefully prepared drive instead of penetrating it with a lightning assault with relatively light forces. This actually astonished us at headquarters." As much as the Germans were astonished, no one was more astonished than Patton. Forced to halt before a retreating army, Eisenhower's headquarters was continually receiving plaintive, pleading calls from Patton.

Westphal states not only that the West Wall was incapable of putting up a determined defense at this time, but that in the vicinity of Koblenz-Trier, it was especially vulnerable. This was the *very area* that Patton was demanding an advance through! Eisenhower and Montgomery laughed off his cries that in two weeks he could be in Germany. Yet Westphal continues, "I would like to state unequivocally that we would have been totally incapable of putting up any serious resistance and foiling a drive across the western boundaries of the Reich had General Eisenhower decided upon a truly determined, ruthless advance at this point [Trier]. At that time, headquarters of *OB West* was located in the vicinity of Koblenz. Whenever after sunset we could hear the rattling chains in the street where the Field Marshal [Model] had his headquarters, he would ask, 'Can this be Patton?' The question was posed in jest, of course, but it did not lack the most serious undertones." Westphal agrees with Patton that had the Allies advanced in the vicinity of Trier, the war would have been over in 1944!

Patton was telling General Bull that the German resistance was "merely a thin crust." Westphal says it was a "very thin front." That the allies mysteriously halted seemed to the Germans – and to Hitler – a miracle. To Patton it was the worst disaster yet.

The allies had lost the chance to end Hitler's evil empire when they left the Falaise Gap unclosed. They lost it again when they decided to give Montgomery the main advance into Germany. The chance was lost yet again when Patton was allowed to run out of gas.

Chapter Twenty Four

PARALYZED

Eisenhower decided to accept Montgomery's plan for a massive attack in the north of Germany. This would require all of First Army[1] to support Montgomery's move for a "lightning dagger-thrust at the heart of Germany." Bradley said it would be more like a butter-knife thrust.

Since Bradley was forced to keep First Army in a "protective" position, he approved Patton's plan to capture the Metz-Nancy corridor. Although theoretically Bradley and Montgomery were equal in rank (they were both Army Group Commanders), Bradley was instructed that his "principal offensive mission" was to guard 21st Army Group. Montgomery was given "supply priority." Under a less audacious commander, Third Army would have sat down to wait for orders and appropriate supplies.

Not Patton. He was convinced that the Germans were in full retreat and would do as much as he could with what little he got. SHAEF[2] had grudgingly approved a small, three corps attack in the direction of Metz. SHAEF knew that they were not giving Patton enough supplies to advance anywhere. But this way they could do what Montgomery wanted without actually issuing orders to halt Patton.

Eisenhower's orders specified that Hodges was to receive 5,000 tons of supplies a day while Patton was only to get 2,000 tons.

---

[1] General Hodges' Army. It consisted of nine divisions.
[2] Supreme Headquarters of the Allied Expeditionary Force

Patton ordered an advance to Reims-Chalons sur Marne-Vitry Le Francois, which lie halfway to and in the middle of the corridor. Once gained, Third Army would be halfway to its objective of taking Metz.

Metz is a city that has historically been a battle ground. This is because the city lies astride the Nancy Gap and leads directly into Germany. It has always been fought over; either the Germans wanted it so as to invade France, or the French wanted it so as to invade Germany. In every occupation the victorious force built strong fortresses in the city. By 1944 it had 21 forts. During the French Revolution, Louis XVI's rescuers planned for him to be taken to Metz, where loyal Royalist soldiers could easily defend him and be reinforced from his wife's homeland – Austria.

Thus this area has always been a keystone to those who had (or wanted to have) one foot in France and the other in the Rhineland. It has also always been heatedly contested, and Patton knew Metz's history well. He therefore prepared by stressing that his troops move so quickly through the corridor that the Germans would not have enough time to man Metz's vast fortress system.

The Germans also knew the value of Metz, and were trying desperately to delay the Third's tanks at Melun and Montereau. The Germans needed to hold them long enough to allow the slow Pas de Calais reserves to arrive and garrison the Metz fortress works. Patton was just as determined to take Melun and Montereau before the reserves got there. To do this, he ordered heavy attacks on the Germans so as to pin them down; then ordered 4th Armored to sneak around to the south of Troyes. This was successful and the armored division ended up deep in the enemy's rear. They entered Troyes, 80 miles southeast of Paris, without a man or vehicle lost.

A large number of Germans were killed or captured. The Germans in Troyes greatly out numbered 4th Armored. They reconnoitred and counterattacked, but 4th Armored was a hardened division and repelled them. Consider what would happen when a division like 4th Armored didn't have enough gas or ammunition to fight. This was the scenario that these veteran divisions would have to face in the upcoming months.

August 25th was not a happy day for Patton – or his staff. It is the job of G-4 to keep the army supplied. Patton had an exceptional G-4. But they could not explain what had happened. They knew that a fast moving army like the Third required 250,000 gallons of gas to keep its tanks moving. But today only 197,000 gallons had arrived. The frightened staff approached Patton, who was furious. He knew that Third Army had reserves which could make up for these losses, but not for long. If Third Army was deliberately being denied gas it would soon roll to a stop.

This same day Bradley asked Patton to meet him in Chartres. On his way, Patton stopped at the famous cathedral of Chartres. They had removed all the glass to protect it from shattering due to the bombs. The cathedral was unharmed and without the glass it was much lighter than usual. Patton knelt down and said a prayer that his army would continue to be successful.

Third Army now had four bridges over the Seine, south of Paris.

Patton then made for Bradley's headquarters where he and Hodges, Bradley's other army commander, would receive their new orders. SHAEF's plan was that First Army, directed by Hodges and comprising nine divisions, would cross the Seine at Melun and Mantes. Patton bitterly records that it was the Third Army that had captured those bridges. It was becoming more and more clear that SHAEF didn't just want Montgomery to have all of the supplies; they wanted Patton to stop. SHAEF approved Patton's advance to the Metz-Strasbourg line, but only as a diversionary effort and did not allot him the supplies for the advance to continue.

Patton drove to Melun where the Third Army soldiers had erected a pontoon bridge and were crossing the Seine. The soldiers cheered as Patton drove through to talk to their commander. Patton surprised the new commander of XII Corps, Eddy, by telling him that he would be moving again in two days. "He is not used to our speed yet, so was a little surprised."

It was now that Bradley began to see Montgomery's true colors. Patton too had been impressed by Montgomery – at their first meeting in N. Africa more than 3 years ago. But Bradley had continued to admire Montgomery's caution, meticulousness and exactitude. It was not until now, when Bradley would lose prestige and men to an arrogant British

Army Group commander, that he was beginning to see Montgomery in a more realistic light. When Bradley awoke to this, he admired Patton's courage and foresight for the first time. In Sicily, Bradley had been contemptuous of Patton's "recklessness." But now it began to look more and more correct as Montgomery's caution showed its lack of fruit.

Now there was a shortage of trucks. Montgomery claimed that he could not accomplish his thrust without American aid in trucking.[1] They took these supply trucks from Hodges. Hodges, though a very mediocre commander, was part of the group supporting Montgomery and so had supply priority over Patton – which meant that to make up for Hodges' deficit, Patton lost vital supply trucks.

The situation was not yet desperate. C-47s would fly to Third Army's front, dropping thousands of tons of supplies a few miles behind the battle front. On August 25th, 207 airplanes dropped 500 tons of supplies of all kinds to the fronts. However this lifeline would be soon cut; Eisenhower, in approving Montgomery's plan, had specified that airborne forces be used to clear the path for the northern thrust.

Gradually, no matter how hard Patton tried, every route would be denied to him. Eventually Third Army's troops would become akin to guerilla warriors; living, eating, and supplied by captured enemy stores. It is sad to think that this had to happen; an American commander who should have enjoyed fully the benefits of American materiel superiority, ousted by a British commander who demanded overstocked supply dumps.

---

[1] This was due to the terrible quality of British lorries.

Chapter Twenty Five

LIVING OFF THE LAND

"It is terrible to wage war by inadvertence and to conquer by deceit."

A few hours after the capture of Troyes, the Germans began withdrawing from Melun and Montereau. The Germans did not have enough time to blow up the bridges, and the Third Army rolled over them into Reims.

Huge German liquor caches had been discovered in the city. Patton ordered that they be kept under guard until Thanksgiving day (which was three months away.) When the holiday arrived, every soldier and officer in the Army received seven bottles of wine or cognac, as he desired. No wonder why morale was so high!

Third Army had now received 135,000 gallons short of the 450,000 gallons that were needed. Patton was alarmed. Army Group had approved their operation, why were they deliberately hampering it?

Despite what is commonly stated, there was no shortage of gas on the continent. In fact, due to an elaborate system of pipe lines which had been laid across the channel, more gas was reaching the front than previously. By September 1st these pipes were supplying an additional 250 tons of gasoline daily. Other lines were supplying an additional 1,000 tons.

Nor was getting the gas *to* Third Army a problem. Many historians state that Patton over-extended himself and that was why he found himself suddenly stranded, 100 miles ahead of the other armies.

Besides what I have already stated about the supply trucks, airplanes were flying 100,000 gallons of gas a day and could have supplied more.[1]

Patton begged Bradley to change Eisenhower's mind. The Germans were retreating in Third Army's area.
"That's their soft spot. They are off balance and we've got them on the run. With three Corps[2] I'm guaranteed to cross the German border in ten days. I'll stake my rank and reputation on that."
Bradley says that though "George habitually exaggerated" he believed him. What was not to believe? Patton had a good track record. He had blazed through France in two weeks; there was no resistance in Germany as there had been in France.

Bradley was nowhere near as enthusiastic about the chances however. Not understanding Patton's capacity for advance, nor the Germans complete and utter panic, Bradley says that, "Never in my wildest dreams did I imagine that we could force the Rhine alone. For if we were to gain that river bank, I estimated that it would be difficult enough to hold the position without reaching for more."

The number of opportunities that Eisenhower and SHAEF are responsible for losing are incredible. Here were the Americans, ready and able to end the war a month earlier, now once again faced with the golden opportunity of entering Germany and liberating Eastern Europe. Maybe this was why SHAEF was making it impossible for Patton to advance.

Com Z,[3] the department whose job it was to keep the armies supplied, used 25,000 gallons to move its Headquarters from war-torn Cherbourg to luxurious Paris. This extravagant waste of gas is even more appalling because it was committed by the men whose responsibility it was to keep the gas flowing to the troops. These same men would claim later that there simply wasn't enough gas to keep all the armies moving.

Though Com-Z's waste of gas was scandalous, Patton found room for humor. Patton liked to joke at his weekly press conferences[4]

---

[1] If only Montgomery wasn't such a supply hog.
[2] XV Corps had been taken from Patton for Bradley's ceremonial march into Paris and had still not been returned.
[3] Com Z is short for Communications Zone
[4] Strictly off the record, of course.

and, according to his aide, he outperformed all of the comedians who were touring the armies, including Bob Hope and Jack Benny.

> "Now as he strode into the tent, mounted the rostrum, seized the pointer, and turned to the map, you could feel an invisible curtain go up. His opener was a snappy bit on the inefficiency of Com-Z, followed by a masterly resume of the shortcomings of S.O.S. As the laughs died down, he turned his attention to Monty. "Yesterday," he said, "the Field Marshal ordered SHAEF to have Third Army go on the defensive, stand in place, and prepare to guard his right flank. The Field Marshal then announced that he will, after regrouping, make what he describes as a lightning dagger-thrust at the heart of Germany. 'They will be off their guard,' the Field Marshal predicts, 'and I shall pop out at them like an angry rabbit.'" At this point I was called away to take a phone call from XII Corps. When I got back, the correspondents were trooping out of the tent. I didn't hear the General's final word, but the [newspaper] man was still weak with laughter. 'Enjoy it?' I said. 'Enjoy it?' he replied. 'Listen, buddy, that guy in there, all by himself, without benefit of high-priced writers, music, or scenery – that guy is EIGHT-EIGHTY ENTERTAINMENT.'" *"Drive,"* by Colonel Charles R. Codman.

German warehouses, filled with choice cognacs, liqueurs, champagnes, and wines (every bottle was stamped *Reserviert fur die Deutsche Wehrmacht*), were captured. Other warehouses full of cheeses, preserves, sardines and other canned delicacies were overrun by the racing columns of Third Army. Trainloads of fine Italian silk parachutes were sent home by Third Army troops and also used for camouflage nets and scarves. Huge depots of clothing, equipment, Nazi decorations and ceremonial daggers, and other trophies were "liberated" by the ton. Third Army was wallowing in captured German goods, which included everything from little pocket-cookers to fur-lined greatcoats (they were used during the Bulge.) These warehouses were lucky gifts because Third Army was desperately short of American goods.[1]

---

[1] Of course all these goods should be expected, since Patton was in the *industrial* part of France and Germany.

What the Americans were denying Patton in the way of food and clothing was easy to make up for from these warehouses. But a providential store of Lugers was also discovered. These were invaluable during the upcoming "lean years" when Third Army was left out of gas, ammunition and also *guns*.

Around this time Third Army captured a huge German meat-refrigerating depot which held over 3,000,000 pounds of beef. Patton ordered it placed under guard and later, when everyone was sinking in the mud and mire of Metz, they were brightened by the fact that though it might be hard to kill the Nazis, at least they could eat his steaks, roasts and stews.

What was most depressing to Patton and the other Third Army men was that, though they had captured 400 miles in 3 weeks, liberated over a third of France, and captured 75,000 German prisoners they were still on the lowest end of supply priority; they were part of the sideshow.

On August 28th, Patton hurtled two prongs of 4th Armored across the Marnes, one at Mairy-sur-Marne, six miles south of Chalons, the other, one mile northwest of Vitry. And a small victory was also achieved that day when the 5th Infantry Division seized Epernay.

Bradley summoned Patton to Chartres on August 30th for a conference with Eisenhower's G-3, Major General Harold R. Bull and Leven Allen. Patton stressed the weakness and disorganization of the enemy in Lucky's zone of advance, the enemy's great strength and powerful positions in the north. The Siegfried Line was not garrisoned, but if Third Army was forced to delay, the Germans would quickly regroup and fortify.

> "I asked to present my case for an immediate advance to the east and a rupture of the Siegfried Line before it could be manned. Bradley was sympathetic but Bull – and I gather the rest of Ike's staff – do not concur and are letting Montgomery overpersuade Ike to go north. It is a terrible mistake, and when it comes out in the later years it will cause much argument."[1]

---

[1] He was certainly right about that!

As far as we can tell from Patton's diary, it would seem that it was today that he and the "lower ranks" would find out about the exact nature of the plans that had been transpiring between Eisenhower, Montgomery, Bradley and SHAEF.

"The British have put it over again. We got no gas because, to suit Monty, the First Army must get most of it, and we are also feeding the Parisians."

When Patton returned from the meeting he was informed that of the 400,000 gallons Third Army needed, only 32,000 had been delivered. Third Army was almost completely out of gas. All supply dumps were dry and unit loads were disappearing. Gaffey was trying to take Commercy, but was told not to by Eddy, on the grounds that when he arrived near the town he would be out of gas. Patton angrily told Eddy that in the last war he had drained ¾ of his tanks' gas so as to keep the other ¼ moving. "We must and will get a crossing on the Meuse."

Patton went out and spoke to the young tank drivers and their commanders. He ordered them to, "Get off your fanny as fast as you can and move on until your engines run dry, and then get out and walk!"

The lack of gas, and thus the lack of advance, was depressing. A picture was taken of Patton and his generals when they were informed that they were out of gas; every man's face looks miserably dejected.

That same day XV Corps was returned to Third Army. Now they had more men to supply on the same thin rations. Life was looking worse.

Chalons and Reims were taken and the key Reims-Chalons-Vitry line was now firmly secured. The Metz-Nancy corridor into Germany had only a retreating enemy fleeing through it. Hoping that a brilliant victory would wake the SHAEF men out of their stupor, Patton was trying desperately to use every ounce of gas towards a tactical (and strategical) miracle.

Towards this end he issued a new directive ordering an advance east to secure the bridge over the Meuse on the Vedun-Commercy in preparation for a drive to seize a crossing on the Rhine between Koblenz and Mannheim.

Also on August 31st, Lucky was informed that its gas would be cut to the bone until September 3rd, and that all supplies would be slashed to 2,000 tons daily. Third Army requirements were 5,500 tons daily including 450,000 gallons of gas. However, no gas was received at all that day. In desperation, Patton called Eisenhower. His voice came out over the dicta-phone in an incongruent high pitched squeak which made his angry words sound funny. "My men cat eat their belts," he stormed, "but my tanks gotta have gas." The armored columns still had some gas in their reserve tanks and they continued lunging eastward, but time was running out.

Chapter Twenty Six

WAGING WAR ON 2 ROUNDS A DAY

Verdun was occupied; St. Mihiel, Commercy and Bar-le-Duc were liberated. Patton had a diminished army and not enough gas to supply it, but the Third Army was still victoriously plunging forward.

The historic lines of the Marne, Aisne, and Meuse, where millions of men had fought in the trenches of WWI, were rent in one blazing week by Patton's Third Army. In that time 5 divisions[1] had bridged the three rivers – the traditional obstacles into Germany, raced through practically the entire battlegrounds of World War I, and were on their way towards victory – or empty gas tanks.

Third Army was extended 475 miles, from Brest, where they were still fighting elements of resistance in the port cities, to the banks of the Meuse, the corridor into Germany.

Early in the morning on September 1st Patton was listening to the radio. Montgomery had been declared a Field Marshal. Eisenhower then added insult to injury by saying that, "Monty is the greatest living soldier." Patton wrote to his wife Beatrice that, "The Field Marshal thing made us sick, that is Bradley and me."

Some people would say that Patton was an egotist, always saying that all credit was due to him. Can anyone deny that Third Army, in itself, was no different from any other army? It was actually quite green,

---

[1] 4th and 7th Armored, 5th, 80th and 90th Infantry

and was passed over in favor of the other armies for the landing assault. Yet in one sweeping month it had distinguished itself as being far and above the best liberating army in France. By being an army, a division, or a corps, these units sacrifice individual qualities for the sake of an efficient, compact unit. This means that they can not utilize one man's particular talent in the way that a guerilla army can. They assume that each enlisted man in the unit had basically no knowledge before he joined and work up. These units, therefore, by *being* an army, a division or a corps are all equal as far as the men they consist of concern. Because of our military system, they can be no better than their leader. Which means that what they achieve, while due to their muscle, is attributable to the brain of the commander and his officers. Therefore Third Army's triumphs can only be due to the skill and audacity of its commanding general. Was Patton an egotist to correctly gauge himself and his skills against his peers? Was it pride that made him believe that he made Third Army what it was?

He observed that he had to persuade his generals and Ike's that audacious tactics work, "They all get scared and then I appear and they feel better."

Third Army was intercepting messages from German commanders slotted to defend the Siegfried line. They wanted to know where their units should be placed. The clock was ticking.

Things were not looking any better for Patton. Third Army was short of gas, rations, and troops. They badly needed replacements. They had not received any since Third Army had become operational. Then it consisted of nine divisions; now it had only five.

Patton wrote to his wife,

"I am headed for the Meuse, which I will get... I have to battle for every yard but it is not the enemy who is trying to stop me, it is 'They.' No one else ever tries as hard. But they are learning. Now the infantry rides the tanks, guns, anything that moves, to get forward. It is not pretty, but it works. Look at the map! If I could only steal some gas, I could win this war. Sad to say a colored truck company did steal some by careful accident."

This stealing of gas is very controversial. At that time, due to prejudice in the armed forces, most black men were put into supply rather than into battle. Since supply priority after Montgomery was Hodges, truck commanders were told to deposit the gas at "First Army." However the black company put up signs that pointed southeast and told the truck drivers that that was First Army. It was actually Third Army. Patton himself was not prejudiced, and this was probably why the supply men decided to help him. The British cried in outrage that Patton had purposely praised the black company so that they would steal for him. Patton may or may not have encouraged them to do so, officially he had to deny it. It is not a crime to steal gas so as to win the war.

It was the beginning of September and the air was getting brisker.

Com Z has become famous for its inefficiency. However a much more grim responsibility lies on their shoulders. They not only failed to supply Patton's men with gas, but they also allowed his men to freeze due to lack of proper winter equipment. Patton had requested Com Z for winter equipment, but none came. Troops were without overshoes, mackinaws, and blankets. Blankets became so critical that for a time they were first priority.[1]

Six weeks after it had become operational, Third Army finally had all of its assigned artillery units. But without the gas to use them, this glimmer of hope was useless. One morning Patton was informed that the weekly ammunition supplied by Com Z was only enough for two rounds per gun, per day! Imagine!

On September 2nd Patton was summoned to Chartres for a meeting with Bradley and Eisenhower. Eisenhower told them that he had approved Montgomery's Pas-de-Calais area assault. "Ike was very pontifical and quoted Clausewitz to us, [we] who have commanded larger forces than C ever heard of. He is all for cleaning up the Calais area." Patton told Eisenhower that this would not be necessary if he were allowed the gas needed to continue surging forward through the Metz-Nancy area. The 15th Cavalry Squadron had actually entered Metz on September 1st and had spent the night unmolested in the Cathedral

---

[1] Shortages like gas and ammo which were necessary for war were put on lower priority than the shortages like blankets and food that were essential for life.

square. Because of lack of gas the squadron had to withdraw.[1] Patton knew better than anyone that it was now or never, "Ike is all for caution since he has never been at the front and has no feel for the actual fighting. Bradley, Hodges and I are all for a prompt advance. Ike did not thank or congratulate any of us for what we have done."

Patton told Ike that if he was given the appropriate supplies, he could break through the Siegfried Line and be over the Rhine in a matter of days. "I'm willing to stake my reputation on that."
"Be careful, George," Eisenhower replied testily, "that reputation of yours hasn't been worth very much."
Patton was naturally hurt by this comment. Had Eisenhower forgotten that Third Army had made the fastest advance in *history?* Patton looked down and responded quietly, "That reputation is pretty good now."

Eisenhower agreed to permit Third Army to continue advancing in order to establish bridges over the Moselle.

> "We finally talked him into letting the V Corps of First Army and [all of] the Third Army attack the Seigfried Line as soon as the Calais area stabilizes. Until this is done we will not be able to get gas or ammunition for a further advance. He kept talking about the future great battle of Germany, while we assured him that the Germans have nothing left to fight with if we push on now. If we wait, there *will* be a great battle of Germany."

What annoyed Patton further was that,

> "He also said that Lee and the Communications Zone[2] have done a marvelous job, whereas we consider that they have failed utterly to keep us supplied with gasoline. As soon as I get sufficient gasoline, I have permission to secure crossings over the Moselle and to attack the Seigfried line."

Eisenhower knew that Patton didn't have enough gas to breakthrough the Seigfried line, and that he wouldn't have sufficient gas

---

[1] Metz would be recaptured months (and thousands of casualties) later when the gas supply was finally adequate.
[2] Com Z

for months. Perhaps he thought he could console Patton with the permission.

Patton had not divulged a little secret to Ike. XII Corps had captured 100,000 gallons of German aviation gas.

As in North Africa, Montgomery wanted all the supplies to be allotted to him. When his advance into Germany began to falter, he claimed that it was because of Patton. Patton was managing to advance so rapidly that it looked as if he had been supplied – and Montgomery been cheated. Monty furiously claimed that SHAEF had taken supplies that were his. SHAEF shrugged its shoulders. They couldn't explain Third Army's advance because they didn't know about the captured gas.[1]

After the war and Patton's death, Montgomery claimed that his attack into the Ruhr area had failed because Patton had been supplied. He claimed that he had been duped into believing that he would get the lion's share of supplies but in September the Americans began supplying Patton again. This interpretation does not stand up under the harsh light of the facts. For Patton had only received 2,500 tons of supplies a day in the first half of September, only 500 tons more than in the last weeks of August when he was halted.

But one does wonder what happened to all the gas, why the reservoirs suddenly dried up at the end of August. It can not only be because Com Z made a stupid move that wasted gas and Montgomery had full supply dumps. There is another far more terribly foolish reason.

This reason rests far more on Eisenhower's shoulders than on anyone else's. Eisenhower approved Montgomery's plan in which large airborne forces would land near Tournai, a city in Belgium south of Brussels. The airborne forces were supposed to aid Montgomery's northward thrust, but as Bradley had predicted, the infantry got there first. The airdrop was cancelled, but the six day preparation for it cost the advancing armies 5,000 tons of supplies. This was enough to launch two armies across the Rhine without pausing, while the enemy was still retreating in chaos![2] Tragically, this gas was also lost – due to Eisenhower's ineptitude. He had a basic lack of knowledge on tactics and

---

[1] Even if they had, they would not have understood since the amount of gas Third Army had captured was about 1/5th of the amount they needed *per day*.
[2] These figures are from Liddell Hart's "History of the Second World War."

on logistics.[1] His was the failure to supply the *advancing* armies with this gas.

Because of a lack of gas, Third Army made penetrations, but no breakthroughs. Supporting columns could not assist because they did not have enough gas. All of Third Army's artillery was immobilized due to lack of gas. The Germans took great advantage of this situation.

Patton had only three corps. He had set himself on crossing at Nancy and Metz. He said he would use his "rock soup method."

> "Once a tramp went to a house and asked for boiling water to make rock soup. The lady was interested and gave him water, in which he placed two polished rocks he had in his hand. He then asked for some potatoes and carrots to put in the soup to flavor the water a little, and finally ended up securing some meat. In other words, in order to attack, we have first to pretend to reconnoiter and then reinforce the reconnaissance and then finally attack. It is a very sad method of making war."

He wrote to his wife the next day that, "We start with reconnaissance but it is terrible to wage war by inadvertence and to conquer by deceit. But Destiny so wills it and quotes Clausewitz – who never commanded a quarter of what I do – to prove it. Omar and Courtney[2] were also quite ill."

The rations were so scarce that they emptied German depots to feed troops. Third Army bakers used captured flour to bake bread. Outraged, Patton declared that, "SHAEF[3] is not only hog-tying us but trying to starve us to death as well." Third Army was forced to fight like a guerilla army, living off the land.

Patton's nephew, Fred Ayer, came to visit Patton at Third Army HQ in Nancy. Ayer wrote that Patton was,

---

[1] Eisenhower wanted to use the airborne forces no matter what; they were a novelty and had barely ever been used. They took so long to get ready for an operation that by the time they could be used the ground forces were always already there. For this reason many of their operations were consistently cancelled.

[2] Bradley and Hodges' first names.

[3] Supreme Headquarters of the Allied Expeditionary Force, Ike's HQ.

"tall, broad of shoulder, immaculate in ribbon-splashed jacket above salmon-pink officer's trousers, and flanked by his country and his Army's flags. His posture was as erect as ever. This I noticed at once. Then, on studying his face closely, I saw that the lines had deepened and that there was a little puffiness about the eyes. He looked tired, or at least discouraged. Of course, he had been in almost continuous battle for two years and had just been halted in his dash for the heart of Germany. He still had his cigar, however, holding it between the long fingers of his right hand on which the gold rings shone. Somehow, they now looked less adornment than brass knuckles. Uncle George did not move forward at first or even smile. His high-pitched voice had not changed at all." *"Before the Colors Fade," by Fred Ayer.*

Ayer worked for the FBI and had recently been made a lieutenant colonel and been put in charge of the FBI agents in the European theater. Patton had wanted him to stay in Washington and "catch Commies."

Ayer asked Patton if he was disappointed that he couldn't drive for the Rhine. Patton answered, "Of course I'm disappointed and angry and it's going to cost us like hell before we're through. But someday, by God, I'm going to beg, borrow or steal enough gasoline, ammunition and aircover to get a big attack going. I've already stolen enough gas to put me in jail for life, but it's nowhere near enough to keep us rolling. Someday I may even steal a whole damned division of armor and bust the heck out of here. Come on with me, and I'll show you exactly just what I'm going to do."

Ayer followed Patton down the hall and into the sentry-guarded "war room." This room was the pride of the Third Army staff. Its walls were covered with detailed, small-scale maps of all territory, Allied as well as enemy which had immediate tactical interest. Every map was marked with new intelligence relating to troop, armor, transport, supply depots, railroads, artillery and air dispositions. There were also contour models of terrain currently being fought over, because Patton believed that terrain influenced the battle more than any other factor.

Patton crossed the room, and he and Colonel Koch slid back the wooden panels on one of the walls to reveal a detailed large-scale map of the eastern border of France and Western Germany. The General stood with a long pointer in hand, and tapped the map. "Now listen carefully," he told his nephew. "What is important is where a roadway exists, or where you can build one. If there is no possibility of either you can't move heavy supplies, or even light ones, in sufficient quantity to support a major attack.[1] That was true in Caesar's day and it's true now. Once the supplies are there, big hills, forests or rivers won't stop a determined army; there is no obstacle that can't be breached if hit hard enough and in depth."

He turned to his nephew, "So now look here. When the day comes, I'm going to move this outfit 26 kilometers in the first 24 hours to this point here." He pointed at the map. For the next 15 minutes, he showed his nephew, division by division, what he intended to do someday.

He did this plan five months later, almost regiment by regiment.

Patton told Ayer and Third Army Staff, "I have studied the German all my life. I have read the memoirs of his generals and political leaders. I have even read his philosophers and listened to his music. I have studied in detail the accounts of every one of his battles. I know exactly how he will react under any given set of circumstances. He hasn't the slightest idea what *I'm* going to do. Therefore, when the day comes, I'm going to whip the heck out of him."

A tragic lesson that illustrates what happens when armies are without gas occurred that September. A battalion of the 80th Infantry Division, in a gallant attack, forced a crossing over the Moselle. But there was no armor or artillery to support the foothold, and the enemy, counterattacking, wiped it out with a loss of 294 men. "All this comes from the fatal decision of the Supreme Commander to halt the Third Army until the Pas-de-Calais was cleared up. A fateful blunder," Patton wrote.

Three quarters of the American supply had been devoted to First Army's northern thrust. First Army quickly became bogged down around Aachen. Liddell Hart concludes that this is because the line of advance

---

[1] And they say Patton never thought about supplies!

between First Army and 21st Army Group[1] was too narrow – a major strategic error. It was impossible for First Army to bypass Aachen and so it became involved in a complex, long-drawn out slaughter war.[2]

In the north on September 4th, Montgomery's 11th Armored Division captured the port of Antwerp. They made no effort to capture the bridges over the Albert Canal intact but simply halted after capturing the docks. Two days later the division tried to advance but found the bridges blown. This is a great example of the difference between Patton and Montgomery – the difference between audacity and caution.

Forty thousand slave laborers were working in Third Army's section of the Siegfried line. Two Infantry and one Panzer division were withdrawn from the Italian front and rerouted to the Saar. German counterattacks were getting stronger and Third Army was getting weaker.

The Germans were taking the greatest possible advantage of the enforced halt. Patton wrote to his wife, "Books will some day be written on the 'Pause which did not refresh' anyone but the Germans." The elements of Third Army that could fight were finding that the Germans were better prepared. They were blowing up bridges and getting ready. Third Army would soon face something new – a forced, pitched battle.

The fall rains were setting in, crippling the air support. For an army like the Americans which depended heavily on aerial bombardment, this was very bad news. But Patton was still determined to force his way to the Rhine.

When Patton had crossed the Seine, Bradley had wanted him to halt there. Patton persuaded Bradley to allow him to go on to the Meuse. When Third Army arrived there it was not supposed to go any further – Bradley's orders. Even if Patton had wanted to, Montgomery and SHAEF all believed that he couldn't advance any further – he was out of gasoline.

But Patton refused to be halted before a retreating enemy and continued advancing as far as possible. On September 4th Bradley arrived

---

[1] Montgomery's Army group

[2] The massacres of Aachen and the Hurtgen forest were also due to failure of the commanders to exploit their initial advantage, when the Germans were still retreating in surprise.

at Third Army. He was issuing new orders giving Third Army half of all 12th Army Group' supplies. If Patton was able to, he was free to cross the Moselle. This reflected a great change in Bradley's outlook.

> "A less aggressive commander than Patton would probably have hoarded the pittance that came his way and halted the line for winter safekeeping behind the Meuse River line. But George plunged boldly on beyond the Meuse 30 miles farther to the Moselle, where he promptly grabbed a bridgehead south of the fortress city of Metz." *"A Soldier's Story" by Omar N. Bradley.*

Bradley was tired of Montgomery and, though he never admitted it, Eisenhower. They had been Patton's enemies ever since he had landed on the continent, halting him at every turn. Now they were favoring Montgomery's Army Group instead of his. He decided that helping Patton was helping the Americans and so decided to do all he could for him.

At dawn on September 8th an SS Panzer Brigade attacked Third Army. This was a new experience, for in the past Third Army had done all the attacking. The SS brigade fired at General McLain's[1] headquarters, broke in and captured classified files, then withdrew to join the main force. This would have been the first German victory of the campaign; but then Third Army asserted itself, counterattacked, and almost completely annihilated the German contingent. The Germans lost 30 tanks, 60 half-tracks, and 900 men.

On this same day the 2nd Infantry of Third Army was at the outer fortifications of Metz. They managed to gain a foothold on the east bank of the Moselle, but four companies were pinned down there. Other divisions tried to push on to Fort Blaise but were unsuccessful. Not only that, but the Germans were counterattacking and were in some areas successful.

However, even though the Germans were defending better than before, it was still true that everything the Germans had was committed. If the Americans broke through the crust that had been built around them, they would find the country beyond unprotected.

---

[1] Commander of Third Army's 90th Division.

On September 12th Patton attended another conference with the Army Group. He was told that Montgomery was insisting that all supplies be diverted to support his offensive. Montgomery was claiming that the gas allotted to Third Army was hampering his operations. Privately, to his staff, Patton said, "That's a terrible lie. We received only 70,250 gallons yesterday and only 65,000 of the 300,000 gallons a day we need. How can these small quantities hold up him or First Army? That claim is absurd!"

"There seems to be a new plan in the offing which will place more emphasis on the First Army. I wish people would stop making plans and changing their minds, particularly when they always seem to do so at our expense. We may now lose the 83rd Division."

However, Patton managed to persuade Bradley to allow him to attack. If, on the night of the 14th, Third Army had not gotten a bridgehead over the Moselle, they would be forced onto the defensive.

Eddy, the commander of XII Corps, was nervous about the operation. "Eddy still thinks my attack is premature. I hope the Germans agree with him." On the 14th he wrote jubilantly, "We have been having quite severe fighting, which is still going on, but we have finally completely crossed the Moselle River which has throughout history been a great military barrier." Four divisions were across the Moselle.

Third Army had captured or killed 10 to 12 Germans per 1 American. Patton wrote to his wife,

"For the last week we have had a desperate battle forcing the Moselle which we could have had for the asking had we not been required to stop... We may be, in fact we are supposed to be, second string for a while, but we may fool them yet, even if the family[1] is jealous of us."

Third Army's 2nd French Armored and 79th Infantry Divisions had penetrated to Epinal, 50 miles southeast of Nancy. The 80th Infantry had cleared the desperately held Foret de Haye and 4th Armored had enveloped and seized Nancy after heavy fighting. 5th and 90th Infantry and 7th Armored Divisions were entirely across the Moselle, 10 miles

---

[1] The "family" or "cousins" are the British.

north and south of Metz. This was deemed impossible by SHAEF. They still didn't know about the captured gas. But they should have known – they knew about Patton.

On September 16th, ten Russian officers came to visit Third Army. Unlike what Ladislas Farago says, Patton already knew of the their cruelty. Like Churchill, Patton knew long before the rest of the world. Unfortunately, like Churchill, he was ignored.

> "Ten assorted Russians are to visit us today, so I won't be here. I decided to go to the front. I had a map prepared for them which showed exactly nothing in a big way. This is what they do to us…"

Montgomery had a new plan. It was the fateful "Operation Market Garden" about which the movie "A Bridge Too Far" was made. Market Garden became the biggest disaster ever suffered by the allies. The plan was for three airborne divisions[1] to land 64 miles behind the enemy lines in Holland, where they would capture 60 bridges. The rest of 21st Army Group would link up with them, thus outflanking the Seigfried line. If successful, this would make Montgomery's drive into Berlin the only feasible one.[2]

"Market Garden," like Montgomery's earlier plans, called for three airborne divisions. These would take more gas from the advancing armies. The parachutists had been slated for many operations – but then cancelled because the infantry got there first. In practically all the cases in Europe, airborne divisions were too time-consuming and costly to be of effective value. Eisenhower did not seem to understand this and he

---

[1] 35,000 men landed behind the enemy lines in Holland during Operation Market Garden. Twenty four different airfields were used for the 2,500 gliders that would carry heavy equipment such as jeeps and artillery. These gliders also carried 1/3rd of the men. Part of the reason for the gasoline crisis was due to the huge expenditure of gas by the 5,000 airplanes and 2,500 gliders. The German General, Model, watched as thousands of Allied aircraft flew above and commented, "I wish I had half of that." So did Patton.

[2] This operation, as Cornelius Ryan points out, could have been perfectly feasible a few weeks earlier when the Germans had pulled out of Holland. But Montgomery, by waiting for the extra supplies and airborne divisions, lost the opportunity for a quick, surprise takeover. The 2nd SS Panzer Corps was resting at Arnhem, the site of the largest and most important bridge. Market Garden's success hinged on this bridge.

wanted to use the airborne divisions because their morale was dropping due to so many cancellations.

Montgomery was presenting a plan, that, unlike Patton's, would use the airborne divisions. Not only that, but for the first time Montgomery was presenting something that seemed really bold. Bradley says that,

> "Had the pious, teetotaling Montgomery wobbled into SHAEF with a hangover, I could not have been more astonished. For in contrast to the conservative tactics Montgomery ordinarily chose, the Arnhem attack was to be made over a 60-mile carpet of airborne troops. Although I never reconciled myself to the venture, I nevertheless freely concede that Monty's plan for Arnhem was one of the most imaginative of the war."

Imagination, however, does not win a war. Creativity needs to be based in reality. Patton's plans were as ingenious as any, but what is distinctive about his plans is that they were bold and creative – and worked, with the fewest possible casualties. Under these harsh rules, Montgomery fails.

Bradley did vigorously oppose "Market Garden." He says that Eisenhower had made up his mind to go ahead with the operation before the plan ever reached him.

> "Monty does what he pleases and Ike says 'yes, sir.' Monty wants all supplies sent to him and the First U.S. Army and for me to hold. Brad thinks I can and should push on. Brad told Ike that if Monty takes control of the XIX and VII Corps of the First Army, as he wants to, he, Bradley, will ask to be relieved... Ike feels that we think he is selling us out but he has to, as Monty will not take orders, so we have to. Bradley said it is time for a showdown. I offered to resign with him, but he backed out." *Patton's Diary*

Bradley was willing to help Patton. Torn between his loyalty to Eisenhower and his loyalty to his country, Bradley decided on a compromise between both. While not directly disobeying Eisenhower nor expressing his disagreement with Eisenhower and Montgomery's union, Bradley quietly decided to help Patton by giving him a freer hand. Bradley would no longer call Eisenhower to clear Patton's plans, but casually slip away for a few hours. When Bradley was ordered to stop a plan, Patton would also "disappear" at the front.

What Bradley and Patton were doing may have been clandestine, but it was certainly not wrong. It is the natural consequence of poor leadership – when a poor leader always chooses what is wrong and harmful to the troops, commanders like Patton are forced to declare either loyalty to their leader or to their men. Patton wasn't disobeying, nor was he lying,[1] but he could not stand by while innocent men were slaughtered due to high-level incompetence.

---

[1] It has been reported that during the supply crisis he called Eisenhower's HQ many times but was entirely disregarded.

Chapter Twenty Seven

DOUBLE-CROSSED

The casualties from Montgomery's Operation Market Garden were higher than those from the assault on Normandy on D Day. The casualties during the 24 hour period of D Day were 10,000 to 12,000. Montgomery's Market Garden reaped a staggering 17,000 in killed, missing and wounded during the nine day venture behind enemy lines. Montgomery did not heed the warnings his Intelligence, and the Dutch underground, had given him. Montgomery chose to believe that the area would offer no resistance. In fact, the 2nd SS Panzer Corps was resting in that very area. The Allied soldiers had fought well, but they could not capture all the bridges that were required for the operation to be a success. After 13,226 of his British troops had died, Montgomery decided to pull out.

The Dutch civilians, euphoric at their "liberation" quickly cooperated as much as possible with the Allies. This was to have terrible consequences after the British withdrew. Many of the Dutch had lost their homes and froze to death that winter; others died from starvation. Some estimate that close to 10,000 Dutch citizens perished that winter due to Montgomery's mission. Bernhard, the Prince of the Netherlands at that time, told Cornelius Ryan that, "My country can never again afford the luxury of another Montgomery success."

Montgomery refused to learn any lessons from this tragedy and insisted that if he had *more*[1] "aircraft, ground forces, and administrative resources necessary for the job – it would have succeeded despite my mistakes, or the adverse weather, or the presence of the 2nd SS Panzer Corps in the Arnhem area." Montgomery's obstinacy blinded him to the truth: out numbering the enemy can *not* solve the basic problems he had outlined above.

It might be ridiculous to wonder why Montgomery was not relieved after this disaster. If Goodwood wasn't enough to relieve Monty, now Eisenhower had the chance of a lifetime. Montgomery had just terminated an operation that was the biggest Allied disaster – *ever*. Perhaps Montgomery was impregnable. Because even though Market Garden had cost the Allies 17,000 men, Montgomery was still an Army Group commander.

Consider this paradox: Patton is almost relieved several times because of press slip-ups,[2] yet Montgomery, a general who repeatedly "slipped-up" with tens of thousands of human lives, gets off with no reduction of power, no humiliating reversal-of-roles with a subordinate, no loss of armies, no "period of punishment" for a year to contemplate his future, not even bad press. To summarize, Montgomery, despite his complete inability to wage war, is considered the "war hero," revered by Eisenhower and the press alike. Montgomery received no punishment, not even a warning,[3] while Patton was constantly being ridiculed by his senior officers and losing corps. Such is justice.

Meanwhile, at Third Army headquarters, food, ammunition, clothes, and gas were in short supply. The hospitals were filled and the supply of personal-effects bags and mattress covers (in which the dead were buried) became so critical that a special convoy had to be sent all

---

[1] Didn't he have enough already? Montgomery had far, far more supplies, air cover, artillery, men (everything) than *any* other commander in the field, American or German. Why did he need 3 times the number of supplies, aircraft and ground forces that the enemy had? Isn't that a flaw in the basic strategy?

[2] He finally was relieved for this reason.

[3] Consider these excerpts from the letter Eisenhower sent Patton during the slapping incident which make more sense addressed to Montgomery. "I must seriously question your good judgment.... I clearly understand that firm and drastic measures are at times necessary in order to secure the desired objectives, but this does not excuse brutality."

the way back to the beaches to secure them! Com Z[1] was too busy supplying Montgomery.

Devers was boasting to Patton about the number of troops "he is going to take from me" in order to bolster his own 6th Army Group. Patton, nervous, flew to Paris in order to talk to Eisenhower. He felt reassured, "Ike hates him [Devers]." Devers and Patch then arrived, but Eisenhower told them to wait. Then he had a meeting "but the question of stealing troops from Third Army did not come up... One has to fight one's friends more than the enemy."

Patton then wrote in his diary about his private meeting with Eisenhower. "Ike still insists, for the present at least, [that] the main effort should be thrown to the British and the north flank of the First Army. However, he was more peevish with Montgomery than I have ever seen him. In fact, he called him a clever S.O.B., which was very encouraging."

Eisenhower called a meeting and informed Bradley that there would be no major offensive operations by Americans until the port of Antwerp was cleared. Eisenhower also told Bradley that 21st Army Group was launching an offensive across the lower Rhine.

> "Bradley was feeling very low because Montgomery has again put it over on Ike and demands the assistance of the First Army to push into the Ruhr. To do this, I will have to send an armored division and also assume a defensive attitude due to lack of adequate supplies. Also, Devers told Eisenhower that since he could easily supply the XV Corps via Dijon it should go to him. Going on the defense and having our limited supplies cut still more is very discouraging. Bradley and I are depressed. We would like to go to China and serve under Admiral Nimitz." *Patton's Diary*

Bradley phoned Patton with the disastrous news that Eisenhower was contemplating giving Devers the XV Corps permanently. Patton wrote one of his most tragic and revealing diary entries after hearing the news.

---

[1] Communications Zone

"I am not usually inclined to grumble or to think that the cards are stacked against me, but sometimes I wish that someone would get committed to do something for me. However, all my disappointments have turned out for the best. I wanted to command in Italy and that turned out badly. I wanted to command the assault on the beaches here. It was also quite a failure. I felt, and with reason, that when the XIX and VII Corps of the First Army turned north, I should have got the V Corps, which was paralleling my left. I didn't get it, and [V Corps'] attack also soured. I should have more faith. If Jake Devers gets the XV Corps, I hope his plan turns sour. The Lord is on my side, but he has a lot of getting even to do for me."

Once again, Third Army would be stripped of its lifeblood and forced onto the defensive while the lesser armies tried hopeless attempts at advancing. Montgomery could, perhaps, be proud that he managed again and again to strip Patton of supplies and men, but one thing is for sure: Montgomery could not be proud of advances, bought at the steep price of high casualties and American supplies. Patton, alone and forgotten in the murky weather of Metz, wrote, "At the moment I am being attacked on both flanks, but not by the Germans. But I may yet make my getaway."

Chapter Twenty Eight

ALONE

Patton had a press conference on September 23rd. It is interesting to see how well Patton covered his disappointment about the devastating lack of supplies. A newspaperman asked Patton, "Are you getting your share of the supply situation?"
Patton replied, "Yes, but unfortunately we cannot make five barley loaves and three small fishes expand as they used to."

At this time, due to the Third Army's relentless attacks, sixty four German Corps decided to surrender. Once again the glory would be stolen unjustly from the Third Army. Suddenly the zone where the surrendering German corps were located was transferred to Ninth Army. Even though the Ninth Army had never been involved in any fighting, it now collected over 20,000 Germans – and their Lugers. To Third Army, the loss of the preciously needed equipment was even more disastrous than the prisoner bag. Why had Third Army's VIII Corps been mysteriously transferred at so strange a time?

Eisenhower officially ordered the Third Army onto the defensive. He ordered VIII Corps transferred to Ninth Army and XV Corps to Seventh Army. Ninth had just become operational and VIII Corps was its only unit.[1]

---

[1] Now Third Army only had *two* corps, XII and XX.

Patton drove to the front and met with his three corps commanders to arrange for their new defensive role. He informed Haislip that he, and his XV Corps, were being transferred to Devers' command. Haislip told Patton that he was "very depressed" about leaving. Patton replied that he was "equally depressed" about losing him.

Though the Third Army deeply resented VIII Corps' sudden transfer and Ninth Army collecting the 64 German corps, there was a hilarious compensation at the surrender ceremony. Lieutenant General Simpson, commanding general of Ninth Army, and many other high American brass were attending the corps surrender. As part of the ceremony, German General Elster made a speech. When Elster concluded Simpson asked the interpreter rather smugly what he had said. The interpreter fidgeted, then hemmed and hawed.
"Well, what did he say?" the generals demanded. "Couldn't you understand him?"
"Yes, Sir," replied the interpreter. "I understood him all right. He said he wanted to make it quite clear that he was surrendering to the Third U.S. Army."

Clearly, despite all Eisenhower did to stop Third Army, the Germans still respected the only army capable of forcing them to surrender. Third Army was still enduring supply shortages that would make any conscientious commander shutter.

Meanwhile at his headquarters, Patton told his remaining two corps commanders that they were to make "limited attacks" so that the Germans would not know of the Third's new defensive posture. There would be no barbed wire strung and no mining of the army's frontier. They had no intention of sitting around there forever. What he told them to do, however, has an interesting strategic significance; they were to make small outposts which could be easily assisted by Patton's powerful tanks in case of a German attack. Artillery was placed wherever it seemed probable that German tanks would strike. The men in Weyland's air force would be ready at a moment's notice to fly in and strafe enemy soldiers. This is the essence of blitzkrieg: constant mobility at a moment's notice; and contrary to the revisionist theory, here Patton was exercising it under defense.

Patton also told his commanders that if they made even a limited breakthrough, they were to exploit it as far as possible. Patton was making the best of a bad situation. "My plan for taking the defense is to...

rectify the line, thereby maintaining the offensive spirit in the troops so that when we will attack, we will not be pacifists."

An amusing episode happened when Patton was revisiting his WWI battlegrounds.

> "The first man I saw in the street there [in Bourg] was standing on the same manure pile which he undoubtedly stood on in 1918. I asked him if he had been there in the last war, and he replied, "Yes, General Patton, you were then here as a Colonel." He offered to show me around the town, which I really didn't need, but nevertheless I permitted him to do this."

On September 27th nine generals called, "it was a big day for visiting firemen." Patton made comments on the other men in his diary, "Spaatz is all for the Third Army. I have the air force in my pocket. As usual, Lee [commander of Com Z] is a glib liar."

Bradley called to inform Patton that Devers was going to take the XV Corps officially. "May God rot his guts. I feel very low, must trust in God and my destiny." Patton visited the front in an effort to feel better. He was very upset about only having two corps, and he avidly punished two officers who were speeding. "Devers is a liar and, by his glibness, talked Eisenhower into giving him the Corps."

It had been a costly advance by Patton's standards. The constant need to halt and wait for supplies had cost lives. But this month had been costlier for the Germans who had committed two supply divisions to Patton's sector. These divisions were composed of cooks, bakers, butchers, administrative officials, clerks and other non-combatant personnel.

The Rhine was only 100 miles away. It could have been a world away. The flow of supplies had dried up. Though Patton ordered several corps to attack as best they could, there was little hope of breakthrough.

Chapter Twenty Nine

BEHIND THE LINES

The Battle of the Bulge is often described as "Hitler's last desperate gamble" or "the last straw at which Hitler grasped;" the battle is depicted as the sort of death-spasm an evil empire like the Third Reich was likely to go through.

These characterizations of the Battle of the Bulge are wrong. The German offensive in the Ardennes was a carefully planned and conceived military maneuver aimed at stopping the Allies by denying them their supply ports, and giving the Germans time to stabilize the Eastern front and sue for peace.

It is important to realize what the Germans were doing at this time so as to have a complete picture. Now we move from an examination of Patton and his Third Army in these dark days when they were halted, to a closer inspection of what was actually transpiring behind Third Army lines.

According to Major General Friederich Wilhelm von Mellethein, the Chief of Staff of General Balck, "…the spearheads of Patton's Third Army were already probing eastward toward the frontiers of the Reich. In September, General Balck received a summons to report at Hitler's headquarters; he was to be appointed to the command of Army Group G in the west, and I was to accompany him as Chief of Staff."

Hitler confided to Balck one of his two greatest secrets of the war.[1] Hitler told Balck that, "The Anglo-American advance is bound to come to a halt on a line running from the mouth of the Scheldt along the West Wall to Metz, and from there to the Vosges due to supply difficulties. I will take advantage of this pause to launch a counter-offensive in Belgium."

Two days before, on September 16th, 1944, Hitler had announced to his military advisers that he was going to "inflict upon the Western Allies a crushing defeat that would influence the outcome of the war." Even on September 6th, 1944 the Sixth Panzer Army had received orders to be reconstituted. This army would become the backbone of the Ardennes offensive.

Hitler's plan was simple. As Ladislas Farago put it,

"He had little fear that Montgomery in the north would break into the area where he planned to assemble his forces for the offensive. On the other hand, he was apprehensive that Patton might, in spite of his supply difficulties, overrun the area centering on Trier." *"Ordeal and Triumph," by Ladislas Farago p. 641*

Hitler informed Balck that November was a likely date for this operation. Von Mellentheim wrote that Hitler then gave Balck his "formal orders."

"'You are to hold Alsace-Lorraine under all circumstances. You have to fight for time. On no account must you allow a situation to develop in which my forces earmarked for the Ardennes offensive would have to be sidetracked to Army Group C.'" *"Ordeal and Triumph," by Ladislas Farago*

Balck had been hand picked by Hitler for this task, and he arrived at his headquarters emboldened. He ordered his first spoiling attack against Chateau-Salins. Patton could have easily taken this during August ... but such was Patton's lot.

---

[1] Hitler's other greatest secret was his surprise attack on the Soviet Union in October, 1940.

Balck also decided that success would hinge upon halting Patton's XII Corps and blowing the American bridges over the Moselle. He sent his First Army and Fifth Panzer Army to begin attacking Patton's 4th Armored. The Germans began attacking on the foggy morning of September 22nd. Wood, the commander of 4th Armored, had not expected the attack – he had told his men to take the day off. Wood quickly retaliated, however, and inflicted such heavy casualties that the 111th Panzer Brigade was left with only 7 tanks and 80 men by the end of that day.

It was a bad beginning for Balck, but hardly an unusual one for the opponents of Patton's army. The battle continued until the 29th when Balck was forced to call it off. Balck went to von Rundstedt and did precisely what Hitler told him not to do – he asked for three more divisions. Von Rundstedt had none to spare.

Balck was satisfied. He thought that *he,* personally, had stopped Patton from crossing the Saar, and possibly even the Rhine. Balck's chief of staff remarked after the war that Patton "might well have [reached the Rhine] if he had been given a free hand."[1] At the time, however, the problem appeared to Balck to be "bad and timid leadership on the part of the Americans…" Little did he know that Patton was being forced onto the defensive by a direct order from Eisenhower, with less supplies than the Germans.

General Von Mellentheim, Balck's chief of staff, wrote a postwar account, and made some keen observations with his unique knowledge of Balck's secret mission and his recently acquired knowledge of Patton's enforced halt.

> "We now know that Patton was compelled to halt by Eisenhower's orders of September 22nd. The Supreme Allied Commander had decided to accept Montgomery's proposal to make the main effort on the northern flank, clear the approaches to Antwerp, and try to capture the Ruhr before winter. Third U.S. Army received categorical orders to stand on the defensive. The rights and wrongs of this strategy do not concern me, but it certainly simplified the problems of Army Group G.[2] We

---

[1] By Allied higher authority.
[2] The group of German armies commanded by Balck and opposing Patton.

were given a few weeks' grace to rebuild our battered forces and get ready to meet the next onslaught."

These weeks were a precious grace to the Germans in which they built up their forces for the Ardennes. They were training their best Panzer forces right in front of Patton's army – forced to remain on the defensive by Eisenhower's orders.

Chapter Thirty

GUERILLA ARMY

At the end of September Eisenhower visited Third Army – for the first time. Third Army's strength was down to 224,785 men. Its proper strength was 346,208. The shortage of men was due mostly to the recent transfer of the two Third Army corps to other armies. Third Army's losses were 2,130 killed, 12,307 wounded, 4,100 missing. Despite the Third Army's appalling supply shortages, enemy losses were still higher at 94,100 captured, 32,000 killed and 96,500 wounded.

SHAEF restrictions permitted only limited objective attacks to improve *local* positions. And to insure that its orders were obeyed all sorts of supplies merely trickled in. Third Army was living hand to mouth. At one point the Army ran completely out of diesel oil, even though it had sent repeated emergency requests. Finally G-4[1] managed to obtain 10,000 gallons from Seventh Army in an exchange for some things they wanted.

The Third Army was so low on ammunition it resorted to using captured guns and shells. Apparently the enemy had had similar supply problems, for Third Army now had to learn to use captured *Russian 76.2mm* as well as German Schneider 155mm howitzers. It is truly

---

[1] Supply

incredible how desperate the supply situation at Patton's army had become.[1]

Few people realize that the Third Army was not only short of gas and ammunition. In fact there was such a shortage of raincoats, boots, jackets, winter clothes, and sleeping bags that troops developed serious sicknesses. Trench foot and respiratory ailments became so serious that emergency measures were resorted to.

Eisenhower's halt order to Third Army had severe consequences. Montgomery had always claimed that it was Patton's advance in the south that made his army unable to advance. But now Third Army was, by Eisenhower's direct orders, stopped dead in its tracks. Montgomery, however, was finding advance even more difficult than before. Little had he realized that Patton's advance had been constantly threatening the German southern flank, forcing them to withdraw in the north or face envelopment. With the Third Army halted, the Germans could entrench before Montgomery without fear of being captured from the rear.[2]

The Germans were now able to reinforce their northern front, which had always been the best organized and of the greatest strength.[3] The Germans stopped withdrawing and began to defend aggressively, quickly causing Montgomery's offensive to peter out; by October 1st the fighting was contained on the Maas and Waal rivers.

There were bad signs in Patton's sector too. The Germans never paused, and while Third Army was forced to halt, they quickly reinforced the Siegfried line directly in front of the Third Army's line of advance. This area of the Siegfried line had always been the most formidable – and now that line was manned.

Patton, anxiously observing the halt which SHAEF had foisted upon him, watched helplessly as the Germans organized, brought in reserves, reinforced, and re-manned their positions. He could not let them dig in or he would face months of static murder war. So he began his "aggressive defense." He needed to keep the enemy unbalanced and

---

[1] Details and figures are taken from "Lucky Forward" by Colonel Robert S. Allen.

[2] As Patton had done at Falaise-Argentan and would do (in smaller scale) again at the Hunsruck Mountains.

[3] It was only well organized and prepared because Montgomery had never advanced.

disorganized, and most important of all, he needed to find an area worthy of resuming the offensive from. Thanks to Eisenhower, he would now have to force the line of the Moselle.

At Metz, the war had degenerated into static house-to-house fighting. Elite SS divisions had been moved in, and they would not surrender until point blank artillery fire blasted them out. After ten days of bitter fighting, half the town was occupied. But costly fighting continued until the end of the month before "Mazie"[1] was cleared.

Fighting was slow and costly. By the end of the month the four divisions[2] had hacked out 5 to 12 miles east of the Moselle. The Third's casualty toll for October was nearly ¼ that of the sweep through France. In those seven meteoric weeks, over 40,000 square miles were liberated. Casualties were 4,575 killed, 23,794 wounded and 6,156 missing. In the 4 weeks of crippling Metz-Moselle fighting, only 125 square miles were cleared with a loss of 1,279 killed, 6,116 wounded, and 822 missing.[3] This was all because when this crucial sector was unoccupied, Third Army had been halted.

Still, German losses were still far higher than Third Army's at 8,481 captured, 9,510 killed and 20,100 wounded.

When Simpson, tall, long-faced and bald visited Lucky, Patton mischievously introduced him to his staff. "Gentleman, this is General Simpson. When he isn't commanding Ninth Army, he acts as an advertisement for hair tonic." Simpson, startled but good-natured according to one observer, joined in the laugh.

At a meeting on October 10th in Verdun Bradley announced the new plan. In the wake of Montgomery's failure in the north, they would revert to their old plan: all the armies all along the Western Front would continue driving into Germany. The main efforts would be by Montgomery against the Ruhr and, due to Bradley's decision, by Patton in the Saar. Patton could not advance until Montgomery's operation got under way, the date for which was fixed as October 23rd.

At last Patton and his invincible Third Army would be allowed a chance to advance.

---

[1] The Americans' affectionate name for Metz.
[2] 35th and 80th Infantry, 4th and 6th Armored
[3] Figures from "Lucky Forward" by Colonel Robert S. Allen.

Chapter Thirty One

PREJUDICED?

Patton is so often accused of prejudice that I feel compelled to devote a chapter to the subject.

In WWII blacks in the army were segregated. They were made to perform all the lowly tasks – cooking, cleaning, driving and emptying supply trucks – and most were not officially allowed to fight.

In October 1944 Patton was in the middle of the desperate supply crisis. Third Army was out of gas, food, clothing, ammunition and in terrible need of replacements. It was at this time that Patton heard of a tank battalion waiting in the rear – strangely unused and uncommitted. This was the 761st Tank Battalion. It was waiting in the wings because its tankers were black – and therefore unacceptable to the other generals. Patton could not believe that while such desperate conditions existed in the Allied ranks, perfectly healthy men were unoccupied merely because of color. He therefore eagerly snatched up the division – the one scrap that SHAEF was willing to throw in his direction.

When the tankers arrived in France ready for service, Patton went to deliver one of his famous fighting speeches. Undoubtedly sensing what these men had been through, he modified it slightly to suit their own unique position. John Long of the 761st Tank Battalion recounts,

"[Patton] told us, 'Men, you are the first Negro tankers ever to fight in the American army. I would never have asked for you if you were not good. I have nothing but the best in my army. I don't care what color you are as long as you go up there and kill those Kraut S.O.B's. Everyone has their eyes on you and are expecting great things from you. Most of all your race is looking forward to your success. Don't let them down, and don't let me down! If you want me, you can always find me in the lead tank. They say it is patriotic to die for your country, well, let's see how many patriots we can make out of the Germans." *"The Invisible Soldier, the experience of the Black Soldier in WWII," compiled and edited by Mary P. Motley. Wayne State University Press, © 1975.*

The men were honored to be fighting for Third Army – Patton undoubtedly made them feel that it was a privilege reserved only for the best. He did not let on that these men were considered "unworthy" of the other armies and that Third Army itself was in such desperate straits it was willing to try anything. According to Horace Evans, another black tanker who attended the speech,

"Patton let us know that he had asked for us. He said he sent a message asking for more tankers. The answer was the best tank unit they had was black; the general only took the best. He replied, 'Who the heck asked for color, I asked for tankers!'"

This was an incredible statement coming from a well-to-do American in the 1940s. Segregation in the military had been introduced only relatively recently, but prejudice – especially among the upper classes – was rampant and unhidden. It has been insinuated by all of Patton's biographers that he also had this prejudice – that he was simply grasping at straws when he heard that the 761st was available.

This explanation may seem plausible – except that Patton did not have to honor these outcast men by speaking to them when they first arrived. More than that, he *actually stated* that he "didn't care what color they were" so long as they could fight. Patton genuinely loved and cared for his men – and these black tankers were no exception.

Patton had never been prejudiced. Several years before WWII, when Patton had been stationed at Fort Riley, Kansas, the white trash of nearby Junction City's honky-tonk row threatened to lynch one of Patton's black non-coms. Patton ordered a squad of cavalry to mount, borrowed a cannon, and moved against the row, warning that he would level the area unless his man was released – which they promptly did.

If Patton initially had reservations about the 761st, they stemmed more from the fact that the worst white officers were chosen to lead the black battalions.

Patton did not tolerate bad officers, though, and he quickly sacked the incompetents. The 761st went on to distinguish itself. It was common practice at the time to allow black companies to fight for towns but then, right after the enemy was defeated, send a white company in to take the area. This was done so that black companies would not receive headlines. Patton broke from this cruel tradition, however, and allowed the battalion to take what it had captured. This raised its morale and made its men revere Patton. It also allowed to battalion, and its men, to earn an incredible reputation.

Their reputation became so good, in fact, that the 761st Battalion was taken from Patton some months later! His men were always coveted – even when they were black in a prejudiced era.

Another honor often denied blacks were medals. In this, like in everything else, Patton was different. Colonel Ivan Harrison (at the time a 1st lieutenant at Patton's HQ) said that,

> "General Patton believed in rewarding outstanding work on the spot. He carried medals along with him and he pinned them on when earned, *regardless of race*. To cite an instance, a Sergeant Johnson of the 761st, who was later killed, fired one round into a German bunker on orders from General Miley. Everyone was sure he had missed it. Johnson assured the general that the one round had gone into the bunker. He was proven to be correct, and the general, following the lead set by Patton, pinned the Bronze star on his dirty uniform right there."

When Third Army was in dire straits and in desperate need of replacements, Patton ordered many rear-echelon people trained as infantry men. This included black men who were then integrated into the ordinary ranks in violation of the current regulations.

Sergeant Floyd Jones was in the black 578th Field Artillery Battalion and was with Patton at Metz. Jones remembered his experience in the Third Army fondly, "We enjoyed being with Patton because of his well-known vocabulary and remarks that were passed right down the line. Patton kept his superiors uptight: they never knew for sure where he was, excepting beyond where he should be." Patton, just like the blacks who served under him, was successful on the battlefield but strangely unpopular with superiors.

These black soldiers express the same opinions as the other rank-and-file in Third Army – and this is the more remarkable because they *were* black. The 578th Artillery Battalion was reattached to Third Army during the Battle of the Bulge and Jones remarks of the battle, "The skies began to clear, and old 'Blood and Guts' arrived. And in his division, I say with pride, was the crack black battalion, the 761st." Horace Evans, expressing the same pride and loyalty as his white compatriots, said, "That Patton was something else. When he got a message asking him if he had crossed the Rhine, he sent the reply, 'Have crossed the Rhine and I pissed in it.'"

The black soldiers of WWII liked Patton so well that during the supply crisis in the fall of 1944 some of them were willing to "steal" gas for him by deliberately misguiding the supply trucks to Third Army depots. Their willingness to take risks for him shows their love and admiration.

Patton clearly did not treat the blacks in his army any differently than the whites. This was in itself special treatment because Patton pampered his men. This is why Third Army men would boast "I was with Patton." It was indeed an honor, an honor that the blacks of the 761st had been lucky enough to receive.

While the 969th Field Artillery was in England, Patton paid a visit. Sergeant Jesse Cumings' memories best sum up those of his fellow black soldiers that served in Third Army,

> "General Patton visited our unit. He told us some of us could get killed, but that was war. He added that we would be better under him, and we were most of the time. This in itself was a compliment to our ability, because it was generally known that Patton would not

accept anything but the best in his command. General Patton was admired by the average dog-face simply because he was always where the fighting was, right in the middle of the fracas. He wasn't a behind-the-lines general with some maps on a wall. I must say that he kept us busy shifting us wherever we were needed. We were so occupied that it was a year before I got a pass and the war was coming to an end. The Germans dubbed the 969th the 'schwartz with automatic weapons.'"

These black soldiers not only show that Patton was unprejudiced but also go far to prove how great a general he was and how highly he was held among the ranks. "He wasn't a behind-the-lines general" is fine praise and these mistreated black soldiers are the best witnesses.

Chapter Thirty Two

PRAYER FOR GOOD WEATHER

Averell Harriman, the American ambassador to Russia, came to visit the Third Army. Harriman told Patton that when he was in Moscow, Stalin had said in the presence of the Chief of Staff of the Red Army that, "The Red Army could not have conceived and certainly could not have executed the advance of the Third Army across France." These were very high words of praise especially because they were uttered by Stalin, a man not in the habit of commending foreign triumphs. In fact, Patton and the feats of his Third Army seem to have been highly complimented by everyone except Eisenhower and Montgomery. This, far from being a discredit to Patton, is actually a measure of Eisenhower's and Montgomery's worth.

Harriman also confirmed Patton's worst fears about the danger of allowing the Allied armies to slow down while the Russians continued to advance. "Stalin," said Harriman, "is a strong, ruthless revolutionist and therefore a very potential threat to future world conditions." Harriman told Patton that the discipline in the Red Army was more rigid and ruthless than any he had ever seen – far worse than the blind obedience which was being exercised by the Germans. The Russian soldiers would fear not only for their life, but the lives of their families, if they dared to dream of disobeying. Thus the officer caste had become a new nobility. "This is a strange result of communism," Patton commented.

Third Army shortages were up to 9,000 men and there were no replacements in sight. "I cannot see why Eisenhower could be caught short on both men *and* ammunition, because after all, these are the two elements with which wars are fought." Patton decided to withdraw 5% of his headquarters personnel and make infantrymen out of them. He only wished Eisenhower would do the same.

Meanwhile both XII and XX Corps had crossed the Saar River. Ordinarily the Saar was 50 feet wide, but due to the incredible amount of rain it had flooded its banks and was 300 feet wide. He sent his men across even though the river was flooded, because he needed his army to keep moving and break through the Siegfried line. Patton wrote to his daughter, "If we get through, we will materially shorten the war – there is no *if* about getting through; I am sure we will!"

The weather had been terrible. For over two months unseasonably bad torrential rains had poured on the soldiers. The number of men who could not fight due to trench foot and sicknesses was as high as those wounded from enemy fire. Patton's army had 40% shortages in every rifle company.

Even so, the forts around Metz were surrendering. The Germans too were cold, wet and tired and were giving up because, as Patton put it, they had a "lack of salt, lack of water, and lack of guts."

Patton instructed his men that their main objective was to capture the Germans and continue through the Siegfried line. "There is no purpose in capturing these manure-filled, water logged villages," he told them. He prohibited them from making frontal assaults on towns and instructed them to keep attacking the Germans.

The rain was still falling incessantly. On the morning of December 8th Patton called the Third Army Chaplain. "This is General Patton," he said, "do you have a prayer for good weather? We must do something about these rains if we are to win this war." Monsignor O'Neill replied that he knew where to find a prayer for good weather and that he would report to Patton's headquarters within an hour. The Monsignor hung up the phone and looked out of his window; the rain was still falling steadily – as it had been for months. He then looked for the prayer that Patton had requested, but could find nothing that would prove acceptable.

"Keeping his immediate objective in mind, I typed an original and an improved copy on a 5" x 3" filing card:

'Almighty and most merciful Father, we humbly beseech Thee, of Thy great goodness, to restrain these immoderate rains with which we have had to contend. Grant us fair weather for Battle. Graciously hearken to us as soldiers who call Thee that, armed with Thy power, we may advance from victory to victory, and crush the oppression and wickedness of our enemies, and establish Thy justice among men and nations. Amen.'

I pondered the question, what use would General Patton make of the prayer? Surely it was not for private devotion. If he intended it for circulation to chaplains or others, with Christmas not far removed, it might be proper to type the Army Commander's Christmas Greetings on the reverse side. This would please the recipient, and anything that pleased the men I knew would please him. 'To each officer and soldier in the Third United States Army, I wish a Merry Christmas. I have full confidence in your courage, devotion to duty, and skill in battle. We march in our might to complete victory. May God's blessings rest upon each of you on this Christmas Day. G.S. Patton, Jr., Lieutenant General, Commanding, Third United States Army.'"[1]

Task completed, Monsignor O'Neill put on his heavy trench coat and stepped out into the rain, on his way to report to General Patton. Patton read the prayer and handed it back to O'Neill. "Have 250,000 copies printed and see to it every man in the Third Army gets one." O'Neill was stunned for a moment, until realizing that the weather was very bad and this was Patton's way of doing something about it. Recovering a bit O'Neill showed Patton the Christmas Greeting he had written on the back of the prayer card. "Very good," Patton said, with a smile of approval.

After signing it, Patton invited the Chaplain to sit down.

"He then rose and walked over to the high window, and stood there with his back toward me as he looked out on the falling rain. As usual, he was dressed stunningly, and

---

[1] The story of the good weather prayer was retold by Chaplain O'Neill. Taken from "The Review of The News: October 6, 1971." This article appeared as a government document in 1950.

his six-foot-two powerfully built physique made an unforgettable silhouette against the great window. The General Patton I saw there was the Army Commander to whom the welfare of the men under him was a matter of personal responsibility. Even in the heat of combat he could take time out to direct new methods to prevent trench feet, to see to it that dry socks went forward daily with the rations to help troops on the line, to kneel in the mud administering morphine and caring for a wounded soldier until the ambulance came. What was coming now?"

"Chaplain," asked Patton, "how much praying is being done in the Third Army?"
"Does the General mean by chaplains, or by the men?"
"By everybody," he replied.
The chaplain hesitated a moment, before replying, "I am afraid to admit it, but I do not believe that much praying is going on. When there is fighting, everyone prays, but now with this constant rain – when things are quiet, dangerously quiet, men just sit and wait for things to happen. Prayer out here is difficult. Both chaplains and men are removed from a special building with a steeple. Prayer to most of them is a formal, ritualized affair, involving special posture and a liturgical setting. I do not believe that much praying is being done."

Patton left the window, and sat again at the desk, contemplating the problem. According to the chaplain, he "leaned back in his swivel chair, toying with a long lead pencil between his index fingers."
"Chaplain, I am a strong believer in prayer. There are three ways that men get what they want; by planning, by working, and by praying. And any great military operation takes careful planning, or thinking. Then you must have well-trained troops to carry it out: that's working. But between the plan and the operation there is always an unknown. That unknown spells defeat or victory, success or failure. It is the reaction of the actors to the ordeal when it actually comes. Some people call that getting the breaks; I call it God. God has His part, or margin in everything. That's where prayer comes in. Up to now, in the Third Army, God has been very good to us. We have never retreated; we have suffered no defeats, no famine, no epidemics. This is because a lot of people back home are praying for us. We were lucky in Africa, in Sicily, and in Italy, simply because people prayed. But we have to pray for ourselves, too. A good soldier is not made merely by making him think and work. There is

something in every soldier that goes deeper than thinking or working –
it's his 'guts.' It is something that he has built in there: it is a world of
truth and power that is higher than himself. Great living is not all output
of thought and work. A man has to have intake as well. I don't know
what you call it, but I call it Religion, Prayer, or God."

As the Chaplain later recalled, Patton,

"talked about Gideon in the Bible, said that men should
pray no matter where they were, in church or out of it:
that if they did not pray, sooner or later they would
'crack up.' To all this I commented agreement; that one
of the major training objectives of my office was to help
soldiers recover and make their lives effective in this
third realm, prayer. It would do no harm to reimpress
this training on chaplains... [Patton agreed, saying] 'I
wish you would put out a Training Letter on this subject
of Prayer to all the chaplains; write about nothing else,
just the importance of prayer. Let me see it before you
send it. We've got to get not only the chaplains but every
man in the Third Army to pray. We must ask God to
stop these rains. These rains are that margin that holds
defeat or victory. If we all pray, it will be like what Dr.
Carrel said [Patton was alluding to an article where Dr.
Alexis Carrel, a foremost scientist of the time, described
prayer "as one of the most powerful forms of energy
man can generate"], it will be like plugging in on a
current whose source is in Heaven. I believe that prayer
completes that circuit. It is power.'"

Chaplain O'Neill returned to his desk and wrote "Training Letter
No. 5" about the importance of prayer. The Chaplain expected the letter
to be circulated merely to the 486 Third Army chaplains, and he was
mildly surprised when Patton ordered it sent to not only the chaplains,
but every organization commander down to and including the regimental
level. Three thousand two hundred copies were distributed to every unit
in the Third Army. The letter was sent out on December 11th and 12th,
only a few days before the start of the Battle of the Bulge – by which
time good weather would be desperately needed.[1]

---

[1] The good weather which came during the Ardennes Offensive turned the tide
of battle in the Americans favor. When the fog lifted, the Americans' were able
to use their massive air superiority. In January Patton thanked the chaplain for

Foreshadowings of the great German offensive loomed darkly over the scene. On December 12th, a German prisoner of war was interrogated by First Army.[1] The prisoner revealed that the elite *Grossdeutschland*[2] division had moved into the area. This area was generally regarded as a "quiet" sector. The next day, the Intelligence interrogators picked up another movement; the 116th Panzer division from Simpson's front into the Eifel. On the 14th a German informant came with information for Middleton.[3] "The Germans have taken bridging equipment from their other fronts to their Luxembourg front on the Our," the man hastily explained. First Army attached a comment to their report of these incidents that states, "A very interesting report. Build-up of troops has been confirmed by [air] and POW statements. Presence of large numbers of engineers with bridging equipment suggest preparation for offensive rather than defensive action." Yet all these warnings went unheeded.

Several weeks *before* these intelligence reports were received, Patton made one of his most incredible predictions. Grounded only in his unique grasp of the military situation and his stunning intuition, Patton wrote that, "the First Army is making a terrible mistake in leaving the VIII Corps static, as it is highly probable that the Germans are building up east of them."

It was the VIII Corps upon which, in only a few hours, the great German Ardennes offensive would be launched! How could Bradley, Hodges, Middleton and, for that matter, Eisenhower and his chiefs,[4] have been so stupid?

From Eisenhower down, almost everyone had caught the "victory syndrome." They had convinced themselves that the enemy was beaten and thoroughly incapable of any action besides retreating. Because of their overwhelming belief that the Germans were harmless,

---

the good weather prayer. Patton said to him, "Well, Padre, our prayers worked. I knew they would." According to O'Neill, he "then cracked me on the side of my steel helmet with his riding crop. That was his way of saying, 'Well done.'"

[1] First Army was commanded by Hodges. It was in his area that the Battle of the Bulge started.

[2] "Great Germany"

[3] The commander of VIII Corps, the corps that was in the very area where the Bulge started.

[4] Who also received reports of build-up.

they let down their guard.[1] Patton always held the belief that he would win – but he also knew that the enemy would put up a fight and thus always prepared for it. In the Battle of the Bulge, Patton made the oft-quoted remark, "We can still lose this war." Because Patton felt that way, he tried his hardest to win it. A casual attitude is the worst possible one for generals and troops alike.

---

[1] This also partially explains why Eisenhower backed Montgomery's plans. He did not feel that he must back the best plan or lose; nor did he feel the incessant ticking of the clock that most generals are forced (by the enemy) to hear.

Chapter Thirty Three

SURPRISE IN THE ARDENNES

It was December 15th. The victory bug was alive and well, but there was only one day of quiet left. Bradley's intelligence officer had cheerfully announced that, "It is now certain that attrition is steadily sapping the strength of German forces on the Western front." Eisenhower's intelligence followed up with a report confirming Bradley's information. Montgomery stated that day that the Germans "*cannot* stage major offensive operations. The enemy is in a bad way." Bradley and Eisenhower were wrong, and Montgomery was more wrong.

Under their very unsuspecting noses were almost 600,000 Germans. Two gigantic Panzer armies had gathered quietly in the Ardennes, awaiting instructions to attack. Montgomery flew over to Eindhoven for a round of golf with the golf pro, Dai Rees. He was interrupted in his game with news from the front and was forced to return to his HQ.

The morning of December 16th Eisenhower, Bedell Smith, and the rest of Eisenhower's staff, attended the wedding of Eisenhower's valet at Louis XIV's chapel at Versailles. This was the first wedding at the palace since the 18th century. The reception was held at Eisenhower's house in Saint-Germain. While Eisenhower and the other SHAEF dignitaries were drinking champagne and partying, green American soldiers were dying in the Ardennes forest.

It was that afternoon when Patton received a telephone call from Bradley at 12th Army Group, his headquarters. Bradley told Patton that he needed Patton's XX Corps[1] to help out his VIII Corps,[2] who were repulsing a "rather strong German attack."

Patton vigorously protested.[3] "We have paid a very high price in blood in the hope of a break though at Saarlautern and Saarbrucken."

Patton needed the armored division to exploit a possible breakthrough. Bradley, Patton says, "admitted my logic but took counsel of his fears and ordered the move. I wish he were less timid."

However, Patton must have rethought his last sentences, for he then added, "He probably knows more of the situation than he can say over the telephone."

These were Patton's forewarnings of the Battle of the Bulge, which had already officially started. In accordance with Hitler's wishes, 25 divisions were assembled in the Ardennes forests. Twenty of these divisions were committed to the attack along a 60 mile front between Monschau and Echternach. The German plan was to echo their first attack against France by a surprise attack in the difficult Ardennes terrain. They then hoped to roll straight across the Meuse and take Antwerp,[4] the port that supplied the Allied armies. By doing this, they would cut the Allied armies in two and slow the advance into Germany, thereby giving Hitler time to negotiate with the Allies.

The German generals knew that the plan was ridiculous. The generals told Hitler that the Allies would cut their attack off from its base and supplies and leave their armies stranded, surrounded by enemy armies.[5] Besides, they protested, the enemy's overwhelming air superiority would make their attack a bloodbath.

---

[1] Commanded by Walker.

[2] VIII Corps was part of Hodges' First Army and was commanded by Middleton.

[3] Eisenhower had had a conversation with Bradley authorizing him to take two armored divisions from Patton. When Bradley told Ike that Patton would be upset, Eisenhower responded, "You tell him that Ike is running this d- war!" He certainly was, and he was running it right into its biggest disaster yet!

[4] Antwerp was almost 100 miles away from the Ardennes.

[5] Although Patton suggested this plan, Eisenhower never seriously considered it. Hitler probably did not underestimate the stupidity of the American high command, but armies should never attempt to use the same plan (in the same place) twice. The enemy just might get smarter.

248

Hitler, however, had thought of that. They would not start the attack until a week of fog was predicted. This would insure that American planes would be unable to see the German troops below, who could then advance unstrafed by the air.[1] The fog would make American air superiority useless. It happened that on December 16th, a week of fog was in the forecast.

The next evening Patton went to visit his Generals Eddy and Haislip. Patton told his generals that he believed Bradley would have trouble warding off the German attack. "One of the attacks is a feint,"[2] Patton said, "and the other is the real thing. If they attack us, I'm ready for them, but I'm inclined to think the party[3] will be up north. Eighth Corps has been sitting still – a sure invitation to trouble." Third Army still did not know that what was to be the "Battle of the Bulge" had already started in the north. But they certainly were guessing at the cause of the sudden movement of troops and the "small attack" that had been launched against Bradley's VIII Corps. And no one guessed more correctly than Patton.

General Bradley had been very foolish. He writes in his book that he could see no reason nor probable objective that could stem from an attack in the Ardennes, and he had accordingly lightly defended it. He had kept VIII Corps "static:" unmoving and untrained in the very area that the Germans had surprise attacked in their first conquest of France!

Bradley called and told Patton to meet him in Verdun at 11am. Bradley also told Patton that, "I understand from General Eisenhower that you are to take over VIII Corps as well as the offensive to be launched by the new troops coming into the area." We should give credit to Eisenhower: whenever something truly catastrophic happened, he knew Patton could rescue the situation. At this time, when everywhere there was panic and mayhem, there was no mention of Montgomery directing the attack.

Because he suspected the immensity of the attack, Patton ordered a meeting of the whole Third Army staff at *8 am*. Patton discussed what they knew of the German attack. They decided on the quickest routes for

---

[1] This is why when Patton said (almost a month earlier) that Bradley was making a mistake leaving VIII Corps static, he was deadly correct. The Germans had been waiting in front of VIII Corps a long time for the weather to be right.

[2] A diversionary attack

[3] The main attack

the 4th Armored and 80th Divisions to come to the aid of VIII Corps. This required canceling their scheduled offensive in the Saar and a big air bombardment that had been prepared against the Siegfried Line. Patton made a "rough plan of operations" based on the assumption that he would use VIII Corps and the III Corps on two or three possible roads.

> "I made a simple code, one copy of which I left with Gay so that if I was ordered to execute the operation, I could call him on the phone."

.   Once again, Patton was one step ahead of his compatriots at SHAEF.

The Germans had obviously massed all of their stored strength into the attack in the Ardennes. What was the best plan open to the Allies – now that the Germans had made this irreversible move? Patton felt that they should let the Germans advance 40 or 50 miles inland. This would be a superficial German victory, because then the Allies could cut off their rear and supplies: cutting the Germans off from Germany.[1] This would end the war (or at least the war on the Western Front) because the Germans had put all of their divisions and supplies into this attack. Yet, even while suggesting it, it is probable that Patton knew that Eisenhower would, as usual, never accept such a bold plan. Patton undoubtedly guessed that Eisenhower would settle for his usual, cautious, "push the enemy back" strategy which would cause thousands more casualties.

It was 9:45, time to attend the meeting between Generals Eisenhower, Bradley, Devers, Strong and Air Marshal Tedder, their aides, and assorted SHAEF and Army Group staff officers. Patton had had only 1 hour and 15 minutes to create three possible plans (complete with code names) for rescuing the embattled VIII Corps in the Ardennes. Yet Patton reached the meeting on time.

The faces of the other generals, always before self-righteous and smug, appeared now nervous and pale. They had never suspected that the Germans could attack in force again, never realized the danger of leaving corps on the defense. Eisenhower was contemplating how he would explain the mess to Marshall, while Bradley nervously worried that he might be relieved for the biggest blunder yet committed by American

---

[1] Incidentally, this is what the German generals thought would happen to them. Hitler told them, that, as usual, they were overestimating Eisenhower's staff.

forces. "I have seldom seen longer faces," commented Patton's aide, Codman.

General Strong got up before a map of the situation and gave a short picture of what was happening at the front. It was grim. When Strong sat down, General Eisenhower spoke.

"George," he said to General Patton, "I want you to go to Luxembourg and take charge."

"Yes, sir."

"When can you start up there?"

"Now."

"You mean today?" asked Eisenhower, incredulous.

"I mean as soon as you have finished with me here."

There was a pause.

"When will you be able to attack?" General Eisenhower asked.

"The morning of December twenty-second," Patton said, "with three divisions."[1]

> "Less than seventy hours. There was a stir, a shuffling of feet, as those present straightened up in their chairs. In some faces, skepticism. But through the room the current of excitement leapt like a flame. To disengage three divisions actually in combat and launch them over more than a hundred miles of icy roads straight into the heart of a major attack of unprecedented violence presented problems which few commanders would have undertaken to resolve in that length of time."[2] *"Drive," by Colonel Charles R. Codman.*

The generals, at first shocked by Patton's answer, began to ask specific questions. "To all of them, the General had specific answers."[3] Within an hour they had decided on which divisions would be employed, where their objectives would be, the new Army boundaries, and how much of Third Army's original front in the Saar would need to be taken over by Sixth Army Group. Virtually all of these questions were settled on Patton's terms – a first in the war. It is no coincidence that this took place in the middle of a tragedy like the Battle of the Bulge. Patton was

---

[1] These divisions were the 4th Armored, the 26th and the 80th Infantry.

[2] Patton wrote in his diary, "When I said I could attack on the 22nd, it created quite a commotion – some people seemed surprised and others pleased – however I think it can be done."

[3] From "Drive," by Colonel Charles M. Codman.

the only one who could move fast enough to rescue the situation; he was the only one with the audacity, the bold nerve to respond with his instantaneous army; the only man who could promise that he would make a 90 degree turn with his army and begin attacking in a different direction more than 100 miles away – within three days.

Patton wrote in his diary of the meeting,

> "Ike had the SHAEF G-2 give the picture and then said he wanted me to get to Luxembourg and take command of the battle and make a strong counter-attack with six divisions. The fact that three of these divisions exist only on paper did not enter his head."

Eisenhower was afraid that an attack with only three divisions would not be strong enough,[1] but Patton insisted that he could beat the Germans with three divisions, and that if they waited for another three divisions they would lose the surprise that they needed.

The proposal put forward by Patton, though it sounds incredible to us, sounded even more incredible to the military minds that were assembled at this meeting. To reorient an army facing east and turn it north (a 90 degree turn) would pose a "logistical nightmare" as Martin Blumenson put it. Divisions would have to be directed down new roads and make sure that supply trucks reached them from "dumps established in quite a different context, for quite a different situation. Altogether, it was an operation that only a master could think of executing."[2] Patton would have to break off his attack in the Saar, race northwards, and attack the German flank while Devers' Ninth Army group filled in the Saar front that Third Army had just vacated.

The meeting broke up and Patton turned to Harkins ordering him to telephone General Gay. "Give him the code name, and tell him to get started." Patton then told Codman to follow him, "We start in five minutes – to Luxembourg."

As General Eisenhower was leaving he stopped and pointed to the five stars on his shoulder strap. "Funny thing, George," he said, "every time I get promoted I get attacked."

---

[1] Patton had been doing such attacks for months and HQ had never bothered to give him more divisions!
[2] A comment by Martin Blumenson in the "Patton Papers, vol. II."

252

"Yes," Patton returned, "and every time you get attacked I bail you out."

Patton and his aide Codman drove north and stopped at Thionville, where General Walker was preparing to move northwards towards Luxembourg. Patton told Walker what had transpired at the meeting and gave him the instructions for the immediate future. Patton planned on driving to Luxembourg that night, but Walker convinced him to wait until the morning when the roads would no longer be icy and dark.

Codman, however, had to drive back to Nancy to get Sgt. Meeks, Patton's orderly, and the rest of Patton's staff and trailer and send it up to Luxembourg. On the ride to Nancy, Codman observed that for the first ten miles, they made good time. But on the remaining twenty, they were occupied with "dodging the hurtling columns of 4th Armored speeding north.... Occasionally my driver, to avoid being overrun, would in desperation momentarily flash on his headlights, an unpopular move, greeted each time by bellows and curses from the exasperated tankers, and once by a short but happily inaccurate burst of machine-gun fire." Here is real-life proof of the speed of Patton's tanks, which were already racing towards the fight.

Luxembourg was no longer in the festive mood it had been in in the summer. Then the grateful citizens had greeted the victorious Allies with American flags, welcoming banners, and even "English Spoken" signs in shop windows. All those were gone now as the nervous citizens paced the streets listening to enemy artillery only 6 or 7 miles away. They counted every American truck and tank that sped through their streets, worrying that it was too little too late. How they feared another, crueler, German occupation!

Meanwhile Patton had been charging up and down the fluid lines of his armored divisions, visiting corps and division commanders, pushing, ordering, relocating, redirecting.

At dinner, General Bradley "was himself commenting on Third Army's spectacular move," wrote Codman.
"All the credit," Patton said,[1] "*all* of it, 100%, goes to Third Army Staff."

---

[1] And it was a characteristic comment, Codman noted.

Lt. Colonel Otto Skorzeny was the German who had flown in and rescued Mussolini from the Italian hotel where he had been imprisoned after his fall from power. Skorzeny was duly rewarded with a risky mission that was unfolding in the Ardennes. English-speaking Germans under his command were paratrooped into the American rear. Their purpose was to sabotage supplies and possibly pick up useful Intelligence. It is rumored that one of their other purposes was to assassinate Eisenhower, Bradley and Patton. Most of them were caught, but panicky American soldiers questioned everyone. The answers to these questions were supposedly known by every American.

Bradley recalls that he himself was not immune from questioning. His questioner asked him what the capital of Illinois was. Bradley answered that the capital was Springfield, but the soldier held out for Chicago. The soldier then asked where the guard between the center and tackle on a line of scrimmage was located, and who was the current spouse of movie actress Betty Grable. Bradley didn't know the answer to the last question; but the soldier, pleased at having stumped him, passed him on.

How much damage the Germans who were dropped into the American camp did is unknown. They certainly did create panic and distrust. These Germans fate, however, was grim. Those who were caught were shot as spies.

On December 19th, in the midst of this desperate battle, the low rumblings of envy and resentment were heard in the Montgomery camp. Eisenhower told Bradley that he would be putting the First and Ninth Armies[1] under Montgomery's command. Bedell Smith informed Bradley that, "Ike thinks it might be a good idea to turn over to Monty your two Armies in the north and let him run that side of the Bulge from 21st Army Group. It may save us a great deal of trouble... "
Bradley replied, "I'd question whether such a changeover's necessary. When we go to drive [the Germans] out of the Bulge, it'd be easier to coordinate the attack from here."

According to Patton, Eisenhower told Bradley that the reason for the change of command was, "Due to the fact that telephonic communications between Bradley and the two Armies was difficult."

---

[1] i. e. The armies north of the bulge

Actually, the telephone communications were fine. As Patton commented in his diary, "It is either a case of [Eisenhower] having lost confidence in Bradley" or Churchill pulling the strings for Montgomery, or simply that Eisenhower wanted some British divisions involved in the fighting. He must have suspected a fourth and unnamed reason, because he added, "Eisenhower is unwilling or unable to command Montgomery."

Truer words about the Eisenhower-Montgomery relationship would be difficult (if not impossible) to find.

Hodges and Simpson were put under Montgomery's command. Hodges would remain there for a month, Simpson until First Army crossed the Rhine. Bradley had effectively been removed from command. Patton[1] was commanding all the armies to the south of the Bulge; Montgomery the north. Was Bradley being punished for the Bulge?

Bradley deserved it, of course, yet Eisenhower would not be so bold as to say that. As Patton had observed, Eisenhower had lost faith in Bradley. Bradley was left, *temporarily*, in command of only Patton's Third Army. Eisenhower had given the northern part of Bradley's command – American soldiers – to Montgomery, a British field marshal. And Montgomery was not planning on returning them...

---

[1] Since Bradley was Patton's superior, the southern part of the bulge was (in a way) under Bradley's command.

Chapter Thirty Four

BLOOD, SNOW AND PINES

The 101st Airborne Division, commanded by McAulliffe and temporarily under Patton's operational command, was hanging on desperately to Bastogne. The Germans' plan to capture Antwerp was very close to succeeding. There was one thing that had not gone according to plan, however – Bastogne, before now a little, unimportant city in the Ardennes forest – was stubbornly resisting even though it was completely surrounded.

Meanwhile Patton was meeting with Major Generals Middleton[1], Millikin, Gaffey and Paul in Arlon. The VIII Corps was fighting very well, but had been virtually wiped out. Patton told Middleton to give ground and blow up bridges so that the Germans would advance more divisions into the bulge. Then Patton, in a master stroke, could cut off their whole task force from Germany.

In a decision that might seem to go against this strategy, Patton decided to hold onto Bastogne. His main reason for this decision was that if the Germans took the city they would obliterate it. Bastogne was also the key to a very important road net and Bradley wanted the city kept in Allied hands.

---

[1] Middleton commanded the VIII Corps of First Army, Millikin the III Corps of Third Army, Gaffey the 4th Armored, and Paul the 26th Infantry Division. Gaffey and Paul belonged to the XII Corps currently under the command of Major General Eddy.

Quickly Patton reorganized his whole army, telling his men to cannibalize their anti-tank gun units in order to fill the ranks with much needed infantrymen. He ordered the 35th division to move to Metz and pick up replacements. He redirected his whole army through only telephoned orders to Gay and his staff at Nancy, giving new objectives, new supplies, and replacements, all over the phone.

Patton wrote to his wife on the 21st of December that,

> "Though this is the shortest day of the year, to me it seems interminable. We shoot the works on a chestnut pulling expedition in the morning.[1] I am very confident that a great success is possible and I hope certain. Yesterday I again earned my pay. I visited seven divisions and regrouped an Army alone. The Bosch landed a lot of paratroops in our uniforms for the purpose of murdering Ike, Brad, me, etc… Remember how a tarpon always makes one big flop just before it dies."

Patton added at the end of the letter, "Destiny[2] sent for me in a hurry when things got tight. Perhaps God saved me for this effort." This was a very characteristic remark attributing his success to God's plan.

Eisenhower and Bull, Eisenhower's G-3, were nervous about Patton attacking too soon. Patton remarked that he had all they could give him and that if he waited for replacements, "I will lose surprise." He noted that the First Army could attack on the 22nd as well, but they had no desire to. Bradley expressed an entirely different feeling on the matter in his book, where he says that if Third Army hadn't attacked right away, Hodges' First Army might have cracked. Talk about "rescuing the chestnuts."

Patton had all the staffs in for a conference. "As usual on the verge of an attack, they were full of doubt. I seemed to always be the ray of sunshine, and by God, I always am. We can and will win, God helping…"

---

[1] Because of the fear that letters would fall into enemy hands, censors would change any reference to a battle or town. Patton called the Battle of the Bulge a "chestnut pulling expedition" so that his wife could figure out what he was talking about without the censors cutting it out.

[2] Destiny, Patton's name for Ike that would avoid censorship.

Tomorrow, the 22nd, would be the day that he had promised Eisenhower his army would be attacking south of the Bulge. "When one attacks, it is the enemy who has to worry. Give us the victory, Lord."

The next day Third Army attacked as promised. There was a snow storm and the advance was slow. The skies were still gray keeping the airplanes grounded. The Germans had demolished everything that would aid the Third's advance. The III Corps progressed seven miles deep on a front of twenty miles. Patton was disappointed, but wrote, "With a little luck, I will put on a more daring attack before Christmas."

Replacements were critical. This is one of the areas (along with supply) that Eisenhower's failure was complete. No one has ever satisfactorily explained why Eisenhower allowed Com-Z's commander to emerge scot-free from his scandalous waste of supply. It was also Com-Z's job to make sure that replacements arrived. Supplies and men are so critical for the proper running of an army that Eisenhower deserves far more blame for their shortage than he is usually given. Patton took 8,000 men from the rear echelons and turned them into regular infantry because of the shortage; he only wished that others would do the same.[1]

Patton was afraid that Millikin would not do well, so he advised him to "go up and hear them [the shells and bullets] whistle. I think he will."

III Corps continued pushing ahead towards Bastogne that night. "It is always hard to get an attack rolling. I doubt if the enemy can make a serious reaction for another 36 hours. I hope by that time we will be moving." Patton understood the true spirit of blitzkrieg; he embodied it. In time of crisis, he was moving. "In case of doubt, attack," was his invention; it is the essence of blitzkrieg. Those historians who say that Patton did not understand blitzkrieg must themselves not understand blitzkrieg; blitzkrieg is literally "fast war." The Third Army advanced faster than any other army in the history of war. Its commander fully understood the nature of war – and its most important facet, the attack.

---

[1] Rear-echelon men were not properly trained for combat. Trained replacements could have won the war with less American casualties.

One hundred and eight battalions of corps and 1,296 artillery pieces[1] were involved in the attack on the 22nd of December. "I don't see how the Boche can take this much artillery," Patton commented. He also observed that "the situation at Bastogne is grave but not desperate."

Things looked gloomy for the Americans that were surrounded in the little town of Bastogne, however, but they resisted anxiously hoping for Patton's armor to reach them in time. The Germans could not understand such desperate hope – or such trust in an army that was reported to be more than 100 miles away. A German carrying a white flag approached the American lines.

"You are surrounded. Surrender!" The German courier waited for a reply while the Americans awoke their exhausted commander. When the Americans brought the answer, the courier's brow wrinkled. What did it mean? The Germans could not understand McAuliffe's reply, "Nuts."

Bastogne was receiving air-dropped supplies from the few airplanes that could take off despite the fog. Patton had advanced another five miles the next day. His men were involved in bloody fighting for every inch of soil. Every snow-covered pine could hide a German; the fighting was reminiscence of WWI. Bastogne was still holding on.

The next day was December 23rd.

"This has been a very bad Christmas Eve. All along our line we have received violent counterattacks, one of which forced the 4th Armored back some miles with the loss of ten tanks. This was probably my fault, because I had been insisting on day and night attacks. This is all right on the first or second day of the battle and when we had the enemy surprised, but after that the men get too tired. Furthermore, in this bad weather, it is very difficult for armored outfits to operate at night. In the XX Corps all is quiet, and a very low grade of troops is opposing Colonel Polk – in fact Polk is insulted because he said, "They are nothing but Poles with ulcers." I believe the German General Staff is running this attack and has staked all on this offensice to regain the initiative. They

---

[1] These artillery were 105mm or bigger!

are far behind schedule and, I believe, beaten. If this is true, the whole army may surrender. On the other hand, in 1940 they attacked as at present, and the came over at Saarbrucken and Thionville to Metz. They may repeat [that] – but with what?"

Patton's estimate of the capabilities of the Germans, their time schedule, morale and their General Staff is nothing short of prophetic.

Patton had arranged for the prayer card was distributed among the troops on December 24th. He had also arranged for all the troops to have turkey sandwiches for Christmas. The card was wallet-size that had a Christmas message from Patton on one side which read,

> "To each officer and soldier... I wish a Merry Christmas. I have a full confidence in your courage, devotion to duty, and skill in battle. We march in our might to complete victory. May God's blessing rest upon each of you on this Christmas day."

On the other side was the prayer, written by Chaplain James O'Neill,

> "Almighty and most merciful Father, we humbly beseech Thee, of Thy great goodness, to restrain these immoderate rains with which we have to contend. Grant us fair weather for Battle. Graciously hearken to us as soldiers who call upon Thee that armed with Thy power, we may advance from victory to victory, and crush the oppression and wickedness of our enemies, and establish Thy justice among men and nations. Amen."

The next day dawned bright and sunny. This was the beginning of the end for the Germans. A few weeks later Patton thanked the chaplain.
"Well, Padre," he said, "our prayers worked. I knew they would." According to O'Neill, he "then cracked me on the side of my steel helmet with his riding crop. That was his way of saying, 'Well done.'"

Chapter Thirty Five

THE THIRD ARMY RESCUES THE AMERICANS

It was Christmas Day, one of the most noisy of WWII. The weather was wonderful, "lovely weather for killing Germans, which seems a bit queer, seeing Whose birthday it is. Last night Codman[1] and I went to the Candlelight Communion at the Episcopal Church here in Luxembourg. It was very nice and we sat in the former Kaiser Wilhelm I's box."

Patton got up early Christmas morning so as to visit all the divisions that were attacking the Germans. All the troops were cheerful, but Patton was not. "We are not going fast enough," he wrote in his diary. But he felt they were doing their best.

Patton's wife had sent him socks, or "sox" as he spelled them. He wrote her a letter thanking her in which he added, "The Lord has given us 3 consecutive days of good weather and things are looking up but so far I am the only one attacking."

The 101st Airborne division in Bastogne had not been re-supplied that day because of the icy conditions in the UK. After Christmas dinner, Bradley and Patton began to talk about the latest news. Montgomery had said that the First Army[2] could not attack for three months. Monty had also theorized that Patton was the only one who could attack, but he was

---

[1] Patton's aide.
[2] Montgomery was now in command of the First Army!

too weak,[1] so they should fall back to the Saar-Vosges line or even to the Moselle.

> "I feel that this is disgusting and might remove the valor of our army and the confidence of our people. It will have tremendous political implications and probably condemn to death or slavery all the inhabitants of Alsace and Lorraine if we abandon them to the Germans! If ordered to fall back, I think I will ask to be relieved."

Patton discussed Montgomery's proposal with his staff. "Now I want your frank opinion," Patton told them, "General Eisenhower has asked me personally to get that opinion for him. Montgomery thinks the First Army has no offensive power left and won't have any for three months. He thinks the only possible offensive is by us – the Third Army. And he doesn't think we have enough troops." He now told them about Montgomery's proposal of falling back and regrouping.

Everyone in the room was stunned. The operations officer was the first to recover. "It's fantastic! The psychological effect of such a plan on our troops would be disastrous!"
"I know," Patton replied, as his high-pitched voice rose shrilly, "Our men aren't trained to withdraw! But Eisenhower wants your opinion. He already knows *mine*. But, if this plan goes through, the war will be over and the Germans will have won it!"
"Those people up north have plenty of offensive power," another staff member said. "All they have to do is get off their butts and fight."
"Of course they have a lot of offensive power," Patton said. "All they need is the order to fight! But of course, Montgomery won't give that order. The SHAEF gentlemen up north have been associated with him so long the only thing they think armies can do is sit on their asses, regroup, and pivot on somebody else." Patton rose to leave the room. "You talk the proposal over among yourselves and give me a brief answer as soon as you can."

The discussion was brief. Patton's staff rejected Montgomery's plan as unsound and ill-advised. Their new plan, unanimously agreed on, was also brief: hold all positions and counterattack immediately.[2]

---

[1] In men and materiel, that is.

[2] Story taken from "Battle: The Story of the Bulge," by John Toland page 280.

It was December 26th; Bastogne was still holding out. At 2:00 that afternoon, Major General Gaffey, commander of the 4th Armored, called to ask Patton's approval for a risky operation. The operation would be commanded by Colonel Wendell Blanchard and would try to breakthrough to Bastogne by a sudden, surprise attack. Patton authorized the operation.

At 6:45 that evening, Bastogne was liberated. "It was a daring [operation] and well done. Of course they may be cut off, but I doubt it … The speed of our movements is amazing, even to me, and must be a constant source of surprise to the Germans."

There is a striking difference in officer's accounts from Third Army and those from other armies. In other armies, when an officer has not been given a town for an objective, or when the town is outside his boundary, he waits for orders directing him to take it. If he is low on ammunition, he waits to be re-supplied. If there is heavy resistance, he waits and digs in. Not so in Patton's army. All the accounts are full of daring attacks taken at the officer's initiative. Majors, lieutenants, and colonels do not wait for orders, supplies, or the enemy. They move, attack, and capture because time is vital. These men were following the example of their commanding officer, General Patton.

Part of the reason why Patton's men did not fear to take the initiative without direct orders is because Patton did not believe in sacking men because of an early failure. Patton said that cutting off commanders' heads too easily made new commanders fear to do anything without permission. By being afraid of creating a disaster, these commanders actually created a worse disaster by waiting. Even though Patton is portrayed as a man who would relieve for almost no reason at all, Patton actually was very careful when he relieved commanders. For this reason, Patton's officers were willing to take risks – knowing that if a disaster occurred they would not be instantly relieved.

Patton taught all of his officers the art of the attack. If a disaster occurs when attacking, it is far better than a disaster that occurs while defending. This is because when you are attacking, you receive a setback on enemy ground, gaining and losing nothing, but if you are defending, you lose the ground you were meant to defend.

Even though Bastogne was liberated, SHAEF was still as nervous as ever. Bradley had telephoned SHAEF asking for Montgomery to help in the attack. "The Germans are pulling out," Bradley told Bedell Smith.

"Oh, no, Brad, you're mistaken," Smith said. "Why, the Germans will be across the Meuse in 48 hours." Smith's head was obviously full of the latest Montgomery reports.

Because the staff officers at SHAEF never visited the front, they were often 2 weeks behind the actual feel of the battle. SHAEF was holding the 11th Armored, the 17th Airborne, and the 87th Infantry divisions in "reserve." "They should be attacking," Patton commented. Patton realized that the Germans had used all of their last reserves on this offensive, and that Bastogne had turned the tide of the Battle of the Bulge. "The German has shot his wad. Prisoners have had no food for from three to five days. We should attack."

> "Ever since the 22nd, we have been trying to relieve Bastogne. Just now at 1845 Gaffey called to say we had made contact. Of course we did not do it with much, but we did it. I hope that the troops making the advance don't get bottled up too. My Prayer seems to be working still as we have had three days of good weather and our air has been very active. Of course they overstate [their hits by] at least 50% but they do scare the Huns." *Patton, letter to Beatrice, Dec. 26, 1944*

By the 27th, the corridor between 4th Armored and the 101st Airborne (holding Bastogne) had considerably widened making the chance of being cut off considerably smaller. Food, clothing, and medical equipment poured into Bastogne as the wounded were evacuated.

The Germans were fiercely holding the inlet of the Bulge so as to prevent another opportunity like the Falaise Gap. It would be quite easy to cut the Germans off, and now was the time to do it...

This is an amusing, interesting description of his fellow commanders that is so Patton,

> "Bradley left at 10:00 to see Ike, Montgomery and Smith. If Ike will put Bradley back in command of the First and Ninth Armies, we can bag the whole German army. I wish Ike were more of a gambler, but he is

certainly a lion compared to Montgomery, and Bradley is better than Ike as far as nerve is concerned. Of course he did make a bad mistake in being passive on the front of the VIII Corps. Monty is a tired little fart. War requires the taking of risks and he won't take them... If I could get three more divisions, I could win this war now." *Patton's Diary*

"The relief of Bastogne is the most brilliant operation we have thus far performed and is, in my opinion, the outstanding achievement of this war," Patton wrote to his wife, "Now the enemy must dance to our tune, not we to his." On the morning of December 30th, Patton was planning a whole new series of attacks which "may well be decisive if I can only get Destiny to use reserves to attack and not to defend... This is my biggest battle."

Patton now had 16 divisions. "...but four strings attached to them." He had to ask permission from all of the higher echelons before he could use them.

Now that things were not as desperate, Patton had time to write his wife descriptions of the latest battles. Five divisions had been in action between Saarlautern and Sarreguemines and by telephone he sent three to Luxembourg to stop the Germans. The staff responsible for all these complicated move had "consisted of myself and Sergeant Mims," his driver. He could have had his army advance toward Bastogne a day earlier, but "the attack would have been a little ragged." He could not believe that the relief of Bastogne had been accomplished so easily, and predicted that if a military student at Leavenworth[1] had proposed a similar solution he would have been sent to the "doghouse or St. Elizabeth's."[2]

Bradley hesitatingly approved Patton's plan for the III Corps to attack and seize the high ground near Houffalize and then continue on to St. Vith. He also approved the plan for XII Corps to take Echternach and then proceed to Bitburg. Middleton, usually under Bradley's command, asked for more detailed instructions, but Patton told him that "he didn't care how Middleton made the attack, but he must make it, and he must take the objective." This was typical of Patton's philosophy: leave the

---

[1] Fort Leavenworth educates officers in the art of command and staff functions at the tactical level, and educates officers in the operational art of war.
[2] The mental institution in Washington.

details to the commanders in charge, the only important thing is to attack, attack, attack!

The next day, the 11th Armored and 87th Infantry carried out the plan and ran right into the flank of a huge German counterattack that was trying to recapture Bastogne.

> "This lucky meeting stopped the Germans and probably corrected a bad situation. Everyone of the generals involved urged me to postpone the attack... but I held to my plan, although I did not know the German attack was coming. Some people call it luck, some genius. I call it determination."

Patton drove to Bastogne and decorated Brigadier General McAuliffe and Lt. Col. Chappuis, the commander of the 502nd Glider Infantry who had repulsed the brunt of the initial German offensive. Patton gave them both the Distinguished Service Cross. They were so delighted with their fortuitous relief by Third Army that they asked Patton to "drive slowly so the soldiers could see" him.

Patton was extremely happy about his lucky attack on the flank of the German counterattack. He wrote to his wife that,

> "Historians will claim that such perfect timing was a stroke of jenius [sic]. It was just mulishness on my part. I had no idea the Germans were attacking. On the other side of Bastogne, they also hit us hard. But we stopped them with the loss of one village to us and 55 tanks to them. Today has been a slugging match, but I got Bob Grow[1] in and things are better. Tomorrow will be the crutial [sic] test. I think, in fact know, we will stop them and attack at once."

That night a heavy snow fell and froze over. The Germans launched a heavy counterattack the next day against the 26th Infantry Division. All their artillery (except for the small pieces) were useless. They had to send a truck ahead with a cable connecting it to the artillery in order to move it over the icy roads. This counterattack was the 17th of the battle, according to Patton's count. They had all been repulsed. "On

---

[1] Bob Grow's 6th Armored Division.

the other hand, we have not gained much ground," the relentless Patton wrote.

Bradley submitted an efficiency report on Patton and labeled him, "Superior." He recommended Patton for command of at least an army or, better, and Army Group. Bradley listed Patton as the Number 1 Army commander in combat.[1]

Considering the circumstances, it would have been impossible for Bradley to do less. Patton had saved more than his hide – he had also saved his reputation.

---

[1] Where else are Army commanders?

Chapter Thirty Six

BLOODY BATTLE IN THE BULGE

On New Year's day, 1945, a message was distributed among Third Army troops from their commander, General Patton.

"From the bloody corridor at Avranches, to Brest, thence across France to the Saar, over the Saar into Germany, and now on to Bastogne, your record has been one of continues victory. Not only have you invariably defeated a cunning and ruthless enemy, but also you have overcome by your indomitable fortitude every aspect of terrain and weather. Neither heat nor dust nor floods nor snow have stayed your progress. The speed and brilliancy of your achievements is unsurpassed in military history... My New Year wish and sure conviction for you is that under the protection of Almighty God and the inspired leadership of our President and the High Command, you will continue your victorious course to the end that tyranny and vice shall be eliminated, our dead comrades avenged, and peace restored to a war-weary world. In closing, I can find no fitter expression for my feelings than to apply to you the immortal words spoken by General Scott at Chapultepec when he said, 'Brave soldiers, veterans, you have been baptized in fire and blood and have come out steel.'"

Patton told the press at Luxembourg that if you have "a monkey in a jungle hanging by his tail, it is easier to get him by cutting his tail than kicking him in the face. The same thing is true here." Patton was still advocating his strategy of cutting the enemy off from his supplies and his homeland. Would anyone listen?

Patton was sure to praise the younger officers and the soldiers, the men who were actually fighting. They were the ones that had accomplished the true miracle. "When you think of those men marching all night in the cold, over roads they had never seen, and nobody getting lost, and everybody getting to the place [Bastogne] in time, it is a very marvelous feat; I know of no equal to it in military history," he told the assembled press. "I take my hat off to them."

A reporter asked him if the First Army would start their attack soon, to which Patton replied, "I'm not my brother's keeper."

They asked him what his future plans were. "We want to catch as many Germans as possible, but he is pulling out."

"But," they protested, "If you pinch off a lot of Germans, is there any chance of the front collapsing?"

"What do you think I went to church for yesterday?" he laughingly replied.

"What about the [German] concentration of armor?" a bold reporter asked.

"They've got very little armor left – unless they have reproductive tanks."

They asked him other questions to which he gave poignant, explanatory and humorous answers.

On January 2nd, the VII Corps was finally attacking in the direction of Houffalize. The VII Corps was part of First Army and therefore under Hodges' command. First Army, though, was temporarily under Montgomery's overall command. "Dear Courtney [Hodges] comes in at long last in the morning, and that will relieve the pressure," Patton wrote.

"I want to attack to the north from Diekirch but Bradley is all for putting new divisions in the Bastogne fight. In my opinion, this is throwing good money after bad. In this weather, on the defensive, the Germans can hold us well enough so that we can never trap them there, whereas if we attack close to the base [of the Bulge] they will have to pull out and we will regain ground and probably catch just as many Germans as the other way…"

The 11th Armored was very green and had taken unnecessary losses. They had also shot prisoners due to their ineptitude. Patton hoped that they would be able to conceal this from the newspapers. The 17th Airborne was also green and had hysterically reported that they lost 40% of their battalions. Patton wrote that 8 to 10% losses could only result from soldiers running or surrendering, but 40% was obviously an exaggeration resulting from inexperience.

The fact is that many troops being put into the Bulge had never seen battle before, many more were poorly trained.

"Bastogne was being shelled when I drove in. The flashes of the shells of our guns on the snow was pretty, but I could have foregone the beauty. We can still lose this war. However, the Germans are colder and hungrier than we are, but they fight better. I can never get over the stupidity of our green troops." *Patton's Diary*

"These Germans are vicious fighters," he wrote, downcast as he pondered the limited success of his green soldiers.

But, perhaps on a happier note, he wrote this letter to Frederick Ayer,

"At the present time the fighting is very hot, but we are retaining the initiative and killing more Germans than I have ever previously accounted for… I really feel that, although the German breakthrough was regrettable, it may terminate the war sooner… because, when they fail, as they will – or as they have – there will be nothing to look forward to. Of course they have an uncanny method of pulling new troops out of the hat, but at the moment it seems to me that they have everything in they can possibly put in[to the battle], while we still have a few cards up our sleeves."

Patton spoke to Bradley on January 5th, and the two agreed that the German resistance southeast of Bastogne needed to be eliminated before they could attack Houffalize. Patton needed to take the 90th division from Walker's corps, and was impressed that Walker did not even complain. "Walker is a very fine soldier. He has never yet complained about any order he has received."

Middleton and Millikin were reprimanded by Patton for being too cautious. They protested that their men were tired, but, said Patton, "so are the Germans."
"We have to push people beyond endurance in order to bring this war to its end, because we are forced to fight it with inadequate means," he told them. There were only three small counterattacks on January 6th. "I fear this means the enemy is getting away."

Patton was downhearted. He did not have sufficient troops, and the troops he received were all inexperienced and green. The weather was bad and favored defense, and his men – Third Army men, were getting tired and cautious.

Chapter Thirty Seven

MONTGOMERY ATTACKS

Patton ordered Middleton to advance until he "bumps" into the Germans. Eddy and Bradley were worried that the enemy would counterattack against XII Corps. Patton thought that the Germans were pulling out of the Bulge – in any case they could hardly muster a strong counterattack. Nevertheless, he alerted two armored divisions to be ready to help Eddy in case the Germans attacked. He was taking no chances.

Patton was running the battle pretty much on his own terms. Bradley's rare interventions were not appreciated by Patton.

> "In one case, while he did not order, he strongly suggested that instead of attacking north of Diekirch and cutting the enemy off at the waist [of the Bulge], we should put in a new division southeast of Bastogne so as to insure the integrity of the new corridor."

He felt he had allowed himself to be "overpersuaded" by Bradley and should not have deployed the 90th Division as Bradley requested. "Had I put the 90th Division in north of Diekirch, I am sure we could have bagged more Germans and just as cheaply."

On January 6th, the British newspaper *Mail* printed the headlines:

"MONTGOMERY: FULL STORY OF BREACH BATTLE
British Halted Drive to the Meuse Line."

The paper's article stated that, "this is the crucial part of the Western Front since General Rundstedt started to push, and the knowledge that Marshal Montgomery is now in full control there will be received with relief in this country."

The next day Montgomery summoned a press meeting. The meeting took place in Zondhoven, Holland, and all correspondents from 21st Army Group were invited. The text of Montgomery's announcement was this:

> "Von Rundstedt attacked on December 16th. He obtained tactical surprise. He drove a deep wedge into the centre of First U.S. Army and split the American forces in two. The situation looked as if it might become awkward; the Germans had broken right through a weak spot and were headed for the Meuse.
>
> As soon as I saw what was happening I took certain steps myself to ensure that *if* the Germans got to the Meuse they would certainly not get over the river. I carried out certain movements so as to provide balanced dispositions to meet the threatened danger; these were, at the time, merely precautions. That is, I was thinking ahead.
>
> Then the situation began to deteriorate. But the whole Allied team rallied to meet the danger: national considerations were thrown overboard, General Eisenhower placed me in command of the whole northern front.
>
> I employed the whole available power of the British Group of Armies; this power was brought into play very gradually and in such a way that it would not interfere with American lines of communication. Finally it was put into battle with a band and today British divisions are fighting hard on the right flank of the First U.S. Army.
>
> You thus have the picture of British troops fighting on both sides of American forces who have suffered a hard blow. This is a fine Allied picture. The battle has been

most interesting; I think possibly one of the most interesting and tricky battles I have handled, with great issues at stake."

Montgomery didn't take any special measures that "rescued" the Americans. In fact, he wouldn't let Hodges or Simpson fight, but forced them to regroup and wait around while their fellow Americans were dying. If only Montgomery *had* "employed the whole available power of the British Group of Armies" the Bastogne battle would have been finished far sooner.

Yet Montgomery, arrogant and ignorant, acts as if the Battle of the Bulge is *over!* It is only January 6th. Patton has taken Bastogne, but the Bulge has hardly been reduced at all! Montgomery speaks as if he has single-handedly won all the battles, yet he has done less than Patton.[1]

But Montgomery didn't stop talking there. He continued "praising" the Americans soldier and then saying,

"I am absolutely devoted to Ike. We are the greatest of friends. It grieves me when I see uncomplimentary articles about him in the British press. When Rundstedt put in his hard blow and parted the American Army, it was automatic that the battle area must be untidy. Therefore, the first thing I did when I was brought in and told to take over was to busy myself in getting the battle area tidy – getting it sorted out. I got my reserves into the right places and got balanced – and you know what happened. I reorganized the American and British armies..."

Who knew that the "right places" for reserves was in the rear! And Montgomery "reorganized" the British and American armies? No wonder Bradley was furious when he heard this speech!

In the rest of the speech he mixed British aphorisms with military maneuvers,

"It [Collins VII Corps] took a knock. I said, 'Dear me, this can't go on. It's being swallowed up in battle.' I set

---

[1] Who admitted that he hadn't won the battle alone.

to work and managed to form the corps again. Once more pressure was such that it began to disappear in defensive battle. I said, 'Come, come' and formed again..."

He summed up his speech with the epitome of his strategy.

"You must have a well balanced, tidy show when you are mixed up in a dog fight. You can't do it nohow – I do not think that word is English – you can't win the big victory without a tidy show."

One of Montgomery's most irritating – and laughed at – expressions was "tidy." Didn't he know that war is not "tidy?" Montgomery believed that whenever a division lost some men, it should be withdrawn from the fight and regrouped. Regrouping is when replacements are added, officers reassigned, and new orders are issued. It shouldn't take a long time to accomplish, in fact Patton's one regrouping took 1/3rd of Montgomery's usual regroup-time. Another "untidy" thing that happens in the battlefield is small groups of soldiers getting lost and reassigned to other nearby units without the knowledge of headquarters. Montgomery even accused the enemy of being untidy. And in order to force the enemy to tidy up, he would have to withdraw and wait.

As a matter of fact, "tidiness" has nothing to do with victory. It doesn't matter if headquarters knows who the new lieutenant in X Division is, as long as the lieutenant aids the victory. If soldiers are scattered all over the hills and accomplishing their jobs, who cares if it doesn't look "tidy" to the commanding general miles away?

Needless to say, American papers were angry. Hugh Shuck of the New York *Daily Times* finished his cable with, "TO BORROW EXPRESSION OF AMERICAN GENERAL TONY MCAULIFFE, "NUTS TO YOU, MONTY."

Patton arrived at Bradley's headquarters on January 8th. Bradley had another plan. He suggested that Patton attack Houffalize that day using the 101st Airborne, the 4th Armored, and the 90th Infantry Divisions. Patton went ahead with this operation, "I said I could, but felt it a mistake as all plans were made for a general attack tomorrow." This operation, conceived by Bradley, yielded a mere 2 miles.

Patton had lunch at Bradley's headquarters with Paul McNutt and the Manpower Board. It was the Board's fault that Patton had received only green troops, when he had gotten troops at all;so it was obvious that the lunch would not be a happy one.

> "McNutt is a pompous fool not at all interested in
> manpower... He told me he knew all about war. I told
> him he knew nothing about it compared to the people
> fighting it, and that he and his Board were responsible
> for the deaths of all Americans who gave their lives due
> to the shortage of replacements. I doubt if he loves me,
> it's mutual." *Patton's Diary*

Patton told them the truth about their responsibility for providing troops and how miserably they had failed.
One of them responded, "But there were laws governing the dispersal of replacements..."
"We are talking in blood," Patton cut in, "and it is on your heads."

The argument must have been very fiery, because a Harvard professor sitting near Patton suddenly said, "You mustn't care at all what people think of you!"
To which Patton replied, "It would depend who the people are. In any case, I probably don't care very much."

Patton was going to tell Gaffey that he would be attacking in a different operation, but as soon as Patton announced that he would be attacking, Gaffey replied, "When? In what direction?"

Patton continued driving and passed the last battalion of the 90th Division driving along the same road. The men in the battalion were sitting in open trucks in the frigid weather and had been for many hours, but they cheered and yelled as Patton drove past. "It was a very inspiring sight."

The B.B.C. was on at Bradley's HQ when the broadcaster announced,

> "It is the most brilliant and difficult task he has yet
> managed. He found no defense lines, the Americans
> somewhat bewildered, few reserves on hand and supply

lines cut…The battle of the Ardennes can now be practically written off, thanks to Montgomery."

"You've got to get something on the record that tells the whole story of the change in command," Bradley's aide Hansen burst out. "Until you tell the story, the American people will have nothing to go by except Montgomery's statement which certainly leaves a questionable inference on the capabilities of the U.S. command."

"Well, I can do one of two things," Bradley replied. "I can take a statement to Ike and ask him to approve it. He may or he may not. If Ike lets me go ahead and we get into trouble over it then he hangs with me. On the other hand, we need not put Ike on the spot. I can release a statement without clearing it at SHAEF and take the consequences myself."

"But you have a precedent," Ingersoll insisted, "after all, Montgomery spoke to the press yesterday."

"Yes, but –"

"Do you suppose Montgomery cleared his interview with Eisenhower?" Ingersoll asked mischievously.

"You know darned well he didn't," Bradley shot back angrily. It was a difficult decision, but Bradley knew that SHAEF would not make an official statement, and it was doubtful that Eisenhower would clear a similar statement by Bradley. "Okay, I'll do it," Bradley said at last.

The London *Mail*'s headlines that day read,

"MONTGOMERY FORESAW ATTACK
ACTED 'ON OWN' TO SAVE DAY"

The 87th and 17th Airborne divisions had "got fairly well chopped up yesterday" because Middleton did not call in the 11th Armored to back up their attack. That night, as Patton was eating dinner at his headquarters, Middleton called up to say that he couldn't possibly attack tomorrow, they should wait until at least 2 days when all the divisions would be rested.

Patton insisted that the attack would go on, tomorrow, January 9th, as scheduled. He admitted that the 87th and the 17th Airborne wouldn't do very well, but they must not stop attacking. After Patton was finished speaking to Middleton, Gaffey called up requesting a 2 day hold-up as well. Patton remained firm. "We simply have to keep attacking or [the enemy] will. I wish that great soldier Sir B.[1] would do a little more," Patton wrote his wife.

He believed that the Germans might try to recapture Metz, although he admitted they didn't have enough troops. After their failure in the Ardennes, Metz would be hailed as a great victory. To guard against this eventuality, Patton ordered Walker to blow the roads in that vicinity.

Suddenly, on January 10th, Bradley's HQ got panicky. They misinterpreted troop movements against Seventh Army and thought that another offensive would be launched at the Saar River in order to retake Metz. Eisenhower decided that he wanted both of Patton's attacks to be stopped and at least an armored division freed for that operation.

At first, Patton agreed. He always thought it was a bad idea to postpone attacks, and as he thought more about it, he doubted if the Germans had the strength to mass a large attack towards the Saar.[2] He asked Bradley to go down and look over the situation personally. He later wrote in "War as I Knew It," "These two instances, for which Bradley was not personally responsible, indicate the inadvisability of commanding from too far back."

Patton had to change his plans due to the cancellation of his two attacks. He had the 4th Armored assemble southeast of Luxembourg because the roads there could easily carry the division to the assistance of either the XX or XII Corps. To accomplish this rearrangement, Patton simply drove to Bastogne and gave the orders to his division commanders. No written orders were issued, or necessary. Everyone knew what to do.

Bradley began his statement to the press trying to explain why Montgomery had been given command in the north. Since he didn't know why, he gave them the reason that was given to him by Bedell Smith,

> "The German attack cut both *direct* telephone communication to First Army and the *direct* roads over which personal contact was normally maintained. The

---

[1] Bernard Law Montgomery.
[2] In other words, although he thought they *might* attack, he realized a whole armored division wasn't needed to repulse that attack.

weather prevented the making of frequent personal contacts with First Army Group by plane. It was therefore decided that the 21st Army Group should assume *temporary* command of all Allied forces north of the salient. This was a *temporary* measure and when the lines are rejoined 12th Army Group will resume command of all American troops in this area."

So Bradley hoped. It was the first time the newspapers heard that the change in command was meant to be temporary.[1] Bradley admits in his book that one of the reasons for this speech was to remind SHAEF that the change in command was only supposed to be temporary.

It was also the first time that the public learned when the change over had taken place. This is significant because during the 4 days between December 16th and 20th, the offensive had lost its momentum and the Germans had lost their battle.[2] The Germans acknowledged later, under interrogation, that by December 19th they were fatally behind schedule. This was 24 hours before Montgomery entered into the battle.

During one of Bradley's more lucid moments in his book, he admits that if Eisenhower had only issued a statement that the change in command was temporary, the bickering would have stopped. Meanwhile Montgomery was campaigning – and most of the British press was supporting him – to be named "top ground commander." Montgomery was again stating that it was impossible for one man to be actual battlefield commander and also coordinate air, navy, supply, etc. He therefore insisted that Eisenhower name him the "top ground commander."

General Marshall had told Bradley, a long time ago, that Americans would never serve under British command. But Bradley was still nervous, and felt that he must state his "position uncompromisingly to Ike." When Bradley raised the issue to Eisenhower, he put it off impatiently with a reassuring reply.

---

[1] In Bradley's book, *temporary* is always in italics!

[2] Although it would take several more weeks to finish the Germans, they could not take the Antwerp port, their objective, within the time slot that they had allotted themselves. All they could do was cause more American casualties; it would have been impossible for them to reach the objective that had launched the attack.

"Nevertheless you must know," Bradley insisted, "after what has happened I cannot serve under Montgomery. If he is to be put in command of all ground forces, you must send me home, for if Montgomery goes in over me, I will have lost the confidence of my command."

Ike flushed. He stiffened in his chair and eyed Bradley hotly. "Well – " he said, "I thought you were the one person I could count on to do anything I asked you to do."[1]

"You can count on me, Ike," Bradley said, "I've enjoyed every bit of my service with you. But this is one thing I cannot take."[2]

Bradley had finally given Eisenhower an ultimatum. Eisenhower had never, ever, thought that Bradley would oppose him. Montgomery's arrogance and his willingness to exploit Bradley's failure in the Ardennes had enflamed Bradley. What angered him still further – and drove him closer to Patton – was that Eisenhower never opened his mouth to defend the truth, nor did he ever silence Montgomery.

As Patton returned to Luxembourg, he drove passed the tanks of 4th Armored rolling towards Luxembourg. He attributed this to Gaffey's remarkable talent of "doing what he is told fast..."

Preparations were underway for the capture of Houffalize and, barring any enemy attacks, XII corps could attack north and cut off the retreating enemy.

---

[1] This is the reason Bradley was put in command of the 12th Army Group, and not Patton. Eisenhower could "count" on Bradley to do anything he asked – no matter how stupid. But Ike could not count on Patton to carry out jeopardizing orders because Patton "would rather resign."

[2] Before going to the meeting, Bradley told Patton of the latest developments. "If you quit, Brad," Patton told him, "Then I'll be quitting with you." Bradley does not say that he mentioned this to Eisenhower.

Chapter Thirty Eight

THE GERMAN OFFENSIVE COLLAPSES

"Wherever we attack, one thing is certain, we should attack, because if we don't the Germans will."

Twelfth Army Group called again with another frantic message. "There is enemy troop concentration near Trier!"
"To me it is patently impossible that the Germans have troop concentrations all over the face of nature – I do not believe it," Patton wrote in his diary. However, he noted, 4th Armored was in a position that it could relieve that threat, too.

> "This is the second time I have been stopped in a successful attack due to the Germans having more nerve than we have – that is, not me, but some others. The ability of American troops to maneuver when properly led is wonderful. Their ability to fight is not so good…"
> **Patton's Diary**

Patton wrote on January 11th that "the end of the Bastogne operation is in sight." He would prefer to attack at once and take the German bridge at Saarbrucken, but of course, Bradley "thinks we had best wait…"

"I believe that today ends the Bastogne operation. From now on it is simply a question of driving a defeated enemy," Patton wrote. But the higher levels of command had always had a hard time "driving," "attacking" and "pursuing." With a panicked Army Group Headquarters, an even more out of touch SHAEF, and stick-in-the-mud Montgomery in the north, it was pretty doubtful that the Ardennes would see any real "offensive" action.

The VIII and III Corps would attack on January 13th and take Houffalize. "That will tidy up that job and, next to the crossing of France, it is the biggest one we have done. I hope we get the credit."[1] Once Houffalize was taken, it would be easy to link up First and Third Armies. This done, First Army, Patton guessed, would be given back to Bradley, which "will be very advantageous, as Bradley is much less timid than Montgomery."

Bradley came over to Patton's HQ that afternoon to discuss long range plans. He wanted to attack east with the First Army going towards Cologne while the Third Army "maintains pressure and really holds a defensive flank." The plan had the advantage of attacking where the Siegfried line had already been breached and using the shortest road to Cologne, but Patton felt that it was "probably sound but slow." He wanted to attack with XX Corps straight east to Saarlautern because it would go through the whole industrial Saar valley and be more crippling to Germany.

"Wherever we attack, one thing is certain, we should attack, because if we don't the Germans will."

On January 12th, Montgomery sent Bradley a letter. It read:

"My Dear Brad,
It does seem that the battle of the 'salient' will shortly be drawing to a close, and when it is all clean and tidy I imagine that your armies will be returning to your operational command.
I would like to say two things:
First: What a great honour it has been for me to command such fine troops.
Second: How well they have done.
It has been a great pleasure to with Hodges and Simpson: both have done very well.
And the Corps Commanders in the First Army (Gerow, Collins, Ridgway) have been quite magnificent; it must

---

[1] "We" as in Third Army. "I believe that the Bastogne operation is the biggest and best the Third Army has accomplished, not excluding the battle of France, and I hope the troops get the credit for their great work."

be most exceptional to find such a good lot of Corps Commanders gathered together in one Army.

All of us in the northern side of the salient would like to say how much we have admired the operations that have been conducted on the southern side; if you had not held on firmly to Bastogne the whole situation might have become very awkward.

My kind regard to you and to George Patton.

Yrs. Very sincerely,
B. L. Montgomery"

It is interesting that Montgomery "imagines" Bradley's armies will be returned when he would be actively campaigning for the next several weeks to keep those armies. Thanks to his efforts, he was able to keep Simpson's Ninth Army for his gigantic Rhine crossing a month away. And it is also interesting how Montgomery says that if Bradley had not held onto Bastogne "the situation would have been awkward" when *he* had advocated retreating and regrouping along the Saar-Vosges line.

On January 13th, Patton launched a new attack toward Houffalize, hoping to quickly link up with Hodges. He ordered his III Corps to attack Wiltz and St. Vith. Since it was impossible to capture Wiltz by the south, he told the corps to circle around the hills and attack from the west.

That same day, at a half-wrecked church in Lower Wiltz, a Nazi policeman told the pastor, Canon Prosper Colling, "I want you to evacuate all your people to Wilwerwiltz by tomorrow morning."

Colling was used to talking back to Nazis. "Impossible," he said, "I can't move 4,000 people that fast."

The Nazi was angered by Colling's tone as well as by his announcement. "An order is an order!" he yelled as he slammed the door behind him.

Colling didn't know what to do. The 4,000 people were hiding in the church cellar, terrified, and if he told them the news he would create a panic.

"I am making a promise to Our Lady of Fatima," he told them. "A promise to build a shrine to the Sacred Heart and Our Lady of Fatima on the slopes of Bassend, if we are all saved." He signed a paper with the above promise on it and handed it to the other men. They all eagerly signed it.

"Go through the town," he told them, "Tell the people I have composed a novena. Every day they should say the Our Father, the Creed, and a prayer of repentance. And they should sing the "Song of St. Sebastian" the patron of this town, and "I'm a Christian and I'll Stay Christian."

Colling figured with this busy program the people of the town would not have time to panic. The news of the novena quickly spread, and by the time it reached Upper Wiltz, people were sure that if they promised to help build the shrine, the Germans would leave the town on the birthday of St. Sebastian, the town's patron. "Almost every citizen believed without reservation that liberation would come on January 20," wrote John Toland.

"The Germans are definitely on the run," Patton wrote to his wife, "I rather fear that out super planners have been more scared than the soldiers have." Patton had given the cakes his wife had sent to some orphans.

There had been three clear days in a row, perfect weather for the fighters and bombers.

On January 16th Patton and Hodges' armies linked up in the little town of Houffalize. A little less than a month ago, the German offensive had begun. One of the Germans' first actions was to take the city. At that time it had been a small village whose main industry was sawing the Ardennes forest that lay around it. Only one intersection broke through the stone houses of the village, and this intersection ran along the Liege road. It was this intersection that cost the little town its homes and buildings, because the Liege road was the Germans route to the west and east of their offensive objectives. Because the Germans needed the road, the Allied bombers destroyed the intersection mercilessly. Many of the bombs missed their targets and by the time the Americans retrieved the town it was only a little heap of rubble.

Patton wrote this poem based on the Christmas song "O Little Town of Bethlehem" when he saw Houffalize almost a month later, on February 2nd,

"O little town of Houffalize
How still we see thee lie;
Above thy steep and battered streets
The aeroplanes sail by.

Yet in thy dark streets shineth
Not any darkened light;
The hopes and fears of all thy years,
Were blown to bits last night."

Now that Patton's 11th Armored and Hodges' 2nd Armored had made contact at Houffalize, Bradley was restored to command of the First Army. This was the end of the German offensive. It only remained to drive the Germans back out of the Bulge and into Germany. Devers,[1] the commander of Ninth Army,[2] was charged with liquidating the Colmar pocket. At first he said he could do it with only one division, but now he needed Patton's 10th Armored Division and 3 battalions of Artillery. Patton had to relinquish them, but he feared that Devers would not return them. "Personally I would rather fight Germans than the inroads of Devers and Monty," he wrote.

In his letters to his wife, Patton began referring to Bradley as "the tent maker." The reason has been obscured over the years.

"I fear we have not got the mental equipment for one big
push. From a material and personnel view point, it could
be done and should be done. Even the tent maker admits
that Courtney is dumb. He is also very jealous of me."

Patton visited Millikin and Middleton at Arlon on January 17th. Patton had congratulated them over the phone, but he made sure that he repeated it in person. "They have done exceptionally well," he wrote, "Of course, Millikin, being a greenhorn, required considerable shoving, but I think he has done a good job." Patton told them they would have to continue the attack, even though they and their men were tired. However, Patton wanted at least 1/3rd of their forces to rest and "warm up, because we are going to attack until the war is over."

Everett Hughes came to visit Patton. Hughes told Patton "with great glee" that Eisenhower had told him, "You know, Everett, George is really a very great soldier, and I must get Marshall to do something for him before the war is over." Eisenhower never "did" anything for Patton except relieve him – and that was after the war was over.

---

[1] No great friend of Patton's.
[2] Ninth Army was now under Montgomery

SHAEF called, ordering Patton to give up another of his divisions to Devers. Patton chose the 101st Airborne because "we will probably lose that anyhow." Walker called late that night to ask if he could press ahead with his attack, and of course Patton gave his permission. "Now is the time to attack and to keep it up," Patton wrote.

On January 18th, Churchill addressed the House of Commons and settled once and for all the question of a special "ground forces commander" under the name of Montgomery. He gave credit to the American armies, and especially "Patton's Army" for closing the Bulge. At the end of the speech he said, hinting to Montgomery and the supporting British newspapers, "Let no one lend themselves to the shouting of mischief makers when issues of this momentous consequence are being successfully decided by the sword."

It was 10am, January 20th, the birthday of St. Sebastian. This was the day the miracle was supposed to take place.
At the partially destroyed Church in Lower Wiltz, the old Canon was singing High Mass. The Canon noticed the people whispering among each other and was about to become angry when he heard something outside – the clomping of hob nails on the cobblestones. The noise was a familiar one: Germans on the march.
Suddenly, someone ran into the church and shouted, "The Boche are leaving!"
The congregation laughed, cried, and hugged one another. Canon Colling closed his eyes and thanked God.[1]

The weather had turned bad again. A soupy fog had settled over the region and rain and sleet beat down on the frozen soldiers scattered all over the Ardennes. Walker was still attacking, but Milliken and Troy were waiting until Sunday. "I always hate not to have a desperate job on my hands," he told his wife, "I guess I am getting used to it." It had only been a month since the Battle of the Bulge had started!

A heavy snow had settled on the armies in the Ardennes, and the snow kept falling throughout the next day. The Americans were still going forward, if only a mile a day. Troy and Middleton began their attacks on the 21st. Patton went out to see their attacks and to "give each officer a pat on the back." They were doing well now, he thought. At one

---

[1] "Battle: The Story of the Bulge," by John Toland

point he had almost relieved General Holbrook, but he was doing well now too.

On the way back to his Command Post, Patton noticed several trucks carrying between 40 and 50 new soldier replacements. They were stuck on a slippery hill and not moving. There were a number of officers present, but "none of them had enough sense to dismount and push the vehicles until Stiller and I did so. Then the trucks got moving fast." Several years later,[1] in the Canal Zone, Mrs. Patton was stopped by a Third Army sentry who inspected her pass. Since he was from Third Army, she asked him if he had ever seen General Patton.
"Oh, yes," the soldier replied, "I knew him, though I only saw him once. We were stuck in the snow and he came by in a jeep. His face was awful red,[2] and he must have been about froze, riding in that open jeep. He yelled to us to get out and push, and first thing I knew, there I was with General Patton pushing right alongside of me."

Patton wondered how the Germans could withstand so many continuous attacks and added, "I hope we get to Berlin first. But if we do, we will have to get a move on." He was already thinking about what would happen *after* they took Berlin, and presumably meant that they would need to "get a move on" in order to beat the Russians to Eastern Europe.

Devers was begging for more troops. He already had Patton's 10th Armored and 101st Airborne (both veteran troops), and Patton was worried that he might lose the 8th Armored.

Patton called Bradley begging him to have all the Armies attack, even though they were tired and under-strength, because "in view of the Russian offensive, now is the time to strike."[3]

Devers got the 35th Division that he wanted – despite the protests of Bradley and Patton. Devers was the commander of Ninth Army

---

[1] In 1948

[2] On January 10th, Patton wrote in his diary, "It was very cold driving, and I may have frozen my face a little." Part of the reason for Third Army's high morale was Patton's willingness to take the same risks and face the same hardships that the men did.

[3] Did Patton mean the Germans would be weaker due to the Russian offensive? Or did he mean that the Allies must hurry before the Russians took more territory? He probably met the first reason, although he may have meant both.

Group. Their objective was to clear the Colmar pocket, and it was turning into a sad fiasco. "It is too bad that the highest levels of command have no personal knowledge of war," Patton commented.

Bradley and Patton were planning their attacks. They had just worked out the boundaries between the armies when General Whiteley, Eisenhower's deputy G-3 called. SHAEF, Whiteley said, wanted Bradley to withdraw additional divisions and transfer them to Devers. Bradley blew up.

"We would be giving up a sure thing for a sideshow! If you want to destroy the whole operation that we've got here, then you can do so, and be darned."

Suddenly Whiteley handed over the phone to his superior, Bull, Eisenhower's G-3.

"I want you to understand," Bradley said to Bull, "that there is more at stake than the mere moving of divisions and corps and the launching of a certain tactical plan. The reputation and the good will of the American soldiers and the American army and its commanders are at stake. As far as I'm concerned, you can take any division or corps in the 12th Army Group and do with them as you see fit, because those of us that you leave back will sit on our asses until hell freezes over. I trust you do not think I am angry, but I want to impress upon you that I am *incensed!*"

Every man in the room stood up and applauded, and then Patton approached the phone. In a voice loud enough to be heard across the line, he said,
"If they remove the divisions, all three of us will resign. I will lead the procession."

Patton wrote in his diary of this meeting,

"For the only time to my knowledge, [Bradley] lost his temper .... It occurs to me that this patent attempt to prevent the attack of the First and Third Armies is a British effort to give Monty the leading role. If our attacks fail after a good try, we will have to give Monty troops, and the Americans simply sit on the defensive while U.S. blood aids British prestige. At the moment four British divisions are out of contact [with the enemy] and Monty says the earliest he can attack is February 8th. Bradley was very firm and even angry."

It was during this dire period, when Bradley was pitted against Eisenhower's inept leadership and Montgomery's greediness that Bradley began to see eye-to-eye with Patton. All along Patton had had to fight Eisenhower and Montgomery for every gallon of gas, every yard of soil, and every fighting man. Bradley had thought, perhaps, that the long tentacles of 21st Army Group would never reach him. Now both Bradley and Patton were opposing Eisenhower's High Command in order to launch an attack – fighting to fight.

Chapter Thirty Nine

DIVERSIONARY ADVANCE AGAIN

"I am convinced that the Germans are pulling out as far as the Rhine," Patton wrote on January 26th, "and if we go ahead, we will get to the Rhine, and very soon. To do otherwise at this moment would, in my opinion, be criminal."

Both First and Third U.S. Armies were attacking eastwards towards Germany. The Battle of the Bulge was officially over, and Patton said good bye to Bradley. Bradley was leaving for his new headquarters at Namur. "He is a good officer," Patton wrote in his diary, "but utterly lacks 'it.' Too bad."

Heavy snow was falling and there was intense cold, but that was not stopping the attack. The Allied armies were back to their old business of trying to storm the Siegfried line. Thirteen divisions of the four corps of Third Army were poised along the Moselle, Sauer and Our Rivers attacking undaunted the Siegfried Line from Saarlautern, north to St. Vith.

Patton drove around in his jeep reviewing his troops and watching their attack. He did this not only to raise morale, but to see that potential problems were corrected in time. Some books and movies have attempted to portray Patton as doing this only for media attention. Patton could not have cared less about what newspapers thought of him; what he cared about was his troops. Even in the freezing weather, Patton could be found out in the cold, leading, directing, organizing: an example for his officers and his men.

Patton, a sixty year old man, drove in the freezing weather of his open jeep for eight hours on January 30th. The next morning when he woke up he had extreme pain in his eyes from the snow and "eyes running like a spigot." He had to stay inside most of that day with barasic compresses on his eyes.

Eddy called Patton complaining that he could not attack until February 6th, but Patton insisted that he attack on the 4th.
"You never give me any time to get ready," Eddy complained. He said that Patton didn't appreciate the time and space factors involved in getting an attack ready.
"If I gave a corps commander the time he asked for," Patton shot back, "we would still be on the Seine."

Only a few minutes later the telephone rang. It was 12th Army Group HQ, instructing Patton to commit no troops for the attack yet. "We will issue orders later," they said. Patton was understandably annoyed. He had to call Eddy and tell him to stop *preparing* to attack.

> "This is another case of giving up a going attack in order to start one that has no promise of success except to exalt Monty, who has never one a battle since he left Africa and only El Alamein there. I won Mareth for him."

Patton had to talk to the commander of the 94th Division, Harry Maloney. Too many of his men had been surrendering, making the division's non-battle casualties higher than their battle casualties. Patton told Maloney that he, too, would become a non-battle casualty if his division didn't shape up. Patton was intentionally rough in order to alert Maloney of the danger. He then talked to the field officers and representatives from every company in the division and gave them his usual fighting talk. He praised them for what they had done, but told them,

> "very frankly that the 94th had lost more men as prisoners of war than all other troops I had commanded during my entire military service and that they must wipe out the disgrace. I then patted General Maloney on the back, and believe that this technique had the desired effect."

When Patton returned to his HQ, bad news awaited him. He would lose the 95th division and also around five or six artillery battalions to Devers' Ninth Army Group. Patton was "quite outspoken" in his objections, but Bradley told him that it wasn't even Eisenhower's plan. It was forced on him by the Combined Chiefs of Staff. Eisenhower had met Marshall briefly as Marshall was on his way to the Yalta Conference. It was then that Marshall ordered Ike to transfer the division.

"I hate this political war. However, the mistakes of the high command have thus far turned to my personal advantage and glory. Here's hoping."

Patton drove by Houffalize and was surprised by the destruction which he deemed worse than St. Vith. The little town was "completely removed."

At Spa, Patton discovered that Hodges' office was in the room where Hindenburg decided WWI was lost. Patton could appreciate this kind of historical irony. He said he could see the lake around which the Kaiser had walked while awaiting word from Hindenburg.

After Bradley, Hodges, Simpson and Patton had lunch together with a few staff officers, they held a meeting. Bradley told them what Marshall had told General Eisenhower. Marshall had ordered Ike to attack – with Devers' Ninth Army Group and Montgomery's 21st Army Group. This attack would all be under Montgomery's command.

The gathered Americans in the room were at a loss. Their attacks were all in progress and succeeding, why give them up for a *planned* attack under a notorious stick-in-the-mud? Montgomery's attack wasn't even scheduled to start until February 10th. Bradley, eager to defend Eisenhower and Marshall, offered that they undoubtedly wanted to get the 14 British divisions that had not fought in the Battle of the Bulge back into the fighting. The words had a hollow ring to the gathered brass.

Montgomery would again make the main attack, again American troops – the Ninth Army – would support them. Since the Ninth Army was only recently established, First and Third armies would contribute the necessary companies. First Army did have a pseudo-part in the plan. They were to guard the right flank of the Ninth Army and secure the Roer river dams.

21st Army Group would attack, Ninth army would protect them, and First Army would protect the Ninth! Patton's Third Army had managed incredible victories with no support at all; Montgomery couldn't achieve a reasonable victory with all the support in the world.

First and Third Armies would be allowed to continue their attacks until February 10th. "Personally, I think this is a foolish and ignoble way for the Americans to end the war. In my opinion, every division should be attacking, and if such an attack were made, the Germans do not have the resources to stop it," Patton wrote. If the Americans did not have enough supplies for all the armies to attack at once, then only the armies successful in attacking should head for the Rhine. And obviously, Montgomery's 21st Army Group was the *most unsuccessful* attacking army in Europe.

SHAEF bureaucrats had been scared out of their wits when the Battle of the Bulge started. Since they had not foreseen it, they immediately thought that soon the Germans would be on the Meuse. They were completely wrong about the capabilities of the Germans then, and they were also wrong about the capabilities and staying power of the individual American soldiers. They guessed wrongly about how quickly Patton could rescue Bastogne, and now, after so many wrong guesses, they decided that they needed a reserve. The German armies had been completely destroyed, but SHAEF refused to learn the lesson it should have learned back in September of 1944. There's a time for an advance – and a time for a reserve. The time for advance is when the enemy is in retreat. In other words, now.

The decision to keep a reserve at this late hour in the game was one of the most ridiculous to come out of the war. Naturally Patton wanted to advance so as to take more of Eastern Europe – but that is a political reason. Are there any military justifications for this decision? Goltz, a famous strategist, said, "When you know the enemy's strength, and he is fully deployed, then you know enough to dispense with a reserve." This is a rare condition in war – one however that the Allies could now meet.

Of course the Americans were not well versed in either strategy or military history and chose caution over a swift advance. The irony is that though they would later protest they had only the highest military considerations in mind, they probably made this decision for political reasons.

Patton's military plan was based on the basic principle that the Germans were retreating – for the time being. He wanted an extra armored division to clear up the Saar-Moselle triangle, but "as usual I was turned down."

It was depressing for Patton to watch his plan crumble as another Montgomery plan was adopted. "Monty is so slow and timid that he will find a German build-up in front of him and will stall," he wrote in his diary. Patton would not give up, however. He decided to start a new attack with XII Corps and not tell Bradley. He knew that Bradley would stop it if he knew of the attack.

Third Army HQ must have been a very unhappy place at this time. It seems that after every great Third Army victory, they were put on defensive and a Montgomery plan was put into action. Third Army was not just put on defensive each time, but placed at the bottom of the totem pole as far as supplies go.

"You may hear that I am on the defensive but it was not the enemy who put me there. I don't see much future for me in this war. There are too many 'safety first' people running it. However, I have felt this way before and something has always turned up. I will go to church and see what can be done. I feel pretty low to be ending the war on the defensive." *Patton, in a letter to Beatrice.*

Little did he know what would await him in Czechoslovakia.

Chapter Forty

DEFYING ORDERS TO STEAL VICTORY

Patton felt that Third Army, though technically on the defensive, might still have a chance of "getting to the Rhine first."

> "I am trying to keep the impending Bitburg offensive secret so that the powers that be will not order it stopped. Therefore I was quite worried when Bradley telephoned and asked if I could meet him and Ike at Bastogne. I trust that it is simply a desire to be photographed in that historic city, but it may be further orders." *Patton's Diary*

He planned on having Eddy start the offensive no matter what happened, but if ordered on the defensive, he decided that he would go to England and visit the Leicester-Warrens and the Stockdales for a few days. "I am not tired but get bored when there is no fighting."

His instinct proved true. The meeting at Bastogne was "purely a social one, but I was more amused than surprised when Eisenhower failed to make any remark about my Bastogne operation; in fact he made no reference whatever to the great successes of the Third Army." This was less than what Churchill had done when addressing the House of Commons a few weeks earlier. "First Army was reinforced with extraordinary military efficiency from the Metz area by General Patton's Army, who hurled themselves on those intruders from outside of Bastogne." After the war, Gerd von Rundstedt would be asked what

Allied commander he feared the most. He answered simply, "Patton, he is your best."[1]

Eisenhower would never admit so much. The reason for Eisenhower's ingratitude, Patton reasoned, was probably simply carelessness, "however it is poor leadership."

> "So far in my dealings with him, he has never mentioned in a complimentary way any action that myself or any other officer has performed." *Patton's Diary*

Eisenhower and his generals were photographed in front of a carefully selected "junk heap." They then drove to First Army HQ. Patton was careful not to mention his secret plan for attack. Patton did mention, however, that if he had to lose a corps, he hoped that it would not be Middleton's. Eisenhower replied that he didn't see why Patton should lose a man that he trusted. Middleton had been under Hodges' command, but was pleased when he heard that Patton had requested to keep him.

Patton awoke on February 6th at 3am in the morning. It had suddenly occurred to him that he could repeat the incredible sweep across France of last August if he had 2 or 3 armored divisions advance in swift exploitation after the VIII and XII Corps.

> "Whether ideas like this are the result of inspiration or insomnia, I don't know, but nearly every tactical idea I have has popped into my head like Minerva and not as historians attempt to describe generals who work out things on paper in a laborious manner."

This was the origin of the Palatinate campaign.

This plan would leave Patton attacking with everything he had with nothing left for defense. He was not worried, the Germans could no longer launch an attack.

> "We are having a very funny battle right now. I am taking one of the longest chances of my chancy career;

---

[1] This answer astounded the reporter, Patrick Mitchell, who had asked it for the *Stars and Stripes.* He thought the answer would be Montgomery or Bradley, Army Group Commanders.

in fact, almost disobeying orders in order to attack, my theory being that if I win, nobody will say anything, and I am sure I will win."

This operation, he felt, he would be his biggest gamble. He remembered that when Nelson was attacking Calvi at Corsica, "he learned that there were twice as many French there as had been reported to his chief, so he kept the secret and won the battle." Patton figured that the stakes weren't too bad. After all, if Gaffey and Grow didn't get through, he would be in the same situation he was already in. Except that he might be relieved...

The attack was going slower than Patton had hoped due to bad weather. He called Bradley , begging to keep the 17th Airborne. "He was no help," Patton wrote. Then he wrote a telling passage about Bradley,

"His success is due to his lack of backbone and subservience to those above him. I will manage without him. In fact, I always have; even in Sicily he had to be carried. Personally I fight every order I do not like, which makes me unpopular but successful."

The Germans had destroyed the Roer River dams in order to flood the ground in front of Ninth Army, making it impossible for the Americans there to advance. This could be the Third's chance to advance and capture Cologne and Koblenz!

The weather was terrible, though, and the roads were disintegrating quickly. The incredible traffic of heavy weight mobiles that had passed through the region had obliterated the local roads. Patton told Middleton to dismount the tank crews and use them as infantry if the roads became unusable. He also ordered Middleton not to give up Sauer River bridge. "I hate to get men hurt [so as] to take a place and then give it up."

The Sauer River bridge was very difficult to capture. The Siegfried line runs along this river and the Americans had to contend with hundreds of pill-boxes. After eliminating the resistance in the Siegfried line, the men had to cross the flooded river which had a current of 10 to 12 miles an hour. The 6th Armored lost 136 boats trying to cross, but eventually were able to build bridges under the enemy's fire.

On February 13th the Third Army stormed the Sauer and Our River's opposite banks and headed into Germany. This was an incredibly quick advance. Patton went up to visit the front lines, which surprised the soldiers. There was a small amount of risk involved, but Patton thought it was worth the morale-booster. The whole time he was at the Sauer bridgehead, the Americans were covering the area with smoke.

Patton lamented that he did not have just one more division – that would be enough for a breakthrough and rapid advance into Germany. "The brains are all set on another fool move which never has and never will succeed, particularly under Sir B. L. [Montgomery]," Patton told his wife.

Patton decided to visit Paris since his attack could not begin until February 17th. He met Bedell Smith at Versailles, who was "very eloquent" and said to Patton that although,
"I suppose you don't know the high strategy, I am convinced that my northern effort with 21st Army Group cannot logistically support more than 35 divisions. Since we have 83 divisions, that leaves quite a few I can use anywhere else, and I want you to be prepared to resume the old effort through Saarlautern and Sargeguemines." Smith was talking as if *he* was the Supreme Commander. "How many divisions would you require?"
"I could attack with five," Patton replied.
"I think you should have twelve," Smith said, acting like he could dispense divisions wherever he chose.

"I have never known how grand he is," Patton wrote sarcastically in his diary. He then went shooting with Smith at one of the old royal hunting preserves and killed three ducks, one pheasant, and three hares.

While in Paris, Patton went with Hughes to the "Follies" theater. Patton wrote that the dancers there were so naked that no one wanted to watch them. When they went backstage, the owners had the usual party for Patton "the liberator." The wife of the manager said, "My dear General, when ever you come to Paris, make the Follies your home. You can rest here always." Patton wrote in his diary that he could think "of no place less conducive to rest."

General Gay had been Patton's Chief of Staff in Sicily. Eisenhower had punished him rather mysteriously by telling Patton that he could not have him for his Chief-of-Staff in France. Ayer thinks that Ike was trying to punish Gay for the slapping incident. Be that as it may, Gay still acted as a pseudo-Chief of Staff even though Gaffey carried the title. Eisenhower arrived for dinner with Patton, and, seeing Gay, said, "Hap, I wouldn't be much of a man if I couldn't admit I was wrong. You did a magnificent job. I am recommending your promotion to Major General and giving you back your job as Chief of Staff." It must have been a happy occasion.

Chapter Forty One

"NOTHING HAS STOPPED US YET"

"To heck with them. They have associates, I have fate."

Patton wrote Bradley a letter stating that all U.S. troops, besides Third Army, were doing nothing. Since he was still attacking, he wanted Bradley to know that he could do a better job if only he had a few more divisions. Three to be exact. Then he could quickly reduce the Saar-Moselle triangle, remove the threat to Luxembourg, capture Trier, and get on with the war. "I wrote this letter in order to get on record as we will be criticized by history, and rightly so, for having sat still so long. Also, I do not want any of my ideas used without credit to me as happens when I give them orally." Patton was right. Those responsible *would* be criticized when the harsh light of historical evidence uncovered the men whose lethargy cost thousands of lives.

Patton was able to secure the 10th Armored "with a string on it – only for this operation. I will be darned if I see why we have divisions if not to use them." Patton had told Bradley that he would use the division for "reconnaissance in force." Armored divisions aren't used for that – but Bradley knew what Patton was doing: his old rock soup method. Bradley could give Patton *one* division for reconnaissance, but no divisions for the continuation of his offensive.

Bradley wanted to give Patton the extra divisions he needed, but the powers that be had forbidden it. He came personally to tell Patton. He looked tired; he had been battling Eisenhower for divisions. As usual, the result of these battles was that Bradley "did not seem at all sure of himself." "Regardless of what you and I think, we are good enough soldiers to carry out these orders," Bradley said. He had lost the battle with the High Command. "Why not rest, refit, and refill the empty gaps in the divisions?" he asked. It was apparent that 12th Army Group's Commander had surrendered to overwhelming force from SHAEF.

But Patton had a plan. He looked at the exhausted, battle-worn Bradley and asked mischievously, "Are there any objections to my making a run for Koblenz *ahead of time*? Or taking Cologne if the opportunity *suddenly developed*?"
The flicker of comprehension crossed Bradley's wrinkled brow. "No, there are no objections."

Patton refused to think of rest. This was the time to act. If time was wasted, it would be duly exacted in American casualties in the upcoming months.

A "typical" day in the Palatinate campaign was February 21st. The VIII Corps' 90th Division captured five towns and cleared a sixth. The 11th Armored captured Roscheid, and the 6th Armored seized two villages and cleared two more. The XII Corps' 80th Division enveloped and destroyed the Germans in the Siegfried line and captured one town – clearing two. The XX Corps' domain, the 10th Division cleared *everything* in their zone all the way to the Saar. And one cannot say that these results were achieved merely because the Germans were retreating – for if so, why was Third Army Eisenhower's only attacking army? Montgomery's vast 21st Army Group sat silently eyeing the enemy; Hodges' First Army front was quiet as well. Only the Third was attacking, and what attacking!

"I had to use deception, tears, and every other means to get one division," Patton wrote to his wife. "One would think people would like to win a war." He told her he was planning on wheedling an infantry division so as to take Trier. There were seven resting at the moment, and it shouldn't be too hard to secure one. What Patton couldn't understand is why some people were trying so hard to prevent him from fighting. Could it have been a conspiracy? After all, it didn't take too much of a genius to figure out that Montgomery would take months to reach Berlin.

Patton wrote of what people said about him, "There is much envy, hatred, and malice, and all uncharitableness.[1] To heck with them. They have associates, I have fate."

Walker and Morris at the 10th Armored Division were visited by Patton. "To my disgust, I discovered that Morris had let his bridge train get lost" and had not crossed at Saarbourg as Patton had expected. Morris had waited long past noon for the train to be found. He had been held up by small arms fire on the other side of the bridge and "mortar fire at the far side of the river." Patton told Morris to cross the river "at once" and fine the officer who had gotten lost. If Patton had, like many other commanders, stayed at his headquarters and waited for news from the front, Morris could have become days behind. This in turn would aid the Germans defense preparations and cause casualties.

Patton, however, felt guilty that he had not been up to the front *earlier.* "Walker should have been on the job too, and perhaps I am also to blame. Had I been personally present, the train would probably never have been lost, and the same thing applies to Walker and then to Morris – all three of us fell down." Again this illustrates the incredible difference between Third Army and the other Allied armies. Patton's army was always fueled by an incredible drive that came from the top down. Because Patton was at the front, personally directing, he infused his men with the spirit of advance. He took personal responsibility for the failure of his men, because he knew that ultimately they had failed because of a *lack of* drive on his part.[2]

The press corps met with Patton. He assured them that this was not the last war, and that "clubs" would not save them from another war. "They are responsible for the deaths of millions of people," he said. "The only thing you can do when a s.o.b. looks cross-eyed at you is to beat the heck out of him right then and there." Patton was already thinking about the end of this war; he was talking about another war, something that would soon get him into a lot of trouble. He then made a startlingly accurate prediction, coming from a cavalryman. "They now say that we've got 3,000 miles of ocean, but 20 years from now this 3,000 miles

---

[1] Patton spelled this line as, "There is much envy, hatred, and malace, and all unchareatableness."

[2] This is the reason why Third Army morale was high. In other armies, the enlisted men complain that officers never did anything to assist them and were often the dumbest men in the lot. Bad officers were always weeded out of Third Army.

of ocean will be just a good spit. This is a very serious thing, and many people don't visualize this very serious danger." He seemed to understand the mentality people would have when the H-bomb was created. "We are prone to think too much that weapons are more important than the knowledge of soldiering... It takes ability to take care of yourself and live under bad conditions, and above all, it means ability to work with other men."

"Are the Germans still building tank ditches?" asked a newspaperman.

Suddenly recalled into the present day, Patton answered, "If they would use all that energy in some other way, they might do much better, but they are still building those things, and the only thing they are good for are toilets."

"Are you going to try to take Trier?"

"I fear we lost the boat on that one," Patton said sadly. "We had a bridge train knocked out – but don't say that. This is the first bad luck the Army has had. Every minute you don't put this operation across, it makes it that much harder. I think it's a very feasible operation, though, and we have done well." Trier had a major railroad system and was still the keystone in the German triangle of Trier-Koblenz.

"SHAEF has a new toy called SHAEF Reserve, and every time they let an Army have a division, they want one in return," Patton wrote in his diary. He wanted to keep the 10th Armored, but SHAEF had told him that he would have to return the 11th, 6th or 4th Armored to the reserve. All of these armored divisions were well placed to exploit their attacks and enter Germany. "I just hope something will turn up to prevent my having to return *any* armored divisions. Bradley had promised Patton 48 hours before he would be forced to return the divisions. He also told Patton that he could have two new infantry divisions – but he would have to return two old ones into the "so-called reserve."

"Remember this," Patton wrote to his son, "no set piece of tactics is of any merit in itself, unless it is executed by heroic and disciplined troops who have self-confidence and who have leaders who take care of them." Patton didn't want to return his veteran infantry divisions to the reserve!

"At the moment, the Third Army is on a sort of defensive job – or at least any other Army would be – but we are still managing to keep pushing and have captured or buried about 20,000 Germans in the last three weeks."

The XX Corps commanded by Walker had bogged down short of Trier. If Patton couldn't get them moving, he would have to return 10th Armored. In fact, he would get in trouble for having tried to keep it!

Trier was a difficult nut to crack. Patton had Middleton, Walker, and Gaffey in for lunch. Bradley called during their meeting to ask if he could join them. Patton and his generals were delighted to have him, and while they waited for Bradley to come, "I coached all three corps commanders and also Weyland what to say in order to sell the idea of continuing the attack to take Trier."

When Bradley arrived, Patton pointed out that they had a chance of taking Trier. "It would be criminal not to do so just in order to comply with the dictum of the Combined Chiefs of Staff, 4,000 miles away in Washington, who insist on a certain number of inactive divisions in a so-called reserve." According to Patton, "they argued hard." Bradley was arguing alone for Eisenhower. A few months ago, Bradley would have taken the 10th Armored and told Patton to shut up. Now, though, the memory of Bastogne was vivid in his mind, along with the warnings about leaving the VIII Corps static. The insults that Montgomery had offered him still stung, too, and Eisenhower had been silent. Besides, Bradley had never been a strong man. That was why he was chosen to lead the 12th Army Group. And that was why, now, he told Patton that he could attack until dark of February 27th. And he offered a difficult condition – Ike would have to let Patton have the 90th division, a SHAEF reserve unit.

Patton was satisfied. This time, Walker's XX Corps *would* take Trier. Patton had staked his reputation on it. "I wonder if ever before in the history of war, a winning general had to plead to be allowed to keep on winning." I don't think there was before then. Now it's become an almost warly occurrence.

"We have just finished a very strange meeting. The tent maker felt that we should stop attacking, and it took me and all three corps commanders half a day to get permission to continue the attack for another 48 hours, at which time if we have not taken a certain town [Trier] we will have to stop. What a war. Well we will do it anyhow. I have never been stopped either by orders or the enemy yet..." *Patton, letter to Beatrice.*

Chapter Forty Two

THE GREATEST COMMANDER

Five months earlier, Patton could have invaded Germany. Now it would be harder because the Germans, though defeated, were not in retreat and were ready for invasion. Rivers were flooded, roads muddy, and pillboxes full, but Third Army morale was high.

Ayer, Patton's nephew, was still working for the F.B.I. in Europe. He found the job very frustrating because they had collected a lot of evidence about Russian intentions on ruling post-war Europe, but could not make the higher authorities believe it. They were forbidden to report or investigate anything that the Russians were doing. Ayer was, therefore, delighted when a message arrived for him from Luxembourg that read,

> "Get off your dead butt and come up here. We're about
> to have a fine war. – Patton"

Walker's XX Corps started to take the Trier-Koblenz triangle. They were more successful than Patton expected. To take Trier, Patton had to pass one division through the supply train of another. Though this was an extremely difficult move, it completely confused the Germans, who had thought that the 10th Armored would attack to the southeast and try to get behind the Siegfried line. That maneuver would have been safer, but the Germans would have expected it. Patton, as usual, did the unexpected and had the 10th Armored attack to the north.

It was February 27th and the Third Army was eight kilometers from Trier. Their time limit was up. Patton called Bradley.

Bradley told Patton to keep on going until higher authority stepped in. To prevent that likelihood, he would stay away from the telephone.

That morning, Third Army HQ received two top-priority messages. The first was from SHAEF, ordering Patton to bypass Trier "as it would require four divisions to capture the city." The second was from General Walker, announcing that they had just captured Trier. Patton sent a telegraph to SHAEF marked "Urgent" as he often did when ordered not to advance. This time, however, the message was quite different.

> "Have taken Trier with two divisions. What do you want
> me to do? Give it back?"

Walker had not merely taken Trier, he had also captured a bridge over the Moselle intact. Third Army had captured over 7,000 prisoners.

> "Tried to get Eisenhower and Bradley on the wire to
> notify them, but was unable to do so and called Smith.
> Later Bradley called me from the Ninth Army and was
> very much pleased, and Beedle and Brad were
> complimentary. Ike was in the room with Bradley; I
> heard his voice – but he did not take the trouble to speak
> to me. I certainly again proved my military ideas are
> correct and have put them over in spite of opposition
> from the Americans." *Patton's Diary*

"Fooled them again," Patton wrote to his wife, "and I had to beg, lie, and steal to get a chance to take Trier." Patton noticed that the Germans had heavily shelled a town at the time he was scheduled to meet there and concluded that the Germans tapped their telephone wires.

The capture of the bridge over the Moselle was achieved by an extremely heroic Lt. Colonel who saw the demolition charges on the bridge. He jumped out of his vehicle and raced across under heavy fire to the other side of the bridge and cut the wires. "The acid test of battle brings out the pure metal," wrote Patton of this incident.

Patton's divisions were swarming towards the Rhine – uncomfortably close to Devers' Army Group. "Tell Devers to get out of the way," Patton reportedly told Bradley, "or we'll pick him up with the Krauts!"

As usual, Patton went among his troops to right any potential problems. Today he brought along with him his nephew, Fred Ayer. As they drove along, they came across a long column of men, trucks, and weapons completely motionless blocking the road for more than a mile. They were a defenseless target for the nearby enemy artillery. Why were they stopped? A 155mm. artillery piece had jammed underneath a concrete railway overpass. Patton angrily sought out the officer in charge of the column. He found the colonel halfway down the column trying to sort out the mess. "Colonel," Patton shouted, "You can blow up the gun, you can blow up the bridge, or you can blow out your brains, and I don't care which. Just get this column *moving!*"

A little further on the trip Patton spotted a tall man in dusty civilian clothes walking on the side of the road.

> "Within seconds, he shouted, 'Stop the car and cover that man.' The man was ordered over. Patton looked him up and down, then called him to attention in German. The man in automatic reflex snapped to a rigid stance. 'You are an Army officer are you not?' Patton snapped at him.
> 'Ya wohl, mein General.'
> Orders were given to have him taken to the nearest P.O.W. camp. I then asked, 'How on earth could you know what he was at that distance and so quickly?'
> 'Freddy, if after all these years I can't recognize a soldier when I see one, I should turn in my uniform.'" *"Before the Colors Fade," by Fred Ayer.*

After taking Trier, Patton had to beg Bradley to attack with all three corps again towards Germany. "I won a decisive battle just now against the tent maker," he wrote to his wife, "so I can now continue my 'passive defense' with renewed ardor." The Third Army had a longer distance to travel to the Rhine and was as always hampered by higher authorities' restrictions.

Amusingly, Bradley writes in "A Soldier's Story" that he told Patton, "Perhaps you'd better get that assault stuff up closer. I want you to take the Rhine on the run. We're not going to stop, give the other fellow a chance to build up..." But as contemporary evidence shows, he was of a much more cautious mind at the time.

Gaffey, commander of XXIII Corps, captured 2,000 prisoners of war on March 6th along with a corps commander and staff. They had advanced 24 miles inspite of the terrible weather conditions. Patton was very proud of them as he wrote that, "We are in a horse race with Courtney [Hodges]. If he beats me, I shall be ashamed." When by an incredible stroke of luck, First Army captured the Remagen bridge across the Rhine, Patton was surprised and pleased rather than jealous.

4th Armored reached the Rhine north of Koblenz advancing 65 miles in only 36 hours – very good for the conditions.

On March 7th Patton was scheduled to review a green division north of Colmar. There was an icy drizzle, occasional sleet and a biting wind. Patton was riding, as always, in his open jeep. On this occasion he did not have his usual driver, Sgt. Mims, but an unfamiliar man dressed only in an Eisenhower jacket. This was his only concession to the cold. After about half an hour of driving in the frigid weather, Patton noticed that the driver was turning a light shade of blue and that from time to time he shivered. Reaching forward, he tapped the man on the shoulder. "Corporal?"
"Yes, sir?"
"Are you cold?"
"Yes, sir."
"Do you have a warm sweater?"
"No, sir."
The General leaned back, unbuttoned his jacket, and turned to his nephew, Fred Ayer, who retold the story. "Help me out of this thing," Patton said, after which he peeled off the sweater and handed it over to the driver. "Well, corporal, you have a sweater now," Patton said.

This was a typical Patton gesture not in line with the "Blood and Guts" caricature of the newspapers. Patton did not sack men without a moment's regard to them, he did not curse like a sailor, he did not believe in "victory at all costs" in spite of casualty lists. He had a paternal care for his men unlike any other great military leader – he knew that little things, like a hot meal and dry socks – contributed more to victory than all the ammunition in the world. Thus Patton resented the image that was fast becoming the only public connection with him. He felt that a better handle would have been "Brains and Guts."

Also on March 7th, William Hoge's combat command bravely stormed the Remagen bridge making Hodges' First Army the first over the Rhine. Patton was genuinely happy for Hodges and wrote in his diary, "9th Armored Division of the III Corps got a bridge intact over the Rhine at Remagen. This may have a fine influence on our future movements. I hope we get one also."

What happened at Bradley's HQ when Hodges got over the Rhine is a telling indictment of the sort of strategy that SHAEF employed. Eisenhower's G-3, Major General Bull, happened to be visiting when Hodges' called with the good news. Bull found no cause for rejoicing however.
"Sure, you've got a bridge, Brad, but what good is it going to do you?" he asked. "You're not going anywhere down there at Remagen. It just doesn't fit into *the* plan."
"Plan – heck," Bradley answered, "A bridge is a bridge and mighty good anywhere across the Rhine."

Many other members of Eisenhower's staff agreed with Bull's take on the situation, however. "Where can you go?" they asked him. "What can you do over there?" Since the bridge wasn't part of "The Plan" they suggested that he retreat and blow it up.

Although *that* decision was overruled and the Remagen bridge was used, their initial reaction shows their vast inflexibility to the natural fluidity of war.

This may be the reason why SHAEF bureaucrats could not appreciate Patton's genius. They needed a "plan" and they felt that all war required a "plan" that should be adhered to, step by step. Improvisation on the plan and exploitation of a newly developed situation could not be appreciated – or tolerated.

Montgomery had assembled *thirty six* divisions for his crossing in the north, but he wanted 60. Bradley's *diversionary* Rhine crossing was limited to *four* divisions because Montgomery feared he would need another ten divisions in case he "smashed through the enemy crust" that had surrounded his massive crossing. Montgomery still had the twelve divisions of Simpson's Ninth Army which he had taken during the Battle of the Bulge. Bradley worried that SHAEF would force him to give Montgomery more and more divisions, but wrote that happily, "The war accelerated too rapidly thereafter for further harassment from the staff at SHAEF."

Patton had heard rumors of the new Montgomery plan. "It is essential to get the First and Third Armies so deeply involved in their present plans that they can't be moved north..." The trouble was that all of the Rhine bridges in Patton's sector had been blown out. Bradley's other general, Patch, said that he could not cross the Rhine until the 15th. Bradley wanted to coordinate Patton's attack with Patch's but Patton was determined to attack immediately...even if alone. "I am going to attack as soon as possible, because at this stage of the war, time is more important than coordination," he wrote in his diary.

History proves that Patton was right. There were only three months left of war in Europe.

The 11th Armored had reached the Rhine at Andernach and captured 8,000 prisoners. "And I had to beg to do it," Patton commented.

At this time a German officer named Lt. Col. Freiherr von Wagentheim was captured. Under interrogation, he gave voice to the common fear of the German Armies.

> "The greatest threat ... was the whereabouts of the feared U.S. Third Army. General Patton is always the main topic of military discussion. Where is he? When will he attack? Where ....? How? With what? Those are the questions which raced through the head of every German general since the famous German counteroffensive last December. The location of the U.S. First and Ninth Armies was well known, but one was not sure where the Third was... General Patton is the most feared general on all fronts. The successes of the U.S. Third Army are still overshadowing all other events of the war, including the campaigns in Russia...The tactics of General Patton are daring and unpredictable... He is the most modern general and the best commander of armored and infantry troops combined."

What is most incredible is not that Lt. Col. Von Wagentheim offered this praise, but that others could fail to. Throughout Patton's audacious advances only the beaten Germans would give praise to the conqueror. Patton's superiors freely admitted that he was "daring and unpredictable" but were more apt to apply those terms to his public relations skills rather than his tactics.

Patton felt, more than any other man, the end of the war approaching. He wrote a letter to Marshall begging that when the war ended in Europe he be allowed to fight the Japanese. "I am sure that my method of fighting would be successful," Patton said. "I am also of such an age that this is my last war, and I would like therefore to see it through to the end."

Somehow Patton seemed to be out of touch with military as well as civilian leaders. While Patton was pursuing a vigorous advance in an attempt to end the war as far east as possible, Eisenhower was speaking of how difficult it would be "breaking through the fortified lines" into Germany; he expected crossing the Rhine to be "a nasty business."

Because Patton had battle experience, he knew how much to expect from his men. The terrain that the XX Corps was attacking in was "terrible, just woods and mountains." Thus he was satisfied that they had advanced 4 miles. Third Army as a whole had taken 89,000 prisoners since the beginning of February and captured 9,000 prisoners on March 13th "the biggest single bag we have had." Such a large increase in prisoners proved that the war was drawing to a close, even if some people at SHAEF didn't know it.

Someone said to Patton that his instructions were always "in a lay-man's language... easily read and understood."
Patton replied that, "We can never get anything across unless we talk the language of the people we are trying to instruct. Perhaps that is why I curse." Thus Patton was truly the quintessential citizen's army leader; he not only understood his men's hardships and tried to minimize them as much as possible, he also spoke their language. Yet he was finding himself more and more alienated from the men that were guiding his country and its armies' fates.

Patton visited Trier "so did Caesar ... whose Gallic wars I am now reading." Some writers are surprised that Patton would re-read Caesar and attribute it to a romantic impulse. The truth is that all good commanders read the writings of past leaders who conquered in the region that they are planning on occupying. It is the soundest military strategy, because, while armies change, the terrain – and man's instinct – does not.

As he walked through Trier with Caesar in mind he noted that "it is interesting to view *in imagination*[1] the Roman legions marching down the same road." Note the words "in imagination." He was not, as some authors believe, saying that he had seen it all before in some past life, but rather *imagining* that he could see the ancient armies. With a touch of the poetic, he added that as he left Trier and followed Caesar's old road he "could smell the sweat of the legions."

Always eager for a contest, Patton hoped that the Third would take Mainz before the Seventh Army. He called Walker and told him to "turn on the heat as I feel we are not going fast enough."

Nine generals had been promoted to four-star. The three Army Group Commanders Bradley, Devers and Clark were among those promoted. Handy, Kenney, Krueger, Mc Narney, Somervell and Patton's air force friend Spaatz were also promoted. Patton phoned Bradley his congratulations; he sent telegrams to Devers and Clark. Though Patton did not complain in his diary about the promotions, he did write that "I hope they don't make Courtney [Hodges] and I on the same list. I think I would refuse." After all, who had wasted the cream of his army on fruitless attacks against the Hurtgen? Who had left the VIII Corps static, inviting the Germans to begin the Battle of the Bulge? And, after all these disasters, who had saved Hodges' and Bradley's reputations when all seemed lost? Or had Bastogne been so quickly forgotten?

Apparently some people's memories were better; the Prince of Luxembourg presented Patton with the Croix de Guerre for his work in saving their country from another German occupation during the Battle of the Bulge. The French, not wanting to be left out, made him a Grand Officer of the Legion of Honor. The Mayor of Metz honored Patton by presenting him with a large bronze medallion. And Patton already had enough "Honorary Citizen" certificates from various cities to wallpaper several rooms.

---

[1] Italics mine.

Marshall and Eisenhower actually had discussed adding Patton *and* Hodges' names to the list of new promotions; the only reason why they did not do so was that they felt it would be a slight to Bradley and Devers. Eisenhower was sorry that Patton didn't command the 6th Army Group because then it would have been politic to promote him. Marshall replied that if they promoted Patton ahead of Devers it would compromise the latter's usefulness. It seems so peculiar these two, so removed from the war, contemplating promotions based on merit and afraid to give them to the meritorious for fear of "upsetting" those already in command of army groups.

Eisenhower had been flying over Bradley's HQ unable to land because of bad weather. Bradley hurriedly called Patton and warned him that Eisenhower would be forced to land in Luxembourg. Patton drove to the airfield and found that Eisenhower and Bedell Smith had just landed. Eisenhower and Patton drove to Trier and discussed the latest strategic developments at the front. Eisenhower stayed over that night. The next morning, Eisenhower paid Patton "the first compliment he has ever vouchsafed."

This is the way Patton's aide Colonel Codman retold this "great moment" for Third Army,

> "At our briefing the next morning, the Supreme Commander astounded us all by rising to his feet and making a speech. 'The trouble with you people in Third Army,' he said, 'is that you do not appreciate you own greatness; you are not cocky enough. Let the world know what you are doing, otherwise the American soldier will not be appreciated at his full value.'" *"Drive,"* by Colonel Charles R. Codman.

Patton's staff was astonished. For so long they had been accused of being too loyal – of thinking of only their army's welfare – that this turn-about was enough to leave them open-mouthed. Was Ike at last acknowledging the Third's gargantuan efforts in every battle since D Day? Were the messages coming out of SHAEF different from Eisenhower's true feelings?

> "He stated that we of the Third Army were such veterans that we did not appreciate our own greatness and should be more cocky and boastful ..." *Patton's Diary*

Later that day General Eisenhower approved Third Army's request for another armored division, the 12th. Was Eisenhower in person different from the calculating "Supreme Commander" of SHAEF who always passed Third Army's requests up in favor of Montgomery's? For, besides approving the request he now "continued in an expansive vein."

"George," he said, "you are not only a good General, you are a *lucky* General, and, as you will remember, in a General, Napoleon prized luck above skill."

"Well," Patton laughed, "that is the first compliment you have paid me since we have served together.

Eisenhower left soon afterwards. At dinner that night Patton was relaxed. "I think Ike had a good time," he said, "They ought to let him out oftener."

"What I can't get over," General Gay said, "Was his statement to the effect that Third Army isn't cocky enough. How do you explain it?"

"That's easy," the General said, stirring his soup, "Before long Ike will be running for President. Third Army represents a lot of votes." Sensing the half-incredulous smiles, he looked up sharply. "You think I'm joking? I'm not. Just wait and see."[1]

This was an incredible piece of prophecy: at this time Eisenhower was vehemently denying any political aspirations and was protesting that he didn't even belong to a political party. Yet Patton saw through his ploy as clearly as he had seen through the myriad of other devices that had been used to deceive him. Though Patton is often described as a glory-seeker, he knew that Eisenhower's honeyed words were calculated for effect. What is more astounding is that Patton realized they were calculated for *political* effect.

I often think that it was Patton's clear-sightedness that ruined his chances for promotion. I feel that this conclusion is heightened by the fact that the man placed in command of Patton was so intellectually dense. Bradley, by his own account, was Ike's best friend, yet he never noticed the political trend; Bradley also never suspected the Russian intent on keeping Eastern Europe.[2] Since men intellectually Patton's inferior were constantly promoted above him, I can only conclude that this was purposeful.

---

[1] "Drive," by Colonel Charles R. Codman.
[2] Read "A General's Life" for more interesting things that Bradley "never noticed."

It is at this time that Ladislas Farago, one of Patton's biographers, states that the Patton-Eisenhower friendship began to crumble. I have found little evidence of a "friendship" between the two men, although Patton did, decades earlier, lend his notes on a strategic class at Fort Knox to Eisenhower, who used them and proceeded to get an "A" in the class. After that the two rarely saw each other. Patton had been Pershing's aide in Mexico and in France during WWI; he had led American tanks in their first attack while Eisenhower was *training*[1] the tankers in the U.S. The two had little in common; Patton had all his life "loved war" and studied strategy, while Ike had joined the army only out of necessity. Thus there was so little in common between Eisenhower and Patton before the war that it is not surprising that they "fell out" during it.

Eisenhower considered his career "ruined" when he was left out of WWI; at the start of WWII he begged Patton to select him as a subordinate commander. From that point on some would say that "in a strange twist of fate their roles were dramatically reversed." I'm not sure how much fate had to do with it: due to Marshall's approving smile Eisenhower began a sudden advance in rank that averaged out to be a promotion *every 6 months* starting in 1942. Yet, either due to fate or purposeful design, Patton was left to prove his worth as a mere army commander.

Patton's XX Corps' advance towards the Rhine was threatening General Balck's entire forces. General Balck, commander of German Army Group G, was determined to slow Patton's crossing of the Rhine. He quickly formed a defensive line in the Hunsruck Mountains in an attempt to protect his north flank. But Patton now used one of his old tricks against a solidly-held German area. He ordered the 4th Armored to cross the Moselle south of Koblenz and dash through the enemy's rear. The XII Corps' Infantry followed closely behind, wiping up any resistance. The XX Corps, which had plunged through the West Wall in the north and was rapidly advancing towards the Rhine, was able to link up with the XII Corps in the south. Because of this two-pronged attack, Third Army captured 10 German divisions in the Hunsruck Mountains. This was Patton's masterpiece; it shows the true genius of his strategy.

---

[1] Strangely, it is an American tradition to leave training the men about to leave for war to the most inept officers.

The Germans desperately tried to hold everything in front of Patton; Mainz and Mannheim quickly fell to the onslaught of Patton's slashing armor. The 4th Armored cut off the Germans' escape crossings across the Rhine.[1] Patton's armored divisions were attacking the German Army Group on three sides. The Germans, surrounded and cut off from their Rhine bridgeheads, began surrendering in the tens of thousands.

The Third Army's campaign in the Palatinate was rolling onwards, more brilliant by the hour. "We are the eighth wonder of the world," Patton wrote to his wife, "And I had to beg, lie, and steal to get started – now every one says 'that is what we always wanted to do.' I hope things keep smooth. It seems to be too good to be true." The 4th Armored was 6 miles from Worms. The XX Corps was nearing Bad Durkeim. Third Army took Koblenz. German Major General Schimpf of the 3rd Paratroop Division called Patton's campaign in the Palatinate "phenomenal."

Suddenly Patton halted his armored columns south of the Nahe River near Bad Kreuznach – only 25 miles from the Rhine. Bradley's staff had been watching Patton's wonders anticipating his next moves and were now anxiously fretting at HQ. "Why doesn't the old boy push on?" one of them asked Bradley.
General Bradley, trusting an uncanny military instinct that he did not possess, retorted, "Patton knows what he's doing. Just keep your shirt on and you'll see." Certainly a different view than he would have expressed a year ago while preparing for D Day.

Within 24 hours from Patton's halt the enemy counterattacked in *that exact sector*. Because Patton had stopped and consolidated that front with reinforcements, he quickly repelled the attack and continued moving. How did Patton know? Unfortunately this incident, which so impressed Bradley, is hardly mentioned in Patton's diary at the time. That is because Patton was spending much more time at the front – and I suspect that that is how he knew of the German counterattack.

The counterattack had not been mentioned in *any* of the intelligence reports "but George had anticipated it with the curious intuition that helped make him a great field commander."[2]

---

[1] Something that the Allies had notoriously failed to due earlier.
[2] Bradley in "A Soldier's Story."

There is a certain amount of sixth sense that a commander needs to have so that he can correctly judge the enemy's intention and dispositions. This sense can be developed through combat experience and visiting the battlefield, but it remains ultimately a talent given by God that cannot be entirely explained or judged. As T. E. Lawrence said, "The greatest commander is he whose intuitions most often happen." Certainly by this standard Patton proved that he was the "greatest commander" to arise out of the war in Europe. The question only remains why he was so often thwarted and deprived of command.

Patton certainly went far to prove his worth; some have speculated that he would not have worked as hard if his career had been certain. This is doubtful; but it is not doubtful that Patton was truly, as the Germans said, the Allies' "most modern" commander. While addressing the press in Luxembourg on March 17th Patton said that, "The Marines go to town by reporting the number killed. I always try to fight without getting our people killed." His strategy of bypassing all resistance cost fewer casualties and gained more ground; if he was a German he certainly would have been a Field Marshal and probably as revered as Rommel.

Still addressing the press, Patton informed them that the Third Army had been operational for 230 days and had 230,000 prisoners – 1,000 a day! Then he added carefully, "Don't say that the Marines advertise casualties. I was merely trying to emphasize my point." He had certainly learned from his last brush with "fate" at Knutsford.
"Which is more important," a correspondent asked, "a bridge across the Rhine or the fighting down here?"
Patton honestly answered, "A bridge across the Rhine."

On March 21st the Palatinate Campaign officially came to an end with Third Army having annihilated every German contingent in the Moselle triangle. "I really believe this operation is one of the outstanding operations in the history of war," Patton wrote in his diary.

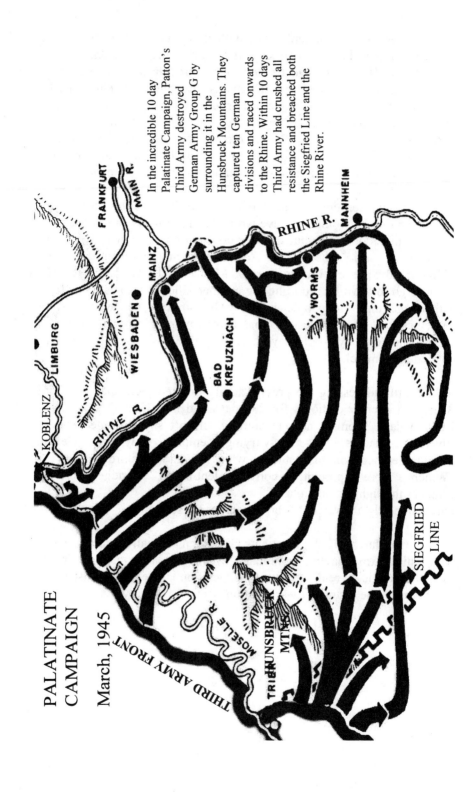

PALATINATE CAMPAIGN

March, 1945

THIRD ARMY FRONT

KOBLENZ
LIMBURG
FRANKFURT
MAIN R.
WIESBADEN
MAINZ
RHINE R.
RHINE R.
BAD KREUZNACH
WORMS
MANNHEIM
MOSELLE R.
TRIER
HUNSBRUCK MTNS.
SIEGFRIED LINE

In the incredible 10 day Palatinate Campaign, Patton's Third Army destroyed German Army Group G by surrounding it in the Hunsbruck Mountains. They captured ten German divisions and raced onwards to the Rhine. Within 10 days Third Army had crushed all resistance and breached both the Siegfried Line and the Rhine River.

Chapter Forty Three

ACROSS THE RHINE AT LAST

Bradley was just sitting down for breakfast on the morning of March 23rd. He was on his second cup of coffee when a telephone call reached him from Patton.

"Brad, don't tell anyone but I'm across."

"Well, I'll be darned – you mean across the Rhine?"

"Sure am," Patton replied, "I sneaked a division over last night. But there are so few Krauts around there they don't know it yet. So don't make any announcement – we'll keep it a secret until we see how it goes."

A little later that day, Patton sent Lt. Col. Stillman to deliver the official message to Bradley. "Without benefit of aerial bombing, ground smoke, artillery preparation, and airborne assistance, the Third Army at 2200 hours, Thursday evening, March 22, crossed the Rhine River." The man who had the aerial bombing, ground smoke, artillery, airborne divisions: in other words the full benefit of Allied materiel supremacy, Field Marshal Montgomery, had been left in the dust by Lt. Gen. Patton.

Patton's 5th Infantry Division had ferried across the Rhine early that morning in rafts and small engineer assault boats. They crossed to find themselves in Germany: the little farming village of Oppenheim to be exact. It had been the first crossing of the Rhine in that vicinity; Patton lost only 28 dead and wounded. "Brad," Patton said, his treble voice trembling across the phone, "for God's sake tell the world we're across. We knocked down 33 Krauts today when they came after our pontoon bridges. I want the world to know Third Army made it before Monty starts across."

Devers had been scheduled to cross the Rhine at Third Army's right, south of Worms, but he was waiting for an air blitz. They waited for 10 days by which time the Third Army had crossed and Devers was somewhat jealous. "We did not wait," Patton wrote, "and caught most of the 15th Panzer division in bed." Patton's strategy had triumphed again.

In his diary Patton wrote, "The 5th Division is over the Rhine. God be praised. It was a fitting climax to the preceding ten days.... I am very grateful to the Lord for the great blessings he has heaped on me and the Third Army, not only in the success which He has granted us, but in the weather which He is now providing." A typically self-effacing passage attributing his success to his men and to God.

"I am really scared by my good luck," he told his wife, Beatrice, "This operation is stupendous." And so it was. Third Army had gas enough for the time being; she was succeeding, wrapped in the robes of triumph and wearing the laurels of victory.

Germany had lost the war. The Red Army was advancing, and in front of it were tens of thousands of German refugees fleeing their homes in hope of freedom at the American lines. These people were called "displaced persons" by the Americans and housed in camps (not unlike prison camps) until something could be done for them. Patton's description of them to his wife is worth quoting,

> "The displaced persons is a problem. They are streaming
> back utterly forlorn. I saw one woman with a
> perambulator full of all her worldly goods sitting by it on
> a hill crying. An old man with a wheel barrow and three
> little children wringing his hands. A woman with five
> children and a tin cup crying. In hundreds of villages
> there is not a living thing, not even a chicken. Most of
> the houses are heaps of stones. They brought in on
> themselves, but these poor people are not responsible.
> I am getting soft? I did most of it."

This letter shows the gradual evolution of Patton's thought. Although he desperately wanted to advance so as to help these poor people escape the Russians, he was aware of the paradox – in the process he was destroying their homes and stocks. And his last comment, "They brought it on themselves, *but these poor people are not responsible*" shows the keenness of his wit but was a remark that was desperately out of sync with the times.

Napoleon, too, had crossed the Rhine near Oppenheim. Patton's son pointed that out to him. He had not known that,

> "I had picked this when I was still in England as the place to cross the Rhine because the terrain on my side dominated that on the other side, as the former was far enough away from the Frankfurt hills to prevent direct fire on the bridges, and because, above everything else, there was a barge harbor there from which we could launch the boats unseen."

Less than ten men died in a military crossing of the Rhine! That is unprecedented in the history of war. That Patton could plan this from simply looking at a terrain map in London is incredible, and shows Patton's genius not just in swift exploitation, but also in *planning*.

The leader of the operation, Major Stiller, requested to cross in the first boat with his men. There really has never been another army like the Third – and it was made that way by its commander. Because in England the Third was considered green and passed over in favor of experienced divisions for the Normandy invasion. The Third Army shows how much a good leader selecting good leaders can do for an army.

The next day, March 24th, Patton officially crossed the Rhine. "Drove to the river and went across on the pontoon bridge, stopping in the middle to take a piss in the Rhine and then pick up some dirt on the far side in emulation of William the Conqueror."

Patton proudly wrote in his diary that Third Army had processed its 300,000[th] prisoner which put it 1,000 prisoners over First Army – even though First Army had had a 59 day bonus.

Montgomery crossed the Rhine in the north at 4 a.m. that day after a huge artillery bombardment of *70,000* rounds, an air bombardment, smoke screens and an airborne landing on the other side to support the crossing.

A sad incident occurred the next day. Col. Jack Hines, the son of Patton's friend Major General Hines[1], had been struck in the face by an 88 armor-piercing shell "which removed his eyes, his nose, and upper jaw, and also took off his left hand. Apparently his wounds had a bad effect on Grow, as the division was very logey today. I told Grow if he did not get into Frankfurt tonight, I would relieve him. I then flew to Bad Kreuznach to see Colonel Hines. When I arrived, he was on the operating table and unconscious. At least if he dies, I can tell his father I saw him."

This incident underlines Patton's hard task, and one for which he is often misunderstood. While he, more than anyone else, felt terrible at what had happened to Col. Hines, it was also his duty as commander to see that Grow did not allow his feelings to get the better of him. Thus he threatened Grow with relief so as to stimulate him to reality, then flew to the hospital.

Col. Hines, incredibly, recovered. He was awarded the Distinguished Service Cross by his father at the Walter Reed Hospital in Washington.

Patton sent Eisenhower a complimentary letter now that the war was almost over. Though he was being flattering, he was careful not to lie. "You have made your Army a fighting force that is not excelled in effectiveness by any other *of equal size* in the world," he wrote. Eisenhower, did not exhibit the same scrupulousness when writing to Marshall. "Patton is a particularly good war friend of mine and has been so over a period of 25 years."

What Eisenhower wrote after that sentence is sickening. "I think I can claim almost a proprietary interest in him because of the stand I took in several instances. In certain situations he has no equal, but by and large it would be difficult indeed to choose between him, Hodges and Simpson... while Patch is little, if any, behind the others." Yet when Eisenhower did have a choice – during the Battle of the Bulge – did he choose Simpson? Could he have chosen Hodges since it was his sector that the Battle started? Why had he so quickly, and unhesitatingly, called for the commander of an army more than 100 miles away when such "equal commanders" were near?

---

[1] Major General Hines had succeeded Pershing as U.S. Army Chief of Staff

330

Sometimes I think that Patton should have waited when that Battle started. He should have waited until things got really desperate, until Eisenhower would have begged on his knees for Patton – maybe even turned over his command to him. Of course, had Patton waited many more of Hodges' men would have died. Patton would never have stood by while Americans died – even when there would have been more glory in waiting.

Patton was soon to be Eisenhower's discarded tool. Used, but then thrown away disgustedly. When war was over, a warrior like Patton had little place, newspapers would say. And Eisenhower would nod his head approvingly. Eisenhower would not recognize Patton's military genius; no one would recognize Patton's political foresight.

We could afford to ill-treat him. After the war he looked old and foolish, a war-monger. Today we have hindsight and can see that not only were his military warnings true, his political prophecies also came true, one by one.

Chapter Forty Four

A DARING ATTEMPT

Allied Intelligence had recently revealed that a camp at Hammelburg, a city that lay in Third Army's path, held 4,700 prisoners. But as Third Army drew closer to the city, Patton began to worry that the Germans would pull out and take the prisoners with them.

One thousand five hundred of these prisoners were American, thus making the camp an even more desirable objective. With Patton's usual finesse for the unorthodox, he ordered Eddy to send an expedition from 4th Armored ahead 60 miles to capture the American prisoners. Hoge, the commander of 4th Armored, and Eddy, as usual, objected.

They told Patton that if he failed, he would be criticized. Patton was used to divisional commanders' objections, and as usual he dissuaded them. "I do not believe that fear of criticism should prevent my getting back American prisoners," he told them, "Particularly because in the last death struggle the Germans may murder our men being held there."

This was a cogent argument. Evidence had already been discovered of Germans' massacring American prisoners during the Battle of the Bulge. Allied pilots who parachuted into German territory were often beaten and killed by the German populace. If this happened when the Germans were doing fairly well, what would happen now that they were losing?

Except for this prisoner-rescuing expedition from 4th Armored, the rest of XII Corps would be advancing northeasterly to join up with Hodges' First Army.

The leader selected for the task force was Captain Baum. Baum was not a career officer. He was chosen for the mission after it was verified that Colonel Cohen was too ill to lead the task force. Patton told Baum that if he pulled the mission off, he'd personally see to it that Baum received the Congressional Medal of Honor. Baum allegedly replied, "I have my orders sir. You don't have to bribe me."

At first the mission went off successfully. German morale was at its lowest. Their soldiers knew that the war was over; their main aim was to stay alive – and away from the Russian front – until peace was declared. When they saw the American tanks of Baum's task force they were convinced that they had seen the last day of the war and were happy to lay down their arms. Since the task force was cut off from the main bulk of Third Army, the American tanks rolled over the German weapons to render them useless. "Now wait here," they said, "Third Army will take you prisoners soon." The Germans hoped so; they did not want the SS to know that they had surrendered.

Baum now foolishly got lost. It turned out he had taken the wrong road – he was on a road that dead-ended in a mine. This cost him time – and time is precious to a task force behind enemy lines. It also cost him gasoline, something he would soon be in short supply of. He had to stop and question wary civilians as to the quickest route to Hammelburg.

However, all was not yet lost. A civilian guide was found and forced to accompany the tanks. The task force had little fighting to do. Everywhere the tanks would begin to fire and the Germans would throw their hands up. As the American tanks advanced further, a German staff car with three occupants drove over the hill above them. The Americans quickly captured the Germans inside, one of whom was General Oriel Lotz. This was quite a prize for the small American task force. Baum ordered the general to sit on the hood of one of the half-tracks. If opposing Germans saw him, perhaps they wouldn't shoot. Better still, they might realize the war was lost.

As the task force wound its way closer to Hammelburg they came upon the town of Grafendorf. Here whole groups of German guards surrendered. The men they had been guarding – starving Russian slave laborers – went wild with joy at the sight of the Americans. The Russians asked Baum if they could take the town, to which Baum replied, "As soon as we get through." He writes in the book "Raid! The Untold Story of Patton's Secret Mission" that he realized how badly they had been treated by the Germans and felt sorry for them. The Russians asked Baum if they could "have" the general. For what torture they had reserved for him is not known; Baum certainly knew that they meant to have their revenge. Baum authorized the Russians to take the town, told them to raid the police station for weapons, and handed over the general along with most of the other Germans the task force had collected to these handful of starving prisoners-turned-occupiers!

The Americans pulled out of Grafendorf and continued towards Hammelburg. Meanwhile, behind them, General Lotz had easily escaped from the Russians and gained contact with the colonel in charge of defense in the area. He alerted the colonel to the fact that the Americans were heading towards Hammelburg; he had heard them asking civilians for the location of Hammelburg many times.

Now that the Germans knew where the tiny American force was headed, all was lost. The Germans knew not only what the task force's objective was, but also that this mission would not be followed up in force by Third Army. The whole virtue of the mission had lain in the fact that the task force was small and mobile and heading for an unknown objective. By the time the Germans knew what had hit them, Task Force Baum would already have reached the Allied lines. Baum had sacrificed the surprise that was so vital to his mission's success. He had handed over the German general – a prize well worth keeping in case things *did* get tight – to a handful of starving, beaten Russian slave laborers without weapons in a *German town*.

Task Force Baum reached Hammelburg safely. The 1,500 American prisoners were delighted to see their compatriots. Baum states in the book "Raid! The Untold Story of Patton's Secret Mission" that he had only been expecting 300-400 prisoners. This is not true. The Intelligence report had suggested that there were around 900 prisoners and this is the number that Patton had planned for. Thus Baum was given adequate transportation for *nine hundred* prisoners, not 300, as he suggests. Still, there was an extra 600 prisoners overlooked by the Intelligence report, as eager for freedom as their fellow prisoners.

The prisoners swamped the half-tracks that Baum had been provided and piled onto trucks, tanks, and any empty space unaccounted for. Now came the second part of the mission: getting out of Hammelburg with the prisoners. Baum sent his light tanks on a reconnaissance around the camp looking for a clear path back to the armies, meanwhile leaving the task force idle outside the camp. This was a mistake. The Germans knew that Baum's objective was Hammelburg; they also knew that the only military significance of the town were its prison camps on the outskirts. While Baum's task force waited outside the prison camp, Colonel Hoepple sealed its fate by posting sentries along all the major roads leading out of Hammelburg.

Instead of fighting through the German barricades, Baum tried to look for another route. Thus he lost men and gained nothing as he tried one road after another, only to find that they had all been blocked. After that, it was easy for the Germans to tighten the ring and wipe up the task force. Of the 294 men that had left for the mission, 268 were captured and 25 presumed killed. The 53 American vehicles assigned to the mission were also destroyed or captured.

Should Patton have sent more men to accomplish the mission? Patton wrote in "War as I Knew It," "I can say this, that throughout the campaign in Europe I know of no error I made except the failure to send a combat command to Hammelburg." But it is still true that Baum's task force should have been successful – and would have been, if he had not foolishly allowed the Germans to know the size of his force and its objective.

Another issue that obscures rather than enlightens the argument over Hammelburg is that Patton's son-in-law John Waters was being held in the Hammelburg prison camp. Some suspect that Patton's reason for rescuing the 1,500 Americans being held there was merely to liberate Waters.

This accusation does not stand up to the facts. John Waters had been captured in Tunisia in February 1943. Patton and his family were not sure if he was in fact a POW or an unidentified casualty. For the time being, they merely knew that he was "missing in combat."

Waters had been transported with other prisoners by his German captors to Italy. Eventually, like many other prisoners, he was moved out of the path of advancing Allied armies to Szubin, Poland. After the

Russian armies took the empty prisoner-of-war camp they found John Waters' name on the roster and reported this to the proper American authorities.

The Soviet report was sent from Eisenhower to Patton in February, the first news Patton had that Waters had been a POW. The report stated that Waters' new whereabouts were "unknown."

Thus it was completely impossible for Patton to have *known* that Waters was in the POW camp. Naturally Patton wanted to have the honor, like a Crusading knight, of liberating his son-in-law from the hands of his captors. But he would not endanger his beloved soldiers in a risky mission behind enemy lines *solely* for his son-in-law.

Proof of this lies in a letter Patton wrote to his brother-in-law Frederick Ayer four days after sending the expedition,

> "Some days ago I heard of an American prisoner of war camp... so I sent an armored expedition to get it. So far I have not been able to hear what they did. *It is possible* that John may be among the prisoners. If so, I will be very delighted to take the place."

The Intelligence report that Patton had received about the Hammelburg camp stated that many of the prisoners there had been transferred from Szubin. This, then, gave Patton at least a glimmer of hope that among the 1,500 American prisoners might be his son-in-law. But based on the number of times Waters had already been moved across Europe by the Germans it made the chance highly improbable.

Patton's nephew, Fred Ayer, believed that it would have been utterly impossible for Patton to have known that Waters was in the camp.

> "From experience in intelligence work, I think [Patton] should be believed. In those days, many tales of atrocities against U.S. prisoners were common fare at the front. Most commanders' immediate human, and humane reaction was to try to free the men as rapidly as possible. Also, I cannot remember a single instance, during those days of movement and confusion, when a command was aware of the identity of individual prisoners in any individual P.O.W. stockade of whose

existence they had just learned." *"Before the Colors Fade,"* *by Fred Ayer.*

In the letters to his wife at this time, Patton refers to "John" in place of the word "prisoners" or "Hammelburg" which would be censored. On March 25th he had written, "Hope to send an expedition tomorrow to get John." Referring more directly to his objective he wrote on the 27th to her,

> "Last night I sent an armored column to take a place 40 miles east of Frankfurt where John and some 900 prisoners are said to be. I have been nervous as a cat all day as every one but me thought it too great a risk. I hope it works. If I loose that column, it will possibly be a new incident, but I won't loose it."

But Patton's specific mention "where John *and some 900 prisoners*" proves that he had no intention of sending a task force to rescue one man. The release of nine hundred prisoners – or 1,500 as it turned out to be – is a legitimate military objective.

There were two major prison camps in Hammelburg, Stalag 13 A and B. Stalag 13B held 4,000 Serbs who had surrendered when the Nazis invaded Yugoslavia in 1941. The first group of American prisoners to be held at Stalag 13B had surrendered during the Bulge and arrived at the prison camp on January 18th. Later that month a group of 20 American officers were interned, along with 800 prisoners that had just completed an arduous trek from Szubin, Poland.

This group of 800 American prisoners, of whom Waters was a member, had a long story. They had just completed a march of over 300 miles from Szubin in Poland to Parchim, Germany on foot. The starving and ill-clad prisoners completed this epic trek in 45 days.

The story behind the march, besides being interesting, goes further to prove my point that Patton *could not have known* where his son-in-law was because that all depended on the German orders of the day. Waters had gone through an incredible amount of prison-transfers in comparison with ordinary POWs who usually sat out the whole war in one stalag.

Patton's rescue mission began in late March. Had it been sent a month earlier, Waters and the 800 prisoners from Poland would not have even been at Stalag 13. For this is the story behind their march: The German guards at the camp in Szubin, afraid of the oncoming Russian armies and rumors of atrocities, forced the 1,400 American prisoners to gather up their belongings and begin marching on January 21st. All who were not too sick to walk began the long march. It was 20° below zero outside the camp and the prisoners had to march through the blinding snow.

For 800 prisoners the journey ended in Parchim, Germany. From there 400 men (including the senior officer of the Americans, Colonel Goode, and his executive, Colonel Waters) were sent in boxcars to the Hammelburg camp. A further 400 marched the rest of the way to Stalag 13. Out of the 1,400 that originally left Szubin, 400 were shipped to a stalag east of Berlin. Waters could just as easily have been in this group. Finally, an additional 200 prisoners never made it to Parchim. Some of them escaped, others were wounded by the fire between the German and Red armies and sent to hospitals, others were killed.

There is a book about the rescue mission sent to Hammelburg called, "Raid! The Untold Story of Patton's Secret Mission." There are several problems with this book. The first is that none of the statements made include sources. Many appear to be eyewitness accounts (since they include the thoughts and feelings of certain men) but they are not referenced. This makes it impossible for me to verify their accuracy. The book is written in a third person fashion, despite the fact that two of the authors are talking about themselves. I find it very hard to believe that certain conversations were held, certainly their wording seems peculiarly after-the-fact. Since the source of the conversations is not listed I can not verify if my suspicions are correct.

However, some statements made in the book are blatantly wrong. One is the assumption, accepted in the book as fact, that the Hammelburg mission was doomed before it ever started. Another is that "this was the first mission attempted behind Allied lines." Market Garden was a whole operation with several divisions executed behind enemy lines.

The authors assume that because their task force was small, they had no chance of victory. Yet a *small force* is just the type that is sent behind the lines, often very successfully. Because it is small, it can be mobile and fluid, its only concern being its supply train. Small forces are sometimes cut-off; yet a great commander often improvises by utilizing an enemy supply dump. When Patton had been out of supplies in September of 1944, he sent several small, guerilla-like bands behind the lines. Their objective was to find gas, ammunition, food and clothing for the starving Americans. These bands were *very successful*. The men in charge of them were true warriors, always eager for a new and difficult challenge. Because they believed that their mission would succeed, and because they were smart and improvised, Third Army managed not to starve that September through November. They even managed small gains.[1]

Thus the statement in the book, "Any time we ever sent someone out through the lines into enemy territory, we darned sure followed, and in force," is completely wrong and shows that the authors were not well-aquatinted with Third Army history. In fact, throughout the fall of 1944 dozens of small attacks were launched and it was impossible to follow *any* of them up due to lack of gas.

The Germans recognized whose army had begun the attack towards Hammelburg. For the German after-battle report says,

> "This surprise push had been made possible by the fact that the bridge south of Aschffenburg was still intact and because of the lack of antitank weapons, no local securities could prevent or stop the push. This *coup de main* (in which the hand of General Patton could be recognized) showed us how the enemy understood the situation within the German resistance and knew of the small possibilities for counter-measures."

The Germans compliment the attack towards Hammelburg and call it a "coup de main." Typically, the Americans attack Patton and call his mission "ill-advised" while the Germans pay him respect and admiringly point to the genius of someone who could understand the turmoil behind the German lines. The German report continues,

---

[1] Hammelburg was not Patton's last raid behind enemy lines. He launched the 2nd Cavalry 100 miles behind enemy lines into Czechoslovakia (in violation of Eisenhower's agreement with the Russians) and rescued the Lippizaner horse breed from extinction.

"When the Army learned that the enemy task force despite the immediate alarming of all rear units, securities and duty posts had pushed through ... the competent *DEP*13AC was asked to concentrate all available force to annihilate the enemy task force which had broken through."

The Germans would not have known where to "concentrate all available force" if Baum had not released his prisoners. Military history is replete with examples of daring missions behind enemy lines – all of which were successful. T. E. Lawrence "of Arabia" turned going behind enemy lines into an art and his fame rests in the success of his raids. But one does find a constant in all of Lawrence's raids – *the enemy didn't know where he was headed!*

It is not difficult to see why a fluid, mobile force behind a disorganized enemy's lines heading for an unknown objective would be successful. The enemy does not know which cities he should defend, cannot block your path because he does not know where you are headed, and has to follow two steps behind your every move... because he does not know what that move will be.

Yet the authors of "Raid!" continually contend that no operation similar to theirs had ever been tried before – let alone successfully. They constantly reiterate that the mission was "impossible" without giving any plausible explanation as to why.

Baum also states bitterly that the whole purpose of Patton's mission was to rescue Waters – as if the other 1,499 prisoners didn't exist. "Trying to liberate a POW camp, even if it seemed impossible, was a noble objective," the authors state pompously. "Sacrificing so many good men on an impossible mission to rescue one man was far less noble; it was criminal." Hammelburg was not attempted – and would never have been attempted – solely for one man. The authors' acceptance of this fallacy is strange but not surprising.

"Raid!" makes several unqualified statements about the mission. The authors do not back up their claims; in fact we don't even know which author is talking. Yet the book speaks as if they were all experts in military maneuvers and history and know absolutely that their mission was impossible and the only of its kind ever tried. I quote this excerpt as an example,

"This was the first time that members of 4th Armored had failed so utterly. Even so, the task force had gotten further than it had a right to, solely by the heroic efforts of its men.... 'Why would [Patton] do that to us?' [Baum] thought. '*How* could he do that to us?'"[1]

Abe Baum had led this task force – and that made it different than the other successful 4th Armored missions. We cannot expect Baum to have behaved like a military genius,[2] but I find his negligence in releasing the German prisoners he had captured unforgivable. On secrecy rested the crux of his success or failure – he had literally handed the enemy a road map to his objective.

Baum's surprising disloyalty in his book is rare for a Third Army man. He expresses a sense of betrayal throughout the book. Its cause is revealed near the end – he did not receive the Congressional Medal of Honor.

Patton had promised Baum the medal if he was *successful*, and Baum is angry that he didn't get it when he *failed*! Baum acts as if he "gave up" the right to get Patton into trouble for the mission because of deference to him. In fact, had Baum started an investigation into the Hammelburg raid *he*, not Patton, would have emerged as the culprit.

"You know sir," Baum said to Patton after the mission's aftermath, "it's difficult for me to believe that you would have sent us on that mission just to rescue one man."
"That's right, Abe, I wouldn't," Patton replied readily.
Apparently Baum never believed Patton. Luckily for him, Patton did not launch an investigation into the mission's failure.

---

[1] "Raid! The Untold Story of Patton's Secret Mission" by Richard Baron, Major Abe Baum, and Richard Goldhurst see page 254.
[2] i. e. with the success of T. E. Lawrence's behind-the-lines raids

Chapter Forty Five

BRADLEY AND EISENHOWER EXPLAIN

4th Armored's advance into Germany was helped by the Hammelburg incident. The Germans diverted their 2nd Panzer division and two infantry divisions to stop Baum's task force because they didn't believe that Third Army was following in force towards Nuremburg. Thus 4th Armored's simultaneous attack in the north found the entire area undefended; they advanced over 90 miles without firing a shot.

The press soon discovered about the Hammelburg task force even though it was classified. They tried to turn it into another incident, but were unsuccessful. Perhaps because Normandy, Hurtgen, Caen, Market-Garden, and the Ardennes battles – all *real* disasters that cost thousands of casualties – were still fresh in people's minds.

Or did the public still remember who had saved them when Bastogne was a tiny, surrounded, embattled little town and Third Army 100 miles away? If they did, their memories were far longer than the press', who tried to make Waters' location seem more than incidental to the task force's mission.

Eisenhower, as usual, felt the need to apologize. He wrote to Marshall on April 15, 1945,

> "He sent off a little expedition on a wild goose chase in an effort to liberate some American prisoners. The upshot was that he got 25 prisoners and lost a full company of medium tanks and a platoon of light tanks.

Foolishly, he then imposed censorship on the movement, meaning to lift it later, which he forgot to do. The story has now been released, and I hope the newspapers do not make too much of it. One bad, though Patton says incidental, feature of the affair was that his own son-in-law was one of the 25 released.[1] Patton is a problem child, but he is a great fighting leader in pursuit and exploitation."

Unlike the Germans and the British, Bradley and Eisenhower speak of Patton in a patronizing, condescending tone that culminates in their reference to Patton as a "child" – and a "problem child" at that. Eisenhower, perhaps feeling a need to justify his position on Patton, reiterates that Patton is a "great fighting leader" – most people would have known that after his incredible race across France a year earlier.

When newspapermen asked Patton about Waters' connection to the task force's mission, Patton replied in anger,
"Has anyone ever known me knowingly to send a force insufficient in strength for its assigned task? Furthermore, no one who knows me would believe that I'd sacrifice Stiller[2] to save my own brother."[3]

Patton was very upset by the task force's failure. It was Third Army's first embarrassment – and however small, it was still embarrassing. Thus Patton counted his failure to send a larger force as his "only mistake."

Bradley, another notorious apologizer for the mistakes of others, wrote in "A Soldier's Story" that he had not known of Task Force Baum until it was on the road two days. "Certainly, had George consulted me on the mission, I would have forbidden him to stage it. But while I deplored the impetuousness that had prompted Patton, I did not rebuke him for it." Why didn't Bradley "rebuke" Patton for his mistake?

---

[1] Waters was actually not released by Patton's task force because he was wounded as he was leaving the camp. He was released by 7th Armored a few days after Patton's task force had surrendered.
[2] Stiller was one of Patton's favorite aides who had captured the bridge across the Rhine by crossing in the first boat. He had accompanied the task force to Hammelburg and been captured when the mission was unsuccessful.
[3] "Before the Colors Fade," by Fred Ayer

Why? Because Bradley had approved the mission. General Hansen, who attended the meeting, recorded it. Bradley and Eisenhower's habit of passing the buck is surpassed only by their despicable lying when missions fail.

Bradley had refused permission to many a successful mission in the past. The fact that he gave this mission his approval is because it was not "impetuous" nor the most incredible "wild goose chase"[1] that "Patton dared during the entire war." Bradley, cautious, stolid, unimaginative: a strictly according-to-the-book commander, would never have approved a mission that was truly daring, dangerous, or impossible. Slogging matches, yes, impossible behind-the-lines missions, no.

---

[1] Oddly, Eisenhower used the phrase "wild goose chase" to describe the Hammelburg raid when writing to Marshall; Bradley was to repeat the phrase 6 years later in his book.

Chapter Forty Six

POLITICIANS AND SOLDIERS

Samplers of opinion asked the public, "What commander serving under Eisenhower do you admire the most?"
The answer that came was invariably, "Patton."

Patton: beloved by the citizens and soldiers of his country, respected by the German High Command, esteemed by the British. There was only one, tiny group that disliked Patton – and their dislike extended to the point of hatred. This group was small yet powerful and was at this very moment planning Patton's demise.

The war was drawing to a close. The Germans were not resisting anywhere.

> "The war looks over to me. We seem to be able to go anywhere, though 'The enemy is still resisting fiercely in front of the British Second Army.' We went 29 miles today and took another 8,000 [prisoners] while doing it. They went 2 miles." *Patton, in a letter to Beatrice*

Bradley had given Third Army permission to advance to the Werra and Weser Rivers. They might then continue toward the Elbe River – but slowly, no more than 15 miles a day. "It would be risky to go faster," Bradley told Patton. Patton knew that that was absurd – the Germans had collapsed and were not putting up a fight anywhere.

"Whenever [Bradley and Eisenhower] get together, they get timid. I am sure that had a bold policy throughout been used in this war, it would have long since been over."

Meanwhile at Eisenhower's Headquarters (SHAEF), a new worry loomed on the staff generals' heads. They believed the rumors that fanatical Nazis would assemble in the mountains of southern Bavaria, western Austria and northern Italy. This was termed the "National Redoubt." Rumors of huge weapon stores, airplanes, and incredible new weapons hidden there abounded.

That these grown men could have believed that the Germans could launch anything like a new offensive while Germany herself was in utter destruction and chaos shows the extent of their stupidity and childish fears. They had invested the Nazis with magical super powers that made them believe these irrational and impossible claims. As Patton pointed out, there were simply not enough Germans left for a "National Redoubt." As usual, Patton's wisdom was ignored by these foolish generals.

The "National Redoubt" has been held up as an example of the boundless stupidity of SHAEF. It is sometimes difficult to believe that they could have been this inane. But even if they did believe in the "National Redoubt," Eisenhower's next move was not stupid but malicious.

Using the "National Redoubt" as an excuse, Eisenhower said that he could not wipe up the resistance in S. Bavaria[1] and continue the offensive eastwards. Hodges' First Army was assisting the 21st Army Group in finishing its offensive along the Ruhr. Eisenhower decided that he could see no earthly purpose in taking Berlin. He called it a "political objective with no military significance." The American and British armies would meet with the Russians somewhere along the Elbe "because it represented a clear geographical boundary" and would prevent the armies from colliding. Once First Army had assembled along the Elbe it would support Montgomery in the north and Devers in the south. Berlin would be left uncaptured in a sea of Red because "in March

---

[1] In other words, the great mass of the Allied armies could not wipe up the "Redoubt" and still advance to the east.

we were 300 miles from Berlin."[1] Eisenhower then sealed Eastern Europe's fate by sending a copy of his plan directly to Stalin.

This was the first time that Eisenhower had ever made a plan unapproved by his superiors. How unfortunate – or is it something more than that – that it was also the first time that he did not get permission before sending it to Russia.

The line that Eisenhower stopped the British and American armies on and the zones of occupations were all part of a British plan drawn up in 1943. A whole year would go by before their armies set foot in France, and two years before they entered Germany. This was still merely an academic plan, a proposal with no meaning nor requirements. At the Yalta Conference in February 1945, this plan was accepted "without further consideration as the *working* basis for the *inconclusive* discussions about the future eastern frontier of Germany," Churchill says.

"Berlin, Prague and Vienna could be taken by whoever got there first," Churchill wrote in "Triumph and Tragedy." Since Churchill was present at the conference, we should conclude that he understood the nature of this basic plan of occupation. Yet Eisenhower writes as if this plan agreed on at Yalta were a solemn declaration and breaking it would be akin to dishonoring a treaty.

> "The agreements and understandings at Yalta, such as they were, had already been broken or brushed aside by the triumphant Kremlin. New perils, perhaps as terrible as those we had surmounted, loomed and glared upon the torn and harassed world." *"Triumph and Tragedy," by Winston S. Churchill*

America refused to take a stand on any of the agreements that the USSR was flaunting readily, meanwhile allowing Eisenhower to send copies of its war plans, unauthorized, to Stalin!

---

[1] This number is purposely deceptive and must have been measured from the corps that was the farthest back. Patton was less than 100 miles from Berlin last September, he had advanced *forward*, not *backward*, in the meantime. Rather than using the closest number, or at least the most representative, Ike here deliberately deceives the readers of "Crusade in Europe."

When Churchill heard of Eisenhower's machinations, he was furious. Eisenhower was making political decisions, Churchill said. Washington replied that Eisenhower had based his decisions solely on military expediency and that they would not interfere with military decisions.

After the war, Eisenhower was to say of Churchill,

"The Prime Minister knew, of course, that, regardless of the distance the Allies might advance to the eastward, he and the President had already agreed that the British and American occupation zones would be limited on the east by a line two hundred miles west of Berlin. Consequently his great insistence upon using all our resources in the hope of assuring the arrival of the Western Allies in Berlin ahead of the Russians must have been based on the conviction that great prestige and influence for the Western Allies would derive from the achievement."

Eisenhower alleges Churchill's only reason for wanting the capture of Berlin was "prestige." No matter how naive Eisenhower would like to convince us he was, he lies when he states that, "I had no means of knowing what [Churchill's] true reasons were." Churchill conducted several frantic telegrams to every echelon of power and watched, like Patton, powerless as the powerful Allied military machine stopped short of Berlin.

While it is not customary to think of Churchill as powerless, during the whole of the military and political negotiations he was handicapped. At the many political conferences, he could do nothing without American agreement. It would be useless if Britain "walked out" in disgust as the Americans made one ominous political decision after another. If Britain and America broke up, Stalin would be delighted. Yet America would not listen to Churchill, they would not listen to Patton: they preferred to hear only the saccharine lullabies of peace that the Russians played upon the flute of "concession." In a way, Churchill was far more helpless than Patton. For he knew the reason behind every decision and could do nothing. Patton, right now, was ignorant – a state Eisenhower preferred to keep him in.

Eisenhower's sympathetic biographers tell us that he was a "simple soldier" who knew nothing of political decisions.[1] They ask us to excuse him; he made merely a military decision.

What is war fought for? The war in Europe was fought for the liberation of the Europeans – or so we are told. What good was it to replace one evil empire with another? At the time, of course, the USSR was not considered "evil" but an "ally." Stalin had not fulfilled any of the Russian Yalta agreements and was attempting to establish a puppet Polish state. Was he still an "ally" and thus impregnable? Churchill felt that as long as Russia violated their treaties, we should attempt to seize as much extra land as possible – if only to coerce Russia into fulfilling her agreements.

Military objectives cannot supersede political ones, because in our world, war is fought for *political reasons*. It has been 800 years or more since soldiers fought simply to fight. If there is a reason behind the fighting, that reason leaves the "purely military" realm and enters the political. It is hard to imagine a virgin military objective since such an objective would have to be purposeless. Patton's war was "political" since he took land so as to cut off the enemy and force that enemy to surrender – surrender, by this definition, would be "political." If war was fought "purely" it would consist only in slaughtering the other side, since slaughter alone has no ulterior motives.

Obviously, a "purely" military objective is difficult to find, and the idea of a "pure" war approaches absurdity. Thus, war is always fought for "political" reasons; that is, reasons other than strictly military. This is why war is regarded as a means to an end. A "pure" war could only occur when war is the end itself; World War II's purpose was not war but peace in a "safe world."

Peace in a safe world. That was not promising so long as the USSR violated its treaties. And if World War II's avowed purpose was to liberate "peoples from oppressive tyranny" it failed miserably.

---

[1] They can not square this with their praise of his Presidency and make some inane comparisons with Grant.

Chapter Forty Seven

THIRD ARMY UNCOVERS GOLD ... AND TORTURE

Meanwhile, the war, or what was left of it, continued as Germany's demise approached.

America felt in debt to Patton and there was talk of publicly acknowledging him. So on March 30th the House of Representatives voted unanimously to express their congratulations to ... Devers, Spaatz, Bradley, Hodges, Patton, Simpson, Brereton, Patch and Gerow. Thus what was meant to be an honor merely stung Patton, and he wrote to his wife that, "There seems to be an attempt to keep all at the same level. Congress voted to thank me and me only, and ended up by thanking everyone."

Writing to his wife, Patton wrote that, "We never met any opposition because the bigger and better Germans fight Monty – he says so. Also he advertises so much that they know where he is coming. I fool them." Since Patton's strategy revolved around *not* fighting the enemy but encircling and cutting them off, Patton's Third Army rarely did fight the "bigger and better" Germans, finding it more desirable to capture them than fight them.

Patton's Third Army had been ordered to wait for the First and Ninth Armies so that they could advance toward the Russians alongside each other. Patton knew that from a "merely military standpoint" the decision was wrong. He sarcastically wrote in his diary, "However, there may be reasons beyond my knowledge which make it desirable to advance [the armies] abreast. By so doing, no one gets undue credit."

On April 6th XII Corps telephoned Patton's HQ. They had overrun and captured the German gold reserve, "or at least part of it. We decided not to notify higher headquarters until we had better information, as it would be stupid to claim we had found the gold reserve and then not have done so." The next day Eddy stated that he had entered the gold reserve vault and had found over a billion dollars in paper money, but that the gold part was sealed in a safe behind a steel door. Patton promptly ordered him to blow the safe open and verify the rumors.

Patton gave Mc Cloy a tour of Frankfurt in which he took the opportunity to point out that the "wanton and unnecessary bombing of civilian cities" was "cruel and wasteful." The American generals were, for the first time, seeing the savage destruction that "indiscriminate bombing" had wrecked upon the German population. Patton felt that bombing should be directed against "selected commodities which are scarce. In the case of Germany, it would be oil." Indiscriminate bombing turned out to be – militarily – a waste. It hardened the local population to unite under their leader and resist, because, as one person put it "we cannot surrender to a bomber in the sky." One bomber took 600,000 gallons of gas on a routine mission, thus wasting this immense supply which could have driven the Allies further onto Eastern Europe.

Third Army had captured 400,000 German prisoners since August 1st. "No one now is in our class," he wrote, no doubt remembering the Representative's "congratulations." No one – and no army – ever had been in the same class as Patton, and even since then no army has traveled faster. Third Army had not only gone farther and faster than any other army in history – they had captured more Germans too. Even with all of the technological advances that we have made, no one has surpassed Patton's unblemished record.

The Third Army was now in the heart of Germany and its culture surrounded them; the writers Goethe and Friedrich von Schiller had lived in Weimar, and so, for a time, had the composers Franz Liszt and Johann Sebastian Bach. Neitzsche, the famous atheist, had died in Weimar. On April 11, 1945, the Americans were approaching Weimar from the northwest. They came upon a wooded hill called the Ettersberg, 8 kilometers north of Weimar. It was at Weimar that Johann Wolfgang von Goethe, the famous writer, had lived from 1775 until his death in 1832. Goethe had particularly loved the Ettersburg; the little wooded hill was his favorite retreat. Then perhaps it had been a solitary, romantic, dreamy spot. Now the forest had been cleared and in its place was Buchenwald – with its torture and its nightmarish horror.

On April 12th Patton brought Eisenhower and Bradley to see the concentration camp. No one had ever dreamed that a civilized nation could wrought such wickedness upon its own population. "The smell of death overwhelmed us even before we passed through the stockade," Bradley wrote. Patton was viewing the camp for the 2nd time.

> "A guard showed us how the blood had congealed in coarse black scabs where the starving prisoners had torn out the entrails of the dead for food. Eisenhower's face whitened into a mask. Patton walked over to a corner and sickened." *"A Soldier's Story," by Omar N. Bradley*

A man who had seen war in all of its gore had never seen anything like this. It was Patton who forced the local population to view the camp and bury the 3,200 naked bodies that were lying in the open. When the mayor and his wife saw the camp they committed suicide.

The man who showed the generals around the camp claimed to have been a prisoner but was "such a well fed looking man that I had an idea he may have been one of the executioners." Two days later he was torn limb from limb by the returning inmates. He showed them many of the contraptions that had been designed to maximize the pain and torture suffered by the prisoners.

Though Bradley and Eisenhower express abhorrence and revulsion, only Patton – as usual – left a vivid account of what they actually saw. In the pictures taken by the press, Eisenhower is in the foreground, his face wrenched with horror. In every picture Patton is very far in the back, presumably he vomited after he saw every ghastly sight.[1]

Patton, the warrior who had seen so much war, describes the experience thus,

> "Just beyond was a pile of about 40 bodies, more or less naked, all of whom had been shot through the head at

---

[1] He actually refused to enter a room in which 20 to 30 naked men were piled, telling Eisenhower that if he entered he would vomit again. Eisenhower entered the room and did not sicken.

short range. The ground was covered with dried blood. These men had become so exhausted as to be useless for labor and were disposed of in this humane (?) manner. In a shed near this place was a pile of about 40 completely naked human bodies in the last stages of emaciation. These bodies were lightly sprinkled with lime, not for the purpose of destroying them, but for the purpose of removing the stench. When the shed was full – I presume its capacity to be about 200, the bodies were taken to a pit a mile from the camp where they were buried... When we began to approach with our troops, the Germans thought it expedient to remove the evidence of their crime. Therefore, they had some of the slaves exhume the bodies and place them on a mammoth griddle composed of 60-centimeter railway tracks laid on brick foundations. They poured pitch on the bodies and then built a fire of pinewood and coal under them. They were not very successful in their operation because there was a pile of human bones, skulls, charred torsos on or under the griddle which must have accounted for many hundreds. In the pit there were arms, legs, and bodies sticking out of the green water which partially filled it. Walker and Middleton had very wisely decided to have as many soldiers as possible visit the scene, which I believe will teach our men to look out for the Germans. The mayor of the town, together with his wife, when confronted with the spectacle, went home and hanged themselves. There are several others in the vicinity who I think will be found dead."

Third Army's advance had been so rapid that hundreds of naked bodies were found lying on the funeral pyre that had been meant to consume them. It is no coincidence that Third Army revealed this horror to the world; for only the Third Army was fast enough to arrive there before the evidence had been obliterated. Patton and his army could have arrived earlier, for there was a time when Germany stood empty before him. That time was September, 1944. Buchenwald was less than 100 miles of undefended territory away. And Patton could not reach them – because Eisenhower's orders had left his tanks out of gas.

Eisenhower, the man who commanded the vast resources and manpower that Britain and America could produce and wielded them in any direction he so chose; Patton, the man whose army had taken France, trapped 11 German divisions at Falaise, traveled faster than any other army in history, captured and killed the most Germans, saved the Allies during the Battle of the Bulge, captured 10 German divisions in the Hansbruck Mountains, crossed the Rhine with only 28 casualties, liberated the first concentration camp, discovered the German gold reserve; and Bradley, Patton's commander, now headed by plane to see another astounding sight that the Third Army had uncovered for the world.

Eddy had blown open the safe as Patton had ordered. At the bottom of the salt mine in the little village of Merkers, $100,000,000[1] in gold bullion was uncovered. Patton, Bradley and Eisenhower went to inspect this reserve. As they began the long, pitch-black descent on a rickety old elevator, Patton looked up at the single, insecure cable that was keeping the ancient elevator from falling into the dark abyss below.
"If that clothesline should part," Patton said as he surveyed the starry shoulders of his fellow generals, "promotions in the United States Army would be considerably stimulated."
Somewhere in the inky darkness of the elevator, an unamused Eisenhower replied, "O.K. George, that's enough. No more cracks until we're safely on the ground again."

They were lowered 2,100 feet into the salt mine, and landed safely. The generals were amazed as they stared at over 4,500 25lb. gold bars. These were packed two to a sack and stenciled in black with the words "Reichsbank." There were also 3 billion paper Reichsmarks, the last reserve the Nazi government had.
"They will be badly needed," the guide said, "to meet the army payroll."
"I doubt that the German army will be meeting payrolls much longer," Bradley replied.

The Third Army had uncovered two important parts of the Nazi governmental machine – its cash reserve and its method of torture for unwanted or uncooperative civilians. It was clear to everyone that the Nazi government had been brought to its knees, and it was also clear that this was mostly the Third Army's accomplishment.

$2,000,000 in American paper money was also stored in the dry atmosphere of the salt mine, along with lesser amounts of British,

---

[1] These values are from 1945.

Norwegian and French money. In a stack nearby the money were hundreds of crates and boxes full of art treasures that had been removed from Berlin for safekeeping.[1] The art that they viewed, Patton estimated, was worth only around $2.50 and was the type that decorated American saloons.

Eisenhower and Bradley spent the night with Patton at his "sparsely furnished commandant's house."[2]
"If these were the old freebooting days when a soldier kept his loot," Bradley said jokingly, "you'd be the richest man in the world."
Patton only grinned.

Patton had been criticized for relieving the reporter who leaked the gold cache story to the press. The story had been censored until it could be confirmed, but this reporter had published the story anyway. Some papers said that Patton's reason for keeping the story secret was that he wanted to keep the gold. His reason for relieving the reporter is much more obvious; disobedient reporters had almost cost him his job twice in 2 years.
"I knew I was right on that one," Patton said as the generals ate their dinner.
"Well, I'll be darned," Ike snapped,[3] "until you said that, maybe you were. But if you're that positive, then I'm sure you're wrong."
Patton winked across the table at Bradley.
"But why keep it a secret, George?" Bradley laughed, "What would you do with all that money?"

> "George chuckled. Third Army was divided into two schools of thought on that issue, he said. One recommended that the gold be cut up into LUCKY[4] medallions. 'One for every s.o.b in the Third Army–" The other suggested Third Army hide the loot until peacetime when Congress again cracked down military appropriations. Then whenever funds got particularly tight, the army could dig down into its cave for more money to spend on new weapons." *"A Soldier's Story," by Omar N. Bradley*

---

[1] Much of it had actually been stolen by the Germans from France.
[2] "A Soldier's Story," by Omar N. Bradley
[3] Bradley's words.
[4] The codename for Third Army.

Ike shook his head, looked at Bradley, and laughed. "He's always got an answer," he said.

Eisenhower did not vomit at the disgusting sights that he had seen at Buchenwald. He was also not as philosophical as Patton. After seeing Ohrduf,[1] Eisenhower was heard commenting to soldiers, "Are you having a hard time hating the Germans now?"
"I can't understand the mentality that would compel these German people to do a thing like that," Ike said as they sat talking at Patton's headquarters.
"Not all the Krauts can stomach it," Patton replied. "In one camp we paraded the townspeople through to let them have a look. The mayor and his wife committed suicide."
"Well, that's the most encouraging thing I've heard," Ike said slowly. "It may indicate that some of them still have a few sensitivities left."

Buchenwald disgusted and sickened Patton more than his fellow generals, yet even in that wretched, squalid place, Patton realized the difference between a people and their leader. "The Nazis are evil," Patton would remark a few months later, "But not all the Germans are Nazis." The Germans, as a people, had suffered terribly for choosing so wicked a leader. It was Patton's idea to show the population of Weimar the camp that had been built on its once lovely wooded hill and to make the Germans bury the emaciated bodies. Thus they were made to realize the full extent of iniquity that had been worked by their own leadership. Patton realized, in a way that Eisenhower did not, that it was not the "*Germans* [who] d[id] a thing like that," but the SS and the Gestapo. Patton was disgusted and literally sickened by the Nazi horrors. His view of them, and their difference from the German people, would not change in the coming months.

Eisenhower and Bradley spent the night at Patton's headquarters. It was now that Patton would learn of the halt that Eisenhower had decided on, and how this would affect Third Army and the Russians. They had a "very pleasant evening," according to Patton, "in the course of which General Eisenhower gave me a proposed stop line and explained his reasons, which it is not expedient at this time to set down."[2] Luckily Gay had no such objections and recorded Eisenhower's words as follows,

---

[1] For this was Ohrduf – a satellite of Buchenwald – that they were viewing.
[2] This is a very strange and untypical comment, I can only surmise that Patton was ordered not to record this meeting.

"From a tactical point of view, it was highly inadvisable for the American Army to take Berlin, and he hoped political influence would not cause him to take the city. It had no tactical or strategical value, and would place upon American forces the burden of caring for thousand and thousands of Germans, displaced persons, Allied prisoners of war, etc.[1]

General Patton replied, 'Ike, I don't see how you figure that one. We had better taken Berlin and quick, and then on to the Oder River.'"

All the reasons for stopping along the Elbe River: that it cut Europe north and south, that it was "a clear geographical boundary" that would prevent the "Allies" from colliding, apply to the Oder River with even more aptness. The only difference is that the Oder is *east* of Berlin.

No one could believe nor understand what was happening, except perhaps a few chosen people at the top. Patton argued to Eisenhower that the Ninth Army could reach Berlin in only 48 hours.

"Well, who would want it?" asked Eisenhower.

Patton did not reply at once, but, placing his hands on Eisenhower's shoulders said slowly, "I think history will answer that question for you."[2]

When Simpson, prepared to advance quickly to Berlin, received for the first time the orders to halt along the Elbe, he asked incredulously, grasping the innocuous note, "Where the heck did you get this?"

"From Ike," was the reply.

---

[1] Strangely, this was one of the reasons that Churchill argued *for* taking Berlin – the more land to the East the Allies captured, the less displaced people there would be, since some of the DPs came from those areas. Displaced People were simply Eastern Europeans fleeing before the Red Army.

[2] Eisenhower, in "Crusade in Europe" says he met few people with such a love and understanding of history and, ironically, compares Churchill and Patton in this sense.

Chapter Forty Eight

AND THERE LIES BERLIN

The Americans stopped along the Elbe because they were afraid. They, or rather their high command, was afraid of running head-long into the Russians. A possibility, though slim, seems to exist here; until one realizes that the Germans had built a mighty fortress around the eastern side of the city, and that the Russians themselves estimated it would take at least a month to crack.

In the end, it is difficult to place the blame for not taking Berlin solely on Eisenhower's shoulders. He communicated by telegraph extensively with the allusive Marshall. Marshall gave his underling, Eisenhower, permission for all of these unprecedented political decisions and so, ironically, Marshall was the cause of the terrible decision not to capture Berlin: a disaster that required the "Marshall Plan" to partially right.

Eisenhower is guilty, like Bradley and Montgomery, of falsifying the after-war record.[1] He guilefully tells us that Churchill was "disturbed because my plan did not first throw Montgomery forward with all the strength I could give him..."

Churchill didn't care *who* took Berlin; he merely wanted it *taken*. Eisenhower knew that Americans hated any troops being given to Montgomery, so, to engage our sympathy, he tells us that this was Churchill's plan. When Churchill heard that the Americans had no

---

[1] See Chapter 62 "Aftermath."

intention of "wasting" any men on the "political" objective of Berlin, he *did* suggest that Montgomery go ahead alone.

This was vetoed by Eisenhower. Churchill independently ordered Montgomery to take the Baltic ports. These, too, were political objectives; Churchill didn't want Russia to have access to the English channel. When Montgomery began to move with his customary lethargy toward the ports, Churchill nervously watched the Russian armies approaching. He then threatened Montgomery with relief; whereafter the 21st Army Group advanced in record time.

Patton, of course, did not know all of this. He now knew that Eisenhower intended stopping short of Berlin, but he could not see the vast political machine[1] working deviously behind the shroud of "diplomacy." He could not "figure" how Eisenhower had made his incredible decision concerning Berlin, but as he approached his death he would begin to see more and more of its devastating results. The terrifying facts concerning the decision would unwind one after another as he began to realize what Eisenhower had done in order to become President.

Although Patton would only hear Eisenhower's side of the story, the story in which the "stop-line" had been virtually written in stone at a meeting between the great powers, he began to realize that Eisenhower was lying, and what was more, that he had betrayed his country. For what? For whom? We do not know. We can not know even if Patton knew, although it is likely. For as his death approached, Patton was constantly reaffirming a burning desire to go home and "tell people" what Eisenhower had done. What this was – and if it was more than we know now – we will never know. All we know is that as his demise approached, Patton was seized as never before with a desire to go home. And he would die the day before he was leaving for America.

It was almost midnight when Eisenhower, Bradley and Patton turned in. They had been up all those hours just talking – undoubtedly about the end of the war. Patton went to his van to go to sleep. He realized that his watch had stopped and he turned on the radio to get the time. An announcer broke in to report the death of President Roosevelt. Patton returned to the commandant's house and knocked on Bradley's door.

---

[1] Or "fate" as he would have called it.

362

Bradley had just climbed into bed and he wearily asked, "Anything wrong?"

"Better come with me to tell Ike," Patton replied, "the President has died."

They stayed up until two talking about what would happen. "We had quite a discussion," Patton wrote in his diary. Roosevelt had made Truman Vice President in order to win the election, and this left Patton worried about Truman's capabilities. "Changing horses" didn't make as much of a difference as he had thought at the time, he was to remark later in "War as I Knew It."

At Mainz, a new bridge was opened and Patton was requested to "cut the ribbon." They handed him a pair of giant scissors especially made for the ceremony. Patton took one glance at the scissors and said, "I am not a tailor! Give me a bayonet." He then cut the ribbon, soldier-style.

Patton now went to see Ohdruf Nord, which was a subdivision of Buchenwald. It is reported to have been one of the worst concentration camps.

"The political prisoners who were sent here to die were fed 800 calories a day and died on the average – so it is said – of 100 a night. I went through two of the buildings. On each side were four tiers of bunks in which the inmates lay at right angles to the wall. They looked exactly like animated mummies and seemed to me on about the same level of intelligence. When we went through they attempted to cheer but were too feeble. We then went to the place where they had apparently put the finishing touches on those who had died or were about to die. In a basement which was entered by a chute, they had a number of iron hooks on the wall like those you hand the side of beef on. To these hooks they had a short piece of stout cord with a loop spliced on each end. This was put around a man's neck. Two men then lifted him and the loops were placed over the hook. If anyone showed signs of life, they had a club like a potato masher with which they bashed in the brains. Upstairs were six furnaces much like a baker's oven, connected with the basement by an elevator.

> Apparently they put 6 bodies on the elevator at a time, hoisted them up to the furnaces, and put them in."
> *Patton's Diary*

He would always remained horrified by what the Germans had done, even while realizing that a new, powerful, and more evil empire was setting up its tyranny in the east.

Patton asked Bradley where Third Army would head after reaching the stop line. Bradley replied that he didn't think the Third had enough supplies to go anywhere.
"You're in error there," Patton said.

Patton reached the conclusion that the higher echelon was merely making an excuse for "lack of any ideas on what to do next." Patton did not record in his diary his opinion of all that was said about the halt along the Elbe, but his mood had considerably darkened and his remarks about Ike had turned from sourly sarcastic to barely disguised contempt. "[Bradley is not solely responsible for the lack of a plan] as it is presumable that the Combined Chiefs of Staff have not yet told Eisenhower," he wrote in his diary.

> "I sometimes get very disgusted with the lack of initiative and drive on the part of 12th Army Group. They now seem convinced that there are some bogies east of the Elbe River which are apt to jump up and destroy us. Personally, I believe that continued vigorous advance would completely destroy what little German resistance now exists."

The Combined Chiefs of Staff, who Patton was now convinced were the real power behind Eisenhower, knew that there was no real "Redoubt." It was simply a convenient way of drawing the Allied armies away from the real objectives in the East. Eisenhower's explanation of these strange events, and all of his decisions that he made which mysteriously favor the Red armies, leaves a lot to be desired. We can not know exactly why these egnimatic maneuvers were executed, nor what force was behind them – all we know is that the office that took the "credit" was SHAEF and the man, or figure-head, was Eisenhower. To what degree he was someone else's puppet and to what end he worked, we will never know.

The newspapers were trying to create a new incident against Patton, hoping again to get him relieved. First they implied that he had meant to keep the Nazi gold reserve secret so as to steal the money that had been discovered. The reporter who disobeyed and published the story – even though it was censored – was treated like a hero while Patton was portrayed as an evil martinet silencing the truth. This newspaperman, by his disobedience, could easily have published a secret leading to the deaths of many Americans. Yet the newspapers glorified him, and Eisenhower "corrected" Patton again.

"Patton must have as many lives as a cat," Ike's naval aide, Butcher commented.

The fact was that Patton was constantly being "skinned" over the strangest public relation faux-pas. Who could really believe that Patton had wanted to keep billions of dollars in Nazi gold as his personal treasure and had thus censored the story? The truth is that no one could, but still the press made it into as big a story as they could.

Patton was the "most popular" commander of the war, and it would take a bigger "mistake" than that to get him relieved. So, never deterred, the papers looked for more "dirt" on Patton. They wanted to find something really evil, something that would poison the public's mind about him. They had just tried to make it seem as if Patton was motivated by money; that hadn't worked. Perhaps women? But Patton was one step ahead of them and had made a strict rule never to allow women at or about his headquarters. Their next move was to give Patton, the greatest and most popular military hero, a disaster – a military disaster.

Since everyone already knew that Patton was a wonderful commander and great strategist and that all of the Third Army's campaigns had been successful, this was a difficult task. But, as usual, the papers rose to the challenge. Clearly, Patton must have had one mistake, one blunder, one accident – the fate of war – and if he had, he must have concealed it. So, all the newspapers would have to do was *reveal* it and make it seem as if Patton was as terrible a commander as all the other Allied commanders, but simply managed to conceal his mistakes better.

Undoubtedly they looked in vain for several weeks. It was clear that the Third Army had never had a comparable disaster to the Hurtgen, or Goodwood, or Market-Garden, or the Bulge. Revealing the Third's worst battle, for Metz, would only reveal that SHAEF had left Patton to starve at the French fortress city; and this, instead of making Patton look bad, would glorify him and blacken Eisenhower. This would certainly not do. Yet, as hard as they looked for evidence to the contrary, the Third's record was clean: full of gleaming successes in the face of appalling shortages.

The only route left to them was to exaggerate. Only one Third Army mission had not been successful. Considering the tens of thousands of men that had died at previous errors of momentous significance, the newspapers' attempts are pretty sad. They must have seemed sadder falling, as they did, upon the ears of men who had fought, died, and suffered with thousands others through these huge disasters. Even so, the papers tried. 294 men had left for a secret mission to rescue Patton's relative, they advertised, and only one soldier had returned to tell the tale. These numbers were paltry then, and seem smaller still when one realizes that 268 of these had been captured and *only 25 killed*.[1]

The newspapers still tried to turn it into a scandal – "an already proven unstable general sent hundreds of men to die in an attempt to rescue his POW son-in-law." Public opinion about Patton, however, remained unchanged. Everyone in Europe noted the Third Army man's extreme loyalty: loyalty that would not exist if Patton were really a cruel, grasping and heartless general who sent his men to their deaths.

Eisenhower was not in any way connected with the men and their opinions because he had remained at SHAEF throughout the war. He got nervous when he saw the headlines condemning Patton. It seems strange, and is truly pathetic, that a man widely hailed as a "commander" would be so commanded by what he perceived to be public opinion. He wrote to Marshall, praising the Allied army and its European commanders, excepting one.

> "There is no weakness except for the one feature of Patton's unpredictability so far as his judgement (usually in small things) is concerned.... Patton's latest crackpot actions may possibly get some publicity .... Three or four newspapers have written very bitter articles about Patton, on this incident, and to my disgust they call it

---

[1] Let's look at some other interesting numbers: 111 Americans were killed and 490 wounded when we accidentally bombed our own troops during Operation Cobra. These numbers were considered incidental.

another example of "Army Blundering." I took Patton's hide-off."

The irony here is that the only examples of "Army Success" had been produced by Patton. It was Patton's Third Army which had surpassed the German blitzkrieg, which had captured or killed 1,000 Germans every day in operation; it was Patton's Army which had taken France, trapped 11 German divisions at Falaise, rescued the stranded Allies in Bastogne, finished off the Battle of the Bulge; his army which had surrounded and captured 10 German divisions in the Hunsruck Mountains, crossed the Rhine with only 28 casualties, liberated the first concentration camp, discovered the German gold reserve: this was the army that had "blundered" by accidentally surrendering 268 men? And the loss of such a small number caused this great army's incredible commander to have his hide "taken off"!

Supreme irony, is, of course, a recurring factor in Patton's WWII career. The more Patton achieved, the more easily he could be relieved. The men whose careers and reputations he had saved would ruin his career and reputation as best they could – once their own were out of jeopardy. Patton was always his own man: he would say, think and act according to what he believed. He had never done anything reprehensible so he could not be bribed into shutting up; and the fact that he would do and say exactly as he thought right frightened SHAEF bureaucrats. "Unpredictable," they cried, as they worried that he would reveal another of their blunders. Yet Patton was perfectly predictable: he would do, say, and act according to his conscience, what he felt was the "best for America." Certainly a frightening thought for those whose power rested at SHAEF.

Patton wrote, "Some times I feel that I may be nearing the end of this life." It was April 17th, 1945.

He had flown to Paris and visited Hughes, where he stayed overnight. The next day Patton's air plane crew heard that Patton had been promoted to full general. They quickly painted an extra star on his plane. Meanwhile, Patton was eating breakfast. Hughes handed Patton the "Stars and Stripes" with the announcement of Patton's promotion, while everyone watched to see what his reaction would be. He read the headlines and threw the paper back on the table. Hughes picked it up and passed it to him again, but Patton merely glanced at it a second time and discarded it. Finally, Hughes picked it up and said "read that," and pointed to the announcement.

> "He did and then leaned back in the chair and amused everybody who had been hovering in the vicinity by saying, 'Well, I'll be –.'" *Hughes, in a letter to Beatrice.*

Patton wasn't too happy about the promotion because he had wanted to be in the initial group of promotions with Bradley, Devers and Clark: the army group commanders. "I have never had an ambition to be an also-ran," he wrote. Hodges had been promoted to 4 star general a day earlier. Patton's staff were happy for him, however, and Codman[1] found the last two 4 star pins in Paris and also a 4 star flag.

Patton's premonition about nearing "the end of this life" almost came true on April 20th. He was flying to the Headquarters of the III Corps in an L-5 cub when he noticed some tracers coming by the right side of their plane. Patton's pilot quickly dove to the ground, where it nearly collided with a plane which looked like a Spitfire. This plane continued to fire at his plane and made a second pass, again firing and missing. By this time, sure that they were being attacked and would probably die, Patton took out his camera and snapped a picture. If they lived, perhaps they would know who it was that had attacked them. While the American plane was doing evasive maneuvers, the attacking plane came in again, flying very fast and firing. Patton's plane, however, was very low to the ground, and the attacking plane was unable to pull out of its dive and crashed into the ground.

> "While Codman and I were engaged in hedge-hopping to avoid this belligerent gentleman, four other planes were circling over us, but did not engage in the attack." *"War as I Knew It," by George S. Patton*[2]

Patton thought that the plane looked like it was from a Polish flying unit in the RAF. He couldn't make out the identities of the other four planes that had been circling above, watching impassively the American plane's death struggle with the fighter. Unfortunately, he had been so nervous when he shot the picture of the attacking plane that he had forgotten to remove the lens on his camera, and he was left with only a blank picture and many unanswered questions. What had a plane,

---

[1] Patton's aide

[2] "War as I Knew It," by George S. Patton, page 306.

apparently a Spitfire, been doing out of its zone? Why had he attacked? Had he misread the markings on Patton's plane? And what of the other 4 planes that had been circling above?

This would be the first of three bizarre brushes with death that would end in his inexplicably fatal car accident.

Willie, Patton's bull terrier, ate something and got paralyzed "but is now better. I would have felt terrible had he died. To him I am always right," Patton wrote to Beatrice.

An old classmate of Patton's, Robert H. Fletcher, wrote to Patton and asked him what effect he thought education had in producing successful generals. Patton replied that according to "old Colonel Feberger" the qualities of generalship were "a desire to fight, good health, historical knowledge, and intelligence." He said that he could "claim some eminence in the first three" but was "not so outstanding" in the fourth. Patton believed that schooling didn't produce combat leaders but simply improved men who naturally possessed the peculiar qualities of combat leadership. What had made him successful, he believed, was self-confidence and "a sixth sense by which I can always know to a moral certainty what the enemy is going to do." The last paragraph of his letter to Fletcher gives the reader an eerie awareness of Patton's uncanny intuition, showing how his "sixth sense" extended far beyond the military sphere.

"The best thing would be [for me] to get a clean hit in the last minute of the fight and then flit around on a cloud and watch you all tear my reputation to pieces or get yourselves torn to pieces defending me."

Chapter Forty Nine

THE THIRD'S LAST MISSION

The Third Army advanced to Bayreuth, Germany on April 14th. Four days later they reached Hof, in Bavaria, only 10 miles from Czechoslovakia. Here they were forced to halt because of Eisenhower's promise to Stalin.

In the little mountain town of St. Martin's in Austria Third Army overran the temporary home of the beautiful white Lippizaner horses. These horses were world-renowned for their intelligence and beauty. They had been trained to do many unique tricks like the *capriole* at the "Spanish Riding School" of Vienna.

Colonel Podhajsky, the director of the school, put on a horse show for Patton. The horses were in grave danger, since all of the female Lippizaners were still a hundred miles distant in Hostau, Czechoslovakia, which lie in the area Eisenhower had promised to the Russians. If these horses were not rescued by the Americans soon, the Russians would slaughter them for meat. Without the male horses, the Lippizaner breed would perish from the earth.[1] The Russians could not understand the vast cultural tradition behind the horses' nor that hundreds of years of selective breeding and years of training had made them among the finest horses in the world. Patton, however, was a cavalryman. If the Lippizaners were to survive WWII, this was Podhajsky's chance.

---

[1] At this time, Lippizaners were the Spanish Riding School's exclusive monopoly and the horse breed did not exist anywhere else in the world.

Unbeknownst to Podhajsky, Colonel Reed, the Commander of the American 2nd Cavalry Group, had told Patton of the Lippizaner's plight nine days earlier. The 2nd Cavalry was in the area and desperately wanted to cross the border and advance the 100 miles so as to grab the Lippizaner mares and foals while there was still a chance. Yet, if they crossed the border, they would be violating an agreement of international proportions. So Reed called Patton. Patton's reply was simple, "Get them. Make it fast." The 2nd Cavalry crossed the border, in violation of the Yalta "agreement" and grabbed the horses.

Patton brought along four generals, four colonels and the Undersecretary of War Patterson to the performance. The white stallions danced to music playing on a record in the background. Patton looked bored as the two horses danced. So now they performed the *capriole, courbette,* and *levade.* These are difficult maneuvers in which all 4 of the horses' hooves are actually off the ground. At this, Patton became interested. At the end of the performance, Podhajsky rode up to face Patton.

> "The Spanish Riding School, this ancient cultural institution, is today the oldest riding school in the world and has managed to survive wars and revolutions throughout the centuries and by good fortune has lived also through the recent years of upheaval. The great American nation, which has been singled out to save European culture from destruction, will certainly interest itself also in this ancient academy, which with its riders and horses presents, as it were, a piece of living Baroque, so I am sure I shall not plead in vain asking you, General, for your special protection and help; for protection for the Spanish Riding School, which will pass the difficult period of transition under American military command, and for help to locate and bring back the Lippizan stud, which is at present in great danger on Czechoslovakian territory."

Patton, of course, gave his protection. "These horses will be wards of the United States Army until they can be returned to the new Austria," he promised. And though the 2nd Cavalry had grabbed the Lippizaner mares, they were still not out of danger.

A Czech rider at the Spanish Riding School was conspiring with the Communists to take the horses at Hostau. Podhajsky informed Patton. There was no time for an ordered move, so an old-fashioned roundup of all the horses was ordered. There were over one thousand of them.

Most of these aristocratic horses had *walked* over 200 miles, but now, behind American lines, they were safe from extinction. Patton's decision to disobey Eisenhower's orders and cross *one hundred miles behind enemy lines* into Czechoslovakia and take the mares had insured that this piece of Austrian culture would not be lost to the Communists.

The Russians complained bitterly about how Patton had stolen the horses, but they were not in a position to do anything about it. Patton, for his part, was unmoved by their complaints. "The beautiful white horses are worth far more, and are much nicer, than the Soviet generals," he said.

Chapter Fifty

"IT IS ALL OVER"

Patton had made a bet that the war would be over before May 10th. He felt the war pulsing to an uninteresting end, an "anti-climax" after the spectacular advances and bloody battles that had been its characteristic.

On May 3rd the German armies in Italy and southern Austria surrendered. Complete unconditional surrender from all of the German forces was only a few days away. Patton wrote to his wife,

> "Last night the German armies in Italy surrendered. Those in front of me will quit to day or tomorrow, and I will be out of a job. I feel lower than whale tracks on the bottom of the ocean. I love war and responsibility and excitement. Peace is going to be hell on me. I will probably be a great nuisance."

Inexorably entwined, the end of the war, the end of the Third Army's glory, and the end of Patton's life drew ever nearer. While the German army in Italy and Austria was surrendering, Patton was driving in his jeep when an ox-drawn cart pulled out of a blind side lane and lumbered onto the highway, pulling directly in front of their jeep. They avoided a crash by inches, but even so the heavy wagon pole which protruded ahead of the oxen team grazed Patton's head.[1]

---

[1] The bull cart pulled out suddenly from a side street, and led Patton to remark "The American soldier is absolutely incapable of enforcing the rule that civilians stay off the roads during active operations."

"After all I've been through," Patton remarked, "think of being killed on the road by a team of oxen."

Out of the blue, on May 4th, the Third Army was given permission to advance into Czechoslovakia. Except for the 2nd Cavalry, all of Third Army had been waiting several days for that order. Patton quickly ordered the V Corps to "get going."[1] Patton and his staff were surprised that they had been given permission, and Patton wrote in his diary, "Things like this are what is going to make the peace so terrible, because nothing exciting will ever happen."

The V Corps would have to halt along the stop line at Pilsen, though. Patton was already writing that, perhaps, they might just be able to "send reconnaissance" to Prague. The people of Prague, seeing the war about to end, had revolted from the Germans' rule, and Patton worried that the Germans might be able to suppress their uprising, resulting in a slaughter similar to the one that had occurred in Poland.

One hundred thousand White Russians were trying to surrender to the Americans. They had fought for the Germans against the Communist Russians, and "are in a pitiable state." If they were returned to their homelands, they would certainly be killed by the Russians. Patton had them moved west of the Czechoslovakian border in an attempt to save them.[2]

That night Patton had an opportunity to speak to the Under Secretary about the post-war world. Patton's aide, Codman, remembers Patton's eye "alight with eloquent argument."
"Mr. Secretary, for God's sake, when you go home, stop this pointless system, stop breaking up these Armies ... send us replacements and let us start training here, keeping our forces intact. Let's keep our boots polished, bayonets sharpened, and present a picture of force and strength to [the Russians.] This is the only language they understand and respect. If you fail to do this, then I would like to say to you that we have had a

---

[1] The V Corps had just been added to Third Army. She now consisted of 18 divisions and over 500,000 men – more men and divisions than Patton had ever commanded before.
[2] These Russians, led by General Vlassov, would eventually be repatriated against their will. They all died at Russian hands. "And the Allied media," Charles F. Marshall remembers, "playing into Stalin's hands, portrayed them as traitors."

victory over the Germans and have disarmed them, but we have lost the war."

The Secretary replied, "Oh, George, you have been so close to this thing so long, you have lost sight of the big picture. You don't realize the strength of these people."

"Mr. Secretary, it is your privilege to say 'Oh, George,' if you wish, but for God's sake listen to what I am trying to tell you."

"What would you have us do, George?" Mr. Patterson replied.

"I would have you keep these Armies intact. I would have your State Department, or the people in charge, tell the [Russians] where their border is, and give them a limited time to get back across. Warn them that if they fail to do so, we will push them back across it."

"You don't realize the strength of these people," said the Secretary.

"Yes, I have seen them. I understand the situation. Their supply system is inadequate to maintain them in a serious action such as I could put to them. They have chickens in their coops and cattle on the hoof – that's their supply system. They could probably maintain themselves in the type of fighting I could give them for five days. After then it would make no difference how many million men they have, if you wanted Moscow, I could give it to you."

The Under Secretary undoubtedly remained unimpressed. Poor Patton! He genuinely believed that the American government might listen to him. How could he know that the same proposal had already been suggested, by no less a person than Churchill, and had been rejected? Patton was still willing to try, however. After all, who was better qualified to speak about the Russian military and its supply system then the only Allied general commended by Stalin.

Patton continued, anxiously trying to convince the impassive man before him. "The Russians lived on the land coming down. There is insufficient land left for them to maintain themselves going back! Let's not give them time to build up their supplies. If we do, then I repeat, we have had a victory over the Germans and disarmed them; but we have failed in the liberation of Europe; we have lost the war!"

His mind was undoubtedly thinking of the hundreds of thousands of "displaced persons" his army was holding – millions of men, women, and children who had fled at the onslaught of the Russian army and the terror of living under Communism. If America did nothing, what would happen to these poor people? Thousands would die, thousands more live under the tyranny of Russian rule.

377

"The Red Army could not have conceived and certainly could not have executed the advance of the Third Army across France." Those were the words of Stalin, and they lend Patton's argument even more poise. If Stalin himself knew the worth of the Third Army, surely he would fear the threat of it invading Russia.

"We, the armed forces of the U.S.A.," Patton argued to Mr. Patterson, "have put our government in the position to dictate the peace. We did not come over here to acquire jurisdiction over either the people or their countries. We came to give them back the right to govern themselves. We must either finish the job now – while we are here and ready – or under less favorable circumstances."

Inevitably, the United States chose the "less favorable circumstances." By the time America chose to fight the Communists – in Korea – the army had bared its ranks, Congress had drastically lowered military appropriations, Bradley was chief of staff of the U.S. army, Eisenhower was the Supreme Commander of NATO, and, saddest of all, our most experienced general, the man who possessed the best sense of history, Patton, was dead.

It was May 8th. Two and a half years ago Patton and his troops had landed in Africa, and "now it is all over."

Chapter Fifty One

GENERAL WITH A CONSCIENCE

The war was over. All of the Third's glorious advances and bloody battles were over. No longer would Third Army march proudly on despite orders to halt, no longer would her General be forced to plead with ·SHAEF for supplies; they would never again experience the nagging fear that on the edge of victory they would be halted, for now there would be no more victories.

None of this was lost on Patton. He knew that for him the war was over; though he vainly begged any general with influence to send him to China.

He attended a press conference on May 8th at which he was asked,
"Could you explain exactly why we didn't go into Prague?"
Patton smiled. "I can tell you exactly why," he replied. All the pressmen leaned forward, anxious to catch this scoop. Patton then said, officially, "We were ordered not to." Obviously they were disappointed, but Patton was not about to get himself into more trouble with the press.
"I don't know the exact reasons," he went on, "but those were the orders."
"Of course there are probably many reasons which we don't know which would explain this," he said, offering them a hint, "as there may be a cause of international incidents up there we don't know anything about."

The Third Hungarian Army had surrendered to the Third American Army around May 8th or 9th. This army had fought the Red

Army in the Ukraine. They had retreated before the Russians and managed to pick up their families on their way westward. It fell to Captain Perry of the 26th Infantry to break the news to them: news that "neither George Patton, nor anyone else in our armies could effect a rescue." Perry was ordered from the higher echelon to turn the poor Hungarian soldiers, with their wives and children, over to the Russians.

The Hungarian general was stunned. "You know, of course, that this signifies enslavement or death, or both, for us."

Captain Perry was struck to the heart, but powerless. "I'm afraid … I'm afraid you might be right," he mumbled.

"I have two requests to make," the general said. "Could you return my revolvers and those of my two deputy commanders?" When Perry hesitated, he said quickly, "Oh, it's not what you think. When we have to turn over our poor people we must have our sidearms as emblems that we still command the authority. They are not to shoot ourselves with."

Perry didn't quite believe him, but he wouldn't deny a condemned man's request. Of course, when the Hungarians were returned, the Russians promptly took the revolvers away.

The general spoke again to Perry, "My second request is this: I have struggled against the Communists at home, and I have fought them as best I could there and in the Ukraine. I know them well. I have kept a diary of all this – in fact I have kept one all my military life. I wish that you would take it and see to it that it reaches your General Patton personally. He understands the problem and he is the general I have studied the most and whom I admire the most in the world."

Perry promised to send the general's diary to Patton. Unfortunately he sent it through regular channels and the diary mysteriously disappeared. Patton's nephew later went through all of Patton's papers in search of the diary, but there was no trace of it. None of Patton's family had ever even heard of it.[1]

Patton's story becomes more and more mysterious as his death approaches. What exactly was in the Hungarian general's diary? And why had he specifically requested that Patton see it? And where did it disappear to?

The Third Army received General Orders No. 98 on May 10th, terminating the war for them. Patton and four other Army commanders

---

[1] This story is taken from "Before the Colors Fade" by Fred Ayer.

along with their air officers lunched with Eisenhower that day. After lunch, Eisenhower,

> "talked to us very confidentially on the necessity for solidarity in the event that any of us are called before a Congressional Committee." *Patton's Diary*

A clandestine meeting led by Eisenhower for the purpose of misleading Congress: how odd. The probable reason behind it was clear to Patton, who felt that Ike's strange talk about "solidarity between the generals" and "cooperation between the Allies" was simply "for the purpose of covering up probable criticism of strategical blunders which he unquestionably committed during the campaign."

Eisenhower gave the assembly a speech which had "the symptoms of political aspirations" about the necessity of cooperation between all the Allies: the British, Russians and the Chinese, but especially the British. Patton wondered whether Ike was really trying to say that his military blunders had been the necessary result of his cooperation with the British.[1] Patton didn't believe a word of it, and listened cynically as Eisenhower and the assembled generals attempted to sew together the "official history" of the war.

When Patton died, an "official history" was indeed agreed upon and corroborated by Bradley, Eisenhower and Montgomery. They blamed each other for various aspects, but in the main part lied about the true cause of each's largest disasters: Market Garden, Caen, Hurtgen, the Battle of the Bulge, the failure to capture Berlin, the failure to keep all of the armies supplied, the failure to take Prague, the failure to close off the Falaise Gap and seal the fate of the 11 divisions trapped there; each had an "official" cause, an "official" whipping boy. Documents from each of these episodes were fudged while others were removed, destroyed and tampered with; and the generals corroborated each others stories in their memoirs.

The reason why the generals cooperated so well on this issue was because each of them had made mistakes. Each had committed an

---

[1] As usual, Patton's intuition was correct, and Eisenhower would always allege that his approval of disastrous schemes like Goodwood and Market Garden had been given only because he did not want to harm the Allies' "cooperation" – in other words he had sacrificed tens of thousands of men for what he called "Allied amity."

atrocious disaster which they felt had to be kept from public knowledge. Only one general, Patton, had never lost thousands of men on a hopelessly mismanaged mission, and thus only he was above corruption. If a spiteful general were to bring up the Battle of Metz, the Third's most bloody battle, Patton could counter that there were 3 dead Germans to 1 dead American, even in that desperate battle. And the Battle for Metz would never be investigated because investigation would only uncover the damning evidence of SHAEF's decision to starve the Third Army, and Com Z's negligence and wastefulness in keeping the armies supplied.

Patton, aside from the fact that he had never caused a disaster and was thus above bribery, was also an extremely honest man. He sickened when he thought of the way Ike, Bradley and Monty had mismanaged the war. And now his conscience was bothering him; he was responsible for millions of refugees, yet he was being given orders to hand them over to their deaths.

Only Patton had the honor to own up to his mistakes, only he would not lie about the cause of the "unquestionable mistakes" that Eisenhower had committed. Only Patton was above corruption, only he would not corroborate his recollection of the war to suit those in power. And only he died.

The war in Europe had only been over for three days. It was May 11th, 1945. Patton gave his nephew, Fred Ayer, a call asking him to come over to General Hughes' room. And it is Ayer who recalled the following incident,

> "General Hughes' billet was in the Hotel Majestic on Avenue Kleber, perhaps 400 yards from the Arc de Triomphe. In the living room of his suite were assembled eight or nine people, including four generals, two aides and some sort of Presidential Assistant, from the White House. His face and name, I am glad to say have vanished from my memory. Everyone seemed in good spirits except Uncle George. This was perhaps because everyone but him was enjoying good whiskey. Patton, on the other hand, held a glass of milk and a soggy chicken sandwich, eyeing both with more than obvious distaste." *"Before the Colors Fade," by Fred Ayer, page 230.*

He turned to Ayer. "Go make yourself a stiff one and don't stare at me. That Hughes won't let me have any bourbon. It's unchristian."

General Hughes grinned. "Of course I won't. George has brought back some recaptured French battle flags to return to Les Invalides. He has to make a speech and kiss Charles de Gaulle on both cheeks. I'm afraid of what he might say."

"Who, de Gaulle?"

"No, your saintly uncle."

Patton, seated in the corner easy chair, shoved the milk glass and sandwich aside, growled at them and lit a cigar. He drew deeply on it, then took it from his mouth, leaned tensely forward, pointing the cigar like a weapon at his host. "Well, by God, Everett, I'm going to say it now. It's all a shame. That's what it is."

Someone asked, "All what's a shame?"

Ayer had never seen his Uncle George so deeply upset. Patton answered in his familiar high, penetrating voice – and that voice trembled. "I'll tell you. Day after day, some poor bloody Czech, or Austrian, or Hungarian, even German officers come into my headquarters. I almost have to keep them from going down on their knees to me. With tears in their eyes they say, 'In the name of God, General, come with your Army the rest of the way into our country. Give us a chance to live before it's too late, before the Russians make us slaves forever.' That's what they tell me, and every one of them has offered to fight under my flag and bring their men with them. Hell, a German general offered his entire air force, the Third, to me to fight the Russians if necessary. Of course he had hardly any planes left, but he had pilots. I would like to take them up on it. I'll feel like a traitor if I don't."

Generals, no matter how they felt, didn't say things like that in public, especially where high officials were gathered. There was an uneasy stir in the room. Most of those assembled sensed what was coming next. None of them quite dared to interrupt. Patton went on, "These people are right. They won't have a chance. We've signed away their lives. We ought to tear up those fool agreements and march right through to the eastern borders ...."

"Uncle George, for heaven's sake," Ayer blurted, "you can't talk that way here."

He glared coldly at his nephew. "Yes I can. I'll talk any way I want. I know what we ought to do. We promised these people freedom. It would be worse than dishonorable not to see that they have it. This might mean war with Russia, but what of it? They have no air force any more; their gas and munition supplies are low. I've seen their miserable supply trains, mostly wagons drawn by beat-up old horses, or oxen. I'll tell you this," he again aimed the cigar at General Hughes, "the Third Army, alone, with very little other help and few casualties, could lick what's left of the Russians in 6 weeks."

He paused here for a few seconds. "You mark my words. Don't ever forget them. Some day we'll have to fight them, and it will take 6 years and cost us 6 million lives."[1]

He may have thought he had a sympathetic listener in Hughes, but this was undoubtedly a fatal mistake. The man was called Eisenhower's "eyes and ears" and Patton himself had called Hughes Ike's "private eye." And who knows what the Presidential assistant thought of Patton's words? There is no doubt that when Patton poured his heart out there in Hughes' room he had sealed the end of his career and maybe his death as well. In four short months Patton would be removed from the command of Third Army.

Yet there was no stopping Patton from making truthful (if embarrassing) remarks; it would be impossible to "shut him up" now. He had been quiet for the duration of the war because he had desperately wanted to fight. Then there had been no great issue to speak out about, except perhaps SHAEF's doling of supplies. But now he was watching with a sense of burning injustice as thousands of refugee families were herded together so as to be returned to the barbaric clutches of the Russians. He could not be quiet while millions were slaughtered because of a political decision.

Bradley recalls how he told Patton, "George, you're going to get yourself in a terrible doghouse if you don't keep your mouth shut." Yet Patton wasn't going to keep his mouth shut, not while millions of refugees were going to be sent back to their certain deaths. He was no longer worried about the "doghouse." After all, the war was over. He wanted to quit the army, go back to America and tell people "what is really going on." He didn't want to keep his mouth shut, he wanted to speak out, he wanted people to listen to him. He had already tried speaking to the higher echelons, but they were oblivious. Now he would

---

[1] This meeting was later retold by Fred Ayer in "Before the Colors Fade." He was one of the nervous onlookers who felt the room come to a standstill as his uncle spoke.

attempt to reach the heart of democracy, the people who had always loved and admired him: the people for whom he had driven his victorious army against the Nazis. These people respected him; for them Patton had captured 1,000 Germans every day in operation. No longer could Eisenhower and Bradley threaten Patton with relief or disgrace. Patton would speak "any way" he wanted to.

No doubt this thought struck fear into the hearts of the SHAEF bureaucrats. All the other generals wanted promotions, to move up into a better and higher position, to be in the public eye. Patton's reputation had already far surpassed his rank.[1] There was nothing left for Patton because he was a warrior and the war was over. But he was also, and far more dangerously, a patriot.

Would he be able to tell the American people what crimes the Communists were committing? Would they listen?

---

[1] Throughout the war, and afterward, Patton's name is mentioned next to those of Army Group Commanders. Patton, Bradley, Montgomery: few people realize how far the rank gap was here, because in German memorandums Patton's name is as frequent as any of these. In fact, before the Normandy invasion, Patton's name received equal mention with that of Eisenhower's. The Germans were convinced that the American's "most modern and experienced General Patton" would lead the assault.

Chapter Fifty Two

THE RUSSIANS – FACE TO FACE

Before he was to go home, Patton had to perform the functions and take care of the duties incumbent on the "Military Governor of Bavaria" – his new title. He was now responsible for 7 million Germans, 2 million refugees, and his own half a million soldiers who were all residing on the 25,000 square miles that Patton was now to govern. It was his duty to take care of the political, social and economic problems which would now be paramount during the occupation.

Nothing in Germany was running. There were no phones, no telegraphs, no transportation, no food, no money, few homes. These were certainly large problems for any man to tackle, but Patton took his new post seriously. He was to rebuild Germany, to make it fit to live in once again. He was appalled at the ruin he observed around him; however he knew the Germans were a "great people" who would assist him in creating a new Germany.

Eisenhower too had a new title, one which carried even more responsibility than his last job. He was now the American member of the four-power "Allied Control Council." The French, Americans, British and Russians each had a representative who dealt with the occupation of Germany. Every decision Eisenhower made would now affect not only the American troops, but the millions of Europeans scattered across western Europe. Ike was now personally responsible for the military government in the American zone, which included the economic, industrial, social and political problems there. He seemed, as usual, little aware of the impact his decisions would make; unlike Patton, who was weighing his every decision in the light of history.

The Americans were poised to "punish" Germany in a vein far worse than that of the Versailles Treaty. They were making no distinction between the Nazis, who genuinely needed punishment, and the ordinary Germans. If the Americans continued, Communism would appear a more favorable alternative. And this was the event that Patton feared; for through the western half of Germany, Communism, like a plague, would spread throughout war-ravaged Europe. The Europeans were in a desperate state; they longed for peace and order. What would happen if they thought that the Russians possessed more justice than the Americans?

SHAEF had issued orders that soldiers were not to "fraternize" with the Germans. The Germans were no longer the "enemy," and thus the order baffled Patton. Were they saying that the Germans were inferior, and thus Americans could not even speak to them? "I think we could do a lot for the German civilians by letting our soldiers talk to their young people," Patton wrote in his diary. He also wrote that if Americans were going to be kept in Europe, they would *have* to have "some civilians to talk to." Of course SHAEF wasn't planning on keeping the soldiers in Europe, so this was hardly one of their considerations.

Non-fraternization was looked upon, by soldiers and officers, as a joke and neither enforced the policy. All across Europe soldiers could be seen chatting with the locals. They were now more like tourists than enlisted men on duty, and they avidly looked at the European landmarks with Europeans for their guides. In the end SHAEF had to revoke their order and conform to the soldiers' wishes, or else they would be forced to admit, as they drove through the towns and cities lined with German-American couples, that their troops had shockingly bad discipline.

A member of the Russian Trade Delegation in London complimented the Americans on their campaign in Europe, mentioning Patton personally. "Patton has shown everyone how the Germans should be fought," the Russian said. And echoing the words of Stalin, he added, "Patton has made a greater advance in one day than the Red Army has ever done." Of course, the Third Army's advance was faster than *any* army in history. What was notable was that the Russians publicly acknowledged Patton. This was very rare for the Russians, and made American High officials realize what respect and esteem Patton was held in. "You seem to be the type of general the Russians like," one commented.

On May 12th Patton met the Commanding General of the 4th Russian Guards Army with the 65th Division providing a guard of honor. The Americans decorated the General and 12 members of the Russian party with different types of the Legion of Merit. Patton then made a speech, emphasizing the "cordiality" of Russian-American relations. After the ceremony, the party went to the officers' club for lunch.

> "The Russians tried to drink American whiskey without water with very bad results. I unquestionably drank the Russian commander under the table and walked out under my own steam. We are going to pay back a call on the 14th, prior to which date I will drink quite a lot of mineral oil, as they will unquestionably try to get us drunk." *Patton's diary*

It was a Russian custom to drink quantities of vodka and have countless toasts when foreign notaries came to call. Since foreigners were unused to the high alcohol content of the vodka and unwilling to miss out on any of the toasts (and thus offer an insult), visitors to the Russians would often enter a quite drunken state. This delighted the Russians who hoped that they would spill important information, or at least be oblivious to what was going on around them. Patton had wisely outsmarted them, and beat them at their own game.

> "Everyone wanted me to get vodka for them to drink but I decided they could drink whiskey or nothing. The results were great. The general went out cold and I did not even have a headache. I kept putting water in my bourbon and he did not. When I toasted Stalin and the 4th Guards Army, I did a skoal with him and then broke the glass. I think I will get a good medal as his aid said that I was the only man he had met with feeling (and an iron stomach). When I broke the glass he embraced me. They are a scurvy race and simply savages. We could beat hell out of them."

It was now time for Patton to repay their call. As he drove to the Russian headquarters at Emperor Francis Joseph's former chateau, every hundred yards were Russian soldiers standing at present arms. The

Russians were trying to impress the Americans with the vastness of their army. The 15 miles of road that Patton drove along had actually been swept. When he reached the chateau, Russian soldiers polished the Americans' boots. "They had a great many women retainers who did everything except wipe your face. They did go to the extent of spraying your head with perfume," Patton recorded. He was received by Marshal Tolbukhim, Commander of the Third Ukrainian Front and second in command only to Stalin. He presented Patton with the Order of Kutuzov (First Degree). The Order of Kutuzov was a huge sunburst on a beautiful wide sash that wrapped around the chest. The encrusted jewels on the decoration weighed several pounds, and everyone admired its beautiful colors, texture and workmanship. It was the 58th issued, which showed the honor for which the Russians held this decoration.

The Russians had a huge party prepared for the Americans. A table that could seat one hundred was prepared, and the Americans were served course after course of sturgeon, veal, whole suckling piglets, and game. After the meal came the toasts. Patton had been prepared for this. He knew that since he had drunk the Russian commander under the table at the last party, there would be a seemingly endless round of toasts at this one. So Patton's doctor, Charles Odom, prescribed mineral oil to the American entourage as an antidote to the vodka.
Marshal Tolbukhim rises, glass in hand. "Premier Stalin," he intones. Everyone rises. Everyone drinks. Bottoms up. More toasts. The President of the United States. The Russian Army. The U.S. Army. The Fourth Russian Army. The Third U.S. Army. Marshal Tolbukhim. General Patton. General Eisenhower. Premier Stalin. "What, again?" think the Americans, hoping that the mineral oil will work.

The Russians did their best to leave the Americans with a good impression. Or at least, an impression of might and civilization. They put on a very good show after the lunch, Patton observed, but it had "unquestionably been flown in from Moscow." There was an all-male choir that intoned Gregorian chant perfectly. After that followed two hours of singing, dancing and sketching. The Russians at first insisted that the musicians were "just ordinary soldiers" but at length admitted that they had come from Moscow.

Thus they did not culturally impress the Americans much. Their next attempts at seeming powerful (like placing troops along all the roads the Americans drove along) only made them seem more menacing.

Patton's entourage missed no detail of the banquet[1] and they noticed how the Russians at the party could not get up or sit down without the Marshal's permission. The Russians all were mortally afraid of him for there his word was law. "Everything they did impressed one with the idea of virility and cruelty," Gay wrote in his journal. Patton wrote in his diary that, "I have never seen in any army at any time, including the German Imperial Army of 1912, as severe discipline as exists in the Russian army." The officer class in Russia had only recently been created, and the officers gave the appearance of "recently civilized Mongolian bandits" who exercised the right to kill their soldiers arbitrarily for minor infractions.[2]

The Russians passed their troops in review for the Americans. Patton was shaken as he watched their "very good imitation of the goose step. They give me the impression of something that is to be feared in future world political reorganization." All together, the Russians had shown the Americans, unwittingly perhaps, their true nature. Brutish, self-assured, powerful and cruel, the Russians were certainly frightening. Seeing them in the face had quelled none of Patton's fears.

---

[1] Because Patton had wisely ensured that they would not be under the influence of vodka.

[2] One American recalls that he complained to a Russian officer about a Russian soldier who had failed to salute him. The Russian officer drew his gun and asked the American to point out the soldier so he could shoot him. The American, with difficulty, dissuaded the Russian officer. It was this fearful type of "discipline" that left the Americans at the party shaken.

Chapter Fifty Three

"I AM NEVER GOING TO SEE YOU AGAIN"

It was now time for Patton's "war bond" tour of the United States. He would be seeing his beloved country for the last time. In Massachusetts he was given a triumphal welcome. An estimated one million people lined the streets to cheer him. He was their hero, as Fred Ayer put it, even if he was Washington's villain. The parade drove through Boston and Patton sat in the lead car, "square-shouldered, trim-waisted, proudly erect, his uniform immaculate and perfectly fitting, all brass and leather highly polished, the ribbons of his medals almost ablaze in color."[1] He was met everywhere along his 25 mile drive by throngs of cheering Americans as his motorcade drove around the Common, near the State House, and on the route to the Hatch Shell on the Charles River Esplanade where 20,000 people awaited him in Boston's most tumultuous reception in history.

He was the conqueror of foreign territory returning to his homeland. Unlike earlier conquerors, Patton was loved and respected by the citizenry. Over a million Americans waved and cheered as his car drove by. Patton looked at them, still mindful of the alarming message he needed to tell them. Ruefully he observed how they honored him, despite all the lies that the press had printed about him. The roar of cheers swelling outside his motor car must have made him wonder whether some of the jubilation was due merely to relief at the end of the war. He hoped they would not fall into the "no more wars" phase they had so easily succumbed to at the end of WWI.

---

[1] "Before the Colors Fade," by Fred Ayer, page 234

After that he was greeted by city and state officials, Patton spoke briefly. About 400 wounded Third Army veterans sat in a reserved section in front of the shell. Throughout the speech, Patton looked directly at the men who had fought with him. His speech was about the bravery of his men, the training they had undergone, and the heroism with which they had faced the battle-hardened enemy.

> "He said, speaking to parents and families ... 'And no matter what you may have read, no matter what they tell you when at last all who survived have returned here, you who have stayed at home will never be able to understand how terrible some of it really was.' He then went on to say that no matter how frightful war might have been it was something which could well come again and that we had best keep our ranks filled and our other defenses strong." *"Before the Colors Fade," by Fred Ayer, page 236*

His nephew remembers "the tall figure, the lined face, the earnest words, but above all, the strange mixture of soaring pride in the men he led, together with the unshed tears which stung his eyelids and burdened his voice and heart."

"With your blood and bonds," he said, "we crushed the Germans before they got here. This ovation is not for me, George S. Patton – George S. Patton is simply a hook on which to hang the Third Army. It is a popular idea that a man killed in action is a hero. Rather a man who gets killed is frequently a fool." Then, looking directly at the wounded veterans of Third Army, he said, "These men are the heroes. Let us not so much mourn the dead as thank our God that such men had lived." He saluted them and then sat down quickly with tears in his eyes, too emotionally shaken to finish his speech.

That evening he attended a state dinner at the Copley Plaza Hotel where his address was greeted by thunderous applause. Here, too, he had choked up at the end of his speech. After sitting down, all eyes were on him as he wiped his face with a handkerchief, pulled up his belt, straightened up and lit a cigar. "That's my Pop," said Patton's son, and the crowd cheered.

They understood Patton's sentimentality. But only the veterans could understand why Patton could both mourn the dead and cheer for the living, cry at the needless brutality of war and proclaim its glory, salute the enemy and declaim him. Only the press did not understand Patton, and one particularly venomous critic, Dwight Macdonald, wrote that he was "brutal and hysterical, coarse and affected, violent and empty." How they misjudged him! Patton was the anti-thesis of the "soldier" legend, he cried freely at the sight of suffering because he *did* have feeling. But certainly Patton did not arrange or pretend to break down, these scenes were not "affected" anymore than those times when he cursed and yelled at a soldier to get moving.

The press had identified Patton as an anti-Communist and thus an immediate target. Hundreds of articles were written attacking him, even though he was at the moment *the* most popular war hero. The press accused Patton of being "pro-German" and "anti-Jew," of being "patrician" and "rich" and disliking the Russians because of their "freedom for the proletariat." Patton, they wrote, was a schizophrenic who could curse and yell, then break down and cry. He was a "war monger" who was attacking the Russians because he could not "live without a war." Their attacks would become more and more vicious in the coming months. All the epitaphs used on Patton by the press were also used against Churchill. Even though it seems absurd, Churchill was also accused of being "pro-German" and a "war monger." Anyone who opposed Russian aims was blasted from the press with one or more of these epitaphs.

When Patton had said to those 400 wounded Third Army veterans that men who are killed are often fools, but those who survive are heroes, the press quickly seized a chance to paint Patton as the vicious martinet who had insulted gold star parents. Like in the slapping incidents, few people complained, but the numbers of those who did were blown out of proportion subsequently by the press and the War Department. One father wrote to General Marshall saying that it was "heartbreaking for my son to lie in his grave in France and for Patton to be alive and telling who the heroes were." This was, no doubt, in reference to Patton's choked words as he pointed at the wounded veterans, "These men are the heroes. Let us not so much mourn the dead as thank our God that such men had lived."

It is hard to see how such words could be taken wrongly. Patton *was*, actually, in a far better position to claim who the heroes were than a father who had stayed at home during the war. Patton had witnessed many heroic actions under fire, he had tearfully pinned the Purple Heart on many soldiers who had not survived; Patton did not, by any means, mean that those who died during the war were fools. But the press wanted him to mean that. They trumpeted Patton's presumed intentions throughout the headlines, trying to turn the only people who respected, loved and admired Patton against him.

They were not successful. All that remains of their efforts are two letters from angry fathers[1] and a number of newspaper articles which appear in the light of hindsight, badly disguised attacks on Patton's character for the purpose of discrediting him and ruining his triumphal welcome in America.

How typical of Patton's fate that while millions of ordinary Americans were thunderously applauding him at parades and speeches, a handful of reporters was working over-time trying to get him into another incident. Macdonald wrote by far the worst of these articles, representative not of the people who were at this moment cheering him, but of the left-wing Communist media. "These utterances of Patton are atrocities of the mind," he wrote, still trying to get people worked up over Patton's remark on fools and heroes, "atrocious in being communicated not to a psychoanalyst but to a great number of soldiers, civilians and school children; and atrocious as reflections of what war-making has done to the personality of Patton himself." Such trash reporting sounds as if it were written right out of the 1960s – Macdonald was ahead of his time.

The next morning Patton spoke to the townspeople of Hamilton where more ceremonies and ovations awaited him. Patton had sold millions of dollars worth of war bonds, which caused Morgenthau, the Secretary of the Treasury to write Patton a delighted little note. He then flew to Los Angeles for more welcomes, speeches, and celebrations. At the Coliseum 100,000 people gathered to hear him speak. Patton was in America giving speeches only for the purpose of selling war bonds, and he was not allowed to say what he wanted. Even so, General Marshall and Secretary Stimson were worried that Patton might say something embarrassing at a scheduled press conference. "Patton might go off his rocker," Marshall told Stimson.

---

[1] Books make it sound as if hundreds of letters were written, but then only quote and name two. Incidentally, one of the fathers undoubtedly hated Patton before this, as he refers to him as the "face-slapping, gun-toting general."

What exactly did they mean? Were they worried that Patton would say something about the Russians or Eisenhower's candidacy? Marshall's idea for preventing Patton from "making a fool of himself" is astonishing. He actually contacted the Surgeon General asking for the best qualified psychiatrist to watch Patton during the press conference and watch for "clues" of mental imbalance. A captain of the Navy Medical Corps, a psychoanalyst who had treated several officers with nervous breakdown, was selected. When Stimson heard of the plan, he vetoed it and suggested one of his own. Patton would not say anything out of line, he promised. He would attend the press conference and answer almost all of the press' questions.

At the press conference, Stimson quickly took over, allowing Patton to comment only on such harmless topics as tanks, horses, and combat psychology. Stimson asked almost all the questions, answered several from the floor, and ruled out of order some questions that reporters did pose. Patton did not mind since the last thing he wanted was another press scandal. He amused and enchanted the reporters who actually met him, as he had always done. Near the end a reporter asked what magic General Patton had that made the morale of the Third Army so high. Patton smiled and said with customary humility, "It was simple, ladies and gentleman. I just had the honor and happiness of commanding some very great men. Thanks to them, we – and by 'we' I mean the Third Army, because I keep forgetting there are any others – well, *we* destroyed 2,300-odd German tanks, including 890 Panzers and Tigers, and we lost half that many."

In California, Patton stayed with his sister Nita, visited Pasadena and the Army Regional Hospital, participated in a ceremony at the Rose Bowl, attended the Church of Our Saviour, stopped in at the Huntington Library, and placed a wreath of roses on the graves of his parents. His sister was delighted at the huge crowds that came to congratulate her brother. "It is your revenge," she said, "on all the slimy, jealous toads who tried to do you harm."

After all the touring for war bonds, Patton spent the next few weeks in comparative quiet with his family. Eisenhower had returned, and the press was busy covering his tour of the country.

The Walter Reed Army Hospital had a special ward for the "multiple amputees." Patton's daughter Ruth Ellen worked in what she called the "saddest ward" of the hospital. She wanted her father to come see the men so as to cheer them up. Patton didn't like visiting hospitals, but he always forced himself to do so. The men were in horrible condition and all sorts of body parts were missing. Many were waiting for their artificial legs and arms to arrive. Patton walked in, Ruth Ellen remembers, like a "one-man parade," then he looked around and stood silent for several minutes.

At length he mustered the strength to speak, "By God, if I'd been a better general, most of you men wouldn't be here."

Unlike the SHAEF bureaucrats who counted numbers of Americans versus the number of Germans and concluded that we would have to win, Patton tried his hardest to win with the smallest number of American casualties. Patton's deeply emotional state was the result of his tender and fatherly love for his soldiers, a love so deep that it almost jeopardized his effectiveness as a commander. Yet it was undoubtedly this love that enabled him to be so successful on the battlefield. Patton could never have entered his men into battle, as some commanders did, with the knowledge that their overwhelming numerical superiority would in the end prevail. For Patton, only the *least* number of casualties was acceptable.

Patton had a difficult time reconciling his love of his men with the knowledge that he had sent many of them to their deaths. He hated to think that he had killed so many young men; and he cursed and acted rather than do what he wanted to do: weep aloud for the men he had sent to death in battle. Though he loved the glory of war, he hated its butchery; and so with the Third Army he had maximized the glory and tried to eliminate the casualties.

There was one other thing that Patton advocated which the newspapers hated: compulsory military service. Patton's reasons for approving of it are clear, "You just wait and see. The lily-livered bastards in Washington will demobilize. They'll say they've made the world safe for democracy again. The Russians are not such fools. They'll rebuild, and with modern weapons. But if we have compulsory universal military service, if we vote for it first at the polls, or in Congress, then in years to come the rest of the world will know that we mean what we say." At the time most church leaders were opposed to compulsory service. Patton set out on a crusade to change their minds. The leaders with whom he did talk were "shaken in their views. He was a most persuasive advocate," Ayer recalls.

One influential leader with whom Patton particularly wished to speak was Archbishop Cushing of Boston. Patton informed the War Department of his intentions, sure that they would approve. It was, after all, in their best interest. He was in for a rude awakening. "I've just been told to keep my mouth shut and that I'm a warmonger," he told his brother-in-law. Patton had been muzzled for most of his trip, but this last bit deeply angered him. He had almost resigned on the spot "so that he might go before the nation and speak his piece on the true nature of the Soviet menace, and the need for the continuance of full-scale national preparedness and alertness."[1] He decided to wait; he would return to Germany and retire soon afterwards. It would have been safer for him to have resigned there.

Governing Bavaria would be his last task, apparently. The only chance Patton had of fighting again was if the Chinese opened a port in the Pacific or if MacArthur became incapacitated. Patton was "depressed with the attitude in the War Department" whose emphasis was on "'planning' and no emphasis at all on fighting." While he was at the War Department, Cook spoke to Patton. "George, you are to be congratulated because Courtney Hodges has gone to China. Courtney will get himself in trouble over there and you will have to go and get him out."

> "As I did in the Bulge, I suppose. Speaking of which reminds me that Courtney Hodges and Omar Bradley got a DSM for their unsuccessful defense of the Bulge, and I did not get one for successfully defending it." *Patton's diary*

Patton had got the message: he was not wanted. Any responsible position needed someone – well, quieter. Not given to "indiscretions." The thought of it made him sick.

Even though Patton had been careful to not speak out directly against the Russians – yet – one more press embarrassment was reserved for him. In his own home town of Hamilton, Massachusetts, Patton addressed an audience of high school students.

> "Standing before them, resplendent in all his medals, stars and sashes, he said, 'You young men and young ladies may well be the soldiers and sailors, the airmen

---

[1] "Before the Colors Fade," by Fred Ayer, page 241

and nurses of this country's next war for survival. As such it befits you to keep your minds and bodies strong, to study the history of your country and of those who would destroy it. There are those who will not agree when I talk of the necessity of a strong citizen's army – that advocating it is an act of belligerence. Well, let me tell you this. I am sixty years old and never in all those years have I known of a single fire that was prevented or put out by discharging the fire department.'" *"Before the Colors Fade," by Fred Ayer*

Patton's meaning was all too clear. The newspapers angrily decried him. Who was he to speak to the young about "another war for survival"? And yet, ironically, there was no man more qualified to speak on the subject. Everyone who met Patton testified that his knowledge of history was unparalleled; clearly he was an expert on the military and wars. The real reason for the press attacks is clear: everyone knew who Patton meant when he spoke of "those who would destroy" America.

Despite all of the bashing in the press, Patton emerges more resplendent, his honor unstained by the "political correctness" that permeated everything in America. One of his relatives remembers that Patton "was quieter, more mature."

It was the night before Patton was returning to Germany. His wife, Beatrice, was upstairs packing his things. His daughters, Beatrice and Ruth Ellen, and his son, George, were gathered around in the living room.
Suddenly he said, "I am never going to see you again. I know this. I am going to be buried in foreign soil."
"Oh, Daddy, don't be silly," Ruth Ellen said, "The war's all over now."
"Yes, I know. But my luck has run out now. That gold Allenby used to talk about is gone.[1] I've spent it all. I have not been a good enough man in my life to be killed by a bullet like General Bee at Manassas. I don't know how it is going to happen, but I'm going to die over there." There was a pause. His children were quiet. They had long ago learned to respect his intuition. "Promise me one thing," he went on, "let me be

---

[1] The famous British Cavalry General, Allenby, had told Patton that everyone has a certain amount of gold (luck). Thus one man could do any amount of daring escapades so long as he still had his luck left, but once it was gone, then he would die. A front-line infantryman spent his "gold" faster than a rear-echelon cook.

400

buried over there. In God's name, don't bring my body home." They promised.

How did Patton know he would die in Europe? This was the same man who had predicted so many other world events. Was his knowledge of history and human nature serving him again? Or was he simply playing for pity? Was he trying to be dramatic? Some have thought so. Ruth Ellen said this about her father's prophetic prediction of his own death,

> "Sometimes Daddy talked just to hear himself, sometimes to shock people. But when he talked like that he gave me the shivers. Sometimes he saw things other people couldn't see. I think that was one of those times."[1]

Patton's prediction of military events, like the Battle of the Bulge and Anzio, is perhaps not surprising. He was, after all, a military man of the finest caliber. But he also was able to predict Eisenhower's Presidency, Montgomery's deceitfulness, and Bradley's ascendancy due to his lack of backbone. This must stem from his uncanny intuition into the minds of other men. He could tell what their motives were and what they were willing to do in order to attain them, just by watching them and speaking to them. His diary is full of his candid observations of the men around him, all of which were later proven true. Thus when he met the Russians, he had no doubt whatsoever as to their objectives. Patton never denied something that was evident before him.

While Patton did record his conclusions, he does not leave us any clues as to how he arrived at them. Apparently he did not tell his children how either. But certainly he could "see things other people couldn't see." The pity was that no one cared.

---

[1] "Before the Colors Fade," by Fred Ayer, page 239

Chapter Fifty Four

THE WORLD FALLING TO PIECES

There was a depressing, lackadaisical attitude in America, a "we're done, we've won" mood that worried Patton. The Americans seemed happy to leave any political troubles in Europe and "get on with life." Yet the soldiers could not entirely remove the "Europe" from themselves. After all, they had lived and fought beside these people for months, they naturally cared what happened to them. An ever widening gap existed between the American who had stayed at home and believed that "the war's over" and the soldier who was returning from Europe who wanted to make sure that the people he had freed would remain free.

Patton knew that it was unlikely, almost impossible, that any Eastern Europeans would be free, especially with the "no more wars" stage having settled unopposed upon his countrymen. As Patton flew over Le Havre on his return trip from America, Sgt. Meeks said, "General, that is France! We sure have done our thirty days in the brig!"

"In a sense I had a similar feeling because with the exception of my own immediate family the whole attitude of the people in America is quite inimical to that which exists in Europe. None of them realizes that one cannot fight for two and a half years and be the same."
Patton's Diary

Perhaps the last slight of its kind was offered Patton at this time. Bradley had rated Patton as the "No. 1 commander in combat" and a paltry No. 5 of 10 generals he knew with comparable experience for "all

403

around duty." Eisenhower had called Patton this "brilliant yet unbalanced officer," and Bradley does not seem to have had any regard for Patton's talents outside the military sphere.

> "colorful, courageous, energetic, pleasing personality, impetuous. Possesses high degree of leadership, bold in operations, has fine sense of feeling of enemy and own capabilities. An outstanding combat leader."

It marked a 180 degree turn in Bradley's thinking. No longer was Patton a publicity-seeking glory hound who skinned his soldiers and forced them to obey his maniacal orders. Something – oh, how much! – had happened since Sicily. Patton had been stepped on, beaten into the dust, insulted and almost relieved, yet he had managed to make a spectacular come-back under his once underling, Bradley. He had broken out across France in a flaming column of victory and headlines, capturing city after city faster than blitzkrieg, and yet – and this was probably what changed Bradley the most – Patton had taken Bastogne, saved Bradley's reputation, and turned around the Battle of the Bulge. He had captured 10 German divisions in the Hunsruck Mountains, and known precisely when to build up the front in participation of a counter-attack that was launched by the enemy within 24 hours. His army had killed or captured 1,000 Germans every day in operation. Yet Patton, the man, was the same. And it was the man that the High Command feared to have with them, hanging about, learning embarrassing facts.

Major General Parks, commander of the U.S. troops in the Berlin Military District, invited Patton to come for a review of the 2nd Armored Division at which the Secretary of War would be attending. And so on July 21st Patton flew over. "We could have gone faster but for the fact that if one flies over Russian occupied territory, they shoot you – nice friends."

He drove to Potsdam and told his wife that the Palace there was "not hurt but all the furniture and rugs have been taken by the Mongols." Patton was beginning to refer to the Russians as the "Mongols," no doubt in order to avoid censorship.

> "We also saw Berlin which is not nearly as much bashed in as represented. The Mongols are a bad lot, even the U.S. sector has [Russian] guards in it, and I had to have a pass. However, I did not need it. I just pointed to my

Russian medal and the world was mine. Berlin gave me the blues. We have destroyed what could have been a good race and we [are] about to replace them with Mongolian savages. And all Europe will be Communist. It's said that for the first week after they took [Berlin], all women who ran were shot and those who did not were raped. I could have taken it had I been allowed."

Patton's mood was increasingly dark. The more he saw, the more he was convinced of American political stupidity and the inevitability of Russian Communist ascendancy. They knew what they wanted; the Americans were dawdling aimlessly.

He was certainly not the only one who felt this way. Churchill had campaigned for "magnanimity" in the treatment of the Germans. If Europe was to resist Communism, Germany must be rebuilt – and rebuilt quickly. He had begged Eisenhower not to remove the American troops from the area that the Russians were claiming was theirs. He was against using German prisoners as slave laborers in France. But Churchill had been ignored by the Americans. And in his own country he had just been thrown out of office and been replaced by a Socialist government. He was in an even more abject state then Patton. Churchill now began writing his history of the war. He was to call this period "Triumph and Tragedy." His feelings about the period are identical to Patton's. "How the great democracies triumphed, so that they could resume the follies which had so nearly cost them their lives," was the theme of "Triumph and Tragedy."

Churchill was in a unique position: he had been through all this before. He had vainly tried to warn Chamberlain's government about Nazism's dangers and evils. Then all the newspapers had scoffed at Churchill and called him a "Jeremiah." Now he was trying to warn them about Communism's thrreat, and again he was being ignored and derided. So instead of trying vainly to appeal to the consciences of statesmen and the sensibilities of newspapers, he began working on a speech entitled "The Iron Curtain" which he would give in Fulton, Missouri in 1946. This would be the first public speech to frankly uncover what the democracies ought to do, and the reason Churchill was able to deliver it was because he was out of public office: he no longer held any official position.

Patton was beginning to realize that that was the only way he could say what he truly believed. He would have to leave the military. Otherwise he would never be free to say what he believed.

"I am afraid that Europe is going to go Bolshevik," he wrote to his sister, "which, if it does, may eventually spread to our country."

Codman, Patton's aide, had remained in America to attend to his sick wife. Patton dutifully wrote to him of what he had seen in Berlin,

> "One cannot help but feel that Berlin marks the final epitaph of what should have been a great race. I really do not see how they can recover, particularly in view of the activities of some of our Allies, and I am not at all sure that we are not stepping out of the frying pan into the fire by concurring in what is going on. However, this is a personal opinion which probably nobody else shares."

Felix of Luxembourg spent the night with Patton. He, too, was distressed over the future of Europe. "So are all thinking men who are not running for office," Patton wrote to his wife bitterly.

Eisenhower, the object of his scorn, invited Patton to dinner on August 1st. They dined alone and Ike had a chance to present Patton with his version of the goings-on.

> "I learned some interesting facts, particularly what impelled him to order us to halt short of the Moldau River when we could so easily have advanced that far.... It seems that when Churchill, Roosevelt, and Stalin were in Teheran in the fall of 1943, Churchill was convinced that even in the unlikely event of the Allies being able to make a landing on the Continent, they would never be able to cross the Rhine River, and he therefore persuaded FDR to go along with him in asking Stalin to have the Russians capture Berlin and Vienna and gave the Russians a line about a hundred miles west of Berlin. Later when we were going along well and could easily have taken Berlin, Churchill asked Ike to do it, and Ike replied by stating that it was Churchill's fault that the line had been established where it was. I believe this was a great mistake on his part because, had we taken the

country to the Moldau River and Berlin, we would have saved a great deal of agricultural Germany and prevented what I believe historians will consider a horrid crime and great loss of prestige in letting Russians take the two leading capitals of Europe." *Patton's Diary*

This, of course, is the same version of the Berlin decision that Eisenhower fed to historians after the war. Patton, for the time being, believed it, but even he realized that it didn't excuse Ike. Ike claims in his book that the "great loss of prestige" that we suffered was not a reason to "waste thousands" of lives on Berlin. And the "horrid crime" part? By now, Eisenhower couldn't tell a crime from a good deed, or an evil empire from an ally.

People at home didn't want a war – no matter what, Patton learned from his wife. "If there ever was a war breeder," Patton wrote to her, "it is the Europe of today. Russia is just like the French Republic of 1870. Germany is out. The Czechs hate every one. The French are Communistic. The British fools. And we, God knows."

When not ruminating on the history of the world, Patton was gathering information from the soldiers so as to compile notes on fighting "because, having studied war since I was about sixteen years old, I have only come across some twelve books which deal with fighting, although there are many hundreds which deal with war. This is because the people who fight either are killed or are inarticulate."

On August 10th Patton heard about the surrender of Japan.

"Another war has ended and with it my usefulness to the world. It is for me personally a very sad thought. Now all that is left to do is sit around and await the arrival of the undertaker and posthumous immortality."

Chapter Fifty Five

SPIES IN PATTON'S SECTOR

Lieutenant General Bishop Gowlina of the Polish Army dined with Patton. Gowlina was, according to Patton, a "very bright man [who] hates the Russians with good reason. He told me some of their methods." According to the Bishop, there were over 2 million Poles in Russia – slaves of the state performing back-breaking tasks. In every case, the Russians had stolen away Poles and split up families.[1] Other Poles had been brutally murdered, raped and some families had been massacred. Patton then went on in his diary to make comments on the Russians. The Russians were devoid of any belief in God or morality and thus the Russian,

> "thinks deviously. We can no more understand a Russian than a Chinaman or a Japanese and, from what I have seen of them, I have no particular desire to understand them except to ascertain how much lead or iron it takes to kill them. In addition to his other amiable characteristics, the Russian has no regard for human life, and is an all out son of a bitch, a barbarian, and a chronic drunk."

These comments may be viewed as racist – until one realizes that Patton really did not mean the Russian race, but the Communist, immoral murdering Russians that he, and his colleagues, were running into. Thus

---

[1] Some writers have laughed at Patton for believing these "rumors;" however they have now been verified.

he wrote to his wife, "Do Americans simply want to destroy our form of government and go Communist? If they knew as much about Russia as I do, they would not be so crazy to be Communists." Thus, for Patton, the words "Russian," "Communist" and "Mongol" were interchangeable.

Another visitor to Patton was Mr. G. A. Kemper, an old acquaintance from his Hawaiian days. Kemper had come to Germany in 1936 as a representative of Woolworth and been run out of business for "not being a Nazi." Kemper told Patton that "our military government is handicapped by the necessity of using dug-out Germans – that is, Germans who are so definitely anti-Nazi that they have not held any office since 1933, and are therefore not only inexperienced in current methods of government but are more or less old, whereas the whole cry is for youth."

> "Under our rules, which demand the total de-Nazification of Germany, we have to remove everyone who has ever expressed himself in any way as a Nazi or who has paid party dues. It is very evident that anybody who was in business, irrespective of his real sentiments, had to say he was a Nazi and pay dues. The only young people who were not Nazis came out of the internment camps and are therefore either Jews or Communists. We are certainly in a hard position as far as procuring civil servants is concerned."

Patton had the German prisoners of war cutting trees, for he rightly anticipated that there would be a heating problem in the coming winter. He also set up groups to begin repairing the telegraph wires, but there was a desperate shortage of workers which would soon turn into a real crisis. At least 80% of Germans had become "Nazis" so as to escape death; Patton couldn't understand what was wrong with hiring them. After all, they had not been indicted of war crimes! They hadn't been members of the SA or the SS or the Gestapo. They were simply ordinary citizens who had joined a political party so as to stay alive. But such concepts as "innocent until proven guilty" were clearly too complicated for SHAEF.

Unfortunately, Patton's clear thinking was to be his downfall. It was all very well for him to realize the absurdity of SHAEF's orders; but the problem was that Patton wanted to have the order reversed. "It is no more possible for a man to be a civil servant in Germany and not have paid lip service to Nazism than it is for a man to be a postmaster in America and not have paid at least lip service to the Democratic or Republican party when it is in power," Patton wrote to Eisenhower.

A few months from now Patton would say the same thing to a group of newspapermen who would quote him and create another furor. Eisenhower, acting as if he was surprised by Patton's words, would relieve him. If Eisenhower had truly been concerned about what Patton thought on de-Nazification, he would have relieved Patton for the letter above, where Patton very clearly states that he thinks the Nazi party is a political party, like the Democrats or Republicans. But Eisenhower didn't relieve Patton because of the thoughts expressed in that letter. Ike didn't even reprove him. And perhaps the reason is not as mysterious as it would seem. Eisenhower, more than any other man, knew that what Patton had said was true.

The French General Juin dined with Patton. It seems that no matter who Patton spoke or ate with, the topic of conversation was always the same. This shows how much the problems of administration, justice (or the lack of it) and Communism were burdening Patton's soul. "It is indeed unfortunate, my General," Juin said, "that the English and the Americans have destroyed in Europe the only sound country – and I do not mean France – and therefore the road is now open for the advent of Russian Communism."

Ladislas Farago writes in "The Last Days of Patton" that Patton now had an "infatuation" with the Germans. This is completely wrong. Patton was trying to save Europe from becoming Communist. He realized that Germany was the most modern of the European countries, and therefore the rapid reparation of Germany was essential. Patton had no more love or hatred for the Germans than for any other race; he was not brought up or taught to think like that.

He made another astonishingly accurate prediction – this time about the atomic bomb.

"The use of the atomic bomb against Japan was most unfortunate because now it gives a lot of vocal but ill-informed people – mostly Fascists, Communists, and s.o.b.'s assorted – an opportunity to state that the Army, Navy, and Air Forces are no longer necessary as this bomb will either prevent war or destroy the human race.

Actually, the bomb is no more revolutionary than the first throwing-stick or javelin or the first cannon or the first submarine. It is simply, as I have often written, a new instrument added to the orchestra of death which is war."

Patton's knowledge of war and human nature again served him, and his comments on the atomic bomb were certainly borne out by time.

One other prediction, this written to Colonel Mc Gee, would also prove true in only a few years.

"In my opinion and strictly for your private ear, we never had a better chance of producing another war than we have in Europe now. I have never seen so much vitriolic hatred, mistrust, and avarice as exists here today. Furthermore, as you know, a certain proportion of the people with whom we are dealing do not have Occidental minds which makes it even more difficult if not impossible to come to an understanding with them. I doubt if the top blows off very soon, but unless something very radical happens and happens within a reasonable time, the top will blow off, probably after we have redeployed our army."

On August 23rd, Eisenhower sent Patton a letter, warning him that "obliteration" of Nazism was a major U.S. war aim and that a Joint Chiefs of Staff directive had clearly prohibited the retention of Nazis for administrative necessity, convenience or expediency. This spelled the crippling of Europe, Patton knew, but he nevertheless complied. Ike wrote that de-Nazification was a "most delicate subject both here and at home" which "our governmental representatives as well as newspapers have been quick to seize upon." Here it was again! Eisenhower was not interested in doing the right thing, only what would yield positive columns. This was the mark of a true politician, Patton thought.

The liberal American newspapers were once again crying for a relief at home. They wanted Patton to remove the civil governor of Bavaria,[1] a man named Schaeffer. Schaeffer was a 57 year old politician

---

[1] Schaeffer's official title was "Minister President of the former Kingdom of Bavaria."

412

that had been highly recommended by the Catholic Cardinal Faulhaber. Schaeffer was competent and knowledgeable, and best yet, from a de-Nazification stand point, Schaeffer had been a prisoner at the Dachau concentration camp. Schaeffer had been in politics since 1918. He was a member of the "archconservative, ultra-Catholic Bavarian People's Party."[1] For this he had been arrested in March of 1933. He was detained for only a night, then arrested again in May for 2 weeks. Schaeffer had so far been able to skillfully bypass prison, but by 1944 there was no more escape and he spent 46 days at Dachau before being liberated. Being a member of the Catholic Bavarian People's Party had ensured Schaeffer a rough ride under the Nazis, and it was this membership that was now provoking a sudden rash of newspaper attacks against "the ruler of Bavaria."

It is now common knowledge that Patton's sector had been flooded with Russian spies, determined to find out what Patton was up to. Based on the agents' information, the Russians reported to Bradley that Patton was not disarming the Germans. In fact, it seemed that he was husbanding them into a private army for some kind of weird adventure of his own.[2] The Russians accused Patton of retaining elite divisions of the Waffen SS[3] that had surrendered in Czechoslovakia in May. They said that the Third Army had never registered the SS soldiers' names in the roster of captured troops, had not dispersed them now that the war was over; in fact, the Third Army hadn't even disarmed them!

Bradley brushed the complaints aside. They were too outrageous to be true. But then the Russians followed up their charges with pinpointed data, giving away the fact that they had been spying in Bavaria. Bradley, alarmed at the Russian reports, warned Patton to release any unaccounted prisoners at once. In response to increasingly urgent Russian protestations, a special delegation of 4 senior G-3 officers led by Colonel Anton De Rohan was sent secretly by SHAEF to Bad Toelz to investigate what was happening with the German prisoners. These secret delegations went to different prison camps.

---

[1] Quote from "The Last Days of Patton" by Ladislas Farago.
[2] This story is taken from "The Last Days of Patton," by Ladislas Farago, page 140.
[3] The Waffen SS were fighting soldiers who had nothing to do with the SS that managed the concentration camps. The "SS" title was merely to mark them as elite.

Immediately an indignant Patton complained to Eisenhower of this needless "harassment." Did they think he was incompetent? Was this their way of saying that they had no confidence in his command?

SHAEF now decided that Patton only complained when he was up to something. If he didn't want their snoops in his territory, the only thing to do was plant more – and this time they did not inform Patton. A task force of officers consisting of a colonel, 2 lieutenant colonels, and three majors were sent to Bad Toelz. These men were basically American spies on Patton. They were ordered to take their findings directly, and secretly, to Bedell Smith.[1]

The American high command had also approved for a man called Professor Dorn to investigate Patton's "soundness." Dorn was a military intelligence officer who hated Schaeffer and was doing his best to see that Schaeffer was removed. The one obstacle in his way was Patton.

There is still no evidence – besides Schaeffer's political association – as to why the newspapers began vehemently attacking him. Schaeffer, the ex-prisoner of Dachau, was even called a "Nazi" and was accused of retaining "Nazis" in office.

Dorn was determined to have Schaeffer removed, even if it meant removing Patton as well. Dorn had decided that Patton spoke and acted as if he were "mad." Dorn's superior, General Adcock, thoroughly agreed, and the two borrowed a psychiatrist from the Medical Corps and sent him to Bad Toelz[2] disguised as a supply officer. Adcock and Dorn then had the Signal Corps place a tap on Patton's telephone and set up secret microphones in the room of his *house in St. Querin!* They justified this clear violation of Patton's constitutional right to privacy by stating that based on certain passages in the Russian communications to Eisenhower, it was clear that the Russians were also tapping and bugging Patton.[3]

---

[1] Eisenhower's chief of staff. Patton may have discovered about this plot, since he told Ike that he would never be seen at the same table with Smith again. Smith was not allowed to visit Patton in the hospital, or attend Patton's funeral. Smith later became *Ambassador to Moscow.*
[2] Where Patton was living
[3] "The Last Days of Patton," by Ladislas Farago, page 208

It was at this time that General McNarney was telling Patton, over the telephone, that he ought to speed up the release of the SS troops. The Soviets are complaining that you're too slow, he told Patton.

"Why do you care what those Russians think?" Patton exploded. "We are going to have to fight them sooner or later, within the next generation. Why not do it now while our Army is intact and the Russians can have their hinds kicked back into Russia in 3 months? We can do it easily with the help of the German troops we have, if we just arm them and take them with us. They hate the Russians."

"Shut up, Georgie, you fool!" McNarney shouted across the phone. "This line may be tapped and you will be starting a war with your talking." McNarney was temporarily in charge while Eisenhower was on leave in America. He may have been aware that the phone was tapped – by the Americans as well.

"I would like to get it started some way," Patton said, "that is the best thing we can do now. You don't have to get mixed up in it at all if you're so soft about it and scared of your rank – just let me handle it down here. In ten days I can have enough incidents happen to have us at war with them and make it look like their fault."

Mc Narney hung up while Patton was speaking. Patton turned to Colonel Harkins, who had heard the whole heated telephone conversation. "We will need these Germans and I don't think we ought to mistreat people who we'll need badly."

What did the Russians think when they heard Patton? "In ten days I can have enough incidents happen to have us at war," Patton had said. And the Russians were well aware of how devastatingly successful the war Patton waged was. Perhaps their taps in his room heard him admit that he'd like to use the Germans, only confirming their suspicions. It's not hard to guess how the Russians felt as they heard the most successful American commander talk of waging war against them with German troops. But it's more difficult to see how the American spies reacted when they heard what Patton had said.

Patton was hardly keeping any of this secret. He would say to anyone who wanted to know that the Russians were despicable and we ought to fight them. And it was Patton's candid speech, uttered to anyone willing to listen, that would be fatal.

Meanwhile at the DP camps, force was being used to evict the Russian refugees and send them back to Soviet Russia. Some of the Russian DP's had opposed Communism in their homelands, and were urgently seeking political asylum. Unfortunately for them, it would be denied, and millions of DP's would be slaughtered after they left American hands. Knowing what would befall them in Communist-dominated Eastern Europe, some sought to deny the Russians the chance of killing them by taking their own lives first.

The Military Government had a meeting in Frankfurt on August 27th. There were a number of speeches by Eisenhower and his assistants which, according to Patton, "were unrealistic and in every case the chief interest of the speaker was to say nothing which could be used against him." The Military Government was still committed to throwing ordinary, un-convicted civilians out of their homes, hiring only those who had left concentration camps, throwing all Germans out of office, and placing all Germans into the "automatic arrest category." What they were doing was "undemocratic," wrote Patton, "and follows practically Gestapo methods."

The Morgenthau plan to utterly incapacitate German industry and turn her into an agrarian state was still in vogue, although it would soon be declared utterly impractical. In 1946 American tax dollars were spent flying food, clothing, wood, and other essentials to Germany because of the ridiculous politically correct decisions which were being made in 1945. Patton saw through the Morgenthau plan, but of course he was ignored, and Americans would pay for this in the coming year.

> "It is patently impossible for Germany to be an agricultural state. First, because there is not enough in Germany for the country to feed itself on such a basis, and second, because if Germany has no purchasing power, we will not be able to sell our goods to her and, therefore, our markets will be very considerably restricted."

Obviously, someone was trying to destroy Germany. The question was: who and why? Eisenhower was carrying out the destructive orders, yet he blamed the newspapers. The newspapers were certainly for the complete annihilation of any kind of working state in Germany, yet, why? Patton thought that it was high-placed Jews, eager for revenge. But he slowly reversed this opinion as he noticed that the orders were aimed at everything that would keep Germany running: everything that would keep her citizens content. Only one group could want this: the Russians. The more he thought about it, the more he

416

realized that Communists in the newspapers were exploiting the soldiers' horror at the Germans' crimes and the Jews' natural feeling of revenge to destroy Germany and open it to Russian invasion.

At the Military Government meeting, Patton stated to the assembled generals and notables that, "In my opinion, Germany is so completely blacked out that so far as military resistance is concerned, they are not a menace. What we need to look out for is Russia." "This statement caused considerable furor," Patton wrote with satisfaction. The bureaucrats, politicians, and generals at the meeting were stunned and they angrily decried him. What fools they look now! Yet at the time, it was Patton who was the lone voice, he who looked the fool.

Depressed at having met his foolish colleagues again, Patton wrote to his wife, "I have been at Frankfurt for a civil government conference. If what we are doing is 'Liberty, then give me death.' I can't see how Americans can sink so low. It is Semitic and I am sure of it."[1]

On August 29th Patton received another order which seemed to verify his suspicion that the Jews had a powerful lobby in Washington thirsty for revenge. He had received a letter in which he was told to give the Jewish DPs special accommodations. "If for Jews, why not Catholics, Mormons, etc.?" Patton wrote in his diary, his sense of justice again horrified. He called General Bull, alarmed at the unjust order, but Bull said that they had looked into the letter and it had "considerable background."

> "Naturally I intend to carry out the instructions to the limit of my capacity in spite of my personal feelings against them and in spite of my fear that in doing such things we will lay ourselves open to just criticism. We are also turning over to the French several hundred thousands German prisoners of war to be used as slave labor in France. It is amusing to recall that we fought the Revolution in defense of the rights of man and the Civil War to abolish slavery and have now gone back on both principles." *Patton's diary*

---

[1] At the time Patton believed what he was being told and assumed that the Jews were trying to revenge themselves by destroying Germany. He would change this opinion in a few months when he realized who the true destroyers of Europe were: the Communists in the press.

The Third and Seventh Armies were warned on August 31st that the care of the displaced persons was a "major military objective." In many cases, they said, Germans living near the DP camps were immeasurably better off. "Where this is so, military government is not doing its job." No DPs could be lodged in tents after September 15th, even if this meant removing German civilians from their homes.

This, of course, would be necessary because no new homes could be built while over 80% of the German population *could not* be hired by the orders of SHAEF. Third Army quickly issued a bulletin complaining that denazification had caused the spread of typhoid and fuel shortages; by SHAEF orders laboratory technicians and forestry experts were unemployed.

As far as building up Europe to resist Communism went, "The Germans are the only decent people left in Europe. It's a choice between them and the Russians. I prefer the Germans. So do our cousins."[1]

Nothing in Europe looked good, and gradually one diary entry merges with another, every letter sounds the same: we are destroying Europe and the Communists will take it over. Luckily for the history of the world, we found our senses and reversed our policies a few months after Patton died.

What was the de-Nazification system and was it really administering justice? All Germans were required to fill out a simple looking questionnaire called a *Fragebogen*. Here they listed their membership in National Socialist and military organizations, associations, employment and salary history back to the pre-Hitler days. At the interviewer's desk the man presented his *Fragebogen* which was quickly examined to determine whether the man was subject to automatic arrest or had technical skills which could be used for intelligence purposes. Most Germans who did not fall into either category could then be released. Charles F. Marshall served as part of the committee that reviewed the *Fragebogens*. He says,

> "When the screening team had a borderline case, and this was frequent, the man was passed on to me. Playing God was never my idea of a good job, but the buck stopped with me and caused me much anguish. A stroke

---

[1] Our cousins: the British.

418

of the pen set the man free; another stroke might result in his eventual execution. And so it went from early morning until evening. And many an evening after supper I spent poring over papers I brought home, racking my brains for the proper solution. Not a day went by that I didn't wish for Solomonic wisdom."
"Discovering the Rommel Murder," by Charles F. Marshall

In another place he says that their power was virtually unlimited, "We were judge and jury." What bothered Patton, and C. F. Marshall, was that these men had never had any training in law. How were they supposed to judge these cases? Patton's affirmation that everyone was "innocent until proven guilty" and that no man should be removed until "convicted in a court of law" would have saved these untrained men a great deal of agonizing.

Eisenhower issued a directive when Patton had been in America in which he stated that "one of the principal objectives of the war is 'to destroy German militarism and Nazism.'" "I can't see what future I have but I am certainly getting a great education in S.O.B.'s," Patton wrote to Beatrice. "I had never heard that we fought to de-natzify Germany – live and learn. What we are doing is to utterly destroy the only semi-modern state in Europe so that Russia can swallow the whole."

An example of the absurdity of "de-Nazification" occurred in Patton's sector. Under the current regulations, it was necessary to remove all Germans from important positions and place them under arrest. But what about the mine director who was the most capable engineer in Bavaria? No one could replace him, and removing him would further intensify the fuel shortage. Gay authorized the man to be placed under house arrest and kept at work. But this was bending the rules. It came down to the simple question: which was more important? Removing nominal members of the Nazi party (80% of the population at least), or preventing starvation and freezing in the coming winter? According to the orders Patton had been issued, "de-Nazification" was *the* most important thing.

Eisenhower wrote Patton a personal letter in which he re-affirmed the "de-Nazification" orders.

"As you know, I have announced a firm policy of uprooting the whole Nazi organization regardless of the fact that we may sometimes suffer from local administrative inefficiency. Reduced to its fundamentals, the Unites States entered this war as a foe of Nazism; victory is not complete until we have eliminated from positions of responsibility and, in appropriate cases properly punished, every active adherent to the Nazi party. I know that certain field commanders have felt that some modifications to this policy should be made. The question has long since been decided. We will not compromise with Nazism in any way. I wish you would make sure that all your subordinate commanders realize that the discussional stage of this question is long past and any expressed opposition to the faithful execution of this order cannot be regarded leniently by me. I expect just as loyal service in execution of this and other policies applying to the German occupation as I received during the war."

What a hypocritical letter! Yet how typical of Eisenhower. He, of all people, certainly knew that the United States hadn't entered the war as a "foe of Nazism." And what exactly was an "active adherent to the Nazi party"? What naivete is shown in the line, "We may sometimes suffer from local administrative inefficiency"! "Local administrative inefficiency"? He was looking at a country at a standstill. *Nothing* was working, *nothing* was running. Hardly "administrative" problems, these threatened to undermine the whole American occupation.

In Berlin on September 6th, Patton represented Eisenhower at the inter-Allied military parade. As the huge Soviet tanks rolled by, Marshal Zhukov said, "My dear General Patton, you see that tank? It carries a cannon which can throw a shell seven miles."
"Indeed?" replied Patton. "Well, my dear Marshal Zhukov, let me tell you this, if any of my gunners started firing at your people before they had closed to less than seven hundred yards I'd have them court-martialed for cowardice."

Patton remembers it this way,

"The R's had a lot of new heavy tanks of which they are very proud. The Marshal asked me how I liked them. I said I did not, and we had quite an argument. Apparently I was the first person ever to disagree with him."

Patton still nourished a hope that he could get Ike to "see the menace of the Mongols." Any particular care on Eisenhower's part for the Europeans had long since vanished, and he was now totally devoted to staying on the press' "good side."

"Sometimes I think I will simply resign and not be a further party to the degradation of my country," Patton wrote to his wife. He was still planning on retiring after he was finished in Bavaria.

Chapter Fifty Six

CLOUDS ON THE HORIZON

The papers began to viciously attack Eisenhower's stewardship of the displaced persons – especially the Jews. They said that the Jews were living in squalid conditions in the DP camps and demanded that the Germans be removed from their homes and the Jews moved into them immediately. This horrified Patton's sense of justice.

> "First, when we remove an individual German, we punish an individual German while the punishment is not intended for the individual but for the race.
> Furthermore, it is against my Anglo-Saxon conscience to remove a person from a house, which is a punishment, without due process of law."

A logical conclusion, but one which would not be carried out.

Nevertheless, due to the press attack, Eisenhower came out to see a Jewish DP camp and inspect the conditions for himself.

> "While waiting [for Ike to land], I talked to Brigadier General Mickelsen ... and he showed me a letter from President Truman to General Eisenhower which was unnecessarily harsh and in much less considerate language than I would have used in cussing out a 2nd Lieutenant. Mickelsen also showed me the report of a man named Harrison on the condition of Displaced Persons in Europe, particularly Jews. Harrison is a

member of the State Department. The report contained many allegations against General Eisenhower, the Army, and the various commanders. One of the chief complaints is the DP's are kept under guard. Of course, Harrison is ignorant of the fact that if they were not kept under guard they would not stay in the camps, would spread over the country like locusts, and would eventually have to be rounded up after quite a few of them had been shot and quite a few Germans murdered and pillaged."

This was what had actually happened before the Americans had had time to round them together. The facts were that while war criminals deserved to be punished, they could not be punished by mob rule like the DP's wanted to do.

Charles F. Marshall, who worked with the DP's, remembers that,

"the people ruined the light wires, tore out telephones, broke windows as fast as they were replaced, set fires, and at times raped, robbed and murdered. Given passes to leave the camp they would visit the nearest towns and pillage. At some camps they formed armed gangs and resorted to outright banditry. They endeared themselves to neither victor nor vanquished."[1]

He contrasts this with the exemplary behavior of the displaced French, Belgian and Dutch laborers who were easily repatriated and hints that the Eastern Europeans were expressing their rage and disbelief at the news that they would soon be returned to their Soviet occupied homelands. If this was their true intention, their efforts failed miserably. They only made themselves appear more undesirable as post-war immigrants to Western Europe.

Patton was also worried how the local population would respond when their homes were stolen away and given to the Jewish DP's. The propaganda they had so recently been taught would undoubtedly flare up, along with their natural resentment at this unfair treatment.

---

[1] "Discovering the Rommel Murder," by Charles F. Marshal, page 163

"I do not see why Jews should be treated any better or any worse than Catholics, Protestants, Mohammedans, or Mormons. However, it seems apparent that we will have to do this, and I am going to do it as painlessly as possible ..."

Obviously Patton was not anti-Semitic. He was the one who had vomited at the horror of the concentration camps. He just couldn't understand why Jews should be treated differently from everyone else, "any better or any worse than" the millions of other DPs. Unhappily, no one else could answer his question satisfactorily. They merely had their orders.

Ike and Patton spent the night commiserating over the terribly contradictory and confusing messages they were receiving from Washington. Ike was "as much under fire as is anyone else" in this case, so for the first time in a long time the two could speak frankly about the stupidity of their orders. Patton spoke about his future, asking if there were any available posts. All posts had already been filled with "general's favorites" so Patton told Ike that the only option he could see was to "go home and retire." Eisenhower, however, asked Patton to remain in Bavaria for at least 3 months. He would be leaving for America and he wanted Patton to "get things running quietly." Patton tentatively agreed. How sad that in fulfillment of this promise, Patton would be relieved by the man who had begged him to stay.

Together the two drove to Munich the next day to inspect the Displaced Persons camps. First they viewed a Baltic one. "The Baltic people are the best of the Displaced Persons and the camp was extremely clean in all respects. We were both, I think, very much pleased with the conditions here."

Some of the inmates at other DP camps were Russian slave laborers who had been living in terribly oppressive conditions in their own homelands. These DP's had never seen electric light or running water. As a consequence they were incredibly ignorant of "modern" inventions and often used toilet bowls as wash bowls.[1][2] Even though

---

[1] Thus Patton's comment that the DP's "Either never had any sense of decency, or else lost it all during their period of internment by the Germans," proved to be stunningly accurate. The Russian slave laborers never had any, and the Jewish concentration camp victims lost theirs.
[2] "Discovering the Rommel Murder," by Charles F. Marshal, page 162

these Russians had been slaves in Germany, they simply refused to return to Russia, preferring suicide.

Eisenhower and Patton then drove 45 minutes to a Jewish camp that had been established in a German hospital. The buildings had been well maintained before, but were now dilapidated. Patton quickly summed up the reason. "This is because these Jewish DP's, or at least a majority of them, have no sense of human relationships." Clearly, their experiences in the concentration camps had left them permanently scarred. "They decline, where practicable, to use latrines, preferring to relieve themselves on the floor." The stench was, therefore, awful, and Patton "lost his lunch" a few hours later "as a result of remembering it."

The thought that human beings could sink so low – even after years of torture – was disheartening, and it was hard for them to believe that "beings alleged to be made in the form of God can look the way they do or act the way they act." It was truly surprising for people to realize that concentration camp survivors would need years of rehabilitation. Unfortunately the higher authorities in Washington could not understand this and blamed the military for the state of the camps.

I must now address a very serious accusation that has been made against Patton. It is said that Patton was anti-Semitic and hated Jews. This particularly nasty deceit was hatched by the liberal newspapers of the time, but unfortunately the accusation has clung tenaciously to the Patton legend. Patton's previous biographers seemed reluctant to clear his name; and in the case of Ladislas Farago, went out of their way to blacken it.

No single Allied general did more to save the Jews than Patton. Only Patton *demanded* advance at every opportunity. Patton, alone, realized that every precious second cost lives. Among all the Allied generals, Patton was also the least race-conscious. He had no problem integrating white and black soldiers, and he happily decorated the deserving black soldiers.[1] For this reason, many of the prejudiced white officers at SHAEF looked down on Patton. Of course, like usual, he did not care – he was winning.

It was Patton who uncovered the first concentration camp. Because he had ordered Third Army to advance so rapidly, there was

---

[1] See Chapter 31 "Prejudiced?" page 217

clear evidence of the systematic methods the Nazis had employed in murdering the inmates. It was Patton who turned white and began retching as he saw hundreds of emaciated bodies. Eisenhower and Bradley may have been horrified at the scenes, but they had not sickened. Patton could not believe his eyes as he saw the living skeletons that could not even walk or speak. He wondered whether they would ever return to normal.

Patton soon learned that they would not – or at least not for years. It was these concentration camp victims who had no compunction to clean the DP camps they were now living in: eating, washing and defecating on the same grounds, even though proper facilities had been provided.[1] When Patton comments in his diary about these Jews, he certainly did not mean these comments to apply to the entire Jewish race or religion. They were addressed to *the Jewish DP's*, in other words, the psychologically damaged concentration camp victims.[2] Some of Patton's biographers have taken these comments out of context and insinuated that they were meant to be about the whole Jewish race. Nothing could be further from the truth. Over the 40 years that Patton kept diaries, this was the first time that he ever said *anything* about the "Jews." And even now that he spoke of them, he was referring to *these* Jews, the DP's, not all Jews. This distinction is very important, because there was a vast difference between most Jews and the Jewish DP's; and thus a vast difference between Patton's opinion about the Jews and his comments about the Jewish DP's.

At this time, Patton believed that certain influential Jews in the United States were seeking revenge on the Germans. He believed they were behind the ridiculous orders that were destroying Germany, and that their vengeful attitude would lead to a quick new leadership in Germany – under the Communists. A month or two before his death,

---

[1] The discovery of the Nazi crimes was so recent, and so earth-shattering, that it was not then known, as it is now, some of the strange effects cruel regimes cause upon people. One of these effects, observed in those who lived under the Communists in E. Europe, is the lack of a normal desire to do *something*; victims refuse even to clean or build (things that would improve living conditions).

[2] Patton's comments are *very clearly* only meant to be about the DPs, and he realized that they were not "subhuman" but that their stay in the concentration camps had clearly damaged them. "Either the Displaced Persons never had any sense of decency, or else they lost it all during their period of internment by the Germans," he wrote.

Patton seems to have realized that there was a very definite *Communist,* not Jewish, influence in the American press, which was causing Germany's destruction. These Communists may have used the Jews natural repugnance of Nazi horrors to encourage a policy of revenge; Patton seems to have thought so. Thus Patton occasionally would refer to the High Command's orders as "Semitic;" meaning that they had been issued with a mind to revenge.

Patton was writing all this in the privacy of his diary. Since it was not meant for the general public, he does not explain his meanings and they can sometimes be mistaken. However, it is usually quite easy to infer what he meant. What Patton said about the Jewish DPs and some Jews in America wanting revenge is not anti-Semitic. Patton disliked their deeds, actions and words: not the fact that they were Jewish. What Patton said was not a blanket statement about the whole Jewish race or religion, only these two types of Jews which he clearly names and whose intentions he clearly sets forth. Thus Patton was not anti-Semitic.

Unfortunately, Patton's "official" biographer Ladislas Farago went out of his way to fabricate incidents about Patton being anti-Jewish. Here is an example of how Farago manipulated Patton's diary and added to the historical source so as to present Patton as anti-Semitic.

> "The compound was a former German military hospital, and Patton was quick to point out to Ike how rapidly it had deteriorated under the new tenants. 'These buildings,' he said, 'were in a good state of repair when these Jews arrived. But look at them now! I'm telling you Ike, these Jewish DPs, or at least the majority of them, have no sense of human decency. They give the impression they've never seen a latrine before. They're pissing and crapping all over the floor!'
> 'Shut up, George,' Eisenhower said." *"The Last Days of Patton," by Ladislas Farago, page 173.*

Patton didn't have to tell Eisenhower what was evident before them: the state of the buildings and the mental and hygienic condition of those that inhabited them. There is, like usual, only one man who recorded these incidents; and that is Patton, in his diary. Patton writes there that Eisenhower was *appalled.* Patton didn't say *any* of the above, and Eisenhower doesn't tell "George" to "shut up."

Farago here creates the false impression that the DP camps were *not* in the horrible state that Patton recorded them in. He also cleverly adds in Eisenhower's "Shut up, George" as if Ike disagreed with Patton. Ike *may* have disagreed with Patton if Patton had actually said what Farago writes, but Patton didn't say or think that. What Patton wrote in his diary (which is very different from saying something aloud), was that the DPs had "no sense of human relationships."

Until Patton's diary was published in 1974, Farago had been the only Patton biographer with a copy. Patton had an uncommonly good perception and was a great observer of people's thoughts and feelings. He records his insights into people as well as the gist of what happened in his diary. Instead of using the diary as a key to the diarist's mind, Farago used it as a tool to help him make up dialogue and insert it into the historical record. "Ordeal and Triumph" and "The Last Days of Patton" claim to be historically accurate works. However, it is clear that Farago did not accurately transcribe Patton's memoirs into dialogue in these books. He went as far as to *come up* with things for Patton to say that do not reflect Patton's outlook at all.

Here is one more example of the fabricated conversation designed to make Patton anti-Semitic. This time there is *no* resemblance to Patton's diary.

> "'I doubt it,' Patton said. 'I've never seen a group of people who seem to be more lacking in intelligence and spirit. Incidentally,' he turned to Ike, 'there's a German village not far from here, deserted. I'm planning to make it a concentration camp for some of these goddamn Jews.'" *"The Last Days of Patton," by Ladislas Farago*

This type of slander really falls into the libel category. Patton never, ever, suggested making *concentration camps* for the Jews; and if he had, Ike could not have stood there mute, as he does in the Farago account. The question really remains why Farago added to the contemporary source, completely made up conversations totally unconnected to the evidence, and blatantly lied so as to make Patton look anti-Semitic.

On September 19th, Raymond Daniell wrote in the New York Times that "Nazis still hold some of the best jobs in commerce and industry." This wasn't true, but that hardly mattered. Daniell claimed that the military was reluctant to weed out the Nazis because they were more interested in "preserving German industrial efficiency." He then accused Patton of being a main-stay in the military's opposition to de-Nazification, and said that he had heard Patton ask "if he did not think it 'silly' to try to get rid of 'the most intelligent' people in Germany."

The press had hatched a plan, diabolical in its conception. Their snares were set, their victim marked. They had only to await the right moment. Dark clouds loomed low on the horizon, foreshadowing the ordeal for Patton that lie ahead. The thunder of the gathering storm could be heard in the distance.

Chapter Fifty Seven

THE LAST FATEFUL PRESS CONFERENCE

Patton was well aware of what lie ahead. But he could only go courageously forward. "If I am not relieved, I will try and get a leave," Patton wrote to his wife.

He spent most of his time hunting and writing. There was little "commanding" to do as most of the soldiers were being returned to America.

> "I think that leaving here sooner than I had intended is perhaps fortunate, as this radical political emphasis on redeployment (spelled votes) is likely to undo all we have done. I think it is the most utterly unpatriotic thing imaginable. No one will say a word – no one!!!" *Patton, in a letter to Beatrice*

Well, excepting Patton. But he would soon be silenced.

Frank E. Mason was in Europe on a confidential mission for former President Hoover. Mason had been a correspondent for the North American Newspaper Alliance, had been president of the International News Service, and had a distinguished career in broadcasting, as well as being a man prominent in public affairs. Mason was privately investigating a conspiracy. It was said that all Germans that held office would be viciously attacked by reporters and then removed if they were unacceptable to the Russians.[1] It was Mason's mission to discover

---

[1] An example would be Schaeffer

whether or not this was true. There were disturbing signs, for Mason wrote to Harbord, Fletcher, and former President Hoover that,

> "The New York Times and the New York Herald Tribune have come to the aid of 'PM's campaign to run interference for a Red government in Germany. I am sure that this is innocent as far as the Times and Trib are concerned at home. But I don't ascribe any innocence to their correspondents over here who are provoking a story."

The liberal New York newspaper "PM" had been criticizing the army's jurisdiction in Europe incessantly for the past few months. "PM" particularly hated the dominant Catholic party in Bavaria which was run by Cardinal Faulhaber. This Cardinal had a record of defying both Hitler and the Nazis, but, strangely, the newspaper began to vilify his reputation. Apparently the Cardinal had not only attacked the Nazis, but also the Communists.

According to Mason's report, only two forces stood in the way of complete Soviet domination of Germany. These were the dominant Catholic centrum party in Bavaria, and the U.S. Army. Mason told Hoover that the attack against these forces could be seen in PM reporter Victor Bernstein's attempt to assassinate the Cardinal's reputation and in the vilification of Patton because he was the only one "daring to block the radicals in running interference for a Red government in Germany."

The press conference that was to disgrace Patton, topple him from his new status as pro-Consul of Bavaria, and remove him from command of his beloved Third Army, had been intended only for local correspondents. These newspapermen had been attached to Third Army for quite a long time and were very fond of its popular commander. Patton used to give them an update of the situation every day, but now that the war was over he usually gave a press conference only once a week or so. At these he would briefly answer the reporters' questions. A notice was posted on a bulletin board four days in advance of the planned conference. Daniell, a correspondent for the New York *Times*, Levin of the New York *Herald Tribune* and Morgan of the Chicago *Daily News*, all liberal papers, saw the sign and decided that this was their chance to trap Patton. They arrived the night before the meeting. The next morning, one of Third Army's regular correspondents overheard Levin, Morgan and Daniell plotting at their breakfast table how they would "needle the General and make him lose his temper."

Unfortunately, no stenographic notes were taken, but according to Gay's diary, Daniell, Morgan and Levin told Patton that the denazification plan was proceeding too slowly. They also told him that Dr. Schaeffer, the President-Minister of Bavaria, should be removed from office because he had publicly disagreed with the denazification plan. Patton replied that all Germans appointed to office did as they were told or were dismissed.

"Suppose," Patton said, "America lost the war. If the conquering nation removed all persons in political power from public office it would have to exclude all the Republicans and Democrats who held government posts." This would leave the country in a terrible state where nothing would work, and no one competent could be hired. Patton reiterated that denazification was going ahead in an orderly fashion with further screenings of Germans to discover Nazis. Getting the Germans back on their economic feet would save the American taxpayers from having to support Germany. At the moment, he told them, he was trying to get enough wood cut and enough stoves provided so that the displaced persons and the German people would not freeze to death that winter.[1]

The three reporters knew that they would have to take Patton's words out of context, and according to Gay, the reporters,

> "making use of only partial truths, construed the answers to their questions to suit their own purposes and ... tried to bring discredit upon General Patton."

This is what happened according to Mason who thoroughly questioned all the newspapermen present. Mason sent a copy of this report to Hoover.

> "the team of Levin, Daniels [sic] and Morgan started to work out on Patton. Morgan's part was to stand close to Patton with a pipe in his mouth and insolently to puff smoke into Patton's face. This was related to me by several newspapermen who were present, and who were humiliated by the scene. Levin and Daniels [sic], using a sneering tone, with the attitude of a criminal prosecutor

---

[1] "The Patton Papers," edited by Martin Blumenson, page 762

interrogating a hardened criminal, and both talking at once at times, went after Patton for permitting a German named Schaeffer to hold public office. The Schaeffer case is confused. He was once in a concentration camp and in wrong with the Germans and at other times held municipal jobs under them. I can't say whether he was a member of the Nazi party.[1] The other correspondents stood back and not one of them got into the cross fire of Levin and Daniels [sic] attacking Patton. Every one agrees that before Patton could answer a question, the other would start up with another question, and as I was told 'crossed Patton up.' Such remarks were made by Levin and Daniels in a condescending tone, such as: 'Don't you know that the directives are that all Nazis should be removed from office?' Levin was so disagreeable in his tone that Patton once said, 'You are so smart. You know everything. Why do you ask me?'
Levin and Daniell jumped at this chance.... Obviously they were trying to get Patton to lose his temper. Some of the witnesses told that despite what the Levin-Morgan-Daniell clique said Patton was really quite cagey in his answers, and that if there had been a shorthand transcript, which there was not, that Patton did not do so badly as they made it sound. Levin and Daniels [sic] would make long involved statements of policy, and then ask Patton to confirm or deny that such-and-such was the policy. Patton said to Daniels, 'Don't put words in my mouth.'"

Mason concluded in his report to Hoover that here was a definite conspiracy on these men's part to get rid of any German officials unacceptable to the Russians and warn other American generals of the consequences of opposing their wishes. This would lead to "the formation finally of governments in German cities in the British and American zones which will be in effect... puppets of Russia."

There are other accounts of the press conference, of course, but Mason's is the most complete. Patton's press officer, Major Deane was to say later that, "There is no denying that General Patton lost his temper

---

[1] Although Schaeffer was accused of being a Nazi, he was actually never a member and had been arrested by the Nazis and held at Dachau during the war.

on that awful morning and put himself into the hands of his enemies, but God knows he was provoked into it deliberately. I'll never believe otherwise."

Patton recorded his reaction to the conference the day of in his diary, before it had created a furor.

"This morning we had the ragtag and bobtail remnants of the great U.S. press present... I always had them on my side. Today there was very apparent hostility, not against me personally, but against the Army in general. The special gripe seems to be that we are backing the wrong horse in the choice of the Governor or President of Bavaria. The temerity of the newspaper man in suggesting that he knew more about it than I do, although I know nothing, made me mad which I think is what they wanted.
The [press] has utterly lost the Anglo-Saxon conception of justice and feel that a man can be kicked out because somebody else says he is a Nazi. They were evidently quite shocked when I told them I would kick nobody out without the successful proof of guilt before a court of law.
If people have time to read anything besides the number of points which will get a soldier home, I will probably make the front page but, frankly, do not give a damn. The attitude of the American people as evinced by the press and the radio is such I am inclined to think I made a great mistake in serving them for nearly forty years, although I had a very good time doing it.
Another point which the press harped on was the fact that we are doing too much for the Germans to the detriment of the DP's, most of whom are Jews. I could not give the answer to that one because the answer is that in my opinion and that of most non-political officers, it is vitally necessary for us to build Germany up now as a buffer state against Russia. In fact, I am afraid we have waited too long. If we let Germany and the German people be completely disintegrated and starved, they will certainly fall for Communism and the fall of Germany for Communism will write the epitaph of Democracy in the United States.

The more I see of people, the more I regret that I survived the war."

A sad and revealing diary entry. Patton must have known that the press were going to misquote him, for he wrote to his wife that very day, "I will probably be in the headlines before you get this. As the press is trying to quote me as being more interested in restoring order in Germany than in catching Nazis. I can't tell them the truth that unless we restore Germany we will insure that Communism takes America."

One attendant of the press meeting recalls the meeting this way. Patton had said, "If a nation conquering America removed all persons in political power from public office it would have to exclude all the Republicans and Democrats who held government posts and nothing would run."
"After all, General," said one of the conspirators, trying to coax Patton into slipping, "Didn't most ordinary Nazis join their party in the same way that Americans become Republicans or Democrats?"
"Yes," Patton agreed. That was it. It was all over. Patton had uttered the fateful word that would cost him Third Army.

For all over the newspapers in America were huge headlines, "Patton compares the Nazis to the Democrats and Republicans," and "Patton says 'This Nazi Thing is Like a Democrat and Republican Election Fight.'" The *Times* headlines read "Patton Belittles Denazification."

It was Victor Bernstein who, on September 24th, had his article printed on the front page of "PM." In the biggest type that could be found, the headlines of the newspaper trumpeted loudly,

"GENERAL PATTON SHOULD BE FIRED."

"General Patton is the issue," Bernstein wrote. Then, appealing directly to the man widely known to have no backbone and a penchant for politics, Bernstein continued, "Eisenhower is responsible. The reputation of the one is as much at stake as of the other." And as if he thought Ike might miss his message, he added, "General Patton should be fired."

Chapter Fifty Eight

HONOR

"Am I weak or a coward? Am I putting my posthumous reputation above my present honor? God how I wish I knew ... "

Another meeting with the press was held on September 25th to clarify the first one. Patton spoke well, denying that his comments reflected on Eisenhower and stating that,

> "Unquestionably when I made the comparison of so vile a thing as Nazism with political parties, I was unfortunate in the selection of analogies. The point I was and am trying to bring out is that in Germany practically all or at least a very large percentage of tradesmen, small businessmen, and even professional men such as doctors and lawyers, were beholden to the Nazi party, particularly for the patronage which permitted them to carry on their businesses and professions, and that therefore many of them had to give lip service, but lip service only, and I would extend this to mean that paying dues was nothing but a form of black mail for holding their jobs. If we kick them out, all this bunch, we will so retard the reorganization of Bavaria that we will certainly be guilt of the death by starvation or freezing of women, children, and old men this winter."

This time the meeting was stenographed, and we have a record of exactly what Patton said and the questions that were asked afterwards. "General," said one reporter, "if you recall, what was that direct quote about political parties?"

"I said that Nazism might well be compared to any of the political parties at home, either Republican or Democrat. I also referred to my cousin who remained a postmaster for years by judicious flip-flops, and I don't consider him a son-of-a-gun either."

The press brought up Schaeffer again, and Patton only reaffirmed that so far he "has not been proved to be a Nazi."

Frank Mason, the investigator for former President Hoover, had a chance to attend this meeting, and he wrote that, "There is not much to report about this conference except that it was decent and courteous in tone. Patton is sound. He is American. He is getting hell for daring to block the radicals [who want] a red government in Germany."

Mason was determined to help Patton, and he gave Ike's adjutant General Lovett and his chief of public relations, Colonel Fitzgerald, a copy of his report on the plot against Patton. He felt that if Eisenhower knew the facts he would better be able to resist the "small but vociferous group of newspapermen led by 'PM' with the 'Stars and Stripes' echo."

That night, as Patton was eating dinner, a telegram arrived from General Eisenhower stating that he had been accused of differing with him on the de-Nazification policy and he was to see Eisenhower at once as soon as weather permitted.

> "It may well be that the Philistines have at last got me. On the other hand, every time I have been in serious trouble or thought I was, it has turned out to my advantage. At least, this time I do not have to go on the defensive." *Patton's diary*

The next morning he wrote to his wife,

> "It may be that I will get home as soon as this. The whole thing is a deliberate misquote with the intent of getting me in trouble because I am not 'pink.' If Ike etc. don't like what I do, they can relieve me. Then I will resign, not retire, and can tell the world a few truths which will be worth having."

That day USFET issued "Military Law Number 8." In a clear attempt to appease the newspapers, this order stated that "In order to further diminish the influence of Nazism in Germany" there was to be no employment for members of the Nazi party or affiliate organizations except as ordinary laborers.

At 11 am Bedell Smith met with reporters at Frankfurt-on-Main. Among them were the conspirators Daniell, Levin and Morgan.

"Tell us General," a reporter said, "whether you think that [the de-Nazification] program can be carried out by people who are temperamentally and emotionally in disagreement with it."

"I don't think we have anybody who is temperamentally or emotionally in disagreement with it," Smith replied.

"Wouldn't General Patton's statement indicate that?"

"No," Smith said.

"Are you familiar with General Patton's statement on Saturday?" a reporter asked insolently.

"I am familiar only with the press reports," Smith returned.

"He said this Nazi thing is just like a Democratic Republican election fight. For this reason, he said, he personally has never seen the necessity for the de-Nazification program..." quipped one reporter.

"Yes and he said he didn't know what reactionaries were," added another, "but he did ask, 'What do you want – a lot of Communists?'"

"And then he said that the Germans are innocent of Nazism until proven guilty," chimed in another newsman, spitting the abominable words as he spoke. Innocent until proven guilty? Incredible!

The reporters then told Smith that the "smart Nazis" were "playing a clever game by allying themselves with the Bavarians" ultra-conservative, Catholic, People's Party, thus destroying the "social democratic and left wing parties" because "we are doing everything that we can to make the Bavarian Peoples Party as strong as it can be."

"Well," Smith said, "we shouldn't do that. That is the reactionary party." Did Smith mean this? What Smith had just said was against Eisenhower's established policy, but the press saw fit not to publish it – because it was in line with *their* policy.

Smith made several other slip-ups during the course of the news conference. Luckily for Smith, his conference *was* stenographed, and the press could not misquote him.

Among the papers of Frederick Ayer is the transcript of, this, Bedell Smith's press conference, along with an unsigned memorandum that reads,

"Daniell, Levin, and Morgan put into effect a definite scheme to undermine and discredit General Patton. Their method was to sow seeds of doubt as to whether or not General Patton was loyal to General Eisenhower... Many influential United States citizens feel that there exists today a well organized group with definitely laid plans to bring discredit upon the Army and the Navy; and that General Patton having news value, like General MacArthur, was one of the first to feel the effect of their venom, and that later this group will attack others, for instance General Bradley, General Eisenhower, and perhaps certain high ranking Naval officers. It is highly probably that Mr. Levin, Mr. Morgan, and Mr. Daniels [sic] are tools of this group but definite proof of this is at present lacking."

Mason had no doubts. He was to write in a letter, also among Frederick Ayer's papers,

"The Dainell-Levin-Morgan plot to destroy Patton ... was successful because Bernstein of PM was the most powerful force in Germany in 1945 because he had the support of Harry Dexter White and Henry Morgenthau... Laughlin Curry, David K. Niles, and Alger Hiss."

Edward P. Morgan, one of the journalist plotters who had attended both Patton's and Smith's conference, wrote "Patton is Called on Carpet" for the Des Moines *Tribune*, September 26th, 1945.

"General Eisenhower has summoned Gen. George S. Patton Jr., to Frankfurt to give an accounting of his 'stewardship' as military governor of Bavaria. This action follows Patton's statement ... that he saw no need for a sweeping de-Nazification program in Germany ... The famous combat soldier is being called on carpet to explain the situation in Bavaria, where a German political scandal of major proportions is brewing... Some leading American newspapers have demanded Patton's removal on the basis of his now celebrated Saturday interview at which he revealed that many of his views clashed with the declared American policy of ruthlessly purging Nazis from any and all important positions in Germany, either public or private ... Patton's remarkable comment to reporters that the Nazi question was as simple as a Democratic-Republican election scrap at home ... may be enough to detonate an explosion in Bavarian politics,[1] which, many observers think, already has been too long delayed – for the general's own "reactionary" attitude ... The original American military government teams ... were primarily concerned with getting some semblance of normalcy established; firing Nazis was a secondary consideration. Since Bavaria is predominantly Catholic, they, not surprisingly, contacted individuals in the traditional Bavaria's People's Party. But, while not out and out Nazis, a lot of these people including Schaeffer had managed to play along with them during Hitler's regime without suffering much personal damage[2] ..."

It is at this point that Morgan reveals the purpose of their attacks on Schaeffer and the Bavarian government and their deliberate baiting of Patton. Mason was not wrong after all. For Morgan continues,

"[Schaeffer's government was] far more afraid now that Bavaria *would go left politically* than they were of playing with the individual Nazis ... Although this pattern was drawn before General Patton moved into the area as commander, his critics charge that he and his officers not only condoned but encouraged this state of affairs, which systematically and deliberately excluded *Communists* and Social Democrats from a large measure of Bavarian political life."

So here it is, at last. The newsmen reveal the true cause of their unending attacks – against both Schaeffer and Patton. Even though they had admitted it, the War Department would continue blindly to punish Patton: even though the newspapers' motives were clear.

---

[1] Morgan certainly hoped so!

[2] Note the words "*much* personal damage." *Much* can be defined however they want, most people would think any time at all in Dachau was "personal damage" of quite a grievous nature.

In November, Marshall, the Chief of Staff, summoned Mason to see him. Mason spoke to him "in order to serve the ends of truth and justice" as he put it, and he spent 90 minutes discussing the whole fateful press conference with Marshall. Mason gave Marshall a letter dated November 4th in which he recapped the whole affair. The service that morning at the church in Leesburg had an unusually apt quote which covered the whole incident. "Then went the Pharisees and took counsel how they might entangle him in his talk," from Matthew XXIII-15 seemed to express best the methods that had been used against Patton, Mason felt. For, continued Mason in his letter, three men and a woman,

> "came down to stage the Patton attack ... Then they went back to General Eisenhower's headquarters to entangle W. Bedell Smith ... I would say that they succeeded with Bedell just about as well as they did with Patton, except that the press was asleep at the switch and apparently did not get the significance of the words finessed into Bedell's mouth. I say finessed because it is conceivable that an officer of W. B. Smith's unusual intelligence and keen mind should have wittingly laid himself open ... The remarks attributed to Bedell Smith that the Catholic conservatives ... are of more concern and more troublesome than Nazis is about on a par with the remarks attributed to George Patton comparing Republicans and Democrats with the Nazis. For sure Bedell Smith isn't setting the United States Army against Catholicism or conservatism per se in order to run interference, in a Kerensky role, for the Sovietizing of the American zone in Germany ... The United States Army is now building a record which will lay itself open to charges of having created such chaos as to make it appear that some of our representatives and officials deliberately desired to throw the American zone into ultimate Russian control."

Smith never lost any prestige because of what he had said, even though Mason pointed out that Smith and Patton's "crimes" were identical. Did the Army really have to worry about what the press thought about Patton? Or was this whole incident a convenient excuse to relieve a man who was too dangerous and too talkative?

On September 27th Murphy, from Washington, came to see Patton. Murphy advised Patton to relieve Schaeffer as Minister-President but keep him as Minister of Finance. He also advised changing "the setup in Bavaria from rightest leanings to more Social Democrats with a little lean to the left." Patton said that he had heard of no charges against Schaeffer, but that if he were ordered by the higher command he would be "removed pronto." It was Patton's steadfast decision to stand by "innocent until proven guilty" with regards to the mysterious Schaeffer that would bring his own downfall as well as Schaeffer's.

Patton had a call from Bedell Smith, complaining about the questions and embarrassing results from the press conferences.
"You're my best friend George," Smith said. "Probably that is the reason why you always give me the worst headaches."
"He's a snake," Patton said to Colonel Harkins when he had hung up, unconvinced by Smith's sweet talk. And why should he have been? Smith was not Patton's best friend by any standard – it was Smith who at this moment was listening to taped conversations from Patton's HQ and home.

On September 28th, Patton answered Eisenhower's summons and drove to Frankfurt. His mind raced through varying topics as he wondered what Ike would say this time.

> "As we drove along, I was following my practice of forty years in deciding how I would attack various positions that presented themselves in the changing landscape or how I would emplace troops for rear guard action in the same country when suddenly I realized that I had fought my last war and other people would be picking the positions." *Patton's diary*

The ride reminded him of his ride to Eisenhower's HQ after the Knutsford incident. He had thought then he would be relieved, if he wasn't tried. "I did not believe yesterday I would be tried, but I thought I might be relieved of command," he wrote in his diary the day after his drive.

The drive, which must have been agonizingly suspenseful, ended after seven and a half hours. Eisenhower was, according to Patton, "quite friendly and gave me a long oration on my inability to keep my mouth shut."

443

"In this particular case the words I am quoted as saying have been deliberately altered," Patton said in self-defense.

Eisenhower didn't hear him. He had rescued Patton many times, and he made it clear that he had had quite enough. Ike's lecture on Patton's "big mouth" continued on and on. "You simply can not keep your mouth shut," Ike said.

"I was thinking yesterday that perhaps my greatest virtue, and also, perhaps, my greatest fault, is my honesty and my lack of ulterior motives."[1]

"No, George," Ike replied, "your greatest virtue and your greatest fault is your audacity."

But it was not audacity that had landed Patton into the press furor that was at this very moment engulfing him. It was honesty. And the reason Patton had been honest? Besides his nature, he wasn't planning on moving up the ranks any longer; he didn't have "ulterior motives."

Eisenhower now insulted Patton by saying that, "I am as much at fault as you are. Knowing your strength and weakness as I did, I should not have put you in as Military Governor."

"It is my opinion that Bavaria is the best governed state in Germany," Patton protested, "We have probably removed and de-Nazified better than any other state!"

Patton's recollection of what happened next is funny in that he saw through Eisenhower's guise.

> "Ike said that had he possessed any adequate command for me at the time, he would have given it to me rather than have me act as Military Governor of Bavaria. He then was apparently struck with an idea, which probably was acting on his part, that since Gerow was going home, it might be a good idea to transfer me to the Fifteenth Army whose mission it is to write the account of the history and tactics of the war. He talked about this and said I might be criticized because I would be taking the place of a three-star General, although he too had been an Army commander. I told him in my opinion I should be simply relieved, but he

---

[1] An insightful comment, even if a little ill-timed.

said he did not intend to do that and had had no pressure from the States to that effect."

"Then I think," Patton said, "I should be allowed to continue in command of the Third Army and the government of Bavaria."

> "He said he felt on mature thought I should certainly continue for ten days or two weeks and then he thought I should take command of the Fifteenth Army because, while he had complete confidence I would do my full duty as I understood it, I did not, in his opinion, believe in the policies being put into effect and that, while I would not have ever expressed these views to my staff, they had all absorbed them from me in the same way they absorbed my battle system."

As a matter of fact, of course, Eisenhower, or at least Bedell Smith, knew *exactly* what Patton was saying because his telephone was tapped and his rooms bugged.

Now came the dilemma. The Third was Patton's Army. He had molded it, taught it, conquered with it. All its achievements were his, and he was as much a part of it as it was of him.

> "At the present moment I am of two minds. If I am kicked upstairs to the Fifteenth Army, should I accept or should I ask for relief and put in my resignation? By adopting the latter course, I would save any self-respect at the expense of my reputation but would on the other hand, become a martyr too soon. It is my belief that when the catchword "de-Nazification" has worn itself out and when people see it is merely a form of stimulating Bolshevism, there will be a flop of the pendulum in the opposite direction. When that occurs, I can state that I accepted the job with the Fifteenth Army because I was reluctant, in fact unwilling, to be a party to the destruction of Germany under the pretense of de-Nazification. Further, that the utterly un-American and almost Gestapo methods of de-Nazification were so abhorrent to my Anglo-Saxon mind as to be practically indigestible. Further, that I believe Germany should not

be destroyed but rather rebuilt as a buffer against the real danger, which is Bolshevism from Russia." *Patton's Diary*

During the "interview," as Patton termed it, Eisenhower called in General Adcock[1] and Professor Dorn. In the final showdown, the men who had been pulling the strings for Patton's relief came to see the humbled General. This, they knew, had been their doing. For months they had tried to trap him, bugging his office and home rooms, tapping his telephone. At last, with a little help from the press, Patton had been toppled. They must have been proud.

Patton didn't know who these men were, though he gathered that Dorn provided General Adcock with his information. He watched and listened as Dorn spoke. His judgement of Dorn's character is nothing short of incredible, considering that Patton had only just met him.

> "He is a very slick individual – I think a pure German, and very probably a Communist in disguise."

During the conversation, Eisenhower brought up that "several" of his staff officers had reported to him that Patton had told them "that we should strengthen Germany because we were going to fight Russia in 5 years." Patton looked at Ike, astonished.

> "The two staff officers who told him that were unquestionably Adcock and Bull, as I never made the statement to anyone else and only made it to them under the erroneous assumption that they were my friends."
> *Patton's Diary*

Patton's "friends" had the extraordinary habit of rapid back-stabbing. But it need not have been them who told Ike. For in the most cunning and original back-stabbing maneuvers in history, it was Bedell Smith who had approved the unconstitutional tapping and bugging of Patton's quarters.

Ike was still talking. He made "the sensational statement" that during wartime, the most important things were order and discipline, but afterwards,

---

[1] Ike's G-5

"the important thing was to stay in with world public opinion – apparently whether it was right or wrong; I suppose on the same basis as Dacatur's famous remark: 'My country, may she ever be right, but, right or wrong, my country.' We could paraphrase that to 'My public, may it ever be right but, right or wrong, my public.'"
Patton's diary

The turnaround had been complete. Eisenhower had lost all moral qualities he had ever possessed, and was now willing to do anything based on the "public" – a politician in the worst sense of the word.

Dorn informed Patton "what the particular gripe on Schaeffer was" and found that he had kept in his cabinet "in minor positions, it is true, some twenty people (16 in Agriculture and 4 in Finance) who were mandatory cases for removal under our instructions. Eisenhower here told Patton that no matter how adversely affected the administration of Bavaria may become, all Nazis were to be removed, because 'it is my experience that there is always some subordinate to take over the job of a superior.'"[1] "In battle I believe this is true and it is probably true in Military Government," Patton wrote in his diary. His next sentences are full of sarcasm,

"It is a strange thing that in battle I am perfectly willing to chop off heads but in peacetime my Anglo-Saxon ancestry makes me reluctant to remove people without due process of law. However, I shall carry out General Eisenhower's wishes to the letter and in the spirit also."
Patton's diary

And Patton takes it from here, recording what occurred next at the meeting in his diary,

"Since it was very evident from General Eisenhower's demeanor that we had to relieve Fritz Schaeffer, I asked him who he wanted for President. He said, 'Ask Dorn,' which I did and Dorn recommended a man named Dr. Wilhelm Hoegner. So I called Harkins at 6:30 and told him to remove Schaeffer, Lange, and Rattenhuber and all members of their ministries in any way tainted with

---

[1] Like Bradley had for Patton, no doubt.

Nazism regardless of the setback it would give to the administration of Bavaria and the resultant cold and hunger it would produce – not only for the Germans but also for the DP's. This seemed to make everyone happy except for myself.

Ike was apparently very anxious that he should not seem too friendly with me because almost the first word he said was, 'If you are spending the night, of course you will stay with me, but since I feel you should get back to Bad Tolz as rapidly as possible, I have my train set up to take you, and it leaves at 7 o'clock.' It was then 6:30. I took the train.

During the whole of the preceding interview Eisenhower was more excited than I have ever seen him, and I believe this can be traced to the fact that he is very much worried about the delay in getting appointed as Chief of Staff at home, and fears that if he stays here, he will lose some of his prestige.[1] I think this fear is well grounded, but I do not believe that a fear psychosis should make him so utterly regardless of his better nature as to make him practically unmoral in his treatment of the Germans."

It was sad but true – Eisenhower had no other desire than to become President and he was willing to do anything to attain that end. The last thing he wanted was bad press, and what did he care about the Germans?

To Beatrice, Patton wrote that he felt resigning at this time would only "discredit me to no purpose." He did not mind too badly his new assignment of "reviewing the strategy and tactics of the war ... Were it not for the fact that it will be, so far as I am concerned, a kick up stairs, I would like it much better than being a sort of executioner to the best race in Europe." The next part of his letter reveals the inner torture that he was going through, wondering whether or not he should resign – whether or not he was compromising his integrity in staying on.

---

[1] This was true – newspapers were calling for Ike's head – unless he did something about Patton.

"Am I weak or a coward? Am I putting my posthumous reputation above my present honor? God how I wish I knew...

P.S. No one gives a damn how well Bavaria is run. All they are interested in now is how well it is ruined."

Another letter written to her on October 1st with virtually the same sentiments,

"In a sense I am glad to get out, as I hate the role we are forced to play and the inethical means we are required to use.... My self esteem would be better had I simply asked for immediate retirement but then anything I said in the future could be attributed to revenge. At the moment I feel pretty mad."

On October 2nd a situation occurred that served to make him even more angry. It is best told by Patton,

"Just as I was about to go home at five o'clock, the telephone rang and General Eisenhower told me... that information of the ensuing change in command had leaked in Berlin and that therefore it might be necessary for him to make the announcement at noon tomorrow. I said I could not see that made any difference. After the conversation ended, Colonel Harkins, who had listened to it, said the only person who could have let it spill in Berlin was Mr. Murphy. I said no, Mr. Murphy I would trust, but I did not trust Beedle Smith. This is interesting as showing how guileless I still am because on the way home the truth suddenly dawned on me that Eisenhower is scared to death, which I already knew, and believes that a more prompt announcement of my relief than the one he had originally planned will be beneficial to him. The alleged leak is nothing but a figment of the imagination which is a euphemism for a damned lie."
Patton's diary

Patton may still have been guileless but he was rapidly learning that to assume anyone else in Europe had the same qualities was foolish. Patton wrote to his former aide, Codman, "Today I am performing with my usual efficiency my duties as undertaker at my own funeral and am at the moment sitting at a perfectly cleaned up desk." Then, in a reference to the people he suspected were behind his removal, he wrote, "I am certain we are being completely hoodwinked by the degenerate descendants of Ghengis Khan. The envy, hatred, malice, and uncharitableness in Europe passes belief." He had written a wryly amused line to his wife in which he stated that while Stimson and Marshall always backed each other up it was interesting to watch "the lobster like agility with which the high command over here backs water when any of us are attacked."

"My head is bloody but unbowed," Patton wrote to Beatrice. "All I regret is that I have again worried you. I was terribly hurt for a few days but am normal again."

It was raining on October 7th, the day for the official change of command ceremony. Patton had attended religious services as usual that morning, while the four corps commanders had assembled in a spacious gymnasium in Bad Tolz. At noon Patton and Truscott entered and marched onto the platform. Four ruffles and four flourishes, in honor of Patton, were played. Patton then made a speech. "General Truscott, Officers, and Men, All good things must come to an end. The best thing that has ever come to me thus far is the honor and privilege of having commanded the Third Army." His speech was short, in which he congratulated his men and praised General Truscott, asking them to serve Truscott as faithfully as they had served him. Fisher recalls that, "Nothing in his dress or bearing reflected the torture of his soul as he stepped forward to hand over the symbol of his command."

> "The Command was again presented, and three ruffles and three flourishes were played in honor of General Truscott. Following this, he made a short speech, which I could not hear as he was very emotional and shouted too loud into the machine. I think he was very much perturbed at taking over the command. Of course he had nothing to do with this and was simply carrying out orders." *Patton's diary*

It was a cruel thing for Eisenhower to have selected Truscott, Patton's loyal general from Sicily and a family friend, to succeed him.

George Fisher remembers that a very good lunch had been prepared but it "deserved a better appetite than most of us could muster.

450

All the old corps and division commanders who could be found were there. Their testimonies varied in length but no wise in sincerity. Some thoughts strayed to George Washington and Fraunces' Tavern [Washington's farewell speech there]. [Chaplain] O'Neill may have remembered the Last Supper."

It was all over – Patton was no longer commander of Third Army. Weyland, one of Patton's friends, wrote him saying, "I feel that the Third Army has died. To me, the Third Army meant Patton." To thousands of others too.

Merle-Smith, Patton's new aide, says that,

> "The General did not weep, even when he handed over his Army's flag to General Truscott, or when all the troops sang 'Auld Lang Syne.' He was quite grim-faced when we left to board the train and obviously hurt. When we reached our compartment he took the seat by the window and sat smiling and saluting to the crowd on the platform. Finally he turned to me and said, 'Pat, I hope to God this train starts pretty soon, but until it does I'm going to sit smiling out this window even if it kills me."

Robert S. Allen writes what Patton, but especially his entire staff was feeling,

> "Patton took the heartbreaking blow in silence. But while outwardly subdued, inwardly he seethed in anguished fury and searing despair. He was baffled as to just where and how he had erred. He could not understand the rancorous storm of abuse and castigation. He had done no more than other Allied commanders administering occupied areas! So why pick him? If he was wrong, why weren't they? Particularly he was cut to the quick by Eisenhower's stinging rebuke in their [dismissal] talk. Patton felt that not only was that wholly uncalled for, but grossly ungrateful and unfair. From Africa to the ETO he had given Eisenhower the utmost in loyal, unstinting and peerless service ... Surely simple gratitude alone warranted more than a humiliating verbal spanking in private and degrading condemnation in

public. For that reason alone, Patton indignantly felt, he should have been treated with more consideration and appreciation. To him the whole debasing affair confirmed strongly a suspicion ... that malicious and envious forces in and out of the Army were determinedly bent on destroying him and discrediting him as a battle commander."

Patton's staff was to maintain this view forever. It was quite simple to them. Eisenhower and his gutless generals had ungraciously and ungratefully dismissed Patton. As part of Patton's loyal team, they had become aware of some disturbing facts. Patton was the only general left with honor.

Chapter Fifty Nine

THE PAPER ARMY

For they have whetted their tongues like a sword; they have bent their bow like a bitter thing, to shoot in secret the undefiled. Psalm 63

In the early hours of October 8th, Patton arrived at his new command, Fifteenth Army. The headquarters was in an old hotel. At lunch time, Patton descended the stairs into the main lobby, which was now the officers' mess. His dog, Willie, preceded him and, sniffing the food aromas coming from within, began running quickly towards the mess. Patton shouted, "Willie!" One hundred officers who had been eating immediately came to attention. Seeing the grim Patton stride into their midst so abruptly made the officers fear the legends about "Blood and Guts" Patton might be true. Eyeing them in silence, Patton said, "There are occasions when I can truthfully say that I am not as much of a s.o.b. as I may think I am. This is one of them." Colonel Allen wrote, "The relieved staff roared with surprised delight. From then on, it was as wholeheartedly for him as the Third Army staff had been."

For days dozens of rumors had been afloat the Fifteenth Army about Patton's authoritarian rules and strict punishments. John Eisenhower, Ike's son, had been assigned to Patton's new headquarters and he writes that,

> "I was unsure of what his attitude would be.
> Nevertheless, his generous nature showed through, and
> as the officers of the headquarters went through the
> receiving line, he pulled me aside for a brief and
> congenial chat."

John did not have to fear that Patton would treat him badly because of his father's abrupt and crushing dismissal. Patton knew of the derogatory remarks which had been published about him, and he clearly saw that his new Army half-believed them. He decided to calm them and give the rumors the lie.

That evening, Patton impishly began his remarks with, "I have been here and have studied your work today." His voice rising, he shouted, "I have been SHOCKED" – and then in a lower tone, "by the excellence of your work."

The officers and men at Fifteenth Army no longer needed to worry. Patton was not a monster.

On October 13th Eisenhower dined with Patton. It was unusually bad timing to begin resuming their "friendship" which had never existed. As they ate, Patton told Ike that he would never again eat at the same table as Bedell Smith. Smith had said at his press conference that the Catholic Bavarian Party was "radical" and needed to be "looked out for." Eisenhower told Patton that Smith felt he had been misquoted and "wished to apologize." Strange that a similar misquote had relieved Patton.

There was a more purposeful point to their little dinner that night, however. "Eisenhower was also quite anxious for me to run for Congress – I presume in the belief that I might help him." A few days later, Patton went to a football game and was seated right beside Ike, the man who had just relieved him of his beloved Third Army. Apparently oblivious to this, however, the two had an enjoyable time.

> "As usual a lot of soldiers with cameras, several hundreds, came and wanted to take pictures but the MP's would not let them get close, so Hughes suggested that Ike let them come up. Instead he decided to go down in front near them. He waved his hand and 'grinned' and they took a few pictures and he came back but the soldiers did not leave and presently they began to shout 'We want Patton!' so I went down and there was really an ovation. Lots of film was used up."

He was still popular with the average rank and file! It must have been heart-warming to realize that despite his humiliating relief, he was still loved by the soldiers.

During the game, Patton had had a chance to talk to Ike. He records in his diary,

> "Ike is bitten with the presidential bug and is also yellow. He has convinced himself that he did me a favor by getting me out of really grave risks entailed by being a governor.
> He will never be president!
> I will resign when I have finished this job which will be not later than Dec. 26. I hate to do it but I have been gagged all my life, and whether they are appreciated or not, America needs some honest men who dare to say what they think, not what they think people want them to think." *Patton's diary*

It is quite clear here that Patton wants to resign and speak out as a direct result of the fact that Eisenhower wants to run for President. What he is saying is obvious: Ike can't win – at least not while I live. "I feel that as an American it will ill become me to discredit him yet – that is, until I shall prove even more conclusively that he lacks moral fortitude. This lack has been evident to us since the landing in Africa but now that he has been bitten with the presidential bee, it is becoming even more pronounced." He outlined his plans as, "It is my present thought ... that when I finish this job, which will be around the first of the year, I shall resign, not retire, because if I retire I will still have a gag in my mouth... I should not start a limited counter-attack, which would be contrary to my military theories, but should wait until I can start an all out offensive." But Patton would never be able to launch his "all out offensive" and tell people his conclusive evidence against Eisenhower because, the day before he was to go home, he was injured in a fatal car crash.

Giraud came to see Patton and told him that he was "shocked to the heart at the treatment accorded to the greatest soldier since Napoleon." "How can one expect any backbone in a man already running for President?" Patton asked his wife, after recounting the incident. The French General Juin was also distressed at Patton's treatment and sent him a letter stating that France and General de Gaulle had always wished to decorate him for his preeminent part in France's liberation, but as a result of the change in his command status, "France was more than twice as anxious to do you the honor."

So on October 25th General de Gaulle gave a special luncheon in Patton's honor. At the end of the lunch, he compared Patton to "everybody from Napoleon up and down." Patton replied in similar terms, returning his compliments. They then went to the Invalides and to the tomb of Napoleon. Patton was allowed downstairs in the normally restricted area, "it was very impressive and we all enjoyed it," he wrote. That night Juin had dinner with Patton. Juin brought up "the Russians whom he distrusts and fears as much as I do." For the next few days he traveled across France where dignitaries made him an "honorary citizen;" there were speeches, dances, lunches, and all types of celebrations. At Chartres he was welcomed in the city hall, taken on a tour of the city, and escorted to the Cathedral for a Mass attended by "at least 5,000 people" and "many more outside who were yelling 'Vive Patton!' – and some of them, to the scandal and disgrace of religion, started yelling in the Church." He returned to Paris where he collected ten more Citizen of Honor certificates and two plaques. Clearly Patton was still popular in some quarters.

The Fifteenth Army was only a "paper" army. It had no troop units. Its mission was simply the preparation of historical and analytical studies on the tactics, techniques, organization and administration of the war in Europe. Patton's days were occupied with writing his memoir, which he tentatively titled, "War as I Knew It: Or Helpful Hints to Hopeful Heroes."

Every letter, every diary entry is a comment on Eisenhower's lack of "moral courage" and "intestinal fortitude." There is also mention of the Russians, and the inevitable war which he could see coming. "As the days passed," Robert S. Allen writes, "Patton became increasingly restless. He took long drives by himself, and at times nervously paced the floor of his office. At dinner, he said little and went to his quarters early. He smoked more cigars than usual. It was obvious that he was undergoing deep and gnawing turmoil."

"The whole world is going Communist," Patton wrote to Beatrice. "Destiny relieved me simply in a state of funk and because he has no moral courage."

Along with those lines was a rather mysterious message that he had just been in an automobile accident which had been reported in the press, but "it was nothing – just a bent fender, so your dream did not

456

work." This accident was clearly a foreshadowing of the fatal one, and Beatrice's dream had simply to wait to come true.

While driving to Mannheim to go hunting, Patton observed the "utter devastation" of Frankfurt and Mannheim. Cities were rubble. People had no homes. And the Americans were doing nothing to remedy the state of affairs. They were, in fact, exacerbating them. "Nothing conceivable could be more apt to bring back a Hitler than what we are doing," Patton commented in his diary.

Belgium, like France, wished to decorate their hero conqueror. On his way to receive the decoration Patton drove through Cologne, Aachen and Liege. Thousands of Belgians had gathered at the outskirts of Brussels "for the ecstatic privilege of seeing me." At the ceremony, he was given the Grand Officer of the Order of Leopold and the Croix de Guerre with Palm of the same order. He was also given a 1940 Croix de Guerre with Palm. "One more sunburst," he wrote Beatrice.

For some time now the newspapers had been calling Patton an anti-Semite, undoubtedly as part of their efforts in smearing him as a "Nazi." Patton, for his part, felt that certain Jews had misled themselves into following the Communists in destroying Europe – especially Germany. Bernard Baruch, the famous Jewish financier, wrote to Patton that he was not part of this clique, and he resented the unfair criticisms which were being made against "a great soldier." Baruch told Patton he had wanted to meet him in the U.S. to warn him of "some of the dangers of the occupation." Baruch included with his letter a newspaper clipping which quoted K. E. Wallach of Galesburg, Illinois, who was recovering from wounds in the hospital.

In the article, Wallach had said, "The attacks on General Patton as an anti-Semite sound strange to a Third Army soldier. Our general was on the record as knowing only good soldiers or bad soldiers and not soldiers of different religious preference. It will be the pride of my life that I had the honor to serve under a man like General Patton." Patton was pleased when he read the note, and wrote to Baruch saying,

> "My sincere thanks for your nice letter.
> I was particularly interested in the clipping which is exactly in accordance with the facts. I cannot understand who had the presumption to attribute to me anti-Semitic ideas which I certainly do not possess.

With warm personal regards, and looking forward to the
pleasure of seeing you on my return to America,
George S. Patton, Jr."

Wallach, the young soldier who had defended Patton, had
impressed Patton. "I am deeply moved by the fact that one of my soldiers
who, so far as I know, I did not have the pleasure of meeting personally
should take this much interest in my career." Actually, every soldier
from Third Army was unanimous. Even newspapers reported that when
soldiers of the Third Army were asked about Patton, their reaction was
always the same, "Oh him! Wasn't he swell?"

Among one of the very few favorable articles written about
Patton at this time is Adolph Goldsmith's "Old Blood and Guts Idol of
His Men" which was published in the *Arkansas Democrat* Sunday
Magazine on November 16th, 1945.

> "Patton is a soldier's general. He did not ask his men to
> fight for him; he asked them to fight with him...
> Much has been written about Patton's ruthlessness and
> disregard for the individual. True, he was daring, rough
> and brutal, but so were his soldiers. They would not have
> defeated the Nazis if they had been otherwise. He
> expected the impossible for the Third Army – and got
> it....
> As for Patton's most recent transfer to the doghouse, we
> are as much confused as the American public. He
> certainly has no love for the Nazis...
> The soldiers of the Third Army are practically
> unanimous in their belief that "their boss" got a d—d
> rotten deal."

A few days earlier, Ike had left for America and Patton was
supposed to be in command of the theater temporarily while he was
away. "Some joke," Patton wrote. If Ike didn't come back, "I will have a
grand house cleaning." "However, since I am simply pinch-hitting during
the brief absence of General Eisenhower, I do not conceive it to be my
duty to make any radical changes pending his return," he wrote in his
diary. He had few tasks to subsume, one was signing court-martial cases.
He was surprised to find that Ike had not been sentencing American
soldiers found guilty of rape to death. "This seemed somewhat at

variance to Anglo-Saxon customs," Patton wrote, and he changed all of the rape sentences to death penalties.

As temporarily taking over for Ike, Patton was in far closer proximity to Bedell Smith than he wished. "Beadle and I will have some fun anyhow," he told Beatrice, "He has never apologized but sent word he had been misquoted.[1] I have never seen him. It is my hope he will be investigated by Congress." In another letter to her dated November 15th, Patton wrote,

> "It is very evident that Beadle really runs the show in so far as it can be said to be run ... The chief interest seems to center on doing nothing positive and never doing counter to what the papers say. Some one proposes something and Beadle makes a speech against it and ends up by saying that while he is against it in principle he will go along with it just this once.
> Of course since we don't get on and are pretty nearly on official terms, it is not very pleasant."

"I really shudder for the future of our country," he wrote a few days later. On the 23rd Patton attended a meeting at USFET where he learned that Eisenhower, owing to a cold, would not be returning to Europe and that General McNarney would be taking over the European Theater's command. Kay Summersby, Ike's amour, was crying uncontrollably "in a high state of nerves as the result of hearing that General Eisenhower is not returning," as Patton put it.

Eisenhower had promised her that he would divorce Mamie and marry her. He had written to Truman stating his desire, and Truman promptly "lost" the file. Ike was undoubtedly informed while he was in America that no divorcee would become President. He never saw Kay again, he never even said good bye to the woman he had promised to marry. Ike's case is strange when you look at it from this perspective, for here he was, totally and completely immoral, willing to give up anything to become President. Kay had watched him ruin and destroy Patton, a general that she respected and admired. Now she, too, would be left by the wayside, an obstacle in his path to the Presidency.

---

[1] Never apologized for his remarks to the press about the Bavarian Catholic Party, that is.

Patton was reviewing his own future. Should he stay in the army or do what was burning his heart and burdening his soul – tell the American people what was happening? He had written asking Harbord for his opinion, and Harbord had replied that he didn't think Patton should resign in order to "speak freely" because the public would want something sensational and would be disappointed. The reaction in the long-run would be unfavorable. Besides, why would Patton want to "backfire" against Eisenhower now? Harbord evidently thought that Patton meant to speak against Ike in a fit of revenge. Whereas Patton wrote back to him saying, "I am not at all discouraged about the treatment I personally have received but I am terribly worried about the situation in America and in Europe." Patton's motives were higher; he was motivated only by sheer patriotism. However undoubtedly the press would say he was merely seeking "revenge," and this was why Patton was looking for more substantial evidence against Eisenhower. Patton was so thoroughly and completely honest and honorable, so lacking in "ulterior motives," that it is indeed a tragedy that he never made it back to America.

> "It may well be that V-E Day is misnamed and simply marking the beginning of a relatively short armistice. I bet Monty a hundred pounds to that effect and he gave me a ten-year limit, so I fear that his Scotch soul is worrying. I hope it is."

Sweden was the next country to host Patton, who had been there for the Military Olympics in 1912. He stopped at Copenhagen for a cocktail party at the American embassy and traveled to Stockholm where he was greeted by the King and the Crown Prince. He lunched with Count Bernadotte, then traveled to the Olympic stadium where the pistol shoot of 1912 was re-enacted and Patton came in 2nd. He attended a banquet hosted by the Swedish-American society where 500 guests waited to hear him speak. The vacation was ruined by three telegrams and a letter from the Displaced Baltic and German people. The messages were frantic requests that he intervene and "prevent their return to the Russians" before they were eliminated. "I could do nothing about this," Patton wrote in his diary, but the appeal shook him. He was powerless to stop their plight, but it distressed him to know that the men responsible were unmoved.

Bedell Smith gave a luncheon for Eisenhower's successor, General McNarney on December 3rd and Patton sarcastically noted that "present were all the youth and beauty of the ETO."

> "With the exception of Generals Keyes, Truscott, Allen, Gay and myself, and a limited number of others, I have rarely seen assembled a greater bunch of sons-of-bitches...
> I had a good deal of fun at lunch quoting from recent articles on the Military Government of Germany, which I had the forethought to take with me, and which removed the appetite from Bob Murphy and the new Commanding General... The trouble with both of them is that their answer is that they could not do anything about it as they were carrying out orders. My answer is that a man who receives a foolish order should not carry it out – but such is not the breed of cats in authority. It is certainly quite a criticism of our form of Military Government to find that the Deputy Theater Commander, General Clay, and the Theater Commander, General McNarney, have never commanded anything, including their own self-respect, or if that, certainly not the respect of anyone else.
> The whole luncheon reminded me of a meeting of the Rotary Club in Hawaii where everyone slaps every one else's back while looking for an appropriate place to thrust the knife. I admit I was guilty of this practice, although at the moment I have no appropriate weapon."
> *Patton's diary*

Clearly the government of Europe would continue in its downward spiral because the new commander was as spineless and immoral as the last one. Patton observes the political-correctness around him with a wry humor, but this entry is seemingly overflowing with sarcasm. If Patton had known this would be his last diary entry, would he have written it any differently?

"I hate to think of leaving the Army, but what else is there?" he wrote to Beatrice. This would be his last letter to her. Patton was given permission to travel to leave Paris on December 14th and fly to the United States for a month's leave. A truck – or the hand of Destiny – would prevent Patton from ever seeing the United States again.

Chapter Sixty

DEATH COMES

It was December 9th – the day before Patton was to go home. He had no intention of returning to Europe; in fact, he had quite made up his mind this time. When he got back to America, he would resign and speak his mind. After all, he had a lot to say, and he was tired of being muzzled by the Army. If he retired, he would still be in debt to them; thus resignation had clearly become his only option, and the one he fully intended to take once he returned to America.

On that fateful Sunday morning Patton had planned to have his last pheasant hunting trip with Gay. The weather was clear and cold, not unusual for December. Patton stopped along the car trip to look at some ruins which were covered in snow. He sat in the front seat of the Cadillac limousine when he returned to dry his feet. Patton's dog, Willie, had been travelling in a truck, but Patton then ordered him placed in the front seat, worried that the dog would freeze. Patton himself took the left passenger seat in the rear. Instead of sitting back in the comfort of the limousine, Patton perched on the edge of the seat looking out as they drove along. This was his favored position.

They continued driving and came across Keyes' broken down car. Patton stopped briefly to make sure that Keyes was okay, only to find that Keyes had hitched a ride and was not there. Patton's concern at his friend's apparent mishap seems ironic in the light of what happened afterwards.

After halting for a train to pass, Patton's Cadillac moved up and an Army truck suddenly, without signaling, made a sharp turn to the left and crashed into Patton's car. The radiator of the car was smashed and the right front fender and the motor were pushed back, but, aside from this, there was not even a scratch on the body of the car. Not a single window of the car had broken because the two vehicles were going 20 miles an hour at the most.

"The driver made no signal," Patton's driver of 4 months, Woodring, recalled, "He just turned into my car. I saw him in time to hit my brakes, but not in time to do anything else. I was not more than 20 feet from him when he began to turn. The GMC was barely scratched, but it hit us solid with its front fender."

Due to the minor damage to Patton's car, most deemed the accident relatively minor. The MP senior officer at the scene, Lt. Babalas, looked into the car.[1] And he was horrified at what he saw. Patton's scalp was torn off and hanging down "in a loop," his entire face smeared with blood. He was bleeding heavily from the wound. "My neck hurts, Lieutenant," Patton said to Babalas. "I'm having trouble breathing, Hap," he said to Gay, "Work my fingers for me." Gay quickly began rubbing Patton's fingers to stimulate his blood flow, but was alarmed when Patton said, "Go ahead, Hap, work my fingers." He had lost all feeling in his hands.

Babalas leaned over and heard Patton mutter under his breath, "What an ironical thing for this to happen at this time!"
"What's that, General?" Babalas asked.
Patton replied, almost ironically, "Nothing, Lieutenant – except that I want to say that this here was a stupid accident – only an accident!"

His hands were not the only thing he couldn't move, and by the time the ambulance arrived he was able to muster in a voice barely audible, "I think I'm paralyzed." The doctor took one quick look at Patton and decided that he should go to the best hospital in the area, which was in Heidelberg, 20 miles away. "He broke his neck," Captain Snyder whispered, "He needs the very best we've got."

The truck that had hit Patton – from the Signal Corps – was never properly identified. In violation of all Army regulations, the driver,

---

[1] On a side note, Babalas had immediately known the occupant of the car because Patton was, as he put it, the only 4 star general left in Europe.

Thompson, had taken the truck on a joyride for an unknown mission with two unauthorized buddies. All three were in the cabin, another violation. However no citation was given. In fact, the driver of the truck, Robert L. Thompson, who was allegedly from Chicago, was never pinpointed with any exactitude and promptly disappeared.

Obviously there was gross negligence in not filing even an ordinary traffic report. Deputy Provost Marshal Shanahan says, "By the time the MPs got there, there was nothing to report. They considered it a trivial accident at the time. No one thought that Patton was hurt at all." This is a lie, since everyone at the scene remembers the horrible condition of Patton's head and his crippling paralyzation. Shanahan continues with the strange remark that, "it was known that General Patton was hated by all his men, including me." Patton was loved by his men, but that makes little difference. Clearly Shanahan hated him.

Babalas did file a report on the incident, however, in which he concluded that both drivers had been guilty of careless driving. He also felt that the severity of Patton's wound was puzzling. No one else in the car had been hurt. Even Patton's dog was unscathed. In January 1971, Babalas became curious about the accident again, and wondered what happened to his report. He asked for a copy of his official report that had been "submitted at the time of the investigation." He received no reply for months, although he repeatedly asked after the report. Finally in July of that year he received a letter from the National Personnel Records Center of the General Services Administration in St. Louis, Missiouri. "A review of the military personnel record of George S. Patton, service number 02605 has been made; however, the report of investigation which you request has not been located."

All documents bearing on Patton's accident had mysteriously vanished, much to Babalas' chagrin. There is nothing bearing on the accident in Patton's 201 File, which contains *all* his personal papers bearing on his career in the Army, including his medical records and efficiency ratings; nothing in the archives of the Office of the Adjutant General; nothing among the documents of the Medical Corps or in the vast collection of the Military Police,[1] nothing in the Army's Military History Center.[2] There is only one document bearing on the accident, and that is a deposition by Patton's driver, Woodring, which is obviously

---

[1] There should have been at least a record here of the accident's occurrence along with more details.

[2] Except, ironically, the post-mortem by Spurling.

doctored.[1] It contains precise medical information that was far beyond his knowledge at that or any time.[2] No one has a reasonable explanation for the disappearance of the relevant documents, or the fact that the only extant document dealing with the incident has been altered.

Meanwhile a severely injured Patton was admitted to the hospital. It had been an hour and a half since the accident, and Dr. Hill found Patton fully conscious and alert, although his skin was pale, his lips blue, and the rest of his head a bloody mess. After examining the head wound, Dr. Hill, the chief surgeon at the hospital, found that Patton's skull had not been fractured but there was a long, deep Y-shaped ragged gash from the bridge of his nose up and over the scalp from which the skin was hanging like a noose. Patton had been thrown forward and upward when the truck hit his limousine, and he either struck the railing above the driver's seat or hit the glass partition between the front and the back of the car. Patton thought he may have hit a clock in the partition.

Dr. Hill was now ready for a thorough examination, and he was dismayed to find paralysis of all musculature of the thorax, abdomen and legs. There was loss of sensation beginning about an inch below the collarbones. He had no sensation to the tip of his shoulders, arms, and legs. Several times Patton coughed and his right leg was drawn up, but when asked to move his limbs, all he could do was a "feeble outward rolling of his right leg." Patton was paralyzed – from the neck down. As Hill examined him, Patton was repeating to himself in a low whisper, "This is an ironical thing to happen to me." Seeing his lips move, an attending physician rushed over and asked him what he wanted. "I don't want a thing, Captain. I was just saying, 'What a nice way to start a vacation.'"

Everyone around him had heard of him – by reputation. They were clearly in awe of his rank and intimidated by rumors of his fearsome personality. So Patton treated them in the same way he had the Fifteenth Army staff. "Relax, gentlemen," he said, "I am obviously in no condition to be a terror." The doctors laughed along with their critically wounded patient.

---

[1] This even Farago admits.
[2] "The Last Days of Patton," page 10.

X-rays revealed that Patton's spinal column behind the neck had been fractured or dislocated at the third or fourth vertebra, and the spinal cord was apparently transected. Because of the damage to his spinal cord, Patton's nerves were paralyzed from the neck down. The doctors decided that Crutchfield tongs would ease the unbalanced situation of his vertebrae. The tongs were placed on his head and set to hold 5 pounds of traction. They cleansed and sutured his head wound and then placed the tongs in under local anesthesia. As the first stitch was inserted Patton exclaimed, "Seventy two!" Colonel Hill asked what he meant, to which Patton replied, "That was the seventy-second stitch I've had in my life."

After 40 minutes the painful operation was over. The next day Patton awoke and was read a telegram from Truman.

> "I am distressed at the painful accident which you have suffered and want you to know that I am thinking of you at this time. You have won many a tough fight and I know that faith and courage will not fail you in this one. I am thankful that Mrs. Patton will be at your side to strengthen and sustain you."

More than the note from the President, the message that his wife would soon be arriving cheered Patton. Meanwhile the doctors' prognosis remained grim. Colonel Hill felt that Patton didn't have a chance.

Of course more prestigious and possibly more competent doctors were quickly being called in. Patton needed a neurosurgeon. The Surgeon General in Washington got in touch with London's War Office to secure Brigadier Hugh Cairns, professor of nuerosurgery at the Oxford University of Medicine and chief neurosurgical consultant to the British Army. On December 10th, Cairns flew to Heidelberg. Colonel Spurling, one of two chief neurosurgical consultants in Europe, was summoned to Patton's bedside. Spurling had been in America and did not arrive until a few days later.

Cairns quickly offered his own recommendation. The Crutchfield tongs kept falling off Patton's head and were not staying in place. They were necessary to correct the dislocation of the vertebrae, so Cairns suggested that they dispense with the tongs and use zygomatic hooks instead. These are exactly like large-caliber fish hooks. The hooks were inserted into Patton's cheekbones under the eyes and were weighted to 10 pounds. The pain from this device was excruciating, but Patton never complained. He had been disciplined all his life, and as a soldier he took this new pain in stride.

In fact, Patton joked with his doctors, nurses, and even the German orderlies who were doing the menial chores. Like everyone else who came in contact with his vivacious and infectious personality, the hospital ward adored Patton. Nurses remarked how he never complained, despite the exquisite torture he was gong through. Dr. Hill recalled,

> "Everybody who was privileged to observe his last battle from close up was awed and fascinated by the incredible contrast between his *joie de vivre* and his inward reconciliation that his end was near. The same afternoon that he entertained me with the tale of the inflammation of his testicles, he told one of his nurses that all the fuss about him was a waste of the taxpayers' money, because he was 'fated to die' within the fortnight. He didn't guess, he didn't contemplate. He knew."

Even while he was dying, the press got Patton's story wrong. And, true to their calling, they once again portrayed him incorrectly. On December 12th the *Stars and Stripes* announced on its two-line banner headline,

FLAT ON HIS BACK, SKULL CLAMPED,
PATTON CALLS FOR SHOT OF WHISKEY

The type used to announce this was considerably larger than the announcement of his accident. The article sited Patton's night nurse, Bertha Hohle, and said that the general, hovering between euphoria and depression, required the constant attention of the nurses because he refused to take any nourishment. "I have to be there," the article quoted her as saying, "because he never wants to eat or drink. He says he won't drink unless he gets a shot of whiskey."

Lieutenant Hohle, the night nurse, just got a taste of the "accurate" reporting Patton had always been subjected to. When she saw the article, she frantically notified the hospital's public relations officer to issue a denial. She "had never said anything like that" to *any* of the reporters. She was horrified at the injustice of the accusation, and how it had so completely reversed the truth. Ward A-1, Patton's ward, was appalled at the article.

"He is a patient patient," Nurse Hohle added tearfully, "ideal, does not complain. If I were in his position with that uncomfortable traction apparatus, I'd be doing a lot more griping than he has done."

The doctors thought Patton looked better, although all night he had been coughing up blood tinged mucus. He had greeted the nurse clearly and cheerfully that morning with, "Good morning, Lieutenant. I feel much better today. Look, I can move the index finger of my right hand." The nurse, Ann Maertz, strained hard and decided that a slight movement was probably there. But then at 1 in the afternoon, Patton's perceived improvement vanished. "I have a queer sensation in my hands," he told the nurse, "as if my skin and flesh are trying to fall off my hands."

The nurse sent for Colonel Hill to come and cheer Patton up. Hill began to quiz Patton about some of his operations before the war because Patton enjoyed amusing Hill with his recollections. Today was different however. Patton answered Hill's questions but with none of his usual cheery banter. Suddenly he said, "You know, Colonel, exactly a year ago, I was approaching the most glorious moment of my service to my country. Unlike the anointed geniuses at General Bradley's headquarters, we at the Third Army had more than just an inkling of the imminence of the Ardennes offensive, what's now called the Battle of the Bulge. On this very day just a year ago, I issued orders to my staff to get ready for it, five days before it came." He paused, coughed up more mucus, then told a story that left Hill listening carefully, enthralled.

"I never told this to anybody before," Patton said, "so you'd better listen carefully, Hill, and make notes, because I don't want this story to go with me to the grave." He chuckled a little, but it was obvious to Hill that Patton knew the grave was not far off. Patton continued his story; the story of how he had gone to warn Bradley not to give the Ninth U.S. Army to Montgomery. "Monty," he told Hill, "was dead set against everything I was doing. He wanted all the available forces, British, Canadian, and American, up in the north under him, for the big crossing of the Rhine that was the brightest gleam in his bloodshot eyes. Actually, I came to think, he was playing into the hands of the Germans. They could never have launched the offensive without Monty." Patton ruminated on these past events, but he seemed depressed to Hill. It was as if Patton was looking back at all of the battles so recently completed, seeing clearly his position in history there, and knowing that he would not live to tell the truth about everything that had gone on. He was already an observer of his own place in history. There only remained for him to die.

Whereas before Patton had gone out of his way to amuse Hill, he now seemed overly preoccupied with the lost opportunities of the past. Colonel Hill remembered that he had a bottle of whisky in his office. He suggested that he go get it, and Patton smiled and nodded. It turned out that the bottle was almost empty, and there was only enough whisky left for the two to have a tiny medicine glass. Hill said cheers and watched as Patton struggled to take a few sips. Patton was amused by Hill's ministration as doctor and medicinal bartender, however, so Hill recommended that whisky become an official part of Patton's medication. Captain Duane ordered a bottle with instructions to give Patton a teaspoonful whenever his condition called for it.

This was the origin of the story that *Stars and Stripes* had printed. When Patton heard about the ridiculously false headlines, he went on one of his "joke binges" with it. Every time he did not feel like taking a sip of water or eggnog, he would tell his nurse, in imitation of the news story, that "I will take only a shot of Scotch." His nurses had thought that Patton was "cute," but they thought his jokes about wanting whisky made him even "cuter."

Reporters left the Nuremburg trials by the dozens to come to the hospital and hear of Patton's tribulations. More and more newspapermen showed up, and by December 10th there were over 30. None of them could see the critically wounded Patton but this did not stop their eager attempts at sneaking into his bedroom as doctors, nurses or patients. In an ironical twist of fate, Levin of the *New York Herald Tribune*, one of the conspirators who had put words in Patton's mouth, showed up at the hospital to hear of his ignominious fate. Two other reporters who had also arranged to trap Patton at that fateful press conference, Kathleen McLaughlin of *The New York Times* and Pierre J. Huss of the International News Service were also waiting outside for news.

Morgan assigned additional MPs to guard Patton's ward; every entrance and exit was guarded. Doors were locked and new press passes and I.D. cards were issued. Even so, reporters seemed to be swamping every part of the hospital. To organize them, General Keyes authorized Colonel Ball to issue daily bulletins detailing professionally and frankly

Patton's progress. Colonel Hill was shocked at the inanity of the questions the press asked him. Was it orange juice or grapefruit juice that Patton had for breakfast? What was the color of his pajamas, and were they his own or government issue? Was Patton swearing as profusely as he used to, and if yes, could they give a
few juicy samples of his expletives? Which of his three nurses was his favorite?

Even this press conference did not satisfy the press' urge for an exclusive scoop, and the correspondents began harassing Morgan, the man whose job it was to keep them at bay. Several newspapermen donned hospital gowns and ran up and down the corridors looking for Patton's room, until they were spotted and evicted. One had the brashness to try bribing the German cook who prepared Patton's eggnog. This German had the special honor of delivering it personally to Patton, and the newspaperman offered a carton of Lucky Strike cigarettes, a couple of pairs of nylon hose, and ten Hershey bars, to deliver it in his place. Fortunately, this "business" deal was caught while still being transacted.

On December 11th at 3:30 p.m. Mrs. Patton arrived at the hospital. When she was taken to Room 101, she saw her husband resting quietly, although his head was suspended by fish hooks into the forbidding traction hanging over him. Patton had requested that they speak together in private, but as the door was closed on the two, they heard Patton say in a firm voice, "Good to see you, Bea. I'm afraid this may be the last time we see each other." What they said for the next thirty minutes will never be known, but when Mrs. Patton emerged she made arrangements for a number of things. She had a list of the books her husband wanted her to read to him. Then she turned to Colonel Hill and said, "General Patton asked me to curtail his visitors somewhat, for the strain is getting too much for him." Her voice hardened considerably as she added, "Under no circumstances does he want to be visited by General Bedell Smith. Please understand, under no circumstances."

What had Patton told her? What did Patton himself know? Why did Patton write, "It is my hope [Smith] will be investigated by Congress"? Had he discovered the bugs in his home and the tap on his phone? Or the spies dressed as supply officers who had been reporting directly and only to Bedell Smith? Or was it something else – something more? We will never know.

On December 12th at 4 p.m. Colonel Spurling, the neurosurgeon, was taken to Patton's room for his first nuerological examination. He noted Patton's excellent demeanor, and was completely surprised when the man reputed to be a curmudgeon even when healthy, said, "Colonel Spurling, I apologize for getting you out on this wild goose chase, and I am particularly sorry since it probably means that you won't be home with your family for Christmas." Patton had blown away Spurling's expectations, proving once again that he was a very considerate man, regardless of what the legends said.

He submitted without complaint to yet another painful examination, remarking once again on the irony of the accident. "To think that after the best of the Germans have shot at me, to get hurt in an automobile going pheasant hunting." Patton was in no pain, Spurling discovered, except for the "rather persistent drag at the site of the traction in my skull." Spurling felt that the doctors already at the scene had done fine and he had no further recommendations to make. Patton was being attended by 3 regular surgeons, 4 nuerosurgeons, an orthopedic surgeon, and 5 or 6 doctors with other specialties.

Spurling was confident that Patton would pull through. Deep sensation was feebly present in both arms, and questionably in both legs. The new X-rays showed a complete realignment of the vertebral bones. Patton's temperature, pulse and respiration had also returned to normal.

When Colonel Spurling returned at ten o'clock the next morning he found that Patton's breathing had become labored, and he became worried that Patton's right diaphragm might also be paralyzed. His recovery, Spurling decided, was "increasingly grave."

Maybe Spurling's face had shown his disappointment at Patton's relapse. Or perhaps Patton had been planning on finding out the truth from this his newest of doctors. A short time after Spurling had left Patton's room he was paged and asked to return to the room alone. Spurling entered to find Patton's room empty. Mrs. Patton had gone to her room and the nurse had left as well.
"Sit down, Colonel," Patton said. After some small talk, Patton came to the point. "Now, Spurling, we've known each other during the fighting and I want you to talk with me as man to man. What chance have I to recover?"
"You're doing so much better than the usual patient with a cervical cord injury," Spurling replied, "that it is impossible for me to give you a

forthright answer. After all, if the cord has been severed or severely damaged at the moment of impact, your chance of recovering would be very slight. On the other hand, if the cord was only shaken up, we might see some rather dramatic improvements in the next 48 to 72 hours."

"Okay," said Patton, "But what chance have I to ride a horse again?"

"None," Spurling answered without a moment's hesitation.

"In other words," Patton said, showing renewed interest, "the best I could hope for would be semi-invalidism."

"Yes," the doctor said. There was a pause. Then Patton said, "Thank you, Colonel, for being honest."

In an instant Patton returned to his jovial mood. "Colonel," he said, "you are surrounded by an awful lot of brass around here – there are more generals than privates cooling their heels, so far as I can gather from the nurses and doctors. I just want you to know that you're the boss – whatever you say goes."

"Yes," Spurling agreed, "your old Army comrades are naturally anxious to see you, sir. They are clamoring for admittance to your room."

"It's your decision, Spurling," Patton said with his familiar laugh. "Whatever you say, buddy, goes. One exception. Did Mrs. Patton tell you that I don't care to see General Bedell Smith should he ever show up? He never was a special friend of mine. It's too late to patch things up, Colonel," he said, with a twinkle in his eye, "it's up to you to keep him out."

"All right," the doctor replied, "no one is to see you except Mrs. Patton, General Keyes, and of course the doctors and nurses on duty. How's that sound, General?"

"I think that is a good decision, irrespective of the medical point of view. After all, it's kind of hard for me to see my old friends, when I am lying here paralyzed all over," he said. Then, as if referring to Smith again, he said, "It may be fatal, if I have to see that old sonuvabitch."

"You need not worry, General. And save your strength sir," the doctor said.

"I will try to be a good patient," Patton replied as Spurling explained the problems that remained to be surmounted.

Four days later, on December 16th, Patton awoke shortly before midnight complaining of pain in his cheekbones. At 5:45 in the morning Captain Duane was called to adjust the traction again. He was sipping coffee through a glass tube at 2 p.m. when Colonel Hill checked in. Suddenly his legs began twitching again. "Will this never end?" Patton asked.

"How do you feel?" the doctor said.

Patton replied eagerly, "Look at the weather, Hill. It's exactly the kind of weather we had a year ago today. The Germans counted on it. It kept all our planes grounded."

Hill looked outside. It was dark and gloomy. A year ago to the day, in the quiet Ardennes sector, the Germans had launched their offensive. At that time Patton was in the height of his glory. He would quickly reorient his army and send it hurtling to Bradley's rescue. Hill thought perhaps a little whiskey was in order, as a sort of little anniversary celebration. "To the Distinguished Service Medal I never got," Patton toasted.

That evening, General Keyes dined with Patton's doctors. He found that Colonel Hill had a radically different opinion than that of the neurosurgeon. Whereas Spurling felt that there had been a "distinct improvement in General Patton's condition," Hill felt that Patton was doomed as the edema was spreading and increasing. "I don't care what you do, gentlemen," Keyes said as they left, "but do your best to keep him alive. He *must* live! It's absolutely imperative that he survive so that he can write his memoirs."

Every day Dr. Spurling dispatched a confidential medical report to General Marshall, the Chief of Staff, the Surgeon General, his superior, and President Truman. There was never any doubt in these reports, Spurling said, but that "General Patton was done for."

On December 17th the fishhook traction was taken off and Patton was fitted with a plaster collar that attached around the neck. He had been positioned in the same 45 degree angle for almost 2 weeks. During this time he had eaten very little, although sipping down soup and drinks. That night they moved him from the air mattress to a hospital bed, and he felt better immediately. Captain Duane found that Patton's condition was "excellent." He was beginning to be able to move his legs and arms – only slightly, but an improvement nevertheless.

When Spurling and Captain Duane dropped in on Patton on the morning of December 19th, it seemed as if Patton might really pull through. He was very alert, cheerful and talkative. He surprised even the pessimistic Hill with his stamina and resilience. "General Patton was a good patient this morning," Nurse Maertz told them happily, "He had a

474

whole egg and a cup of coffee for breakfast, and he wasn't making any fuss."

"I am feeling really well, Ann – for the first time," Patton told her, and Captain Duane noted that Patton had "had the best night so far."

Duane told Spurling that evening that Patton was clearly aware of the extent of his paralysis but "he's obviously determined to grin and bear it. He's checking up on us stealthily, testing out everything we tell him. Occasionally he may be a little confused or perhaps distracted, but only for a moment or so. On the whole I'd say he is normally alert."

Patton's vitality amazed his doctors. His vital organs were functioning fine. His heart and blood pressure were normal. Spurling was so encouraged that he made arrangements for Patton to be transferred to a hospital in the United States on December 30th. Sgt. Meeks, Patton's orderly, was taking a crash medical course so that he could function as a nurse during the trip home.

Harkins, who would also accompany Patton, came to see him at the hospital. "Don't show that you're upset by what you see," a doctor told Harkins before ushering him in. When Harkins walked in he saw Patton, the famous general, pallid and helpless, propped up in bed with an enormous collar around his neck. "Good afternoon, General," Harkins said.

"How do I look?" Patton said, perhaps sensing something in Harkins' face.

"You look fine, General," Harkins replied very quietly.

Patton broke out into laughter. "Paul, you never were any good at lying."

Harkins was brought to the verge of tears, and he left the room abruptly. He never saw Patton again.

That night, a little after ten, Patton was awakened by a violent coughing spell. For minutes afterward he strained to catch his breath, and his nurses, alarmed, sent for the doctor. Duane had been taking it easy because of Patton's apparently imminent recovery. When he arrived he found that Patton's skin had turned a bluish-gray color from his lack of oxygen. His breathing was difficult and labored. Patton's spinal condition, however, was fine. But now his heart was faltering under the strain of his difficult respiration.

The doctors were worried that a piece of clotted blood would travel through his bloodstream and block a major vessel – perhaps his brain, lungs, aorta, or an artery in the leg or thigh. If a major vessel became blocked, a pulmonary embolism would result and he would die within seconds. Patton had been coughing up blood, a sign that worried Spurling.

Another day passed by, and Patton's lease on life was nearing its end. He was sleeping more and talking less. By December 21st, the doctors had pronounced his condition hopeless. Patton had told Nurse Maertz several times that day that "I am going to die." Then to Nurse Rondell, who changed shifts that afternoon, "I am going to die," he said, "today."

Beatrice, his wife, was reading to him "Through the Fog of War," by Liddell Hart. She had just started the chapter called "Three French Soldiers" when it seemed that Patton was again asleep. To test him she went back to the top of the page, but as she read the opening sentence, Patton opened his eyes and said, "Oh, Bea, don't read me that again."

Mrs. Patton doubted the doctors hopeless verdict because Patton had been sleeping so quietly throughout the day. At 5 p.m. she sat crocheting by her sleeping husband when he awoke. "Are you all right, Georgie?" she asked. She patted his hand gently, and she heard him say, in a distant voice, with some difficulty, "It's so dark." Then, a moment later, "It's so late."

The words had come only with difficulty and their meaning was difficult to decipher. Those were his last words. He drifted off to sleep again, and Mrs. Patton left the room. She would never hear him speak, nor see him alive again.

At 5:45 p.m., only a short time after Beatrice had left, Nurse Rondell looked up, because a sixth sense told her that Patton had just died. She beckoned to Captain Duane who summoned Beatrice. Dr. Spurling followed shortly behind her. He had died from "sudden stopping of the heart" due to "pulmonary edema and congestive heart failure."

At last, after 12 days of excruciating pain, Patton had died. Like a true soldier, he died uncomplaining.

Chapter Sixty One

TRIBUTE TO THE MAN

"Last night one of the greatest men that ever lived died. That was Patton. The rest of the world thinks of him as just another guy with stars on his shoulders. The men that served under him know him as a soldier's leader. I am proud to say that I have served under him in the Third Army.
It sure looks different here. All the flags are at half-mast. We are making every [German] that passes stop and take off his hat. They can't understand our feelings for him. I don't know whether or not you can understand them either."

That was simply an anonymous private, yet his thoughts were echoed by thousands of men who had served with pride under General Patton. Patton had come to symbolize a true soldier, patriot and man. One Lieutenant Colonel Montgomery C. Jackson remembers that over 50 British officers were inquiring about Patton's condition because they regarded Patton as their favorite general.

After Patton's death there was talk of a conspiracy – that his accident was planned. This unfortunately was compounded by Mrs. Patton's decision not to conduct an autopsy.

On Saturday, December 22nd, the day after Patton's untimely death, his body was placed in state at the Villa Reiner, a pretty house on a mountain overlooking Heidelberg. On Sunday the casket was closed and escorted by a platoon of cavalry and pallbearers to the Protestant Church in Heidelburg for the Episcopal funeral service. Hundreds of flowers donated by various organizations and friends surrounded his casket. There were official delegations from Britain, France, the Soviet Union, Sweden, Belgium, and Luxembourg, as well as from the major American military commands in Europe. After the service, the body was escorted to the train station. As the train pulled away, an artillery battery fired a 17 gun salute.

One of those in the mourning party was General Truscott. He had been an old family friend, but he was afraid that Beatrice would not speak to him due to Ike's cruel decision to put him in command of Third Army. "When I offered him my hands, he threw his arms around me and burst into tears," Beatrice recalled later. He had not wanted to take the Third from Patton.

When they arrived at Luxembourg it was dreary. A steady rain was falling. After his casket was lowered, Master Sgt. Meeks, Patton's orderly of 10 years, presented Mrs. Patton with the flag that had been draped over the coffin. There were tears in Meeks' eyes. He saluted her stiffly, then turned away, overwhelmed. A 12 man firing squad fired a three round volley after which a bugler played "Taps."

One of Patton's generals, Walker, had flown from Texas at his own expense to be at the funeral. The weather was so bad that he could not land and all he could do was fly above the funeral cortege. The members of the mourning party could hear his plane although they could not see him through the thick fog. Five years later to the day, Walker was to die in a tragic jeep accident.

At Fifteenth Army headquarters 200 big bags of candy arrived from Creed, Patton's former Third Army cook. The story behind them was this: A few months earlier, Creed had been trying to return to America, but his orders were always delayed. When Creed told Patton, Patton had the orders filled while they were waiting. Creed asked Patton if there was anything he could do in return.
"Yes, there is something you can do for me," Patton answered. "There is a Catholic orphanage outside of Frankfurt. Could you send over a bunch of hard candy for the children?"
When Creed got back to America, he sent 200 big bags of candy. But by the time it arrived, Patton was already dead.

When Mrs. Patton heard the story behind the candy, she went over to the orphanage and handed it out in his name to all the little German kids. "That's the kind of people [they] were," Creed said later.

Hundreds of letters of regret poured in. One staff sergeant who was struggling with the English language wrote a mostly inarticulate letter, at the end of which he added, "I love him." From London, one soldier wrote insightfully and eloquently,

> "His personality is more firmly fixed in our minds than any other military commander of the late war, and therefore his memory will remain with us and our children for generations. He came to us fellows in the 12th Evac. Hospital and he told me in plain words, 'Don't you lose that leg, I need you.' But I let him down. I had to lose it. I did love him as a leader, and I believe that every man under him did. I will never forget the feelings of the men in my battery when, after reaching the Rhine, we were informed the division was being transferred to another Army. They were afraid the General thought that we were not good enough for him. The fondest memory I have of the war just finished is the thought that I was a member of the Third Army. In the earliest days of the Ardennes, we green troops were righting with desperation, and in the darkest moments of the worst hours, the news came that we were in the Third Army and that help was coming. It would have warmed your heart to see the hope that came with that simple announcement. The Third Army meant the 'old man,' and he meant hope, success and victory ... I feel that I am a better man because of the General, and he will be a source of strength for the rest of my life. He held all the lore and wisdom of America's past and stood face forward. Germany never terrified him. Russia never mystified him, the future came to him as nothing strange. Out of the mud of vilification a great man and soldier has arisen. It's a shame that death should have been necessary to clarify his true value and virtue."

A former army mess sergeant said as late as 1972 that, "I still can't think of Patton as being dead, a man like that. I expect to turn around and still see him standing there."

Brigadier General Chynoweth, a friend of Patton for 37 years, wrote rebutting the Washington *Post*'s accusations with,

"You state that 'Patton the man never lived up to Patton the soldier.' I fear that it was not your privilege to know Patton the man. The man who deliberately and continually courted every form of personal danger, in peace and war, in order to crush out of his own heart any vestige of the fear which he knew to be the greatest of all enemies in war... You state that he 'was made for no other purpose than for war.' Please let me inform you that he was also made for friendship, for kindly affection, and for sympathy with the underdog. I have never known a friend upon whom one could count more surely for disinterested help in time of trouble. This soldier and man has passed on, leaving in the lives of his friends and in the service of the nation a vacancy that cannot be filled except through a reflection upon his heroic example."

The myth that Patton was only a soldier, who could not comprehend either world or political problems, is one that has survived and which is distressing to not merely his friends who knew him while alive, but also to those who learn about him now that he is dead. For here truly was a man worthy of imitation, one in whom honor, courage, honesty and bravery were not merely time-worn expressions but virtues lived to the fullest.

Patton was essentially, as the hospital staff found out, a good-natured, intelligent, highly disciplined and honest man. These qualities were sometimes difficult to reconcile with his job as Army commander for Eisenhower. Yet he managed to escape with his dignity and candor intact. No other army commander could say the same; and none can boast his excellent military record either. Patton combined his virtues with a military genius of unequaled caliber. Unlike other authors, though, I find it impossible to simply label him a genius for war because Patton was, first and foremost, an intellectual and historian. He possessed a keen sense of human nature, and this is what made him such a great combat leader. It also made his superiors uneasy around him. He was so accurate at predicting peoples ideas, aspirations, and goals that often his intuition must have seemed nothing short of uncanny. Patton was a fine governor of Bavaria, and his talents served him well for the short time that he held the position. One of his virtues – honesty coupled with justice – was not conducive toward the retention of that position. Patton will always be regarded as a soldier, a warrior; but it is very important to remember that he was also a highly virtuous man, with honor and dignity, and that he possessed a remarkable intelligence and quick wit.

Chapter Sixty Two

AFTERMATH

When Patton had voiced objection to the de-Nazification orders he had been publicly castigated, ridiculed, and relieved. Yet, only weeks after he was removed from command of Third Army, Eisenhower reversed those orders and declared that for the better running of Germany, nominal Nazis would be allowed to keep their posts. Patton had been relieved for *suggesting* that idea!

Everything Patton advocated was borne out over time. His renunciations of the Russians, at that time wildly politically incorrect, would soon find favor as the U.S. woke up to Russian atrocities. Patton knew, before them, that Russia wanted "world domination," but it seems to have been Patton's fate to be ahead of his time. Throughout his life he had been persecuted for saying his opinion; then a few years later the establishment would come around to his point of view. Saying the truth, honestly as he saw it, caused Patton to fall from favor, promotion lists, and eventually command. Being ahead of his time had not served Patton well, because in a strange way honesty is timeless: and accepted by no time.

Churchill, too, spoke ahead of his time; but he was in a position of respect and when he expressed his opinions they soon became publicly acknowledged – if not accepted. In 1946 Churchill delivered his "Iron Curtain" speech – the West's first acknowledgment that they were not in full accord with the Soviet Union. Gradually after this speech, the Western powers took their heads out of the sand and admitted that they had an evil and unruly power to contend with. If Patton had lived, would he have given his own version of the "Iron Curtain"?

Germany, which had sunken to the depths of death and despair under the alleged "de-Nazification" orders, would soon require the drastic and expensive Marshall plan to rescue it. Even though Ike had repealed the de-Nazification order, it was far too late and Germany was far too advanced in decay. Millions of American tax dollars were spent feeding Germany that winter of 1946, and millions more would be spent repairing it to working condition – all because Eisenhower's foolish and unworkable orders had been blindly obeyed by his subordinates. No one else had been brash enough to speak out against what was obviously unjust and harmful to America. Because no one else had the courage to stand up with Patton against the idiotic orders of USFET, America would pay the price – that year, and years to come.

One of the reporters who had been guilty of purposely trapping Patton at the press conference in Bavaria later felt such remorse at having destroyed a great man that he went and apologized to Patton's widow.
"It is probably too late, but I want to tell you, Mrs. Patton, how much I regret having had anything to do with that fatal[1] press conference. After I had spent more time in your husband's presence and observed the problems he faced and how he handled them, I came to admire him greatly."
Beatrice answered typically. "It's still too late," she said. I wonder if she, too, felt that the press conference had been more than fateful: did she think it had been fatal?

Eisenhower and Bradley proceeded to remove, tamper and "lose" documents – especially those connected with the Battle of the Bulge. Together with Montgomery they hatched a version of the war, unique only in its outright dishonesty.

No longer did there live a man honest enough to combat their efforts, and for years their history remained on the books. There were some obviously manufactured parts of it, though, and generations of historians have peeled away at its fabrications.

---

[1] An interesting choice of words.

484

Bradley would become the first permanent chairman of the Joint Chiefs of Staff from 1949 to 1953. He was promoted to 5 star General in 1950 and he retired 3 years later to become a business executive.

A motion was put forward in Congress to make Patton a posthumous 5 star general. It was rejected because they decided that there would be no more 5 star generals. This honor was reserved only for those who had already received it – Bradley, Eisenhower and MacArthur. In a seeming burst of belated gratitude, there was also a bill in Congress requesting that Patton receive a posthumous Medal of Honor. If only they had appreciated this man of worth while he lived. But perhaps such gratitude can only be awarded posthumously.

Eisenhower became President of Columbia University for a very brief time before assuming "supreme command" again – this time of the new NATO forces being assembled in 1951. True to Patton's prediction, Eisenhower ran for President in 1952, after being persuaded that he was a Republican. Because Patton had never been able to tell people in America about what Eisenhower was doing in Europe, the soldiers voted overwhelmingly for him.

Meanwhile, Patton's family fearfully refused to print Patton's diary or personal papers. They authorized the publication of "War As I Knew It" – but not before removing most of the "objectionable" material that would have made it, like Patton, honest and different from the other memoirs. His family had learned, unlike Patton, to be afraid of too much honesty in the face of treachery.

Montgomery became a Knight of the Garter and was made a Viscount in 1946. He served as Chief of the Imperial General Staff from 1946 to 1948. He was made chairman of the Permanent Defense Organization of the Western European Union from 1948 to 1951. As always, Montgomery managed to make it to deputy commander – this time of NATO, from 1951 to 1958. He wrote his "official history" *Memoirs* in 1958. He also wrote a few other books on the history of war and strategy which serve merely to illustrate the lengths to which he failed to grasp these subjects. He died in 1976.

On March 28th, 1969 Eisenhower died. A few years later, Patton's family allowed Martin Blumenson, the Third Army's official historian, to edit and publish Patton's diaries and letters. At last Patton could be heard and read in his own crystal clear, candid style.

After the dust of the armies settled and the clouds of political-correctness evaporated, only one man emerges unstained: uncompromised by his position of power and his duty to truth and justice.

Colonel Harry Semmes delivered an address at the American Legion's ceremony in which he ended, "George Patton, your old comrades-in-arms and friends, both living and dead, salute you. A thousand years of unborn Americans will look down on what you have done and find it good."

MONTGOMERY

Sir Bernard Law Montgomery is a character that, like Eisenhower, dominates the scene of the war in Europe. However, unlike Eisenhower, there is less popularly known about him. Patton knew little about him besides his tactics.

But it would seem peculiar to most that Montgomery would obstinately stick to a doomed strategy. It would seem stranger still that Montgomery, out of personal spite towards Patton, failed to allow him to close the Falaise Gap. Montgomery's continual criticism of Eisenhower comes as a surprise – considering how lenient Eisenhower was when he dealt with him.

Here are examples from Montgomery's life that prove that Montgomery was a bitter, vindictive man with an ambition that far outpaced his talents.

When Montgomery was a student at Sandhurst, Britain's military college, he led a gang of rowdy cadets in a series of practical "jokes." One of these consisted of tying up a successful cadet while Montgomery lit fire to his uniform. The cadet suffered very serious burns and under ordinary circumstances Monty would have been expelled. Montgomery's father was head of the Anglican Church's Society for the Propagation of the Gospel and the school tried to save him from scandal.

Montgomery's brother said that when Monty attended St. Paul's school he first showed a "streak of showmanship he never had before."

At Sandhurst, and out of his parents' supervision, he had developed a brash and caustic attitude when speaking to superiors. Montgomery came to regard all of his superiors with contempt, and unlike other men, he did not hold *any* of them in high regard. His own high opinion of himself offended everyone that he knew. This, coupled with his harsh treatment of underlings, made him a very acerbic leader.

In WWI Montgomery's men were brought to the verge of mutiny because of his arrogant behavior.

In the 1920's, following the aftermath of the WWI bloodbath, many officers were reviewing their strategies. What could have caused such a colossal disaster? Their conclusions would determine their future strategies. In Britain, J. F. C. Fuller and Liddell Hart were developing a revolutionizing strategy. Liddell Hart termed it the "expanding torrent" theory, the idea that in the next war *tanks* would move in a rapid advance to the enemy's rear, cutting him off from retreat and escape. This idea meant that in the next war *advance*, not numbers of men, would be the deciding factor. Fuller and Liddell Hart campaigned vigorously that a rapid advance with tanks and strong air cover would be decisive for victory in the wars of the future. In Britain the two were ignored by the high command which had decided that all future wars would be the same as the last – a bloody struggle between two head-on infantry armies. In Germany the officers were avidly reading Liddell Hart's books and adopting his theories. They correctly realized that rapidity of movement was vital to all future operations. The British blindly ignored their countrymen, to their detriment. Field Marshal Rommel said that, "The British would have been able to prevent the greatest part of their defeats if they had paid attention to the modern theories expounded by Liddell Hart before the war."

Montgomery was thoroughly convinced that he knew why WWI had caused so much bloodshed. He said it was because of lack of communication between the front lines and the rear. He believed that a central intelligence would save lives in the next war. Montgomery, like most of his British contemporaries, did not believe in *mobile* warfare. Liddell Hart met Montgomery in 1920. He says that,

> "At that time Montgomery was still a captain, with a brevet as major, and a student at the Staff College. Viewing his perky manner, peaky face and small stature it seemed amusingly apt that in the Battle of the Somme

he had been a staff officer in what was called 'the Bantam Division'. He did not show the natural signs of leadership, or a knack of handling men – indeed, when he was eventually given command of a battalion, after sixteen years on the staff, he brought it to the verge of mutiny by misjudged handling. But even in 1920 he showed the dynamism and determination that carried him to the rank of field-marshal and the position of Commander-in-Chief of the Allied Army Group engaged in the cross-Channel attack of 1944.... In particular, he learned the methods by which Napoleon and other 'Great Captains' had impressed themselves on troops *en masse* and evoked an enthusiastic response from their armies. Monty provides an outstanding example that a 'born commander' can be surpassed by a 'made commander – made by concentrated application to the job and the problem. Even in the nineteen-twenties, however, he showed one of the characteristic tendencies which became a handicap in reaping the harvest of his victories – and for which he came to be widely criticised during and after World War II, especially in American quarters."

In 1924, Montgomery sent Liddell Hart "Tactical Notes" on methods of attack and defense for Liddell Hart to critique. These notes were from a course he was giving officers which consisted of four lectures on tactics. Liddell Hart had expressed surprise that he had not dealt with the problem and need *of exploiting successes* when gained. Montgomery's reply was that:

"I have not mentioned exploitation anywhere. Perhaps I should have done so, and if I ever get out a revised edition I will do so. I was anxious not to try and teach too much. The first thing to my mind is to get them to understand the elementary principles of attack and defence. But I think you are probably right, and exploitation should have been brought out."

This was a crippling mistake. An attack without exploitation is not a victory. But now Liddell Hart assumed that Montgomery knew.

Seven years later, a dismayed Liddell Hart was reviewing Montgomery's new draft of the official manual. It had been sent to Liddell Hart by Brigadier Fisher for criticism.

> "My chief criticism was that in all the parts dealing with attack scant attention had been given to exploitation. I had a letter back from B[rigadier] Fisher saying: 'I had a long talk with Montgomery, and we went carefully through all your criticisms of the new infantry Training – with the result that the great majority of them are being incorporated in the final proof. The importance of "the expanding torrent" is being specially emphasised.' I also had an appreciative letter from Montgomery to the same effect. Yet when the new manual was issued I was dismayed to find that such exploitation had not been adequately emphasised, nor apparently grasped. That became evident again at El Alamein, eleven years later, and in subsequent battles, where the opportunity created by the break-in was repeatedly missed, and the enemy slipped away to fight another day. Such a persisting blind spot of Montgomery's was the more remarkable because in his early tactical lectures he showed the same thorough grasp of the requirements of the break-in and set-piece battle as he did in his battlefield performances."

It is quite incredible that Montgomery could read strategy books and not grasp their key components. In his "A History of Warfare" Montgomery discusses historical campaigns and what caused their failures and successes. Written as late as 1968, Montgomery shows a thorough lack of understanding with regard to many important campaigns. One example is the Middle Eastern campaign led by Lawrence in 1917 in which Montgomery completely misunderstands the purpose of Lawrence's "indirect" method of war. Lawrence realized the futility of continually attacking Medina. A very similar situation occurred in France in 1944, where the Allied armies bombarded the coastal ports in an attempt to take them by storm. Their attempts were completely useless, and the ports, like Medina, did not surrender until after the war. Montgomery did not understand why Lawrence did not take Medina, and he could not understand why the head-on attacks of the French ports would fail; clearly because he could not understand the strategy involved, he could not learn from history.

During the Battle of Britain, Montgomery was ordered to plan the coastal defense. He needed a place to plan at but was unable to find a hotel large enough. His aide decided to ask a member of the House of Lords who had a large country house in the area if he would mind inviting the general as a houseguest. The lord replied that he would love to be host to Montgomery for a few days. The aide returned to Montgomery, satisfied with the arrangement. Montgomery, however, felt that the lord would interfere with his work by talking to him at mealtime and intrude upon his privacy. Montgomery then suggested his own solution. He would take over a wing of the house, and bring his own army cook so that he could eat his meals separately. The aide, apprehensive, returned to the owner of the estate. The would-be host was quite upset. "It is not customary for my guests to make demands." But, said the owner, it was war, and he understood that there were times when a general needed to be alone to relax and think. After all, it would only be for a few days.

The aide reported back to Montgomery, delighted at having smoothed over the relations. He found that Montgomery had other plans. "From what you tell me," he said, "it is a lovely place... has nice gardens and everything... maybe we will stay for three or four weeks. Yes, we will – we will be staying for a month. Go back and tell him I have changed my mind and that we are going to bring a couple of servants as well." This time no helpful aide could quell the owner's anger. The lord of the estate told Montgomery's aide quite unequivocally that he would not be treated like that in his own home. Not only that, but he withdrew his invitation altogether.

The downcast aide reported back yet again to Montgomery and told him the news. Montgomery then took out a map of the area and decided that the house was in a restricted zone. "Kick him out at once," he ordered. "We can't have him in the way of an invasion." The member of the House of Lords was ejected from his country estate and Montgomery moved in, handing it over to the army for the duration of the war when he was through with it.

Montgomery frequently treated those above him with insolence and disrespect. He was arrogant and boastful and had been known to relieve officers for showing up a few minutes late to a meeting. Churchill had once called him "a little man on the make." Montgomery had humiliated many of those beneath him who hated him in return. Since

Montgomery liked to surround himself with yes-men who would look pale in comparison, he would often relieve career officers for minor infractions. Five decades after the end of WWII, Norman Gelb, author of "Ike and Monty: Generals at War" says that while researching an account of the Dunkirk evacuation he had encountered the son of a man who had been a commander of an elite British regiment in the war. "An officer himself, he told me until the day his father died he had despised Montgomery with a passion for the way he treated officers of whom he disapproved."

During the campaign at El Alamein, Nigel Nicolson records that,

"In the field he made it clear that nobody existed for him except the troops of his own army. I retain in my mind a sharp picture of his arrival on the plains of Kairouan in Tunisia where Eighth and First Armies joined hands, both of them then under Alexander's command. We in [British] First Army had won our own small battle at Fondouk and had every right to pursue the enemy across the poppy-fields, but they happened to lie in the path of Eighth Army's advance from the south. Montgomery drove up in an open staff-car like a Roman consul, his knuckles showing white on the rim of the windscreen as he raised himself to bellow, 'Out of my way! Out of my way!' accompanying his words with dismissive sweeps of his arm, as if First Army were a bag of refuse which a garbage-truck had accidentally dropped on his doorstep. The joy of the occasion, the pleasure of setting eyes upon this famous man, and momentarily the unity of the two armies, were simultaneously shattered."

Montgomery, the son of a strict Protestant preacher, believed that drinking and smoking were wrong. When Churchill visited him in N. Africa he asked Montgomery if he would like a drink. Montgomery, insolent to the last, replied, "I neither drink nor smoke and am 100% healthy." Churchill quickly rejoined, "I both drink and smoke and am 200% healthy."

In Tunisia, Montgomery made a bet with Bedell Smith that if the Eighth Army entered the city of Sfax by April 15th a Flying Fortress would be put at his personal disposal for the rest of the war. Eisenhower's chief of staff did not think that it was a serious wager for he had made it jocularly, and there was no suggestion that Montgomery would have to forfeit something if he lost the bet. However, on April 15th, British troops entered Sfax and a cable from Montgomery reached Smith with the words, "Please send Fortress." At first Smith was amazed that Montgomery was serious, then he tried to joke Montgomery out of it. Montgomery told him harshly that a bet was a bet, not to be welched on. However this was certainly a different type of bet, because unlike betting money, Smith was not in a position to give out Flying Fortresses. Bedell Smith felt obliged to inform Eisenhower. When Brooke[1] heard of it he sharply chastised Montgomery. Eisenhower says that he was "boiling over with internal anger," but instead of leaving this "inside the family" he decided that he didn't want anything to ruffle British-American feathers. Since he had the power to, he sent the bomber and an American crew to Montgomery's headquarters. Monty didn't relinquish it until late in the Sicilian campaign when he admitted that a Flying Fortress was a little big for most airfields. Was that the end of it? No. Eisenhower exchanged it for a small Dakota.

Montgomery was, unlike Patton, of small stature. He would attract attention by wearing his uniform in public, even after the war. And to distinguish himself he would wear the red tanker's beret that did not properly belong to an infantry general's uniform. His boastfulness and self-displaying was such that some thought he was headed for politics. A popular joke from the time goes like this: Churchill was telling the king, "I'm worried about Monty. I think he's after my job." The king replied, "Thank God! I thought he was after mine."

Sometimes Montgomery would give a speech without properly evaluating its effect on his men's morale. In an address to a grenadier battalion before Mareth he told them that, "When I give a party, it is a good party. And this is going to be a good party." His men remembered his words when 200 of their number didn't return alive. At Market-Garden, a terrible disaster-plan of his in France, he told his men that he "wouldn't want to miss this party." Almost 2/3[rds] of them didn't return.[2]

Montgomery always depreciated his men and so turned the spotlight of the press upon himself alone. This understandably also lowered their morale. In N. Africa Montgomery only gave credit of victory to his army – the Eighth – even though there were many other

---

[1] Brooke was Chief of the Imperial General Staff and Montgomery was his protégé.
[2] An astounding 17,000 men!

British armies fighting along side him. Alexander, who had the difficult job of being his superior in Africa and in Italy, once remarked that, "Monty has a lot of personal charm – I always like him best when I am with him. Yet he is unwise, I think, to take all the credit for his great success as a commander entirely to himself. His prestige, which is very high, could be higher still if he had given a little credit to those who had made his victories possible, and there are those besides his own fighting men to whom he owes something."

Montgomery's behavior was a source of embarrassment many times. Churchill once said that Monty was, "In defeat, indomitable, in victory, insufferable." When Montgomery was in hot water for dining with Von Thoma, a defeated German general in N. Africa, Churchill told the House of Commons, "Poor Von Thoma. I, too, have dined with Montgomery."

Of course, none of these personal characteristics are important if a commander can bring victory. Which unfortunately is not true of Montgomery. In his one allegedly great battle, El Alamein, he allowed Rommel's vastly inferior and under-supplied troops to slip away uncaptured. In strategy, that is an unpardonable mistake. The Germans knew they could count on Montgomery's limitless caution. For Rommel says,

> "I was quite satisfied that Montgomery would never take the risk of following up boldly and overrunning us, as he could have done without any danger to himself. Indeed, such a course would have cost him far fewer losses in the long run than his methodical insistence on overwhelming superiority in each tactical action, which he could only obtain at the cost of his speed."

Montgomery never advanced quickly because he insisted on having three times the necessary number of supplies and then moving forward "with caution." "War requires the taking of risks," as Patton said, "and Monty simply won't take them." Rommel commented, "Montgomery had an absolute mania for always bringing up adequate reserves behind his back and risking as little as possible." Rommel had exploited Monty's "mania" to the full.

Compare Rommel's notes on Montgomery with his comments on Patton. "We had to wait until the Patton Army in France to see the most astonishing achievements in mobile warfare." Clearly the Germans regarded Patton as a modern commander who fully understood the British-invented blitzkrieg, whereas Montgomery was an old-school WWI commander who would plod bloodily from battle to battle.

The numbers speak for themselves. In Operation Goodwood, Montgomery had 1,500 tanks and 250,000 men attack the German defenses which, due to over a month of Monty's inactivity, had hardened around Caen. 45,000 shells were dropped on the 2nd SS Panzer Corps alone. Over 800 fighter bomber missions flew to support Montgomery's men while 1,800 RAF and RCAF squadrons flew against German tanks and artillery emplacements. At the end of the operation, Caen, the largest northern harbor in Europe was still uncaptured and desperately needed for Bradley's ever extending lines. Seven thousand tons of bombs had been dropped in the most elaborate bombing of enemy front-line positions ever accomplished and Montgomery had only managed to take *seven miles!*

Most of Montgomery's operations were more like Goodwood. Tons of supplies wasted, little captured. An extreme example of the flaw in his strategy, though, must be Operation Market Garden. The casualties of this doomed escapade were higher than those from the assault on Normandy on D Day. Montgomery's Market Garden reaped a staggering 17,000 in killed, missing and wounded during the 9 day venture behind enemy lines. Montgomery did not heed the warnings his Intelligence Corps and the Dutch underground had given him. He chose to believe that the area would offer no resistance. In fact, the 2nd SS Panzer Corps was resting in that very area. The Allied soldiers had fought well, but they could not capture all the bridges that were required for the operation to be a success (this was a basic flaw in Monty's plan). After 13,226 of his British troops had died, Montgomery decided to pull out and labeled the mission a "success." This time he had captured *nothing.* An estimated 10,000 Dutch civilians who had cooperated with the Allied forces perished that winter after Monty pulled out. Bernhard, the Prince of the Netherlands at that time, seems to sum it up. It was he who said, "My country can never again afford the luxury of another Montgomery success."

BRADLEY

It is worth reviewing the personality of another famous commander, General Omar N. Bradley. Six years after the war he wrote a careful "official history" book entitled, "A Soldier's Story." He attacks Montgomery and his plans viciously, yet defends Eisenhower's actions – sometimes even when these actions were to support Montgomery. However at occasions there is a break in the "official history" where we get a real glimpse of his thoughts. Unfortunately for us, Bradley did not keep a diary. If he had, we would have seen his day to day thoughts and what he was really thinking. Instead, we know only that both Eisenhower and Montgomery published their "Histories of the War" first, and that it some cases[1] Bradley scrupulously "corrected history" and corroborated Eisenhower's version.

Patton is the only clear voice that remains from WWII without need of deciphering. We are extremely lucky that Patton followed General Pershing's advice and kept a diary. Without Patton's diary, we would not have clear proof of his incredible "sixth sense:" his accurate guesses as to the intention of the enemy. It is easy for a commander to say, years after the war, that he "knew all along" the enemy was about to attack. That commander must be able to *prove* that he knew – and the best proof is a day-to-day account in a war diary.

In "A Soldier's Story," Bradley praises Patton with what would seem mollified respect. But in 1983 Bradley wrote another vicious book

---

[1] For instance, the Falaise Gap

that fiercely attacks Patton called, "A General's Life." The tone used in describing Patton, while in the first book admiring, has changed to bitter hatred. In his second book, Bradley attacks Patton where in the first book he seemed to approve. Read these two passages describing the same event.

> "Patton telephoned me that evening from Lucky Forward[1] near Laval. 'We've got elements in Argentan,' he reported. 'Let me go on to Falaise and we'll drive the British back into the sea for another Dunkirk.'
> 'Nothing doing,' I told him, for I was fearful of colliding with Montgomery's forces. 'You're not to go beyond Argentan. Just stop where you are and build up that shoulder. Sibert tells me the German is beginning to pull out. You'd better button up and get ready for him.'" *"A Soldier's Story," by General Omar N. Bradley*

> "I had a sharp telephone exchange with Patton that morning. He further infuriated me with his boastful, supercilious attitude. 'Let me go on to Falaise and we'll drive the British back into the sea for another Dunkirk.' I replied coldly and firmly, 'Nothing doing. You're not to go beyond Argentan. Just stop where you are and build up that shoulder.'" *"A General's Life," by General Omar N. Bradley*

And while in the first account Bradley seems happy that Patton recalled Haislip "without a word," in the second account, Bradley is "furious" that Patton did not ask to advance Haislip in the first place. There is a very clear difference in Bradley's attitude towards Patton in both books. Why?

It first must be realized that Bradley lived into the 1980s – long enough to see the collapse of the post-war reputations. Bradley had lived a long and prosperous life. He had commanded in Korea and had been promoted to five-star general. Bradley knew that he had risen higher than Patton would ever have been allowed to go. Yet Bradley must also have known that he was eclipsed by the genius of the man whom he had commanded. Bradley must have read many of the books by historians who had begun to realize that Patton had been unjustly cheated of many opportunities – like Falaise – for winning the war.

---

[1] The code name for Patton's command post.

Bradley lived to read books by historians who had uncovered evidence that Eisenhower and Montgomery were bad commanders who had purposely "lost" files pertaining to their disasters. "Patton's Gap," with its evidence that Bradley had changed his version of events to match Eisenhower's, had been published as well. There were some cloudy circumstances around his own Hurtgen Forest and Battle of the Bulge, too.

Patton had emerged the true hero of WWII – Bradley was only a five star general who had survived the war. Historians already knew that one of the reasons Bradley was promoted was because he was so weak-kneed. Did Bradley read the books that proved Patton was denied gas for his attacks? Or the books that showed he had ignored Patton's timely advice predicting the Battle of the Bulge?[1] It would have been difficult for Bradley to ignore the evidence that Eisenhower's, Montgomery's, and his own reputation were not going to last beyond his lifetime.

It seems to me that "A General's Life" was Bradley's last, desperate "vindication" of the men whose reputations were falling apart around him. Bradley would have went down with far more grace if he had let history uncover itself; but instead in his 2nd book, like his first, Bradley tries to obscure the gradually emerging truth by defending Eisenhower tooth and nail.

Bradley had another unique experience – reading Patton's diary. Since Patton's diary was a record of his intensely personal and often critical thoughts and comments, it was not published until after Eisenhower's death. Patton had often criticized Bradley's timidity and mediocrity in his diary. Bradley writes of reading Patton's diaries and letters,

> "He wrote obsessively candid self-congratulatory (or self-abnegating) letters and diaries, which have recently been edited and published in two volumes. Reading these volumes was one of the most astonishing literary experiences of my life. It would seem that no thought George ever had in his life – however trivial or magnificent – went unrecorded, that his sense of

---

[1] In his book, Bradley makes reference to these books among others: Ladislas Farago's "Patton: Ordeal and Triumph," the book and movie "A Bridge Too Far," and "Drive," Patton's aide's recount of the war.

greatness and destiny demanded a full accounting to the public."

Bradley does not seem to realize that Patton wrote his diary with no intention of ever releasing it to the public. The thoughts and impressions recorded there were his real opinions – he was not trying to show-off to the "public."

There was much in Patton's diary that, while interesting from a historical perspective, was hardly flattering. For instance, Patton wrote about Bradley,

> "His success is due to his lack of backbone and subservience to those above him. I will manage without him. In fact, I always have; even in Sicily he had to be carried." *Patton's Diary*

True, but undoubtedly infuriating to its subject.

It seems that after Bradley read Patton's diary, he bitterly hated Patton and wished to criticize Patton "for the record" in his new book. One particularly jarring account is coupled with the announcement of Patton's death – a death that does not seem to have upset him at all.[1] He writes that,

> "It may be a harsh thing to say, but I believe it was better for George Patton and his professional reputation that he died when he did. The war was won; there were no more wars left for him to fight. He was not a good peacetime soldier; he would not have found a happy place in the postwar Army. He would have gone hungering for the old limelight, beyond doubt indiscreetly sounding off on any subject any time, any place. In time he would have become a boring parody of himself – a decrepit, bitter, pitiful figure, unwittingly debasing the legend." *"A General's Life," by General Omar N. Bradley, page 464*

While obviously Bradley's opinion of Patton had soured with age, Bradley never truly appreciated Patton's worth. In Sicily, Patton had been in command of Bradley. Patton forced Bradley to employ daring end-run tactics which eventually led to the capture of Palermo and

---

[1] Bradley does not mention Patton's death at all in his first book.

Messina. Nevertheless, Bradley resented Patton's "meddling" in his command. Bradley was the military adviser for the *Patton* movie. As Carlo d'Este pointed out, Bradley seems the hero, always advising Patton not to be foolhardy – "Those out-spoken comments will eventually catch up with you!" "George, you're going to get yourself relieved if you don't shut up!"

Interestingly, one of the most inaccurate scenes of the movie *Patton* was protested against by the actor who plays Patton, George C. Scott. The scene occurs in Sicily, where Patton tells Truscott that if his conscience will not let him conduct the risky end-run operation, "I will relieve you and have someone else do it." Patton says that he doesn't care how many men die, because he must take Messina before the British. Scott believed the scene did not properly represent Patton's character and that it suggested Patton was indifferent to his men's welfare. Even though Scott protested the scene, the studio owners wouldn't change it. It strikes me that the military adviser for the movie, General Bradley, who was there in Sicily in 1943 and knew the scene to be false, did not protest it as well.

Bradley did not see fit to protest the many inaccuracies of the movie even when George C. Scott did, and so the studio owners kept the inaccurate Sicily scene. Scott, however, did not give up easily. He decided to purposely play the scene reclining on the couch, hoping that people would realize the scene's falsity. When I first watched the movie, the fact that Patton was saying things he never said while *lying down* particularly galled me. I did not know this interesting side of the story.

Obviously, Bradley must have had some reason that made his hatred blind; what it is, we shall never know. It may have been jealousy[1] at Patton's fame, anger at Patton's descriptions and predictions in his diary, loyalty to President Eisenhower, or all three. Bradley says in his book, "A General's Life,"

> "Patton and I were closely associated at Fort Benning for
> a period of almost a year. It was during this time that I
> first got to know him well. Thereafter our professional

---

[1] Patton seems to have believed Bradley was jealous of him, at least during the Battle of the Bulge. "Even the tent maker [Bradley] admits that Courtney [Hodges] is dumb. He is also very jealous of me," Patton wrote. And even though Bradley says he thought Hodges and Patton were equal, he would have been a military idiot to think that they were of equal value.

lives would become interwoven in war. He would be my boss; then in a kind of Greek drama, I his. As a result I probably knew Patton as well as any man."

True, but Bradley did not see fit to defend him even when Scott, who did not know Patton, did.

Here is Bradley's description of Patton. Historically it is not worth much, but it may be helpful in understanding the man who wrote it.

"As a soldier, a professional officer, Patton was the most fiercely ambitious man and the strangest duck I have ever known. He appeared to be motivated by some deep, inexplicable martial spirit. He devoured military history and poetry and imagined – in the spirit of reincarnation – that he had fought with Alexander the Great, Genghis Khan, Caesar, [sic] Napoleon.[1] He dressed as though he had just stepped out of a custom military tailor shop and had his own private bootblack. He was unmercifully hard on his men, demanding the utmost in military efficiency and bearing. Most of them respected but despised him. Although he could be the epitome of grace and charm at social or official functions, he was at the same time the most earthily profane man I ever knew. I sometimes wondered if this macho profanity was unconscious overcompensation for his most serious personal flaw: a voice that was almost comically squeaky and high-pitched, altogether lacking in command authority. Like Douglas Mac Arthur, Patton was a born publicity hound, a glory seeker." *"A General's Life," by General Omar N. Bradley, page 98.*

I cannot help but wonder if Bradley here disguised his own thoughts about Patton as Patton's men's; it seems it was really Bradley who "respected but despised" Patton.

---

[1] This description contains many errors that he must have gained from reading Patton's biographers. For instance, Bradley says that Patton believed in reincarnation but does not provide conclusive evidence here, or anywhere else, that he did.

BIBLIOGRAPHY

Alexander, Bevin, "How Great Generals Win." W. W. Norton & Co., NY © 1993.

Alexander, Bevin, "Lost Victories, The Military Genius of Stonewall Jackson." Henry Holt & Co., NY © 1992.

Allen, Colonel Robert S., "Lucky Forward." The Vanguard Press., NY © 1947.

Ashley, Maurice, "Churchill as Historian." Charles Scribner's Sons, NY © 1968.

Astor, Gerald, "The Bloody Forest." Presidio Press Inc., CA © 2000.

Ayer, Fred Jr., "Before the Colors Fade." Houghton Mifflin Co., Boston, © 1964.

Barber, Noel, "The Week France Fell." Stein and Day, NY © 1976.

Baron, Richard, Baum, Major Abe, and Goldhurst, Richard, "Raid! The Untold Story of Patton's Secret Mission." G. P. Putnam's Sons, NY © 1981.

Blumenson, Martin, "Patton, the Man Behind the Legend." William Morrow & Co., Inc., NY © 1985.

Bradley, General Omar. N., "A Soldier's Story." Henry Holt and Company, Inc., NY, © 1951.

Bruer, William B., "Unexplained Mysteries of World War II." John Wiley and Sons, Inc., NY © 1997.

Ciano, Count Galeazzo, "The Ciano Diaries: 1939-43," Edited by Hugh Gibson. Doubleday and Company, Inc., NY © 1946.

Churchill, Winston S., "Memoirs of the Second World War." © 1948. 1959 edition published by The Riverside Press, Cambridge and also by Houghton Mifflin Company, Boston.

Clausewitz, Karl von, "Principles of War." The Stackpole Co., PA, Copyright © 1960.

Codman, Colonel Charles R., "Drive." Little, Brown and Co., Boston © 1957.

Cohen, Eliot A. and Gooch, John, "Military Misfortunes: the anatomy of failure in war." The Free Press: a division of Macmillan Inc., NY. © 1990.

De Gaulle, General Charles, "The Call to Honour: the War Memoirs of General de Gaulle." Viking Press © 1955

De Weerd, H.A., "Great Soldiers of the Two World Wars." Published by W. W. Norton & Co., © 1941.

Dunnigan, James F. and Nofi, Albert A., "Shooting Blanks; War Making That Doesn't Work." William Morrow and Co., Inc, NY © 1991.

Dunnigan, James F., "Victory and Deceit: Dirty Tricks at War." William Morrow and Co., © 1995.

Eisenhower, Dwight D., "Crusade in Europe." Doubleday & Co., Inc., NY © 1948.

Ellis, John, "Brute Force: allied strategy and tactics in the Second World War." Penguin Group, NY © 1990.

Essame, H., "Patton: A study in Command." Charles Scribner's Sons, NY © 1974.

Farago, Ladislas, "Patton, Ordeal and Triumph." Astor Honor Inc, NY © 1964.

Farago, Ladislas, "The Last Days of Patton." Copyright 1981. Published by Mc Graw Hill Book Co., NY © 1981.

"Frederick the Great on the Art of War," edited and translated by Jay Luvaas. The Free Press, NY © 1966.

Fuller, J.F.C., "A Military History of the Western World ," Volume 3. Funk and Wagnalls Co., NY © 1956.

Gavin, Major General James M., "On to Berlin," Published by The Viking Press, NY © 1978.

Gelb, Norman, "Ike & Monty: Generals at War." William Morrow and Company, Inc., New York, © 1994.

Gilbert, Martin, "In Search of Churchill: A Historian's Journey." John Wiley & Sons, Inc., NY © 1994.

Hapgood, David, and Richardson, David, "Monte Cassino." Congdon & Weed, Inc., NY © 1984.

Hanson, Victor Davis, "The Soul of Battle." The Free Press, a division of Simon and Schuster Inc., NY © 1999.

Harkins, General Paul D., "When the Third Cracked Europe." Stackpole Books, © 1969.

Hastings, Max, "Overlord: D Day and the Battle for Normandy." Simon and Schuster, NY © 1984.

"The Invisible Soldier, the experience of the Black Soldier in WWII," compiled and edited by Mary P. Motley. Wayne State University Press, © 1975.

Irving, David, "The War Between the Generals." Congdon & Lattes, Inc. © 1981.

Keegan, John, "The Battle for History; re-fighting World War II." Vintage Books, NY © 1995.

Keegan, John, "The Mask of Command." Penguin Books, NY © 1987.

Keegan, John and Wheatcroft, Andrew, "Who's Who in Military History." William Morrow and Co, Inc., NY © 1976.

Kemp, Anthony, "The Unknown Battle." Stein and Day, NY © 1981.

Liddell Hart, B.H., "The Defense of Britain." Random House, NY © 1939.

Liddell Hart, B.H., "History of the Second World War." G. P. Putnam's Sons, NY © 1970.

Liddell Hart, B.H., "Strategy." Frederick A. Preager Publishers, NY. © 1968.

Liddell Hart, B.H., "War in Outline: 1914-1918." The Modern Library, NY © 1936.

Macksey, Kenneth, "Military Errors of World War Two." Arms and Armour Press, Great Britain © 1988.

Manchester, William, "The Last Lion: Winston Spencer Churchill." Volume I: Visions of Glory, Volume II: Alone. Published by Little, Brown and Company, Boston © 1988.

Miller, Merle, "Plain Speaking: An Oral History of Harry S. Truman." G. P. Putnam's Sons, NY © 1973.

Montgomery, Viscount Bernard Law, "The Memoirs of Field-Marshal Montgomery." The World Publishing Co., © 1958.

Moorehead, Alan, "Don't Blame the Generals." Harper and Brothers, London © 1943.

Nobecourt, Jacques, "Hitler's Last Gamble: the Battle of the Bulge." Schocken Books, NY © 1967.

Nicolson, Nigel, "Alex, the life of the Field Marshal Earl Alexander of Tunis." Athenium, NY © 1973.

Overy, Richard, "Why the Allies Won." W. W. Norton and Co., London © 1995.

"The Patton Papers," edited by Martin Blumenson. Houghton Mifflin Co., Boston © 1974.

Perett, Bryan, "Desert Warfare." Thorsons Publishing Group, Northamptonshire, © 1988.

Perett, Bryan, "A History of Blitzkrieg." Stein and Day, NY © 1983.

Pilpel, Robert H., "Churchill in America." Harcourt Brace Jovanovich, NY and London © 1976.

Pogue, Forrest C., "Ordeal and Hope: George C. Marshall." The Viking Press, NY © 1966.

Preder, Nathan N., "Patton's Ghost Corps." Presidio Press, CA © 1998.

Province, Charles M., "The Unknown Patton." Bonanza Books, NY © 1983.

Rohmer, Richard, "Patton's Gap." Beaufort Books, Inc., NY © 1981.

"The Rommel Papers," edited by Liddell Hart. With the assistance of Lucie-Maria Rommel, Manfred Rommel, and General Fritz Bayerlein. De Capo Press, NY © 1953.

Roosevelt, Eleanor, "This I Remember." Harper & Brothers, NY © 1949.

Root, Waverley, "The Secret History of the War." Charles Scribner's Sons, NY © 1945.

Ryan, Cornelius, "A Bridge Too Far." Simon and Schuster, NY © 1974.

"The Seven Military Classics of Ancient China," translated by Ralph D. Sawyer. Westview Press, San Francisco © 1993.

Shirer, William L. "The Rise and Fall of the Third Reich." Simon & Schuster, NY © 1960.

Strawson, John, "Churchill and Hitler." Fromm International, NY © 1997.

"The Sword and the Pen," edited by Adrian Liddell Hart. Thomas Y. Crowell Co., NY © 1976.

Taylor, Robert Lewis, "Winston Churchill: an Informal Study of Greatness." Doubleday & Company, Inc., © 1952.

Thomson, R. W., "Churchill and the Montgomery Myth." Copyright 1967. M. Evans and Co., Inc., NY © 1967.

Toland, John, "Battle: the Story of the Bulge." Random House, NY © 1959.

Tzu, Sun, "The Art of War." Translated by Samuel B. Griffith. Oxford University Press, © 1963.

Van Creveld, Martin, "The Transformation of War." The Free Press, a division of Macmillan, NY © 1991.

Verrier, Anthony, "Assassination in Algiers." W.W. Norton & Company, Inc., NY, © 1990

Von Manstein, Erich, "Lost Victories." Henry Regnery Co., Chicago © 1958.

"Warrior, the Story of General George S. Patton," by the Editors of the Army Times. G. P. Putnam's Sons, NY, © 1967.

Wedemeyer, Alber C., "Wedemeyer Reports." Henry Holt & Co., NY © 1958.

Weighley, Russell F., "Eisenhower's Lieutenants." Indiana University Press, Bloomington © 1981.

Welles, Benjamin, "Sumner Welles: FDR's Global Strategist." St. Martin's Press, NY © 1997.

Whiting, Charles, "The Battle of Hurtgen Forest." Orion Books, NY © 1989.

Order a copy of *Patton Uncovered*
for a friend or relative!

You can order online at www.pattonuncovered.com or fill out the coupon below.

Check out the author's website at:
www.barbaraboland.com

You can find updates, information, news about the author and more about Patton at:
www.pattonuncovered.com

Save $5 off the cover price of *Patton Uncovered*.
Name: _____
Address: _____
City: _____ State: _____ Zip: _____
Mail this coupon to: Melody Publishing Co., P.O. Box 221, Voorhees, NJ 08043 along with a check for $30.
($25 for book and $5 for shipping and handling.)

Available only to U.S. residents.

Offer: B66K